in the
circle of
mysteries

Praise for *In the Circle of Mysteries*

"Fr. Bleichner's work *In the Circle of Mysteries* presents a fresh synthesis of the Catholic faith, pulling together the central mysteries from a historical perspective in a way that is accessible to Catholics today. Using Sacred Scripture, the documents of the Church, and the great theologians of history, Fr. Bleichner presents the faith as a systematic whole with the goal of leading the believer to an ever deeper act of faith. For anyone looking for an engaging and faithful presentation of the Catholic faith, *In the Circle of Mysteries* is a welcome and fresh contribution."

— Most Reverend Donald W. Wuerl,
Archbishop of Washington, D.C.

"Fr. Bleichner sets forth a symphony of salvation with clarity and depth. He shows that it all fits together into one breathtaking composition, a kind of theological fugue of which the Lord is both composer and performer. This work should be a source of inspiration for any serious believer or for anyone who longs to be a serious believer."

— Most Reverend Daniel E. Pilarczyk,
Archbishop of Cincinnati

in the circle of mysteries

the coherence of
CATHOLIC BELIEF

HOWARD P. BLEICHNER

A Herder & Herder Book
The Crossroad Publishing Company
New York

The Crossroad Publishing Company
16 Penn Plaza – 481 Eighth Avenue, Suite 1550
New York, NY 10001

Printed in the United States of America.

The text of this book is set in 11/14.5 Galliard.

Cataloging-in-Publication Data is available from the Library of Congress
ISBN-10: 0-8245-2447-0
ISBN-13: 978-0-8245-2447-0

1   2   3   4   5   6   7   8   9   10   12   11   10   09   08

To Family and Friends
In Remembrance and Gratitude

CONTENTS

Part One
ORIGIN AND DEVELOPMENT
OF CHRISTIAN BELIEFS

I. Yahweh, God of the Tribes of Israel / 14

Exodus, Sinai, and the Land, 16; A Law of Development: Yahweh and the Community, 18

THE EXODUS: "WHAT ACTUALLY HAPPENED?" / 19

The Journey to the Monarchy, 21

II. Yahweh, God of the Nation / 24

Jeremiah and Ezekiel, 26; Second Isaiah, 30; Other Voices, 34; Job, 35

THE FOURTH SERVANT SONG (ISAIAH 52:13–53:12):
"WHO HAS BELIEVED WHAT WE HAVE HEARD?" / 37

III. Yahweh, the Only God, Lord of the Nations,
Creator of the Universe / 40

A Question of Identity, 40; The Editing of the Pentateuch, 41; Ezra and Nehemiah, 42; The Vision of God, 44; The Maccabean Revolt, 47; The Community, 47; Apocalyptic, 49

Part Two
THE DEVELOPMENT OF
CHRISTIAN DOCTRINE: THE CENTER

Part Three
THE DEVELOPMENT OF
CATHOLIC DOCTRINE: CLOSING THE CIRCLE

ACKNOWLEDGMENTS

It has struck me forcibly more than once in recent years that writing a book is of its nature a collaborative effort. An author is far too close to the text to have good perspective about its strengths and weaknesses for any sustained period of time. Such closeness brings, rather, myopia that is remedied only with the help of friends and associates who truly become collaborators in a common project.

Therefore I wish to acknowledge and thank those friends and colleagues who have assisted me with their insights, encouragement, and suggestions. In the early stages of the project, I thank Fr. Robert F. Leavitt, SS. In the middle stages, Frs. Thomas R. Hurst, SS, and Ronald D. Witherup, SS, have gone over the entire text several times, and their help has been invaluable. In a special way, I thank Fr. John S. Kselman, SS, who was the first reader of most chapters, for his insight and acumen. Sister Mary Ann Donovan, SC, has been helpful not only in regard to patristics, which is her specialty, but also to the project as a whole with her thoughtful perspectives. I thank as well retired archbishop of San Francisco John R. Quinn for reading the manuscript and for his comments and observations. John Jones of Crossroad Publishing Company has been a steady and constant support. John Eagleson has been a highly effective copy editor whose good service I wish to acknowledge. At every stage of the process, Dr. Cecil White and the staff of St. Patrick's Seminary and University in Menlo Park, California, have offered me kind assistance and efficient services. The corrections and improvements of the text are the fruit of my collaborators' good efforts. The errors, mistakes, and shortcomings of the book are mine alone.

I celebrate the Eucharist each Sunday at St. Joseph's Parish in Capitola, California. The prayers and good wishes of the parishioners have sustained my efforts over the years in this project. The support of the Sisters of the Holy Names of Jesus and Mary at Villa Maria del Mar in Santa Cruz, California, has been a great gift for many years. While I dedicate this book to "Family and Friends in Remembrance and Gratitude," I think here in a special way of my sister, Joan B. Stanley, a good sister and a great friend.

INTRODUCTION

The Aims

The dogmatic constitution *Dei Filius* (*Son of God*) of the First Vatican Council (1870) outlines a fruitful approach for understanding the mysteries of the Christian faith: "If reason illumined by faith inquires in an earnest, pious and sober manner, it attains by God's grace a certain understanding of the mysteries, which is most fruitful both from the analogy with the objects of its natural knowledge and from the connection of these mysteries with one another and with our ultimate end."[1]

In this book I wish to follow the constitution's approach. In particular, I will seek to the trace the connection of the mysteries of the Christian faith with one another in light of our ultimate end. I regard this as a useful method that may be followed in different ways.[2] This introduction outlines the particular way in which this book will explore the interconnection of the Christian mysteries.

The book begins with the understanding of God in the Old Testament. Then a chapter on Jesus and one on Jesus as the Christ follow. Subsequently, I examine the doctrines of the Trinity, of Christ and church, of Mary and of the last things. I seek to trace how these beliefs developed, how they interrelate, and what they mean. The book closes with the topic of faith, what it means to believe in this tradition whose lineaments I have sought to trace.

The approach is broadly "historical" — something that deserves its own word of introduction. I think that the ordinary reader of the Old Testament recognizes that there are large differences between the story of creation, the journey of the patriarchs across the Fertile Crescent, and the beginnings of the monarchy under David and Solomon. I suspect that readers instinctively know not to read the entire story in the same way. Rather, the mind shifts gears almost automatically, making adjustments. In other words, the modern application of "literary forms" to biblical texts makes sense in large measure because of the different ways in which the Bible was written in the first place and how it is normally read. Therefore, in order to speak of a historical tradition and to trace its origin, one must acknowledge first of all that the word *history* has several meanings. Simply put, it is used *analogously*. The epic events of the exodus and the founding of the monarchy, for example, mean to tell a story of events that actually happened. But the story is quite different in each case. Hence, if we seek to trace the historical development of doctrine, the terrain will change along the way, calling for different approaches.

Consequently, the book will shift back and forth between different methods. Sometimes we will look through the text to the history behind it, but also we will regard the text as a literary unit with its own integrity. The story of the exodus illustrates the point. On one level, we may fairly ask, What actually happened to those first Israelites who fled from Egypt? Were there as many as the Bible recounts? Precisely 603,550 adult men, according to the book of Numbers (Num. 1:46)! But another question arises as well. How is the story told in the book of Exodus and what is its meaning as it stands, apart from such historical considerations? The problem arises in a critical way in regard to the New Testament. What do we know about Jesus himself? How does the early community understand him after the resurrection? Can we separate these strands of the tradition in the same text to answer different questions?

I take this approach because it best accords with what Vatican II's constitution on revelation, *Dei Verbum* (*Word of God*), writes about theology: "The 'study of the sacred page' should be the very soul of sacred theology."[3] The story of God in the Old Testament is linked at every point to the history of Israel as a tribal league, a nation, and then a religious community after the exile. In turn, this story is connected to the death and resurrection of Jesus and the rise of the Christian community in the New Testament. The Christian faith subsequently unfolds through the first four ecumenical councils until A.D. 451 in order to achieve *relative* stability. In other words, the Christian faith from its first beginnings in the Scriptures is embedded in a history in which its meaning is narrated and then confessed. I take this to be the heart of the Christian faith and the best and most natural way to explain it. In effect, history seems to be both the medium and the message. This also seems clear from the historical grid that undergirds the creed: from God and creation to Christ, then to the Holy Spirit and the church, and finally the last things.

In taking this approach, I seek to follow the "plain sense" of the biblical text and of the writings of the church fathers, using all the critical means available.[4] Yet this book is consciously not a scholarly piece but rather a popular one, aimed at believers who seek a better understanding of their faith. It is also an essay in faith seeking understanding, of "reason illumined by faith," in the words of *Dei Filius,* and that too should be clear. The Scriptures, written *in* faith, reveal the intention of their authors in a special way to those who read them *with* faith. The first intent of this book is to explain the meaning and plausibility of Christian doctrine. Inevitably, however, that makes the book into an apologetic of sorts, and I acknowledge this intent as well. Apologetic motifs will appear more explicitly in part 3, "The Development of Catholic Doctrine — Closing the Circle."

These various emphases establish my target audience. The book is written for Catholics, especially young Catholics, who have zeal and enthusiasm but whose actual knowledge of the faith may not match the level of those first qualities. It is also written in the conviction that a Catholic consciousness is complex and differentiated.[5] Countless examples over the centuries — Augustine (354–430), Thomas Aquinas (1225–1274), Blaise Pascal (1623–1662), Cardinal John Henry Newman (1801–1890), G. K. Chesterton (1874–1936) — display this quality. Chesterton explains why. If the problem is complex, the human predicament, then the answer must be complex as well, redemption in Christ and its continuance in the church. It is the madman, he writes, who lives "in the clean and well-lit prison of a one idea."[6]

For the same reason, this book consciously seeks to tie the articles of the faith together, seeking the *nexus* of the Christian mysteries of which Vatican I speaks. Now, almost two generations after

Vatican II, Catholic theology has increasingly become a matter of specialized study. The Scriptures, Old and New Testaments, are studied for themselves. Likewise, systematic theology comprises a series of subdisciplines on God, Christ, grace, faith, revelation, and other such topics. Such specialization certainly is legitimate, but a synthetic moment is sometimes lacking when all parts of the faith are seen together. From a believer's point of view, this synthesizing moment is crucial. The act of faith is made not in fragmentary pieces of the creed but rather in the whole of it. And there is a strong conviction that the articles of faith flow from a common source and that they belong together. These factors conspire to make the scope of this book quite broad. But if it examines a wide gamut of topics, it is finally to bring them together into a single object of faith.

The difficulties of a book such as this should be acknowledged. How does one cover such a wide swathe of history? How to do justice to primary sources? How to integrate even a portion of the secondary literature? The dangers of easy generalizations are clear. In this regard, Albert Schweitzer's famous image still stands as a fair warning to those embarking on voyages like our own. Those who booked "through-tickets on express trains" — broad generalizations in order to write lives of Jesus based on the "historical character" of Mark's Gospel — were brought up short by the rediscovery that Jesus' preaching of the kingdom of God was close to an announcement that the world was soon to end, an emphasis that Mark reflected.[7] Such baleful news effectively ended express service and broad generalizations. The image contains enduring wisdom on one side of the ledger. Those who piggyback on the research of others are never guaranteed a risk-free ride.

But concerns on the other side of the ledger bring us to run these risks. In the thicket of technical exegesis and scholarship on every aspect of the Bible, can we at times miss the forest for the trees? As specialized discussion among professionals predominates, may religious concerns sink below the surface? What begins as a chapter *on* Jesus, for example, easily becomes a discussion of the literature *about* Jesus, with the principal actor caught in the amber of disputed questions. The discussion also becomes increasingly abstract as theories grow, one upon another. Whatever began as fresh and green in the discussion of Jesus becomes pale and gray as hypotheses mount. What was once the cornerstone of the church and the believing community now becomes grist for the mill of the scholarly establishment. Our own first concern here is religious and theological, and although due respect is given to the critical discussion of the Scriptures, that is not the primary focus of this book.

Therefore my aims are relatively clear: a generalist's sketch of specialized research; historically accurate yet written in a believing spirit; a plain yet differentiated presentation of Christian faith; an essay that seeks to retain some of the freshness of the original sources, illuminating the connection of the mysteries of Christian belief as a single object of faith.

Beliefs and Doctrines

It remains to define my primary terms — *belief* and *doctrine* — and then, in that light, to sketch the main divisions of the book. Jaroslav Pelikan (1923–2006), in the first volume of *The Christian Tradition: A History of the Development of Christian Doctrine,* describes doctrine as what the church *believes* in its worship, spirituality, and life of prayer; what the church *teaches* in biblical interpretation, catechesis, and theology; what the church *confesses* in apologetics and in its creeds.[8]

Clearly, while every point in this definition pertains to the Christian church, what the church believes, teaches, and confesses also *predates* its own existence. The church preaches about the God of the Old Testament and what this God has done in the life, death, and resurrection of Jesus of Nazareth. In other words, the origin and development of Christian faith extend to the beginnings of Israel's faith, encompassing also the ministry of Jesus and the life of the early church. Part 1 of this book, the chapters on God, Jesus, and Christ, explores the sources of the Christian faith.

The development of doctrine, as such, begins with the church. Part 2 examines the topics that naturally follow: how doctrines develop, and then how the doctrines of the Trinity and of Christ and the church have evolved. I will follow a three-step approach in tracing the origin of the tenets of belief. I begin in each case with the scriptural basis, seeking to approximate as closely as possible the originating *experience* of Christian faith. I take this to be the seedbed of later developments.

Theology arises on the next level as a way of explaining Christian experience. It is motivated by a series of factors, both internal and external to the original experience. The message itself presses toward more coherent articulation. Conflict and contradictions in Christian belief must be resolved. Apologetics seeks to explain the faith to others. The witness of prayer and worship has its own voice.

Doctrine arises on still another level.[9] Here decisions are made about which theological viewpoints are acceptable and which are not. Such decisions are often hotly contested and only slowly accepted, sometimes not accepted by all Christians. But for the majority, doctrines lay down markers for the future that theology is asked to respect as it continues to explore the meaning of Christian doctrine. These, then, are our categories: *Scripture and experience, then theology, and finally doctrine.*

In part 3, other factors appear. Here I continue the discussion of the Roman Catholic Church and its beliefs about the Virgin Mary into the modern era, down to and including the Second Vatican Council. I seek to "close the circle," as it were, and bring the discussion full term to the present situation of the reader. Ultimately, I do this for the sake of the topic that closes the book: the question of faith. In the last analysis, the act of faith cannot be vague, diffuse, and generic. On the contrary, in order to be a live option, the question of faith must be focused, specific, and particular. We do not believe in Jesus Christ as he exists in textbooks, and no one believes in the Christian church in general. One believes in Christ as he is confessed in a particular community in which faith in him is kept alive. Thus I pose the question of faith from the vantage point that I know best and in which I myself stand. Do I believe in the God of Jesus Christ as this God is confessed in the Roman Catholic Church?

A Précis

Thus far our considerations have been formal ones, the considerations under which this book is begun. I change the focus here to more substantive ones. If the object of this book is to explore the nexus of the Christian mysteries, how, in a preliminary way, would we describe this nexus? This question becomes in brief a statement of the book's game plan and a précis of the whole.

We begin with Israel's belief in one God whom Christians will call God the Father. This God is the bright light that illumines all parts of the story. If God the Father is light, the creeds call the Son light from light. I would describe the connection here this way. Jesus' life, death, and resurrection become the prism that the light of God strikes full force. So much so, in fact, that Christians will subsequently say that in the life of Jesus, God reveals his *face*. I will describe Jesus' death and resurrection as the prism that catches the light of God and then refracts it outward in a rainbow spectrum of different but related colors. These colors comprise the topics of this book.

Let me shift the image to illumine the process of refraction. The bodily resurrection of Jesus in the experience of his first followers may be likened to a dense ball of explosive experience whose outward thrust gives birth to the mission of the church. This dense ball of experience carries within itself a series of implicit questions that must be answered for the mission to occur. Surely, the first and most obvious one is this: *Who is Jesus?* This question is the relentless focus of the Gospels, beginning with the Gospel of Mark. It is the question that Jesus himself bluntly poses at Caesarea Philippi: "Who do people say that I am?" (Mark 8:27). And then to the disciples: "But who do you say that I am?" (Mark 8:29). It is the question that the high priest poses to Jesus: "Are you the Messiah, the Son of the Blessed One?" (Mark 14:61). And Pilate too: "Are you the King of the Jews?" (Mark 15:2). These are questions about Jesus' identity, and all four Gospels are built around them.

The Gospel of John represents a certain culminating point. Here Jesus is described as the preexistent Son of God. The question posed at Caesarea Philippi will be answered by Thomas's exclamation: "My Lord and my God!" (John 20:28). This is a closing verse of the original ending of the Gospel that matches the way the Gospel began — in other words, the response of the entire Gospel of John: Jesus is *God*.

But if this represents a culminating moment, it also is a new starting point. If we wish to remain true to Israel's faith in one God yet confess that this God has become so transparent in Jesus, that he too in some sense is God, then we open a new chapter. In other words, our original question — *Who is Jesus?* — gives birth to a second one: *Who, in light of Jesus, is God?* The light of this one God is so thoroughly absorbed and refracted in the death and resurrection of Jesus that God himself is *experienced* in a new way and then *rethought* in a new way as well. In short, the clear confession of the divinity of Christ leads in a straight line to the doctrine of the Trinity. But the path here is also a long and arduous one that unfolds in the life of the church to achieve first stability in A.D. 381. In another sense, the question can never be answered definitively. The Trinity therefore represents not a human explanation of God but rather a way of recasting the mystery that human words may touch but not encompass.

Yet the original question — *Who is Jesus?* — is still more complex. If the question of Jesus' identity reflects upward to our understanding of God, it refracts downwards to our understanding of Jesus' followers. In other words, the way we define Jesus carries within itself a self-definition of what it means to follow him. The connection is clear in Mark: "If any want to become my followers, let them deny themselves and take up their cross and follow me" (Mark 8:34). Jesus is a crucified Messiah. His followers must share the cup of suffering as well. Therefore the question *Who is Jesus?* contains still another one: *Who, in light of Jesus, are we his followers?* This is the question of the church.

Josiah Royce (1855–1916) describes the church as a *community of interpretation,* and this represents a fruitful perspective.[10] But the church can function as a true interpreter only if it is in a deeper and prior sense a community of presence in which Jesus' spirit remains alive, above all, in the church's prayer and worship. This means that the church does not first speak about itself. It is not self-referential. Rather, it seeks to describe what God has accomplished in the death and resurrection of Jesus for the sake of our salvation.

Our topic now bifurcates into two natural parts. Paul will describe the *community* of believers in 1 Corinthians as the body of Christ, the first of a series of images that seek to capture the mystery of the church. But this question remains: What does it mean for an *individual* to follow in Jesus' footsteps? Here Jesus himself is the first teacher. It means to pray to God, as *Abba,* Father, and regard ourselves as God's children. The *child* is the first image of Jesus' followers. The preaching of Jesus abounds in family images, of father, mother, sister, and brother. Indeed, believers who hear the word of God and keep it comprise a family whose bonds are stronger and deeper than those formed by blood kinship. Mary, the mother of Jesus, becomes the exemplar here. She is the mother who becomes offspring, child, to her own Son's preaching. Indeed, the conception of Jesus is the fruit of Mary's discipleship. She hears the word of God spoken by the angel Gabriel and obeys it. At the cross in John's Gospel, Mary becomes the mother of the beloved disciple and hence herself a model of discipleship. She is living proof that the bonds of discipleship are deeper and stronger than the natural ties of a mother to a son. She is first disciple, then mother.

The final question to be posed, like the others, is contained in the first one in quite explicit terms: *What, in light of Jesus, may be our hope?* This is the question of salvation, and essential elements are clear from the start. The resurrection of Jesus is never considered an individual affair. Rather, Jesus is the first of many brothers and sisters to follow him into the kingdom that he preached, whose portals he opens. He now awaits us in the banquet feast of heaven. The resurrection of Jesus in the church's meditation becomes the keystone that defines and distinguishes the nature of Christian hope.

Yet the meandering path of these questions is not fully answered by understanding their first beginnings. The message has traveled a long distance in the course of two millennia. Initial starting points begin the journey and set the trajectory. Prompting circumstances and the movement of grace — in John Henry Newman's phrase, "chronic vigor" — determine the course of subsequent development.[11] As noted, we will follow two of these mysteries — the church and Mary — down to the present.

The book concludes with some reflections of faith. What does it mean to believe in this long tradition whose winding path we have sought to follow? The question of faith may be broached at the beginning of a book such as this. This is how the creeds begin. "We (I) believe" and such represents a time-honored starting point. I prefer to pose the question at the end, when all or almost all of the cards are face-up on the table.

Part One

Origin and Development of Christian Beliefs

Chapter One

ONE GOD

Credo in unum Deum. The Latin phrase rings with stately sonority. "I believe in one God." Although creeds phrased in the singular play an important role in baptism, the great creeds of the councils of Nicea and Constantinople begin not in Latin but Greek, not in the singular but in the plural. They also reflect Eastern practice, asserting the belief in "one God, the Father Almighty, maker of all things visible and invisible."[1]

More to the point, this article of faith did not drop down vertically on these early councils. Nor was it the invention of its earliest defenders. On the contrary, the article encapsulates in a handful of words a long history, never a matter of sudden discovery but rather of protracted effort to discern the nature of God's revelation. In one sense, one can say that the Christian doctrine of God began with the first words of the book of Genesis. And God remained at the heart of Israel's meditation for more than a millennium. And while that meditation was broad and capacious, it was never dilatory or wandering. Otherwise, it could not be finally captured in a phrase. For our purposes, we can narrow the focus even more to a single word, the adjective *one*. How did Israel come to believe in *one* God?

In this chapter, we will seek to disassemble the confession of *one God* into its component parts and then trace how they came together. We do so as Christians who will ultimately view Israel's faith in light of the birth of Christ and the subsequent development of the doctrine of the Trinity, the subject of chapter 5 of this book. In effect, we wish to trace in broad outline the *sources* of that faith which the church

confessed at the Council of Nicea in A.D. 325 and amplified at the
Council of Constantinople in A.D. 381.

I distinguish three stages in the journey that this chapter seeks to
trace. Although Israel's faith may go back further, we begin the story
at Sinai when God reveals his name to Moses. Here Yahweh emerges
as *the God of the tribes of Israel*. The advent of the monarchy marks a
second stage. Now Yahweh appears as *the God of the nation*. The final
phase emerges after the exile, completing the first article of the creed.
Here Yahweh emerges as *the God of Israel, the one God, Lord of the nation
and Creator of the heavens and the earth, Maker of all things visible and
invisible*.

I. Yahweh, God of the Tribes of Israel

Searching out the Scriptures for the best place to begin, one could
scarcely find a better one than the moment at which the God of Israel
steps forward to introduce himself to Moses at the burning bush.

> When the LORD saw that he had turned aside to see, God called
> to him out of the bush, "Moses, Moses!" And he said, "Here I
> am." Then he said, "Come no closer! Remove the sandals from
> your feet, for the place on which you are standing is holy ground."
> He said further, "I am the God of your father, the God of Abra-
> ham, the God of Isaac, and the God of Jacob." And Moses hid
> his face, for he was afraid to look at God. . . .
>
> "The cry of the Israelites has now come to me; I have also
> seen how the Egyptians oppress them. So come, I will send you
> to Pharaoh to bring my people, the Israelites, out of Egypt." But
> Moses said to God, "Who am I that I should go to Pharaoh, and
> bring the Israelites out of Egypt?" He said, "I will be with you,
> and this shall be the sign for you that it is I who sent you: when
> you have brought the people out of Egypt, you shall worship
> God on this mountain."
>
> But Moses said to God, "If I come to the Israelites and say to
> them, 'The God of your ancestors has sent me to you,' and they
> ask me, 'What is his name?' what shall I say to them?" God said
> to Moses, "I AM WHO I AM." He said further, "Thus you shall

say to the Israelites, 'I AM has sent me to you.'" God also said to Moses, "Thus you shall say to the Israelites, 'The LORD, the God of your ancestors, the God of Abraham, the God of Isaac, and the God of Jacob has sent me to you': this is my name forever, and this is my title for all generations." (Exod. 3:4–6, 9–15)

The passage gives every sign of careful, deliberate editing, authors and editors aware of the high-voltage electricity of the text. Generations of commentators — all of the high Scholastics, for example — grasped the same point. Its subtlety is everywhere evident. God introduces himself by a verbal phrase, using an archaic causative form of the Hebrew verb *to be,* that can be variously translated: "I am he who causes to be"; "I am what I shall be"; "I am what I do." The Greek and Latin translations narrow the original focus, placing the accent on existence. English follows: "I am who I am." The phrase clearly is enigmatic.

Also clear is that this enigmatic verbal phrase is finally compressed into a single, personal *name:* "Yahweh." This is the larger import of the text. The phrase becomes a name. The lines of continuity with the God of Israel's ancestors are clearly delineated: "I appeared to Abraham, Isaac, and Jacob as 'God Almighty,' but by my name 'Yahweh' I did not make myself known to them" (Exod. 6:3). But the break is also recorded. Here for the first time, before the exodus from Egypt, the God of Israel steps forward to reveal *his proper name.* By any measure, this marks a momentous turning point, carefully carved into the text.

An obvious commentary on the revelation of the name is the first commandments of the Decalogue. This is the God who brought Israel out of Egypt, and the nation is to have no other gods. This comprises no denial of the existence of other gods for other nations. This is not the concern. The focus here is simpler. Yahweh is the God of Israel. Even more striking is the prohibition of images, a command that contains several levels of meaning. In the most obvious sense, there is nothing around to form a comparative likeness of this God. He is not like anything in the heavens or on the earth. But an image is also an avenue of access. The prohibition of an image also means that from the start, Yahweh is not at Israel's disposal, not the nation's totem. In simplest terms, Yahweh is experienced as *other* — different from all other things around and not the guardian of Israel's self-interest. Here is the root of a fundamental characteristic of God in the Christian tradition that later thought will seek to capture with the abstract term *transcendence*. Yet the philosophical translation is rooted in a primitive experience of Yahweh's simple *otherness*.

If the experience of otherness represents one pole of the revelation of the name, it is inextricably bound to another. As God reveals his name, he steps forward as a distinct personality. Significantly, Yahweh is everywhere described in the Old Testament in human terms. He becomes angry, feels remorse, knows sadness. We hear of his arm, hand, finger, and face. The obvious conclusion of so much human attribution is that Yahweh is experienced as a *personality*, a personal God with his own name. This sets him off in another way. Nature gods are experienced as impersonal forces, the rhythms of wind and weather. Not so the God of Israel. And although the imagery of the Canaanite deity Baal, god of storm, is appropriated, this appropriation finally serves to enhance Yahweh's personality, as in Exodus 19 when Yahweh, thunderous lawgiver, steps forth on Mount Sinai in smoke and fire to bestow the Decalogue.

In sum, by revealing his name, God reveals both his *otherness* and his *personality*. When we place these characteristics together, they define exactly the *social* role that Yahweh plays in Israel's life. He is a transcendent personality who steps forward at the exodus as a warrior God to lead Israel out of Egypt. Then as lawgiver, he sets down this fledgling people's constitution. Finally, he leads them into the promised land. The social role that kings play in other nations is played in Israel by Yahweh, who has revealed his name at Sinai.

Exodus, Sinai, and the Land

The best commentary on the nature of this God who has revealed his name are the great nation-founding events of the exodus from Egypt, the covenant at Sinai, and the gift of the land. In effect, these events become categories. In so doing, they participate in a normal, ordinary form of human identification. When we meet people, we invariably search out those gestures that most aptly characterize them. Then we interpret the rest of their behavior through the optic of those actions. Nations and communities do the same. The Glorious Revolution of

1688 provides a foundational event through which subsequent English history is interpreted. Their French and American counterparts of 1789 and 1776 do the same. And who could think of the Duke of Wellington apart from the battle of Waterloo, or George Custer distinct from the Last Stand? In the same way, the beginning of Israel's history — exodus, Sinai, and the land — become Yahweh's signature gestures, establishing a fundamental paradigm for understanding the nature of this God. These events become categories of perception for organizing the nation's past, interpreting its present and looking into future, ways in which God's action toward Israel become characteristically clear. In effect, they form a permanent set of spectacles that the tradition cannot remove. Positively, they represent fixed points of reference to which the tradition always returns when it seeks to speaks seriously about God. And while philosophical categories may seek to distill the essence of God *behind* appearances, events-become-categories work the opposite way. They illumine the past and then open the future. They therefore disclose more fully the nature of God who has revealed his name at the burning bush. The revelation of the name is only the beginning.

Thus, that God reveals himself as an exodus God indicates more broadly that he will be a God who saves and protects Israel. If the event is the exodus, the category is salvation. Although the enemies change — Egyptians, Philistines, Assyrians, Babylonians, Syrians, Romans — the expectation remains the same. Yahweh is a saving God. Likewise, the covenant remains a permanent way to understand God's relation to the nation. As Israel seeks to organize its past tradition, it will see covenants extending covenants back to Abraham and to Noah, a running thread to its beginning. When it turns to the future, the monarchy will be justified by a covenant, and the community after the exile brought back to life by Ezra's renewal of the covenant. Although circumstances change and covenants change as well, the modality remains the same. The covenant also underscores Yahweh's character from another angle. Covenants are not made with nature gods, who are everywhere like wind and weather; rather, they are made between independent parties in which the connection is conscious and deliberate. Yahweh, the God of Israel, has deliberately chosen to covenant with this people, thereby bringing them into existence. Here Yahweh's transcendence is everywhere assumed.

The entry into the promised land, a land overflowing with milk and honey, serves as an image of fulfillment, salvation on the other end. In one sense, the land, because it represents actual geographic territory, can never fully be spiritualized. Yet, because Israel's actual possession of it was ever tenuous, the land carries from the start a heavy symbolic valence. Its possession, loss, and return become fateful gestures of God's benevolence, anger, and generosity.

According to the book of Exodus, the revelation of the name brings Israel into existence as a nation, and hereafter the nature of this God and the fate of the community to which he pledges himself are inextricably bound. Hence, while the first commands of the Decalogue enshrine an experience of this God, they give way to other commandments that regulate the social life of the community. In many ways, these are fundamental cross-cultural rules of civilized life. What sets them apart here is that they are given as commands of God. They thereby gain a new status. In this regard, form follows function. The "words" of the Decalogue are issued without justification or explanation. They are apodictic laws. What other kind of commands could God utter? In other words, their simplicity reflects the nature of their author. Noteworthy as well, ethical strictures are thereby woven into the fabric of God's revelation. That the Decalogue is given twice — with the people's idolatry and the subsequent shattering of the original tablets in between — becomes an eloquent statement that future failures are foreseen and already reckoned in the bargain between Israel and its God.[2]

A Law of Development: Yahweh and the Community

I would set forth the following as a significant rule of development in Israel's understanding of God. The revelation of the name opens a new chapter in Israel's understanding of God. Simultaneously, the same revelation sets the stage for a covenant, bringing Israel into existence as a people. The mutual interplay between the God Yahweh and the community to which he has committed himself establishes the fundamental dynamic of subsequent theological reflection. As Israel's understanding of God changes, the shape of the community will shift. As the community changes, its understanding of God will develop. Hence, Israel's understanding of God will be framed at every point against the background of the community in which its faith is confessed.

Therefore, Israel's faith does not develop as the result of armchair musings. Nor does it ever comprise a rolling series of philosophical statements on the nature of God, though it will have such implications. Rather, Israel's understanding of God takes on its characteristic features as it seeks to grapple with two existential dilemmas, one more serious and threatening than the other: first, the journey from a *tribal league to a dynastic monarchy;* second, and by far the greater, *the fall of Jerusalem and the loss of the land.*

While tracing the development of Israel's understanding of God, we should acknowledge that Israel's faith did not accord the same importance to creedal statements as Christianity did almost from the start. True, there are confessions of faith in Israel's tradition, perhaps the most famous, the Shema (Deut 6:4–9), and the "historical credo" of Deuteronomy 26:5–9 (see also Deut. 6:20–24; Josh. 24:2–13), but this was not its characteristic or exclusive path of development.[3] Nevertheless, in various forms, Israel's faith remained *coherent* and *consistent,* and these will be the characteristics that we will trace as the community threads its way through the obstacles and dilemmas of its history.

The Exodus
"What Actually Happened?"

Scholars have long debated how much actual history stands behind the events of Israel's founding. Our concern is primarily theological. We seek to isolate Israel's fundamental theological template, and our focus is not finally with Israel's origins, but rather, looking in the other direction, we seek to understand the God of Christian revelation who nevertheless assumes at every point the God of Israel.

Still, the text's theological claim is to relate a form of epic protohistory. And the modern reader invariably asks questions that the ancients did not. How much actual history, in our sense, stands behind the larger-than-life episodes of exodus, Sinai, and the land? What actually happened?

Two generations ago, William Foxwell Albright (1891–1971), dean of American archaeologists and Old Testament scholars, was confident that the journeys of the patriarchs reflected the migration of ancient peoples across the Fertile Crescent in the early second millennium B.C.[4] *This view was typical of the time — a general belief in the historical reliability of the biblical text and a proclivity toward early dating of the events it narrated. George Mendenhall saw parallels between biblical covenants and ancient Hittite suzerainty treaties of the thirteenth and fourteenth centuries.*[5] *His findings seemed to be independently confirmed by Klaus Baltzer.*[6] *Conclusion: biblical covenants were ancient and original as they stand in the biblical text.*

When it came to Israel's entrance into the land, Albright and his students favored the account in the book of Joshua. The tribes of Israel invaded Canaan and took the country by conquest. In the 1920s and 1930s, German scholars Martin Noth (1902–1968) and Albrecht Alt (1883–1956) proposed an alternate model of peaceful infiltration.[7] *Nomadic tribes from semiarid regions of Transjordan settled in the fertile, well-watered hill country of Canaan, and these were the proto-Israelites. Mendenhall rejected both the conquest and peaceful infiltration models. Instead, he proposed in 1962 that Israel originated in a series of peasant revolts.*[8] *The people of Canaan overthrew their local rulers and joined together, forming a new group that had no king but Yahweh. Norman Gottwald took up the same theme in 1979, this time from a Marxist perspective.*[9]

The foregoing picture has changed considerably in the past twenty-five years. The arguments for the antiquity of biblical covenants on the basis of their parallels with ancient suzerainty treaties no longer find the same support. Rather, some argue, biblical covenants may be the result of prophetic preaching from later centuries, read back into the story of Israel's founding — in effect, Julius Wellhausen's (1844–1918) thesis revisited. In general, the proclivity toward early dating of biblical events has given way to one that favors later dating. If early dating often served conservative theological opinion, later dating sometimes reflects a skeptical cast of mind. Thomas Thompson sees no actual history behind the Pentateuch, only a myth of origins, written many centuries after the exile.[10] *Such views produce their own problems, above all, a new form of argument from silence: what is not positively known to be early must therefore be late. Still, archaeologist William Dever sees a growing consensus around a modified version of peasant revolt.*[11] *He quotes historian J. Maxwell Miller, whose words stand as a good summary of informed opinion about Israel's origins at this time:*

> *In any case, earliest Israel was probably a loose confederation of tribes and clans that "emerged" gradually from the pluralistic population of the land. Accordingly, Israel's ancestors would have been of diverse origins. Some may have been immigrants from Transjordan, possibly even from Egypt. But basically Israel seems to have emerged from the melting pot of peoples already in the land of Canaan at the beginning of the Iron Age. Accordingly, their lifestyle and material culture were essentially "Canaanite."*[12]

What about the exodus? Joseph Blenkinsopp writes, "It seems plausible that some Hebrew ancestors of the Israelites spent time in Egypt, together with other Western Semites, and were engaged in building projects."[13] *It is difficult to imagine a momentous theological tradition such as the exodus built out of whole cloth. But for the same reason — because the theological overlay is so thick — it is also difficult to trace in detail the voyage of these first Israelites from Egypt into the land of Canaan.*

The Journey to the Monarchy

Israel enters the land of Canaan as a loose confederation of clans and tribes. The accounts of its entrance vary. The book of Joshua tells a story of outright conquest, redolent of the larger-than-life deeds of the nation's founding. The book of Judges carries a more modest tale, closer to actual events and similar to what follows in the biblical record. Israel's progress in the land of Canaan is slow. Warfare, the peaceful absorption of the other peoples, and the attraction of a group that has no king but Yahweh each play a role in an extended social process extending down to the time of the monarchy, roughly two hundred years.

But, in truth, the tribal league's strengths and weaknesses are identical. The loose league of tribes attests to its faith in Yahweh as its principal source of strength and sustenance. Indeed, the uniqueness of this God is exactly mirrored in the unique social reality of these tribes whose king is their God. In times of trouble, Yahweh raises up "judges," local charismatic leaders, to face the crisis of the moment.

When the situation is resolved, it returns to the *status quo ante bellum*. In this way the tribal league is able to cope with the patchwork of Canaanite city-states. But the combined pressure of Philistine and Ammonite expansion exposes the inherent weakness of the loosely organized Israelite confederation. The Philistines conquer the shrine at Shiloh in 1050 B.C. and seize the ark of the covenant, Israel's emblematic symbol. The fledgling nation is faced with stark alternatives: either risk extinction or move toward a king, a stronger and more stable form of government. But in doing so, does Israel betray its own founding vision?

Both *ark* and *king* are potent symbols. Kingship is reminiscent of Egypt, of the pharaoh, and of all that Israel left behind. A king has always been an easy, natural symbol of God, an identification that has recurred in human history countless times. So much power — economic, military, political, administrative — concentrated in a single pair of hands! Indeed, we continue unabated to give near religious veneration to vast concentrations of power and wealth in single individuals. Certainly, wealthy benefactors to schools and churches are regularly accorded near religious devotions when they write out a check for seven figures, with hushed administrators at their side in quiet attendance. This is one kind of revelation, and it is easy enough to understand. God as the most powerful being in the heavens is revealed in the most powerful figure on earth by human reckoning, in the king. By contrast, the ark makes quite another statement. It is a symbol of Israel's God — a transcendent personality — who himself is different enough. The ark is also the receptacle of the Decalogue, the covenant between God and the nation. Here ethical commands outweigh the dictates of power or wealth. Was Israel now to betray this legacy (Judg. 8:22; 1 Sam. 8:7; 10:19; 12:12, 17–20)? Such were the sentiments of Gideon and Samuel (Judg. 8:22–23).

The founding of the monarchy resembles in its own way the founding of the nation. If Yahweh steps forward at the exodus to reveal his name and disclose his *personality,* the latter is also the running thread in the turn toward kingship. The story is traced through four *personalities* — Samuel, Saul, David, Solomon — reaching a climax in the person of David. The principals themselves are surrounded by a cast of memorable characters. The prophet Samuel presides over the transition, giving voice to traditional misgivings about kings (Judg. 17:6; 21:25; cf. 18:1; 19:1). Kings take sons for warfare and daughters for the household, he tells the Israelites. Kings take the best of your land and your crops and give little in return. And if the step is once taken, there is no turning back.

The actual turn toward the monarchy is personified in the lives of three people over three generations: Saul, David, and Solomon. Each is a unique personality, each a stage on the journey toward dynastic monarchy. Few pages of the Bible glow with such luster as those which portray the turn to the monarchy. Long gone is the heroic protohistory of exodus, Sinai, and the land in which Yahweh himself led Israel out of Egypt. Now, as Yahweh moves to the background, these human personalities step to the fore, each more finely sketched than the other. The central narrative, the so-called Court History of King David (2 Sam. 9–1 Kings 1–2) has often been attributed to the hand of an eyewitness, most recently to a Davidic princess.[14] That such a thesis regularly recurs — apart from its truth — carries its own message. These seem like events that actually happened. Their "gritty historical realism," as Robert Alter calls it, rebuts all attempts to reduce them to the creative imagination of a later scribe.[15] But the point is not the genius of the narrative; rather, only events of extraordinary magnitude could have inspired such a chronicle in the first place. Indeed, the founding of the monarchy was as extraordinary in human terms, as the founding of the nation was as its divine equivalent. That much was at stake!

David is the centerpiece. He exemplifies the maxim that large personalities carry the fault of every virtue. David is generous yet avaricious, forgiving but vengeful, shrewd yet foolish. But at every turn, the simple largeness of his personality stands out, and this fits exactly the task that he is called to discharge on the historical stage. David defeats the Philistines and establishes his capital at Jerusalem, a city that belonged to no tribe and henceforth is called the "city of David." Then he transfers the nation's symbol, the ark of the covenant, to Jerusalem. Finally, he set in motion an institutional change that only a charismatic personality of the highest caliber could accomplish: he founds a dynasty. In terms of Israel's logic, God established a covenant with the house of David. It is not David who will build a house, a temple, for Yahweh, but God will establish a covenant with David's house, his family (2 Sam. 7:14; 1 Chron. 17; Ps. 89). This covenant is also different. A covenant with God's "son," as the king is called, even an adopted son, like the kings of Israel, is unconditional. In sum, only an extraordinarily charismatic personality could accomplish what heretofore seemed unthinkable in Israel, the founding of a dynastic monarchy.

In Solomon, the transition is complete. It is not Solomon's personality that stands out, but rather his accomplishments. He builds palaces and a temple. He establishes a full-fledged court, complete with foreign wives. He concludes treaties with other nations. Internally, he establishes new fiscal districts for tax purposes, cutting across old tribal boundaries. He institutes forced labor, the hated *corvee*. At every point, Solomon acts against the older traditions of the tribal league, anxious to establish Israel as a full-fledged monarchy, an imperial power of the second rank, Israel now a nation like other nations. However, the cumulative effect of so much change was to spin the nation dizzily on its axis, far beyond its ability to absorb so much novelty and disruption. In a rush, Samuel's warnings about a king come true.

II. Yahweh, God of the Nation

Israel has now become a kingdom, ushering in a new set of characters into the nation's life and onto the historical stage. Prophets enter with kings. The wisdom tradition comes into its own in court life. The construction of a temple, finished by Phoenician artisans, and a change in priestly leadership create a new class of priests. But overshadowing all such factors is a far simpler equation. *As Israel becomes a nation much like other nations, does Yahweh come to resemble a national god?* Originally, Yahweh's uniqueness was anchored in the unique social character of the tribal league. Now the magic circle is broken. Instead, Yahweh is now placed on comparative display, and his uniqueness is not guaranteed. Consequently, apostasy, idolatry, and the worship of other gods now loom in a new way as dangerous and menacing to the nation and to its God. Whose deity is stronger? The new picture could not be more clearly portrayed than in the face-off on Mount Carmel between

Yahweh the God of Israel and Baal Melqart the god of Tyre. The worship of this god had accompanied Jezebel south when she became the wife of King Ahab of Israel (ca. 868–850 B.C.), and the situation had become intolerable. But on Mount Carmel the prophet Elijah makes short work of the competition. The priests of Baal are unable to ignite the bull of sacrifice, but the God of Israel accomplishes the feat effortlessly on the first try. Clear as well, this comparative display is a public one.

The event illumines the problematic for this new chapter in Israel's understanding of God. Yahweh's victory over the Baal of Tyre was evident enough. But what if the tide turns against Israel and its God?

In sum, the road ahead: the united monarchy of David and Solomon lasted a scant seventy-eight years, breaking down into its natural, constituent parts. The house of David continued in the smaller, southern kingdom, Judah. The kingdom of the north, called "Israel," continued under kings closer to the charismatic leaders of the tribal league. Although these kingdoms knew prosperous days — and at roughly the same time, the reign of Jeroboam II in Israel (786–746 B.C.) and of Uzziah in Judah (783–742 B.C.) — the overriding factors augured otherwise. The great empires of Assyria and then Babylon cast long shadows across the Near East, playing a baleful role in the fate of the two nations. The Assyrian empire captured Samaria in 721 B.C., ending the life of the northern kingdom. In 587 B.C., Jerusalem fell to the Babylonians. Judah ceased to exist. If Israel's history began in its glorious deliverance from Egypt, it ends in ignominy in Jerusalem, its final spasm described in the last chapter of 2 Kings. Here the Babylonians mete out to Zedekiah, the last king of Judah, his fate: "They slaughtered the sons of Zedekiah before his eyes, then put out the eyes of Zedekiah; they bound him in fetters and took him to Babylon" (2 Kings 25:7).

This train of events represents not merely a neutral précis of Israel's decline but rather a religious dilemma of the first order that the nation is forced to confront. If the God of Israel is linked to the fate of the nation at every point, where is Yahweh in this tale of defeat and destruction? If he is an exodus God, a saving God, where is he when the lights of Jerusalem go out? If the God of Israel is a covenant God who had chosen Israel as his own, where is he when all visible signs of this election — the dynasty, the temple, the covenant with the nation, the covenant with the house of David — are obliterated? If Yahweh remains a God of the promised land, what can this mean when the land itself is lost? Or has the God of Israel been publicly discredited in the nation's defeat and humiliation?

The horns of this dilemma dare not be blunted. Israel and its God are forced to navigate the treacherous waters between Scylla and Charybdis, and there is no escaping this harrowing passage. Israel's faith has to face this stern test before it can once again glimpse the light of day on the far side of these events. And it was never the same afterward. The helmsmen of the journey are the prophets, and their role is crucial. In Israel's earliest history, Yahweh revealed himself as a God who acts *into* the course of human events in miraculous episodes like the exodus, events that were largely self-explanatory. That has changed. Now God's activity merges in the flow of ordinary events. But where and how in the course of such events is Yahweh's action discernible? Here the prophets enter. In this sense, the prophets are not predictors of the nation's future; rather, they glimpse Yahweh at work with his heavenly court and interpret the course of events accordingly, declaiming God's presence in the otherwise tangled skein of human history. In this sense, Max Weber's observation is correct: the first concern of the prophets is international affairs, for this is the venue in which Yahweh and Israel are preeminently tested.[16]

Not surprisingly, there were several interpretations of the fateful events surrounding the fall of Jerusalem. In one sense, they represent successive stages of digestion as the nation seeks to grapple with its fate. In another sense, they catch and magnify different sides of the dilemma. Only time would tell which mixture of interpretations would be adequate to interpret the fate of the nations and its abiding faith in Yahweh, God of Israel. But this much is crystal clear: a credible interpretation of the fall of Jerusalem is a *sine qua non* for the life of the community to continue. In that sense, theological reflection is nothing less than a lifeline to the future. The past was now irrevocably lost.

Jeremiah and Ezekiel

By any measure, the prophets Jeremiah and Ezekiel offer a far more penetrating analysis of the nation's misfortunes than the interpretation that reformers in the reign of King Josiah (640–609 B.C.) proposed.[17] In this regard, despite their obvious differences, Jeremiah and Ezekiel are linked by common features: a word of judgment and then one of hope. They are also prophets whose personalities leap from the page of the biblical text. In both cases, the personality of the prophet blends with his message. In effect, the unrelieved word of judgment, to be credible, requires that message and messenger become one. The burden of the prophetic office grows accordingly. Jeremiah's rueful lament to Yahweh catches the sentiment: "Truly, you are to me like a deceitful brook, like waters that fail" (Jer. 15:18). Gerhard von Rad (1901–1971) writes, "If it is only with Jeremiah, and not earlier, that the earthly vessel broke, the reason is primarily that the prophetic office assumed by Jeremiah was far greater in its range and depth than that of any of his predecessors."[18] Much the same could be said of Ezekiel.

Their message is a simple one: Israel's fate is sealed, and its judgment fully merited. Indeed, there never was a time when the nation was faithful to the covenant, says Ezekiel, not even at the beginning at Sinai in the wilderness. There never was a honeymoon in the marriage. And by now, these failures have acquired a long history. Hence, even the signs of nation's election — the temple and the dynasty — have become filled with corruption. The failure of kings is well known. Jeremiah scorns those who cry, "The temple of the LORD, the temple of LORD, the temple of LORD," hoping in vain to save themselves by invoking the temple. Ezekiel's vision sees the temple infested with foreign idols, with the gods and goddesses of Canaan and Egypt. For him in a special way, "the cause of Israel's approaching fall lay quite indubitably in a failure in the sphere of the holy."[19] Hence, the prophet sees Yahweh's presence — the "glory of the LORD" — abandoning the temple in Jerusalem altogether to be with the exiles in Babylon. Jeremiah counsels those in exile to settle in, plant their garden, and pray for their rulers. Their stay will not be brief.

The destruction of these former signs of election delivers a clear message: resistance to the enemy is useless. Jeremiah is a leading voice of the party of appeasement in the reign of King Jehoiakim (609–598 B.C.). The prophet himself thereby becomes a hated figure. In the last analysis, there is scarcely an inch of light between the life of the prophet and the stern message of judgment that he delivers.

Yet where, one may ask, is Yahweh, God of Israel, in the midst of the nation's travail? Here the prophets answer with one voice. He is indeed active. But in this case he is acting on the side of Israel's enemies. He is using the nations as his chosen instruments to mete out punishment to Israel for its failure to live up to the covenant. Hence, the counsel to surrender to the enemies flows from this deeper insight that, at the moment, the nations are the special instruments of Yahweh's judgment on the nation.

We also witness in this insight the growth and expansion of Israel's insight into the nature of its own God. It had been clear from the start that the God of Israel was not the nation's totem, never identified with its group self-interest, no matter how closely the two were allied. The book of Kings also recounted that the prophet Elijah had used Hazael, king of Damascus, against the house of Omri. Now this latent potential is reawakened. Now the prophets see Yahweh of Israel using Assyria and Babylon as the special tools of his will. *But if the God of Israel can use foreign nations, then he must be their God as well.* Is the God of Israel somehow the God of Assyria and Babylon? Where, then, can his domain cease? So, in the waning days of the monarchy, as Jerusalem falls, as all visible signs of election collapse; as the land itself is lost, the God of Israel seems to disengage slightly and ascend above the chosen people to reveal himself in their defeat as the Lord of all nations. This did not mean that Yahweh sundered his bond to the community; however, of necessity and as a consequence, the bond will need to be understood in a new way.

Yet equally, and remarkably, Yahweh remains God of the exodus, a saving God in the midst of Israel's travail. The prophets are no less faithful to this side of their legacy. Beyond a message of doom, each carries one of hope. Their convictions here are simple too. Even in their defeat and exile, Yahweh has not abandoned Israel. He will act again on Israel's behalf. And so the events of Israel's founding — exodus, Sinai, the land — swing this time toward the future, defining the new way God will act. In effect, they become categories of expectation that define the nation's hope. There will be a new exodus, the prophets foretell, a new covenant, and a return to the land. The visions of the prophets are all the more remarkable, given the message of unrelieved doom that to varying degrees they also proclaim. They resemble shafts of light that, breaking through dark clouds, appear all the brighter and more shimmering by virtue of the contrast. In each case, they swing toward the future across a hiatus that describes the present moment. Indeed, they must become larger-than-life visions, vast hopes, because nothing less can nourish the sprouts of new life.

I quote two of those visions. The first is from the book of Jeremiah, probably the work of an editor during the exile, and the second from the book of Ezekiel. These are not the only visions in these prophetic books. Characteristically, Ezekiel dreams of a new and purified temple (Ezek. 40–48) to which the "glory of God" can return. And in chapter 37, he delivers his famous sermon on hope, "O Dry Bones, Hear the Word of the Lord."

> The days are surely coming, says the LORD, when I will make a new covenant with the house of Israel and the house of Judah. It will not be like the covenant that I made with their ancestors when I took them by the hand to bring them out of the land of Egypt — a covenant that they broke, though I was their husband, says the LORD. But this is the covenant that I will make with the house of Israel after those days, says the LORD: I will put my law within them, and I will write it on their hearts; and I will be their God, and they shall be my people. No longer shall they teach one another, or say to each other, "Know the LORD," for they shall all know me, from the least of them to the greatest, says the LORD; for I will forgive their iniquity, and remember their sin no more. (Jer. 31:31–34)

Ezekiel writes in a strikingly similar vein:

> I will take you from the nations, and gather you from all the countries, and bring you into your own land. I will sprinkle clean water upon you, and you shall be clean from all your uncleanness, and from all your idols I will cleanse you. A new heart I will give you, and a new spirit I will put within you, and I will remove from your body the heart of stone and give you a heart of flesh. I will put my spirit within you and make you follow my statues and be careful to observe my ordinances. Then you shall live in

the land that I gave to you to your ancestors; and you shall be
my people, and I will be your God. (Ezek. 36:24–28)

The visions share common features. They arc far above the present
baleful situation, hoping thereby to throw a bridge across troubled
waters in order to reach a distant shore on the far side of the nation's doom. Each assumes a hiatus. The original covenant with Moses
was carved on stone, meant to found a community in which the message was passed down from generation to generation. That covenant is
now broken, and there is no return to it. By contrast, the covenant in
Jeremiah and its equivalent in Ezekiel (see Ezek. 34:25) are radically
internalized, written in the heart of each individual. Indeed, it need
no longer be taught, for all have it inscribed within them, its fidelity
thereby guaranteed. In Ezekiel, each Israelite is given a new heart and
a new spirit to follow God's commands. The element of continuity
in difference could not be plainer: a new covenant for a new age in
which humanity is changed for the better. Likewise, Ezekiel's sermon
on hope is preached to a field of dry bones. This is the prophet's situation. "Our bones are dried up, and our hope is lost; we are cut off
completely." The nation is literally brought back to life, piece by piece,
until new life can be breathed into it. This is the chasm that the vision
seeks to bridge. In none of these cases is the message one of reform.
Such days are long gone. Instead, these are words of consolation and
visions of hope in which the high arc of the vision's trajectory stands
in contrast to the trackless wasteland below it. Only the highest of
hopes can carry across such bleak terrain.

Second Isaiah

The Talmud links Jeremiah, Ezekiel, and Second Isaiah this way: "Jeremiah is all doom; Ezekiel begins with doom but ends with consolation;
while Isaiah is all consolation."[20] Significantly, the personalities of the
prophets who carried a message of judgment are heightened. Second Isaiah, the author of chapters 40–55, by contrast blends into
anonymity as one author of the great book of Isaiah. Perhaps a
message of consolation may carry by itself.

Second Isaiah is the interpreter of Israel's restoration from exile.
Yet the prophet assumes at every point the message of Jeremiah and

Ezekiel with which the Talmud links him. The words of those prophets have been vindicated. They predicted that Yahweh was working on the side of Israel's enemies, that the nation's defeat and exile were inevitable, and they were right. Israel's defeat is God's vindication. But if Yahweh can use the nations as tools of chastisement, he can also use them to restore Israel. And this is, of course, what happens and is the central event that Second Isaiah seeks to interpret. Cyrus of Persia, Yahweh's "anointed" (Isa. 45:1), his messiah and shepherd (Isa. 44:28), has been the chosen instrument to defeat Babylon and restore Israel. And this turn of events, no less than the exile itself, demands interpretation. How many nations have been conquered and consigned to oblivion? The number is legion. How many have been restored? Very few. Second Isaiah is fully aware of the wondrous nature of this turn. He therefore looks to Israel's deepest hopes to interpret it. This is truly a "new thing," he says (Isa. 43:19). The images used to describe it proliferate. This is a new exodus, a new sojourn in the wilderness, done not in haste but rather in leisure and in grand style. The hills bow down and the crooked ways are made straight before these returning exiles.

This dizzying display of Yahweh's power, first in defeat and then in restoration, propels Second Isaiah's vision of God. In the face of these events, there can be only *one* God in all the universe. All other so-called gods are simply creatures of wood and stone, human effigies and no gods at all, the object of scorn and derision (Isa. 40:19).

In effect, Second Isaiah's breakthrough to a pure monotheism has been forged in the furnace of defeat and restoration (Isa. 48:10–12). The latent potential in Israel's original vision of God has thereby been fully actualized. Its defining characteristics are here given clearest and fullest expression. On the one hand, Second Isaiah, along with Ezekiel and Jeremiah, become architects of the sheer upward vault of God's transcendence, hereafter a hallmark of the God of Judaism and of Christianity. What began long ago at Sinai as the experience of "otherness" — what Yahweh was *not*, a negative valence — is here endowed at every point with positive meaning. Yahweh of Israel is the great creator God. His first action is the creation of the universe. Within this context, the exodus comes into proper perspective. Here Yahweh, creator of the universe, intervenes to save Israel from the hand of the Egyptians.

If transcendence is balanced by personality at Sinai, this side of Israel's original vision is given equally remarkable expression. This towering God displays tender solicitude, now all the more striking given Yahweh's overwhelming power. Isaiah 40 begins with these words to the divine council which proclaim its central theme: "Comfort, comfort my people, says your God. Speak tenderly to Jerusalem and cry out to her that she has served her term, that her penalty is paid, that she has received from the Lord's hand double for all her sins" (Isa. 40:1–2). Yahweh, creator of the universe, displays toward Israel the tender solicitude that a mother shows toward her nursling child: "Can a woman forget her nursing child, or show no compassion for the child of her womb? Even these may forget, yet I will not forget you. See, I have inscribed you on the palms of my hands" (Isa. 49:15–16).

Such words are all the more astonishing when spoken by the one God, the only God, Creator of the universe and Lord of the nations! If *otherness* (transcendence) and *personality* (immanence) are enduring characteristics of the God of Israel, now they are teased in dialectical counterpoint to their widest extremes in Second Isaiah's exalted vision of Yahweh. Here the creator of the universe is mysteriously concerned with the fate of Israel as a mother might love a special child with particular devotion.

Yet if defeat and restoration have brought forth a new sense of Yahweh's full dimension, they also underscore another conclusion: the ways of this God are inscrutable. "His understanding is unsearchable" (Isa. 40:28). "For my thoughts are not your thoughts, nor are your ways my ways, says the LORD. For as the heavens are higher than the earth, so are my ways higher than your ways and my thoughts than your thoughts" (Isa. 55:8–11).

If Yahweh is the one God, the only God, what is the new role of Israel? Certainly, the special choice of Israel seems enshrouded in the mysterious nature of Yahweh himself. Why has the all-powerful God chosen this nation among all the nations of the earth? And how does Israel relate to the other nations that ultimately share the same God? Yahweh no longer stands in a hostile relation to other gods now reduced to mere idols, creatures of wood and stone. Can Israel's relation to the nations remain marked by antagonism, not least of all because the community has been restored through the agency of the great Persian Empire and its reigning monarch Cyrus? Finally, what do these answers bode for the actual establishment of a new community in Israel after the exile?

Second Isaiah turns to some of these questions in the figure of the "servant of Yahweh." The term *servant* carries its reverse surface connotation. A servant is one chosen for an especially important mission. In this sense, Moses, Joshua, prophets, and the kings are ranged among God's "servants." In the so-called Servant Songs — independent poetic units within Second Isaiah (Isa. 42:1–4; 49:1–6; 50:4–9; 52:15–53:12) — especially in Isaiah 42–50, the servant is practically identified with Israel. The servant may seem more like an individual in the fourth Servant Song. Yet the servant, even as individual, remains a symbolic figure of the nation with exemplary status, endowed with multiple levels of meaning. The great themes running through these chapters are inseparable. What is the role of Israel? What has been the meaning of its suffering?

Isaiah 2 suggested a more positive tack between Israel and the nations, envisioning a double movement. "In days to come, the mountain of the Lord's house will be established as the highest of mountains" (Isa. 2:2). All the nations will stream toward the mountain of the Lord. In turn, instruction will go forth from Zion. A peaceful vision emerges. Swords are beaten into plowshares, precursor to the peaceable kingdom of Isaiah 11. But when such themes appear in Second Isaiah, they are broached differently. This time, what are the implications for Israel of Yahweh's emergence as the only God?

> You are my witnesses, says the LORD, and my servant whom I have chosen so that you may know and believe me and understand that I am he. Before me no god was formed nor shall there be any after me. I, I am the LORD, and beside me there is no savior. I declared and saved and proclaimed when there was no strange god among you; and you are my witnesses, says the LORD.
>
> (Isa. 43:10–12)

Israel was deaf and blind. Now it sees clearly what for others may remain obscure. Therefore Israel should be the first to recognize

Yahweh's uniqueness and witness to it before the nations. Above all, Israel is a witness in its own fate. In defeat and exile, Israel exemplifies God's justice. In restoration, Israel testifies to God's mercy. If Israel is to act as Yahweh's chosen servant, this is its special role. Israel is to be "a light to the nations" (Isa. 42:6). Even in the third Servant Song (in which the servant is identified *with* Israel, while retaining a mission *to* Israel), the theme of a light to the nations continues, so that God's "salvation may reach to the end of the earth" (Isa. 49:6). "See, you shall call nations that you do not know, and nations that do not know you shall run to you because of the LORD your God, the Holy One of Israel, for he has glorified you" (Isa. 55:5).

Therefore Israel has an exemplary status. In Third Isaiah, the people of Israel act as priests and ministers to the nations (Isa. 61:6). Just as the status of Israel's God is exalted, so too the role of Israel is elevated. Israel receives a double portion in its restoration, as Isaiah 40:2 promised. Israel, the servant of the Lord, is the first witness to Yahweh as the one God, the only God. This is Israel's special honor.

Other Voices

Yet nagging questions remain. Is it all fair? Had Israel fully merited this degree of destruction, earned this measure of God's wrath? What *else* may the fall of Jerusalem, the destruction of the temple, dynasty and nation portend about the God of Israel? Were these events perhaps signs of Yahweh's weakness? Did God see or even care about what is happening? And granting the truth of the prophets, why must *this* generation pay for the accumulated sins of its ancestors? This seems the logical conclusion of Ezekiel's view that Israel's infidelity goes back to the beginning. A proverb of the day catches the nagging question. Why must the children of this generation grind their teeth on the sour grapes their ancestors have eaten? (Jer 31:30; Ezek 18:2)

Both Ezekiel and Jeremiah respond to the proverb. No one is punished for another's sins. The children of this age do not grind their teeth on the sour grapes their ancestors have eaten. Conversely, no one is saved by the righteousness of another. True, in the days of Abraham with Sodom and Gomorrah it may have been different, the inhabitants of those towns saved by ten righteous Israelites. But that day is gone. The older notion of communal solidarity in blessings and curses now gives way to an individual approach. Each one earns his or her own salvation, no more and no less.

Such a view surely reflects the destruction of the community's social fabric under the accumulated weight of defeat and exile. But it represents a large historical turn as well. The Sinai covenant was made first with the community within which the fate of the individual was enfolded. Now the individual steps to the fore in a new way. How is the justice of God to be reckoned in this new situation in which the fate of the individual becomes paramount?

Job

We place the book of Job in this context. Scholars agree that it is impossible to date the composition of the book of Job with any certainty. There are no internal indices to outside historical events and no references to Israel's history within it. Indeed, Job and his friends are identified as non-Israelite. The conscious effort to remove all fingerprints from the text heightens the role of the individual and the symbolic struggle he wages. Gerhard von Rad writes of Job's situation, "It is in an existence totally without community or saving history that Job in steely isolation carries on his struggle with God."[21]

Job is an innocent man whose family and possessions have been taken away and destroyed as a test, unbeknownst to Job himself. But in Isaiah Berlin's (1909–1997) famed image of the hedgehog and the fox, Job is the hedgehog who knows one great thing, his own innocence. Circling like foxes, his friends offer standard answers about why people suffer: because of their secret sins or the sins of their ancestors. Although their answers vary, they lead finally to one conclusion: if Job suffers, then one way or another, he must have sinned. However, he answers with a steadfast no.

If Job's innocence is one fixed pole of the discussion, God's justice is the other. His friends *presume* it at every point. Job asks for *demonstration,* while realizing that no higher tribunal can stand above or even be equal to this towering God in order to judge his actions. In claiming his own innocence so steadfastly in the face of God's exalted justice, does an element of hubris enter Job's case?

With a clear sense of exasperation, God — here called "Yahweh,"[22] his name to Israel — responds in Job 38:

Then the LORD answered Job out of the whirlwind: "Who is this
that darkens counsel by words without knowledge? Gird up your
loins like a man. I will question you, and you shall declare to me."

(Job 38:1–3)

In one sense, Job's question and God's answer pass like ships in the
night. Jack Miles neatly sums up the situation: "Job speaks at length
about justice and demands that God responds. God refuses. God speaks
at length about power and demands that Job respond. Job refuses."[23]
In the end, God does not answer Job; God silences him.

But God does not simply reduce Job with a blunt demonstration
of power. Rather, he proceeds through an inventory of creation —
how the earth was made, the heavens created, the waters separated,
how the animals were fashioned, the mountain goat, the wild ox, the
ostrich, the horse. These events revealed God as a skilled artisan of
enormous originality, always acting with a purpose. It is not simply a
demonstration of might; it is one of the elegance of God's creation,
above all, of the steady, guiding intention undergirding it. In this sense,
the God of Job is not simply powerful, but awesome. As Yahweh draws
himself up to full stature, displaying the wonders of creation, Job's
questions shrink by comparison. It is not simply that God silences Job;
God has shrunk his questions. By contrast, Job remains the child of
the principle of individual responsibility. And steely isolation is hardly
a good venue from which to pose large questions. Ultimately, Job's
is a Hobson's choice. If he is right, then he is an innocent man who
suffers for no reason. His sufferings are meaningless. If his friends
are right and Job suffers because he is a sinner in some sense, then at
least his sufferings gain some measure of meaning. In this sense, the
final conclusion of the book of Job follows logically enough. God's
demonstration is not without effect. "I had heard of you by the hearing
of the ear, but now my eye sees you" (Job 42:5). What Job knew
before secondhand, he now sees for himself. Therefore he repents.
God restores him twofold, as he promised to Israel in Isaiah 40.

In another sense, this answer only raises other questions. The God
who speaks in the book of Job is a God of nature, reminiscent of El,
the God of Israel's Canaanite forebears who displays his wonders in
creation. The omission of a God of history is enormously significant.

Indeed, if such a God cannot enter the story of Job — only the name "Yahweh" — can he enter Israel's history at a later moment?

I described Second Isaiah as erecting the upward vault of God's transcendence. But in Second Isaiah's vision, Yahweh's *power* as creator of the universe, the Lord of the nations, was balanced by remarkable *solicitude* for Israel as a mother who cares for an infant at the breast. That was inscrutable enough. Now the element of solicitude disappears. Instead, in the book of Job, the same towering figure of God the creator enters in full plumage. For his own reasons, he chooses to afflict an innocent man. The *comforter* is now replaced by an *afflicter.* With that turn, the figure of God in the book of Job disappears behind the vault of his own transcendence. God's ways are *truly* not our ways. They are hidden and inscrutable far beyond our reckoning. Who can trace out the purposes of God in the suffering of this one innocent man? *A fortiori,* who can trace out the purposes of God in the history of this community with which God has chosen to associate himself? That question now seems unanswerable. But, once posed, the question cannot be withdrawn. Even with the adjustments of the final chapter, the book of Job stands among Israel's sacred writings as a permanent question mark about the intelligibility of God's action in human history.

In sum, we close this second stage of the development of Israel's understanding of God on an unresolved note. While Yahweh, God of Israel, has assumed his rightful place as the one God, Lord of heaven and earth, the community in which this confession originated lies in shambles, now just returned from exile in Babylon. These elements comprise the starting point for the final leg of our journey.

The Fourth Servant Song (Isaiah 52:13–53:12): "Who Has Believed What We Have Heard?"

The fourth Servant Song of Isaiah bristles with problems of historical exegesis and textual interpretation. The reader is referred to specialized literature on these subjects.[24] The focus here is on Isaiah 52–53 as literary unit and why it fits the context of Israel's exile and restoration at this point in the story.

See, my servant shall prosper; he shall be exalted and lifted up, and shall be very high. Just as there were many who were astonished at him — so marred was his appearance, beyond human semblance, and his form beyond that of mortals — so he shall startle many nations; kings shall shut their mouths because of him; for that which had not been told them they shall see, and that which they had not heard they shall contemplate.

Who has believed what we have heard? And to whom has the arm of the Lord been revealed? For he grew up before him like a young plant, and like a root out of dry ground; he had no form or majesty that we should look at him, nothing in his appearance that we should desire him. He was despised and rejected by others; a man of suffering and acquainted with infirmity; and as one from whom others hide their faces he was despised and we held him of no account.

Surely he has borne our infirmities and carried our diseases; yet we accounted him stricken, struck down by God, and afflicted. But he was wounded for our transgressions, crushed for our iniquities; upon him was the punishment that made us whole, and by his bruises we are healed. All we like sheep have gone astray; we have all turned to our own way, and the Lord has laid on him the iniquity of us all.

He was oppressed, and he was afflicted, yet he did not open his mouth; like a lamb that is led to the slaughter, and like a sheep that before its shearers is silent, so he did not open his mouth. By a perversion of justice he was taken away. Who could have imagined his future? For he was cut off from the land of the living, stricken for the transgression of my people. They made his grave with the wicked and his tomb with the rich, although he had done no violence, and there was no deceit in his mouth.

Yet it was the will of the Lord to crush him with pain. When you make his life an offering for sin, he shall see his offspring, and shall prolong his days; through him the will of the Lord shall prosper. Out of his anguish he shall see light; he shall find satisfaction through his knowledge. The righteous one, my servant, shall make many righteous, and he shall bear their iniquities. Therefore I will allot him a portion with the great, and he shall divide the spoil with the strong; because he poured out himself to death, and was numbered with the transgressors; yet he bore the sins of many, and made intercession for the transgressors.

Words of Yahweh begin and end the song. They thereby witness to its drama that they enclose and bless. The song turns on the fate of an individual who has suffered innocently and on the astonishment of those who realize that they have profited from his suffering. "Who has believed what we have heard?" Their astonishment then gives way to insight. This despised and wretched man did not suffer for his own sins; rather, he was afflicted for the transgressions of others. Indeed, by his bruises they were healed. He took upon himself their sins. He gave them his innocence, and so they were restored. All of this is amazing enough. Still more amazing, God did not watch this transaction at a distance. Indeed, it was his will to bruise the servant. His suffering was somehow part of God's plan.

The song turns on these two reversals. What makes it powerful is that it does not attempt a general statement on suffering. Instead, it takes an individual life — the lingua franca of Ezekiel, Jeremiah, and Job — and tells of things that are true yet, by the same token, amazing. Indeed, they seem to defy understanding. This amazement also constitutes the song's suggestiveness. Who has believed what we have heard? Who would have guessed it? What else can it mean? The figure of the servant who bore the sins of others in order to give them his innocence opens other levels of astonishment, wonder, and puzzlement. What can it all mean? And the divine benediction around it is also amazing. No doubt it was this suggestive quality that spoke to the early church and perhaps to Jesus himself to understand his own innocent suffering. Amazement is the keynote of the song as it discloses levels of meaning and significance that no one suspects are there.

In what type of community would such a vision originate? In the same one as that of Ezekiel and Jeremiah, perhaps a generation later. In a fractured society, hammered by the blows of defeat and exile, each individual must be responsible for his or her own deeds, and God will not ask more. Hence the message of individual responsibility makes sense. But the same pulverizing blows of defeat, exile, and restoration may pierce the surface of the ordinary social world in another way. Only in times of crisis does the normal social fabric grow not only thin, but also diaphanous. On a few occasions — in individual cases like the servant's — it may reveal deeper levels of human solidarity than anyone would suspect, rare glimpses of a mystical unity in sin and suffering that undergirds and supports the human family and the fate of individuals. At this deeper level, the sufferings of the innocent not only have meaning, but also may work toward the salvation of others. Not only that: if God's ways are not our ways, then his plans for human salvation may be much more complex and hidden that we imagine or suspect. The fourth Servant Song produces first astonishment and then, in a limited way, insight into these other, deeper levels of reality. "Who has believed what we have heard?"

III. Yahweh, the Only God, Lord of the Nations, Creator of the Universe

A Question of Identity

The breakthrough of the prophets has won the day. Yahweh, God of Israel, is recognized as the one God, the only God, Lord of the nations and Creator of the universe. Yet, how is this lofty vision of God to form the actual basis of a community after the exile? That question remains. Recall that the kingdom of Judah before the exile was a nation like other nations, with its own king, court, temple, and priests. It had fixed geographic boundaries, and national identity was a simple given. One was born an Israelite, cosseted in a society with its own institutions and customs. This kind of identity has now largely disappeared. Instead, a new sense of identity will emerge only slowly — indeed, a hard-won achievement over many generations.

Clearly, the community that returned to the land after the exile is languishing. A brief resurgence of the house of David occurs, as it turns out, the final flicker of a dying dynasty. The last of the prophets appears. The temple is rebuilt in 515 B.C., and the priesthood continues. Yet these factors do not suffice to found a new community, no longer a national state but now a religious community, a dependent province of the reigning empire. In short, while the kingdom of Judah as the last remnant of *Israel* has disappeared, the *Jewish* community as a viable entity has not yet emerged. The issue of intermarriage, which looms so large in the books of Ezra and Nehemiah, gives us a clue to the problem: the community may be on the verge of dissolution, amalgamating with the local populace.

Therefore, turning this lofty vision of God into the basis for a new community is not a simple task; it is one that requires a *genius turn*. This takes place in the editing of the Pentateuch and the subsequent work of Ezra and Nehemiah.

The Editing of the Pentateuch

The shape of the Jewish community that emerges after the exile is bound up in every way with the growing clarity of its theological vision. The spearhead here is the natural desire to edit and revise Israel's sacred writings in light of the nation's exile and restoration. In turn, these cataclysmic events leave their mark on the community's written traditions, above all in the benchmark editing of the first five books of Moses, the Pentateuch.

These books contained the story of Israel's founding, probably originally carrying the narrative from the days of Abraham to the time of Joshua.[25] The covenant with Abraham at Shechem, promising land and children, was fulfilled when Joshua conquered the land and returned to Shechem. The circle is complete. But, remarkably, this continuous narrative is now interrupted when these chronicles are edited in the exile. Instead, the book of Deuteronomy is interposed, concluding the chronicles of the nation's founding in a different way. Israel's founding now stops short of the entrance to the land. Instead, it ends with the death of Moses, who *sees but does not enter* the land. By any reckoning, this constitutes a momentous turn. With the stroke of an editor's pen, a clear line of demarcation is thereby drawn between Moses and the founding of the nation and the traditions of the conquest, the monarchy, and the temple. The former comprise the Torah. The latter are classed as "early prophets," important but secondary traditions by comparison.

This editorial decision casts long shadows in all directions. The unrivaled hero of Israel's founding is Moses, prophet and prescient lawgiver. For he does not only deliver the Ten Commandments on Mount Sinai; a veritable torrent of law codes tumbles from his mouth in a steady stream from Exodus 25 to Numbers 10. The effect is magical. Moses on Mount Sinai now emerges as the law-giving founder of the community who, in the wilderness of Sinai, foresees all the legal and cultic regulations necessary to sustain the fledgling Jewish community after the exile. Thus it seems possible to draw a connecting line between Israel's founding and its present situation. By contrast, the traditions of the land, the monarchy, and the temple remain. But they pertain not to the nation's *esse,* its existence, but rather to its *bene esse,* its well-being as important traditions from the past.

The book of Deuteronomy also changes the status of law. The term *law* no longer refers first to individual statutes; instead, the law indicates God's will for the nation, calling for a corresponding and appropriate response. The word *Deuteronomy* literally means "second law," capturing this new status. All particular laws are enclosed in this newly elevated sense of the law itself as God's will. The Torah thereby becomes the lodestar for the Jewish community after the exile, and its purpose is clear. What Frank Moore Cross wrote of the priestly source achieves its goal: "It was designed to provoke overwhelming remorse in Israel and sought by the reconstruction of the age of Moses, its cult and law, to project a community of Israel in which Yahweh could return to 'tabernacle' in their land."[26]

The editing of the Pentateuch adds the final touches to the nation's theological vision. In the hands of the prophets, the events of Israel's founding — exodus, Sinai, and the land — were projected into the future as categories of hope. Yahweh will act again. There will be a new exodus and a new covenant. Now these same events become ways to interpret the community's existence after the exile. Accordingly, the historical chronicle of Israel's founding remains but steps to the background. The Torah as guidebook for the emerging Jewish community moves to the fore. Ironically, as the story of Israel's founding crystallizes, its historical voice falls silent. The story of the community continues through the work of Ezra and Nehemiah. Then the community sinks for long stretches below the level of continuously recorded history. And even when history is remembered, it is no longer reckoned "saving history" as in its halcyon days.

The editing of the Pentateuch creates another perspective. The Jewish community after the exile looks back to the events of its founding as a *golden* age in which God had acted definitively and spoken clearly. They now live in a *silver* one whose task is to compile a faithful record of the golden age, to treasure its memory and live up to the standards it had set.

Ezra and Nehemiah

In this context, the pioneering work of Ezra and Nehemiah becomes clear. Both are sent from the Persian court to stabilize the languishing

Jewish community in Palestine as a standard part of Persian policy. Nehemiah is twice governor of Judah, newly separated from the province of Samaria. He rebuilds the walls of Jerusalem, rendering the city defendable again. The dates of his tenure are relatively certain, 445–433 B.C., roughly three or four generations after the first Jews returned to the land. But Ezra is the presiding genius of the new community in its formative stages. The book of Ezra (Ezra 7–10) and the book of Nehemiah (Neh. 8–10) movingly recount how Ezra reads some version of the newly edited Torah to the languishing Jewish community. With the people in tears and rejoicing, the covenant is renewed in these new circumstances after the exile.

But this covenant and its renewal are surely different. Above all, the relation between the individual and the community is now reversed. The Sinai covenant was made first with the community. Ezra's covenant is renewed in the new era in which the individual plays a larger role. Indeed, the consistent practice of individual Jews in obedience to the law is what brings this new kind of community into existence. When we place together the issues on which Ezra and Nehemiah insist — an end to intermarriage, observance of the Sabbath and other festivals, the payment of tithes and temple offerings — the shape of the new community emerges. The community is held together by a coherent set of religious observances to which individual Jews pledge themselves. These practices are strong enough to forge the common social bonds of a community. They can ground the Jewish community in Palestine. They are also flexible enough to connect it to the Jewish community in the Diaspora. This is also a feature of the new situation. Not all Jews return from exile. Instead, a Jewish community in Babylon flourishes. Later, a Jewish community will prosper in Alexandria. Ironically, the scenes of Israel's earlier exile now become venues where Jews voluntarily choose to dwell. So as the God of Israel becomes a universal God, Judaism also begins to emerge as a worldwide community of faith. Not surprisingly, the Jews of the Diaspora establish their own distinctive institutions, such as the synagogue (third century B.C.), which only later take root in Palestine. Regular study of the Torah and habits of prayer take on new importance as well.

The Vision of God

Still, Israel's vision of God is not yet complete in its own right. Clearly, the vision of the prophets has succeeded. There is but one God, Yahweh of Israel, Lord of the nations, Creator of the universe. All other so-called gods are creatures of wood and stone. Yet the overwhelming triumph of such a vision creates its own complex legacy. The emergence of Yahweh as an all powerful, transcendent God has the secondary effect of producing a vacuum around him that begs to be filled. In other words, if the monotheism of the prophets crushed all other coequal deities, it creates a need for other heavenly beings, less than God but more than humans.

If the human analogue of God was a king, now it changes to that of an emperor. If God's will for the Jewish community is contained in the Torah, what of his plans for other nations? The God of Israel now has these wider concerns. If Cyrus of Persia and Alexander of Macedon need personnel to staff their far-flung empires — the Persian emperor sends Ezra and Nehemiah to settle his affairs in Judea — Yahweh of Israel will need new ways to oversee his universal domain. Now Yahweh sends out his own messengers, angels, to discharge his will.

Thus the recognition of God's overwhelming transcendence goes hand in hand with the development of the doctrine of angels after the exile. The angels never compete with, but rather they enhance and complement, Yahweh's overwhelming majesty. The God of preexilic Israel may have been surrounded by a court of faceless angelic attendants, but the postexilic emphasis on the individual makes itself felt here as well. Angels take on names. Such befits their specific tasks and distinct personalities. Uriel regulates the movement of the stars.[27] The great archangels, Raphael, Gabriel, and Michael, emerge as heavenly protectors, Michael as the angelic prince of Israel in its hour of need. Raphael refers to himself as "one of seven angels who stand ready to enter before the glory of the Lord" (Tob. 12:15). Angels are God's messengers to specific peoples or nations. Later, they become messengers of revelation to apocalyptic visionaries. In turn, they carry messages back to God. Above all, they surround the heavenly throne, continually singing God's praises, enhancing the majesty of God far beyond the human capacity to do so. Malign forces also emerge more clearly. Satan (literally, "the accuser") was still a member of the heavenly court in the book of Job. Now "Satan" becomes a proper name. In effect, the forces of evil assume greater personality as well. All together, these heavenly forces — the faces of good and evil — crowd the heavens. In apocalyptic literature, they seem like armies massed in the wings for a final showdown, a clash between good and evil both in heaven and on earth.

Significant developments in the wisdom tradition belong in the same context. Wisdom before the exile was what the term normally implies: maxims about wise and prudent ways of living. By definition, they could not be made into a system. The thicket of human life was far too dense and confusing for such. Rather, they constitute the "art of steering," of making one's way through the hazards of human life.[28] Yet, if no system can be made of such practical maxims, a common assumption undergirds them: there is a "hidden order in things and events" that can be discerned slowly, patiently, and at a price. This "hidden order" serves as the link to the development of wisdom after the exile.

In an obvious sense, personified wisdom helps Israel to understand Yahweh's new function in creation, a legacy of his exalted status after the exile. Wisdom therefore plays a *cosmological* role, explaining God's purposes in the universe. Job 28 may serve as a starting point to discern its lineaments. "Where does wisdom come from? And where is the place of understanding?" (Job 28:20). It is hidden from sight like wisdom in human experience. But God knows the way to its dwelling place. It is found among *the secrets of creation.* "When he made a decree for the rain and a way for the thunderbolt, then he saw it and established it, and searched it out. And he said to humankind, 'Truly the fear of the LORD, that is wisdom; and to depart from evil is understanding.'" (Job 28:26–28).

In Proverbs 8, Wisdom speaks for herself. Since the words for *wisdom* in Hebrew (*hokma*) and later in Greek (*sophia*) are feminine, she speaks as Woman Wisdom. The context here is striking and is destined to become famous in the Arian controversy. "The LORD created me at the beginning of his work, the first of his acts of long ago. Ages ago I was set up, at the first, before the beginning of the earth" (Prov.

8:22–23). Later in the chapter, Wisdom is described as God's "master worker" or alternately as his "little child."

Personified Wisdom can also take on a *historical* role. Sirach 24 sketches an even more comprehensive picture in which Wisdom herself became self-reflective. "Wisdom praises herself and tells of her glory in the midst of her people. In the assembly of the Most High she opens her mouth, and in the presence of his host she tells of her glory: 'I came forth from the mouth of the Most High, and covered the earth like a mist'" (Sir. 24:1–3). Wisdom is made before creation. When she seeks a dwelling place among the peoples of the earth, the Creator commands her, "Make your resting place in Jacob, and in Israel receive your inheritance'" (Sir. 24:8). Wisdom is here identified with the Torah, "the book of the covenant of the Most High God" (Sir 24:23).

The book of Wisdom translates traditional picture imagery about wisdom into a more abstract frame of reference. Here Wisdom's spirit is described as "intelligent, holy, unique, manifold, subtle, mobile, clear, unpolluted, distinct, invulnerable" (Wis. 7:22). The capstone of the passage describes Wisdom as the "breath of the power of God, and a pure emanation of the glory of the Almighty; therefore nothing undefiled gains entrance into her. For she is a reflection of eternal light, a spotless mirror of the working of God, and an image of his goodness" (Wis. 7:25–26).

Clearly the intent of wisdom speculation is to make sense of God's most encompassing purposes in creation. In doing so, wisdom is pictured as separate from the creator himself as the first of God's creatures (Prov. 8:22) or as a pure emanation of the glory of the Almighty (Wis. 7:25). What is the status of wisdom so described? In one sense, wisdom is a far more adequate mediator between God and humankind than angels, who inevitably resemble larger-than-life human beings. But it was surely the biblical author's intent to use wisdom simply as a metaphoric way of speaking of God's purpose in creation. Yet when those metaphors are translated into something closer to conceptual language in the book of Wisdom, they provide a way not simply of *imagining* but rather of *conceiving* of God's activity in creation as simultaneously one with God but different too. What was originally a metaphoric explanation about God's purposes can easily become an exploratory probe into God's nature. Certainly, in Israel's reflection on wisdom early Christians found ready at hand an arsenal of concepts when they chose to cross the line between metaphor and reality in order to think through Christ's divinity, one with the Father yet different too.

The Maccabean Revolt

The Maccabean revolt in 167 B.C. represents a dramatic turning point and, in a sense, a concluding chapter both for the Jewish community and its vision of God. It began with a change of policy. After the Jewish exile (587–539 B.C.), the Persians had devised a winning formula for dealing with the Jewish community: grant religious toleration and local autonomy in exchange for the recognition of the empire's authority. The formula builds on Jeremiah's advice to the first exiles in Babylon, and it worked well. And so Judea was, for the most part, quietly passed down as a dependent province of the Persian Empire, then briefly of the Greeks, and then to Alexander's generals, first the Ptolemies of Egypt, finally the Seleucids, Macedonian Greeks ruling Syria.

In 168 B.C., the infamous Seleucid king Antiochus IV Epiphanes (ca. 215–163 B.C.) departs from the formula. He erects an altar to Olympian Zeus in the temple precincts, the "abomination of desolation" of the book of Daniel (Dan. 9:27; 11:31; 12:11; see also 1 Macc. 1:57; 2 Macc. 6:1–7). This was the capstone of his attempt to forcibly Hellenize the Jews, forbidding the practice of their religion. We should be clear on the precipitating offense. The temple had been plundered before; Antiochus Epiphanes *desecrates* it. Indeed, this is the first time the Jews were persecuted for their religion, the first attempt to extirpate their faith. Understandably, these actions leave indelible marks in the Jewish community and on its theological vision. On the one hand, they provoke a successful rebellion against the Seleucid kings. But the aftermath of the revolt produces only political disillusionment. It finally contributes to the *splintering* of Jewish society into the parties familiar to us from the New Testament. But it also *crystallizes* a special theological vision contained in apocalyptic literature.

The Community

The first book of Maccabees begins its account of the revolt against Antiochus IV Epiphanes with the reign of Alexander the Great (356–323 B.C.), connecting the two in a straight line. In doing so, it sets the right context to understand why the Maccabean revolt was so explosive and its impact in Jewish society so profound.

In his twelve-year reign, Alexander of Macedon had conquered the known world, extending his domain to the borders of modern Afghanistan. Yet if Alexander had conquered the East, the East exacted its revenge after his death. The great intermingling of Greek and Eastern cultures called "Hellenism" rolled like an avalanche from east to west across the known world, bringing in its wake a new language, *koine* Greek, and creating distinctive styles of philosophy, literature, law, art, and architecture, extending down to fashions in clothing and pottery as well.[29]

Therefore Hellenism's inroads into Jewish society *before* the Maccabean revolt were substantial. Indeed, the very kind of society that Judaism represented — a community held together by the fragile walls of social practice — seemed especially vulnerable to the inroads of this cultural juggernaut. Jewish society and the later books of the Old Testament are therefore shot through with Hellenistic influences.[30] In effect, the original dilemma that faced the Jewish community after the exile — affirm an identity or face dissolution — is now replayed in a higher key. Granting the inroads of Hellenistic culture all around — an omnivorous cultural melting pot on every side — how is it possible to maintain an authentic Jewish identity? Traces of the conflict are evident in the biblical record (1 Macc. 1:13–15; 2 Macc. 4:10–15). Some Jews wished to assimilate more fully, denying the marks of their own identity (e.g., circumcision). Others resisted. Hence, the crisis that erupts in 168–167 B.C. had been incubating in Jewish society for more than a century. In other words, Antiochus Epiphanes' attempt to forcibly Hellenize the Jews built on a deep dilemma *within* Jewish society between those who wished to assimilate and those who desired an even more radical return to traditional Jewish customs.

Given the provoking circumstances, the revolt against Antiochus Epiphanes begins with a sense of high purpose and noble dedication. Pious Jews flock to its banner. Mattathias, of the Hasmonean clan, and his five sons lead the fight. After Mattathias's death in 166 B.C., his son Judas Maccabeus ("the hammer") takes command. But what begins as a revolt against the Seleucids on religious grounds eventually ends in the successful establishment once again of an independent

Jewish state under Judas's family, the Hasmoneans. The latter ruled as priest-kings from 164 to 63 B.C. In sum, what begins as a noble religious quest quickly devolves into politics as usual and the family ambitions of a newly minted dynasty. In the last analysis, the Maccabean revolt represents a *revolution without resolution,* the fissures of earlier days soon reappearing. The Hasmoneans quickly reveal themselves to be thoroughly Hellenized rulers. Pious Jews withdraw their support. Expelled from the temple by the priest-king Hasmoneans, the traditional Zadokite priesthood decamps to the desert.

Soon the groups emerge that are familiar to us from the New Testament. Other Zadokites *may* have been ancestors of the Sadducees. The latter's history remains obscure. The New Testament sees the Sadducees in conflict with the Pharisees on the status of the Torah, the resurrection of the dead, and other doctrines. Sadducees are portrayed as strict constructionists on the law. They appear as priestly aristocrats, inheritors of an enhanced priestly role in a Jewish temple-state, presumably the party of conservative accommodation. Most, but not all, priests were Sadducees. By contrast, the Pharisees hold that the ancestral wisdom contained in the oral tradition is as binding as the written Torah of Moses. If the Qumran community chooses to withdraw, the Pharisees seek to extend the canopy of law from priests to people in order to sanctify daily life through a circlet of ritual practices. The majority of the populace, the so-called people of the land, probably fall between the lines of all such parties.

Such a society is pluralistic in a limited sense. While lines of agreement and disagreement crisscross, they also form a dense web of affiliation among all groups around the twin pillars of the community: the law and the temple. Equally all parties witness to the pervasive and, for many, contaminating influence of the surrounding culture and its reigning empire, which in the hands of Seleucid kings had once been forged into a weapon of persecution. That memory remains when Palestine passed into the hands of the Roman hands and those of their client-kings, the Herods in 63 B.C.

Apocalyptic

The same actions that bring Judas and his brothers to take up the sword prompt others to take up the pen, giving birth to a new kind of literature called "apocalyptic." While the roots of apocalyptic extend back to the prophets and the wisdom literature, indeed beyond the bounds of Judaism, the actions of Antiochus Epiphanes in 168–167 B.C. — the desecration of the temple and the attempt to forcibly Hellenize the Jews — are decisive for its crystallization in the book of Daniel. It is hard to image a worse turn of events, and it is easy to grasp the logic of apocalyptic thinking in these circumstances. Antiochus is called not only "Epiphanes," a revelation of Olympian Zeus, but also "Epimanes," a maniac. Still, it is difficult to attribute such malevolence to the human will alone, even that of a madman. Does it not rather seem that cosmic forces of evil surface in this signal gesture of offense against Israel's God? And not for the first time. If Judea has been delivered as a dependent province from one empire to another, slumbering below the surface of these peaceful transfers is a long history of insult and resentment going back to Babylon. How long will Yahweh, the one God, tolerate this state of affairs? Can he tolerate the intolerable in the actions of Antiochus? Or will God himself and his angels intervene in a great cosmic battle and finally right the balance? Surely the time for peaceful reform is long past, and *political* rebellion will not cure *cosmic* evil. And so the author of the great canonical apocalypse of Daniel 7–12 comes to a single conclusion: Yahweh himself will shortly intervene. Nothing less will solve this cosmic corruption. The true judge will shortly appear in this world to deal out justice to the nations. Yahweh has been provoked.

No better example can be given of the message and technique of apocalyptic than that found in Daniel 7:

In the first year of King Belshazzar of Babylon, Daniel had a dream and visions of his head as he lay in bed. Then he wrote down the dream. "I, Daniel, saw in my vision by night the four winds of heaven stirring up the great sea, and four great beasts came up out of the sea, different from one another. The first was like a lion and had eagles' wings. Then, as I watched, its wings were plucked off, and it was lifted up from the ground and made to stand on two feet like a human being, and a human mind was given to it. Another beast appeared, a second one, that looked like a bear. It was raised up on one side, had three tusks in its mouth among its teeth and was told, 'Arise, devour many bodies.' After this, as I watched, another appeared, like a leopard. The beast had four wings of a bird on its back and four heads, and dominion was given to it. After this I saw in the visions by night a fourth beast, terrifying and dreadful and exceedingly strong. It had great iron teeth and was devouring, breaking in pieces, and stamping what was left with its feet. It was different from all the beasts that preceded it, and it had ten horns. I was considering the horns when another horn appeared, a little one coming up among them; to make room for it, three of the earlier horns were plucked up by the roots. There were eyes like human eyes in this horn, and a mouth speaking arrogantly.

"As I watched thrones were set in place and an Ancient One took his throne; his clothing was white as snow, and the hair of his head like pure wool; his throne was fiery flames and its wheels were burning fire. A stream of fire issued and flowed from his presence. A thousand thousands served him and ten thousand times ten thousand stood attending him. The court sat in judgment, and the books were opened.

"I watched then because of the voice of the arrogant words that the horn was speaking. And as I watched, the beast was put to death, and its body destroyed and given over to be burned with fire. As far as the rest of the beasts, their dominion was taken away, but their lives were prolonged for a season and a time. As I watched in the night vision, I saw one like a human being, coming with the clouds of heaven. And he came to the Ancient One and was presented before him. To him was given dominion and glory and kingship, that all peoples, nations, and languages should serve him. His dominion is an everlasting dominion that shall not pass away and his kingship is one that shall never be destroyed." (Dan. 7:1–14)

Under the camouflage of apocalyptic imagery, the message of the vision is clear enough. The four beasts that emerge from the sea are the four empires that held sway over the Jewish community: the Babylonians, the Medes, the Persians, and finally the Macedonian empire of the Seleucids. The tenth horn with the eyes of a man symbolizes Antiochus

Epiphanes. The beasts' emergence from the sea underscores their personifications as evil forces, coming from the region that was *controlled*
but never fully *subdued* by the God of Israel.[31] Hence, eruptions of
cosmic evil in human history always remain possible. But because the
situation has now become intolerable, Yahweh himself has decided to
intervene. He himself will preside as just judge, opening the books
for a final reckoning on these kingdoms. Then one like a Son of Man
will appear on the clouds of heaven, in this context a symbol of Israel.
In the finale of the chapter, power and dominion are taken from the
beasts of the sea and given to one like a Son of Man. Now Israel is
given dominion and kingship in perpetuity. Since the lines between
kingdom and king are easily crossed, it is not difficult to understand
the transition from the Son of Man as a *corporate* symbol of Israel to
the Son of Man as an *individual* figure of salvation in the future. The
question is about when it occurred.

The individual elements mentioned in this concluding section on
Israel's understanding of God come together into a *tableau vivant* in
this great apocalyptic vision. Yahweh as the one God, the only God but
still the God of Israel, emerges in a new light. He has finally decided to
act in gestures as large and bold as his original deeds at Israel's exodus
from Egypt. He will vindicate his name as Israel's savior. He will deal
out justice to the nations because he is their God as well. As God's
messengers and helpers, angels play a prominent role in the book of
Daniel. The two angels mentioned by name in the New Testament —
Gabriel and Michael — make their appearance here.

If there is a great overriding theme that held all parts of the apocalyptic vision together, surely it was that of justice. In the vision of
Daniel 7 the great empires of the world are judged and punished. Some
are destroyed outright. Others have their lives prolonged for "a season
and a time." Israel is vindicated. The same theme of justice brought
the author to address the fate of the individual. Daniel 12:2 speaks of
the resurrection of the dead: "Many of those who sleep in the dust of
the earth shall awake, some to everlasting life, and some to shame and
everlasting contempt." The hope of the mother who sees her seven
sons go to their death rather than forsake their religion is vindicated.
Her response: "Therefore the Creator of the world, who shaped the
beginning of humankind and devised the origin of all things, will in

his mercy give life and breath back to you again, since you now forget yourselves for the sake of his laws" (2 Macc. 7:23). The hope of the resurrection enunciated in more general terms in the apocalyptic passage Isaiah 24–27 (see especially 26:19) is here made specific and individual. And so the fate of the individual is given a more adequate response. If true justice is to be given to each person — good deeds rewarded and evil ones punished — then the dead must rise to new life in a realm in which justice reigns. It is hardly an accident and much more a matter of consistency that Daniel's great vision of justice to the nations in Daniel 7 is complemented by the resurrection of the dead in Daniel 12.

What role did apocalyptic play in the tradition? The answer depends on the direction in which one looks in answering the question. Looking to the Pentateuch and Israel's classic tradition, the answer would be a small one. Though there are apocalyptic passages in individual books, the book of Daniel represents the sole apocalypse in Israel's canon of sacred writings. Looking to the future, the answer changes dramatically both in Jewish and Christian circles. Jesus' preaching of the kingdom belongs under the general heading of apocalyptic. The book of Revelation, the apocalypse of John, continues the genre, the four beasts of Daniel merging into one, the Roman Empire. Indeed, broader than a single book, Jewish apocalyptic was described by Ernst Käsemann (1906–1998) as "the mother of all Christian theology."[32] In short, if the message of apocalyptic strikes resonant chords in Jewish circles, especially in the literature between Old and New Testaments, it will be even more central to Christian tradition.

This centrality may be simply put. In the religions of Israel's neighbors — in Babylon, for example — creation is the scene of a titanic battle in which cosmos or order is wrested from the forces of chaos by the victory of one god and the defeat of another. Marduk slays Tiamat, and the world is born. By contrast, in the book of Genesis creation is portrayed as an effortless display of the power of Yahweh, who brings the heavens and the earth quietly into being by the force of his word. But even in Israel, the necessity of a battle is *postponed*, not eliminated. In Jewish and Christian apocalyptic, the great battle finally takes place at the end of time. Although this clash was first adumbrated in sectarian literature, the Gospels and Christian tradition elevate it to a central role. So too the resurrection of the dead. A deeper logic prevails here. Eschatological future and primordial past stand in equilibrium: they must resemble one another. Indeed, the circle is complete only when they meet. Jon Levenson writes, "The central affirmation of apocalyptic is that the evil that occurs in history is symptomatic of a larger suprahistorical disequilibrium that requires, indeed invites, a suprahistorical correction. As evil did not originate with history, neither will it disappear altogether *in* history but rather *beyond* it, at the inauguration of the coming world."[33]

Chapter Two

JESUS

We turn now to the person of Jesus. We begin first by examining two reigning assumptions about Jesus in contemporary scholarship. The topic here is the rich, voluminous literature *about* Jesus. I wish to locate our own discussion in the context of this larger conversation. How much can we know of Jesus? What was central to his message? How did he see himself, and how did he understand his own death? We also begin this way to free ourselves in the second section to follow a continuous story *of* Jesus from his baptism by John the Baptist to his death on the cross as King of the Jews. I mean this straightforward narrative to lead finally to the third section, on the resurrection, God's action in raising Jesus from the dead.

In chapter 1 we traced the story of God in the Old Testament, and here we might compare Israel's vision of God to a beam of light that is now refracted through the life of a single individual, Jesus of Nazareth, as he was known during his lifetime and then in his death and resurrection. If Jesus' life becomes a prism for this light, the resurrection represents the point where that light, having passed through his death, is refracted out again in a series of related colors across a broad spectrum. The subsequent chapters of this book on Christ, the Trinity, the church, Mary, and the last things may be likened to individual colors in this spectrum.

This image of a beam of light from Israel, striking the life and death of Jesus and then refracted out in multiple directions in light of the resurrection, is the *Leitfaden* driving the subsequent chapters of this book. The present chapter represents the pivot, just as the final

Origin and Development of Christian Beliefs

one on faith and the last things brings the discussion to an end in its own terms.

I. Assumptions about Jesus

The title of this section may strike the reader as an odd one: assumptions about Jesus. But assumptions are factors operating below the surface that determine the drift of a discussion. Two large assumptions have controlled much of the scholarly conversation about Jesus in the twentieth century, and they need to be clearly identified.

The first was introduced by groundbreaking theologian and exegete Rudolph Bultmann (1884–1976). Reacting to the so-called Quest of the Historical Jesus conducted in the nineteenth-century, Bultmann voiced such characteristic sentiments as these: "I do indeed think that we can know almost nothing concerning the life and personality of Jesus, since the early Christian sources show no interest in either, are more often fragmentary and often legendary; and other sources about Jesus do not exist."[1]

But these are not the sentiments of a skeptic. On the contrary, it suffices for Bultmann to know only *that* Jesus existed. Jesus himself belongs to the *presuppositions* of Easter faith. He is not its object. That honor is reserved for God's action in raising Jesus from the dead, the heart and soul of the church's preaching and the true focus of faith. To reach "behind" the resurrection — in Bultmann's view, to attempt to "prove" faith on historical grounds — is a misguided venture, doomed from the start. In truth, Bultmann's pious agnosticism about the historical Jesus is firmly grounded in his own Lutheran piety and its theological tradition — *Sola scriptura, Solus Chistus, Sola fide.* Faith alone saves.

Pious agnosticism is buttressed from another side. Bultmann was also a pioneer in the use of the form-critical method to interpret the Synoptic Gospels. According to its tenets, a threefold "context" (*Sitz*) situates any proper discussion of the gospel message. There is the "context" in the Gospel itself (*Sitz im Evangelium*), the place where a saying or event occurs in the written Gospel. Then there is the "context" in the life of the early church (*Sitz in der Kirche*). This is the prompting circumstance that causes the Christian community to remember this event and place it in this setting. Finally, there is the "context" in the life of Jesus (*Sitz im Leben Jesu*), what Jesus said or did that stood behind the memory. Significantly, the form-critical method is designed to take the exegete from the context in the Gospel to the situation in the early church. The final leg of the journey — back to Jesus himself — remains precarious. The criterion of dissimilarity — attributing to Jesus what could not be explained in terms of Judaism or the early church — is not the only guide to locating a genuine memory of Jesus, but probably the most probative one.

In effect, pious skepticism for religious reasons is joined to formal skepticism on methodological grounds. Indeed, it is the combination of faith and methodology that makes Bultmann's position so formidable. The result places the early church and its faith center stage. Jesus, on the other hand, is largely reduced to an elusive presence in the wings, overshadowed at every turn by the church's preaching. The criterion of dissimilarity distances him further, denying Jesus a platform to make sense out of what he said or did. Jesus becomes not simply a cipher, but one who emits discrete, not always intelligible blips. But the simplicity and coherence of the Bultmann's position should not be underestimated.

Its anomalies also become apparent. Beginning in 1953, Bultmann's students begin to distance themselves from their teacher.[2] The preaching of the early church is indeed interested and grounded in the historical Jesus, they argue. Bultmann had also led the way in demythologizing the supernatural elements of the Gospels, no longer believable to modern men and women who use electric lights and ride trolley cars.[3] But he stops short at the event of the resurrection. It is an easy step for others to demythologize the resurrection as well. Bultmann's students then face a stark choice: either buttress the connection to the historical Jesus or risk the drift of Christian faith into the realm of modern myth, one more dream about "human possibility."

But the lingering effects of Bultmann's view continue. It still seems as if the genius moment in the rise of the church lies with the early Christian community, the work of the apostle Paul or of the author of Mark's Gospel. If Jesus is no longer a cipher behind the gospel, he still does not seem a strong enough figure to believably anchor the mighty tradition that springs up about him after his death. Harald

Riesenfeld puts his finger on the point: "New Testament Christology is too potent to be adequately explained without the seminal initiative of an equally potent, creative personality. In this regard, however, the more recent portraits of Jesus are far too superficial and hesitant to be credible."[4] And on methodological grounds, Jesus still seems a remote figure hidden behind dense epicycles of Gospel redactions. The closer we come to him, the more he seems to recede behind less and less reliable reconstructions of the written text.

But not remote to all.[5] Martin Hengel argues, "The time between the death of Jesus and the fully developed Christology which we find in the earliest Christian documents, the letters of Paul, is so short that the development which takes place within it can only be called amazing."[6] Hengel follows up such insights in a series of monographs in which he sketches the portrait of Jesus as the ground and source of the church's faith.[7] One way or another, it seems clear that a developed Christology sits on a weak foundation if Jesus is reckoned a *cipher.* It sits more securely on the assumption that Jesus is a *large figure* strong enough to inspire the developed interpretation of him that sprang up so quickly in the early church. This also restores perspective to the biblical text. The Gospels seem to be primarily about Jesus, who seems larger than life, by turns unpredictable, surprising, and compelling.

These considerations lead to the second assumption about Jesus. It is connected in large measure to the so-called Third Quest of the Historical Jesus. A hallmark of this quest has been the rediscovery of the Jewishness of Jesus. This supplies a context in which to understand Jesus' words and deeds. The efforts of the Jesus Seminar are part of this quest. Their debunking agenda is not small. Their resulting portraits of Jesus differ widely.[8] Yet the work of James D. G. Dunn, Larry W. Hurtado, John P. Meier, Ben F. Meyer (1927–1995), N. T. Wright, and others comprises a formidable block. These scholars, though they may differ significantly, share important assumptions about Jesus.[9] Their critical works are still appearing. Their future impact will be considerable. The common assumption is that Jesus must be placed in the context of Second Temple Judaism to be understood. Dunn and Wright argue that the dependability of oral tradition has been seriously underestimated by those who approach the tradition from the viewpoint of a written text. Hurtado takes worship in the early church as his focus. The names of Peter Stuhlmacher,[10] Heinz Schürmann, Birger Gerhardsson, and Rainer Riesner probably should be mentioned in the same context, and that of Pope Benedict XVI as well.[11]

For these authors, Jesus is no longer regarded as a cipher behind the gospel; he is its main actor, who is available to us in the writing of the New Testament, above all, in the Synoptic Gospels. In effect, Jesus is a strong figure in his own right.[12] His disciples are therefore anxious to preserve his memory. The Synoptic Gospels, while they represent the preaching of the early church, contain reliable historical memories of Jesus' actual words and deeds.[13] Indeed, the early church's interpretation of Jesus may have grown from powerful indicators about his identity that Jesus himself provided.[14] In this vein, Peter Stuhlmacher writes, "The decisive origins of the synoptic tradition lie in the 'school' of Jesus who taught as the 'messianic teacher of wisdom.' The *paradosis* or traditions of this school were transmitted to the primitive church in Jerusalem by the *mathetai* whom Jesus himself called."[15]

What can be said about Jesus in the brief span of these pages to which authors have dedicated volumes of scholarship? While scholars sift through the details of the Gospel tradition, I seek to state as simply as possible what Ben Meyer, James D. G. Dunn, N. T. Wright, and others call the "aims" of Jesus. I think that they are clearly discernible, few in number, and can be stated briefly. Our ultimate concern here is the impact of Jesus on his first followers. For our purposes, the simpler, the better.

II. The Ministry of Jesus

Jesus and John

Just as Jesus sends out his disciples two by two, he himself first appears with another, John the Baptist. Their lives and their fate are inextricably linked at every point. Jesus is baptized by John in the Jordan. Matthew and Mark identify John as Elijah the prophet come back to earth to prepare the way for the Messiah. But the baptism remains somewhat of an embarrassment. Jesus must be baptized "to fulfill all righteousness," Matthew explains (Matt. 3:13–17). John's Gospel places an even greater separation between Jesus and John. John attests that he himself is not the Messiah, not Elijah, not the prophet (John 1:19–28). After giving witness to Jesus, the Baptist concludes, "He must increase, but I must decrease" (John 3:30). Indeed, Jesus himself draws the line in Matthew: "Truly, I tell you, among those born of women no one has arisen greater than John the Baptist; yet the least in the kingdom is greater than he" (Matt. 11:11).

This dividing line is significant. John preaches a stern message of repentance in preparation for the coming of the kingdom of God and the day of wrath that precedes it. He preaches in the Jordan Valley, not in Jerusalem, offering the repentance of sins not through the usual way, the system of temple sacrifices. John also gather disciples, some of whom — Peter, Andrew, Philip, and Nathaniel — become Jesus' first followers (John 1:35–51). Finally, John is killed by Herod Antipas for disparaging the lawfulness of the king's marriage to his brother's wife (Mark 6:18). The Jewish historian Josephus recalls that John was a popular figure, perhaps considered a rabble-rouser, and this played a part in his death (*Jewish Antiquities* 18:118.) In truth, the two accounts may not be far apart.[16] John is a precursor and also in a sense a template for Jesus.

The Kingdom of God

The principal link between Jesus and John is the preaching of the kingdom of God. It is also what divides them. They stand on different sides of the kingdom. John preaches a message of repentance in *preparation* for the kingdom; Jesus announces the kingdom's *arrival*. "Reign" of God better captures its dynamic quality; God's rule is making itself known. But spatial elements are unavoidable. The kingdom "has drawn near" (Mark 1:15//Matt. 4:17). People "enter into it" (Matt. 6:33//Luke 12:31). The kingdom is seized and suffers violence (Matt. 11:12//Luke 16:16). People "recline at table" in it (Matt. 8:11//Luke 13:29; Mark 14:18). People are not "far" from the kingdom. But, above all, the kingdom of God is now in their midst. "But if it is by the finger of God that I cast out demons, then the kingdom of God has come to you," says Jesus (Luke 11:20//Matt. 12:28). Therefore, the kingdom of God has a present dimension. It is an event breaking through in the ministry of Jesus. Yet the kingdom has a future *denouement,* a grand finale. The message of judgment so prominent in John's preaching does not disappear in Jesus, but it does not strike the first note. Jesus' is a joyful announcement of God's forgiveness, a hallmark of the kingdom's appearance. Like John, Jesus is an itinerant preacher whose ministry largely takes place in Galilee. Like John as well, Jesus announces the forgiveness of sins outside the system of temple sacrifices.

But the preaching of the kingdom is not simply the link between Jesus and John; it is Jesus' *aim* par excellence. Jesus is utterly single-minded in the announcement of God's kingdom. Thus the kingdom defines Jesus' mission. It also defines Jesus' self-understanding. It explains both his consistency and his impact on his followers. It provides the key to how Jesus understood his death. In other words, the preaching of the kingdom is the *universal joint* that holds all the pieces together in the story of Jesus.[17]

Jesus' preaching of the kingdom must also be placed against the backdrop of Israel's oldest hopes. Originally, Israel was a league of tribes with no king but Yahweh. This was an ancient anchor that was never forgotten. The preaching of the kingdom must also be ranged with the great hopes of the prophets at the time of the Babylonian exile, hopes never realized in the life of Second Temple Judaism. Finally, it must be placed against the backdrop of Jewish apocalyptic expectations, but apocalyptic of its own kind. There is no speculation in Jesus' preaching about when the kingdom in its fullness will occur. On the contrary: "But about that day or hour no one knows," says Jesus, "neither the angels in heaven nor the Son, but only the Father" (Mark 13:32). There is also no heavy dualism in his preaching of the kingdom, although such elements are not absent.

Significantly, Jesus does not explain the expression "kingdom of God." He announces its advent, presuming that his listeners understand. Whether the kingdom taps into a grand narrative of Israel's hopes, consistently disappointed in postexilic Judaism (N. T. Wright), or whether those expectations were more diffuse (James D. G. Dunn), the term strikes immediate resonance with Jesus' listeners.[18] Although the actual phrase "kingdom of God" is quite rare, the audience knows what it means and what it is about.[19] If Jesus' announcement contains the reversal of expectations at key points, such only makes sense from a common base of assumptions between Jesus and his listeners.

Miracles

The preaching of the kingdom explains the role, indeed the importance, of miracles in the ministry of Jesus. They are never simply displays of messianic power, mere feats of superhuman strength. Such is the core of the temptations, recorded by Matthew and Luke, that Jesus firmly rejects, indeed a test by Satan to abuse such powers. Rather, miracles in the Synoptic Gospels are called *erga* (works) or, closer to the point, *dynameis,* acts of power in the service of the kingdom. They are specific cases in which the kingdom of God triumphs over Satan. If it is by the finger of God that a demon is expelled, then the kingdom of God has scored a public victory. Hence, healings and exorcisms are tangible signs that the kingdom is actually erupting in the events of Jesus' ministry. They therefore vindicate his announcement of the kingdom. And far from being convincing displays of power, they require faith. Miracle stories often end with the statement "Your faith has made you well" (Mark 5:34; 10:52; Matt. 9:22; Luke 17:19). And where there is no faith, Jesus cannot perform miracles (Mark 6:5–6; Matt. 13:58). They are also open to other explanations. Is it perhaps by the power of Beelzebul, the prince of demons, that Jesus casts out demons? But much more likely, it is by the finger of God that the sick are healed and demons are expelled.

Jesus' reply to the disciples of John the Baptist, "Are you the one who is to come, or are we to wait for another?" (Matt. 11:2), dovetails with his announcement of the kingdom: "Go tell John what you hear and see: the blind receive their sight, the lame walk, the lepers are cleansed, the deaf hear, the dead are raised, and the poor have good news brought to them" (Matt. 11:4–5). At the synagogue in Nazareth Jesus announces, "The Spirit of the Lord is upon me, because he has anointed me to bring good news to the poor. He has sent me to proclaim release to the captives and recovery of sight to the blind, to let the oppressed go free, to proclaim the year of the Lord's favor" (Luke 4:18–19). Both cases describe events that are happening in the ministry of Jesus. Both allude as well to the words of the prophet Isaiah (Isa. 35:5; 61:1). The hopes of Isaiah now reach concrete fulfillment in the events of Jesus' ministry when the blind see, the lame walk, and lepers are cleansed.

God as Abba

If miracles and exorcisms are essential signs of the kingdom's advent, so too is Jesus' special awareness of God. In the most obvious sense, if the kingdom of God is breaking in, then that must mean that God himself is drawing closer. Jesus prays to God as *Abba*, Father. If this is not unique to him, it surely is characteristic. Although the word *Abba* appears in the Gospels only in the scene of the agony in the garden in Mark (Mark 14:36), it probably stands behind the Greek *ho pater* of the Lord's Prayer, and its appearance in Romans 8:15 and Galatians 4:6 is quite amazing. "When we cry, 'Abba! Father!' it is the very Spirit bearing witness with our spirit that we are children of God" (Rom. 8:15); "And because you are children, God has sent the Spirit of his Son into our hearts, crying, 'Abba! Father'" (Gal. 4:6). Such passages witness to the importance of *Abba* in the earliest traditions about Jesus. The easiest and simplest explanation of these instances is that they reflect how Jesus himself prayed. Thus Jesus offers no new concept of God, and it is misguided to play off Jesus' *Abba* against a distant, transcendent God of Second Temple Judaism. Jesus assumes the God of Israel at every point. But when the kingdom of God appears, God himself draws near and is available in a new way. The context of the Lord's Prayer in Luke is instructive (Luke 11:2–4). In a world filled with prayers, Jesus' disciples ask for a special one. They want to pray as Jesus does because he seems to pray in a different way. He seems to have a unique awareness of God's presence captured in the family word *Abba*. It is significant as well that the Lord's Prayer is a prayer for the coming of the kingdom. Jesus teaches his disciples to pray with him that God's kingdom come and his will be done on earth as it is in heaven.

Yet while the disciples imitate Jesus in the way they pray, Jesus consciously avoids the use of "our" Father to include himself and the disciples. They may pray "our" Father, but Jesus' relation to God — "my Father" — remains unique, perhaps closer to the words of the Matthew 11:27: "All things have been handed over to me by my Father, and no one knows the Son except the Father, and no one knows the Father except the Son and anyone to whom the Son chooses to reveal him." And this makes sense. Jesus is the unique messenger of the kingdom in whose ministry God's reign is manifest. It seems right that Jesus' awareness of God would remain unique as well, that he regards himself as God's "son" in a special sense. This designation is deeply rooted in the tradition and flows most easily and naturally from Jesus' prayer to God as *Abba*, Father. In the Gospel of John, "Father" and "Son" become synonymous terms for God and Jesus, so deeply has Jesus' original sense of sonship penetrated the tradition.

Jesus as Teacher

What Mark's Gospel says about Jesus should be taken literally: "They were astounded at his teaching, for he taught them as one having authority, and not as the scribes" (Mark 1:22). Jesus appears preeminently as a teacher with special authority. If Jesus' followers regard God as *Abba*, "Father," and see themselves as "children" of God, they see Jesus as "teacher" and regard themselves as his "disciples."

Not surprisingly, *what* Jesus teaches and *how* Jesus teaches are inseparable. Nowhere is the combination more clearly displayed than in the antitheses of the Sermon on the Mount in Matthew's Gospel (Matt. 5:21–48). In each case, Jesus quotes a familiar command of the Torah: you shall not kill, you shall not commit adultery, you shall not swear falsely. However, to each of them Jesus now appends, "But I say to you." In each case the command of the Torah is thereby radicalized: not just murder, but unjustified anger; not just adultery, but lust; not just casual oath-taking, but all oath-taking. In the case of divorce, the taking of oaths and perhaps the dietary regulations (Mark 7:1–37), the actual law itself seems abrogated. But what Jesus intends is clear enough. When the kingdom of God draws near, the law can no longer be read in the usual way. Instead, the letter of the law must consistently give way to the spirit, as the deepest intent of the law penetrates, making an ever more radical claim.

The antitheses of the Sermon on the Mount are also intimately connected to Jesus' special awareness of God as *Abba*. If God is to the disciple an *Abba* — an intimate presence, penetrating to the heart — then the only kind of claim that such a God can make is a radical one. If God is a presence close at hand, then the only kind of obedience that God asks will be radical. The same reading of the Torah stands behind Jesus' response that love of God and love of neighbor are the sum and substance of the law of Moses (Matt. 22:35–40//Mark 12:28–31//Luke 10:25–28). Here the Torah is give a radical center in terms of Deuteronomy 6:4–5 and Leviticus 19:18 and a focus of interpretation. If these two laws are fulfilled, then all the demands of the law are met as well.

Hence, when the kingdom of God approaches, the commands of the Torah are radicalized in every way. Note that Jesus does not quote authorities or schools of interpretation. He quotes himself, thereby placing his own authority as a teacher on the same level as that of the Torah. His claim here is a high one, but in context it is intelligible enough. If Jesus is the one to whom God has entrusted announcing the advent of the kingdom, it is no surprise that he appears as a teacher of unrivaled authority, one who can command demons, even the forces of nature. Likewise, he instructs his listeners on how the law of Moses should now be regarded in light of the kingdom's arrival. Jesus' use of "Amen" to begin and not end a sentence is also characteristic: "Amen, I say to you." In John's Gospel the "Amen" is doubled: "Amen, Amen, I say to you," fittingly enough because Jesus in John's portrayal is a figure of unrivaled authority. Here, as the tradition gains increasing strength, it surely builds on the memory enunciated in the first chapter of Mark's Gospel. Jesus appears as a teacher with unique authority. He announces the inbreaking of the kingdom. He regards himself in a unique way as God's Son. From these sources flows his special authority as a teacher.

At the same time, while Jesus radicalizes the demands of the Torah, he does not intend thereby to abrogate the law; otherwise, the protracted debates in the early church on the status of the Mosaic Torah would be unintelligible.

Jesus teaches in parables. The parables themselves encompass a broad range of forms, from proverbs, maxims, and brief metaphors to more elaborate stories, such as that of the sower and the seed (Mark 4:3–20), that lend themselves to allegorical interpretation. Jesus uses parables to teach about the kingdom of God: its appearance, the crisis it provokes, and the judgment awaiting us in light of our response. The key issue here is to locate the right *genre* to interpret the parables.

Clearly, they are not example stories, although they can be used that way (e.g., the parable of the good Samaritan appears as a response to the question, "And who is my neighbor?" [Luke 10:29–37]). Rather, the parables resemble freestanding windows through which one looks in order to get a firsthand glimpse of the kingdom. They address first the imagination. The attempt to exhaust their content through discursive thought — abstract statements about the kingdom — misses the point. They are a series of perspectives that disclose the kind of world that the advent of God's kingdom reveals, invariably containing a measure of *double entendre*. Matthew 13:44–45 compares the kingdom to a treasure hidden in a field, a pearl of great price, items that in turn change the value of everything else. One sells everything to purchase the field or buy the pearl.

Certain connecting threads run through Jesus' preaching on the parables, which is as much systematizing as they will allow. The kingdom of God is not of our making. We do not create it or determine when or how it appears. The kingdom is found or discovered, perhaps something lost that is recovered, like the lost coin or the lost sheep (Luke 15:3–10). Indeed, the kingdom seems to appear where we might least expect it and grows by its own measure like the mustard seed (Matt. 13:31–32//Mark 4:30–32). Even the seed that falls on good soil produces a harvest that is quite beyond the capacities of fertile soil.

Isaiah 6:9–10 is widely associated with the parables — ears that do not hear and eyes that do not see. This theme follows easily enough from another one in the parables: the first will be last and the last will be first — the great element of reversal (Matt. 19:30//Mark 16:31//Luke 13:30). The appearance of God's kingdom forces us to radically revise our normal expectations about the world, certainly assumptions about who or what is important. Depending on who is on the receiving end of such reversals, Jesus' parables could be offensive. Thus it is easy enough to grasp why some ears were especially closed and some eyes tightly shut. The parables retain the ability to confuse, if not offend, because the great theme of the kingdom's reversal still pertains. The invited guests to the wedding banquet do not appear, so the host sends his servants to the highways and byways and invites others to come (Matt. 22:1–14//Luke 14:15–24). When you give a dinner, Jesus advises, invite the poor, the crippled, the lame, and the blind because they cannot repay the kindness. In effect, the standards by which the world judges and measures people are turned upside down. When the kingdom appears, a Samaritan is termed "good" (Luke 10:29–37), and the prayers of a tax collector are preferred to those of a pious Pharisee (Luke 18:9–14). Indeed, on the great day of reckoning, a poor man such as Lazarus will rest in the bosom of Abraham while the rich man languishes in hell (Luke 16:19–31).

What makes the parables so much more powerful than abstract statements about the kingdom is that they provide actual snapshots of this new reality. The viewers also glimpse themselves as in a mirror. The sight is not always consoling. In this sense, the parables are meant to be interactive. They also do more than indict individual conduct. They may carry a social commentary. An early telling of the parable of the vinedresser likely contains a reference to Jesus' own ministry (Mark 12:1–9 pars.). The owner of the vineyard sends out his slaves to the tenants, and the emissaries are rejected. Then he sends out his beloved son, whom they seize and kill. What will be their fate? The image of God in the parable of the prodigal son clearly mirrors the loving *Abba* of Jesus' prayer, the welcoming father who kills the fatted calf on the return of the prodigal son. N. T. Wright suggests that the prodigal may be an image of Israel, finally returning home from exile, welcomed back to the promised land by God the Father.[20]

Finally, there are numerous parables that speak of a judgment still outstanding when the master returns home and asks for a reckoning (e.g., Luke 12:34–48). Are the listeners prepared for the final day when the God of Israel will judge all people by the standards of the kingdom? In many cases, prudent conduct is rewarded — for example, the parables of the wise and foolish virgins, the buried talents, and the dishonest steward (Matt. 25:1–13; Matt. 25:14–30//Luke 19:11–27; Luke 16:1–9). But in other cases, God's justice eludes our ken. The workers hired at the last hour are paid the same as those who toiled the entire day. The parable ends with a characteristic final line: "So the last will be first, and the first will be last" (Matt. 20:1–16). And who cannot hear in the single voice of the older brother in the parable of the prodigal son a veritable chorus of disgruntled people who played the game by accepted rules and now are forced to grind their teeth on God's inexplicable generosity to sinners? The scene of judgment in Matthew 25 captures the point. Both sheep and the goats do not remember the actions on which their fate is now decided. They inquire as to when they saw Jesus hungry or thirsty or a stranger or naked or sick or in prison. Jesus responds, "Truly, I tell you, just as you did it to one of the least of these, you did it to me" (Matt. 25:31–46).

Jesus' Actions

Jesus' actions match his words. The impact of both is thereby enhanced. Jesus teaches that the first invited guests to a supper should be the poor, the crippled, the blind and the lame. These are also the people with whom he associates. The Gospels echo an epithet that authentically reflects events in Jesus' ministry. He is a "glutton and a drunkard." He not only associates but also dines with "tax-collectors and sinners." The malodorous reputation of tax collectors is understandable enough; they functioned as tax farmers for the Romans. The term *sinner* is broader. It surely includes prostitutes. But it extends more widely and is largely a matter of perspective. Those whom one regards as "sinners" reflect a point of view about the people who are beyond the pale of society.

Here Jesus functions at the borders. He touches and cures a leper (Mark 1:40–45). He touches and heals a woman who has long suffered from a hemorrhage (Mark 5:25–34). He takes the hand of a young girl pronounced dead (Mark 5:41). He exorcizes a legion of unclean spirits from a man with who lives among the tombs (Mark 5:2–13). Having expelled unclean spirits on all fronts, Jesus himself, not surprisingly, is accused of being possessed by one. Such gestures rendered Jesus ritually impure. They connect with other deeds.

Jesus cures a man with a withered hand on the Sabbath (Mark 3:1–6). His disciples casually pluck heads of grain on the Sabbath. Jesus says, "The Sabbath was made for humankind, and not humankind for the Sabbath" (Mark 2:27). He disregards matters of ritual purity — for example, hand washing (Mark 7:1–8, 14–23). In regard to this scene in Mark 7, James D. G. Dunn writes, "Even if Mark has highlighted the theme by his structuring of the narrative and sharpening of the issue, the theme itself is clearly and firmly rooted in the tradition. It is not a matter of much doubt that Jesus was remembered as casual in regard to ritual purity."[21]

Such gestures are enormously significant. They mark the borders between those who were acceptable to society and those who were not. In the first instance, then, ritual impurity may spell social ostracization. Within society, it draws a line between groups, separating, for example, Pharisees from Sadducees. Such gestures pertain then to social identity. Marcus Borg speaks of the "politics of holiness."[22] That Jesus undertakes to ignore such matters publicly in the company of his disciples gives additional scandal.

The truth is that in a society with a deep sense of profanation, Jesus seems to cross such lines without so much as a second thought. He seems to have little instinct for matters that are quite important to others. Jesus associates with just about everyone. And although his mission is to the lost sheep of the house of Israel (Matt. 10:6), he cures a Syrophoenician woman (Mark 7:24–30) and a Roman centurion (Matt. 8:5–13//Luke 17:11–19). The logic here is clear enough. When the kingdom of God approaches, the human divisions between parties and factions lose their importance. Yet again, as in the case of the law, if Jesus meant to disparage all forms of ritual observance, it is difficult to explain the conduct of his followers after the resurrection who clung unselfconsciously to such customs.

Jesus' actions constitute parables in action about the kingdom. He teaches about the least. He breaks bread with them as well.

The Twelve

Jesus calls the Twelve, an action equally emblematic of the kingdom. The New Testament contains four lists of the Twelve (Mark 3:16–19//Matt. 10:2–4//Luke 6:14–16//Acts 1:13). The Gospel of John also mentions the Twelve (John 6:67; 20:24), as does Paul (1 Cor. 15:5). The most prominent are Peter, James, John, Andrew, and, of course, Judas Iscariot. Yet as important as individual names may be, the number *twelve* is key. The number is reminiscent of the twelve patriarchs and the twelve tribes of Israel. In light of the kingdom's arrival, these twelve represent the nucleus of a new and revived people of God that will blossom when God's reign comes in its fullness. They are the starter shoots of new growth, expected shortly to expand into a new Israel. Therefore, as much as the miracles of Jesus' ministry, the call of the Twelve is a tangible sign of the kingdom's arrival and a harbinger of its future.

The stern demands of the kingdom fall first on the Twelve. They do not come to Jesus; rather, he calls them with the peremptory words "Follow me." The command brooks no delays. A follower who would bury a parent is told, "Let the dead bury the dead" (Matt. 8:21–22), a statement without parallel in Judaism of the day. Its brutal simplicity is testimony to the urgency of the moment. Jesus never explains why he has chosen these twelve. There is simply the command "Follow me." The Gospels hold up two images of his followers. They are called to be fishers of people, to be missionaries. They are also sent to the lost sheep of the house of Israel (Matt. 10:6) as shepherds or pastors (John 21). Accordingly, Jesus sends them out two by two to continue his preaching of the kingdom, to heal and exorcize demons in light of its coming.

Luke mentions the sending of a further seventy(-two) (Luke 10:1). He may seek to foreshadow here the Gentile mission in Jesus' own ministry. The truth is that the Twelve were surrounded by other circles of followers and sympathizers, indeed, circles within circles. Within the Twelve, Peter, James, and John play a special role. Then there were other disciples, followers and sympathizers who remained at home without being able to draw clear lines between these groups. In these circles, women play a notable role; Mary of Bethany and Mary Magdalene stand out.

Just as the kingdom dissolves old boundaries, its advent creates new ones. Nowhere is this more evident than in demands of the natural family versus the claims of discipleship. In the first instance, the two are sharply opposed. The opposition here begins with Jesus himself. His family comes to take him away because some say that he is out of his mind (Mark 3:21). In response, Jesus asks the crowd, "Who are my mother and my brothers?" And then, looking at those sitting around him, he says, "Here are my mother and my brothers! Whoever does the will of God is my brother, and sister, and mother" (Mark 3:33–35). The demands of discipleship take precedence over claims of blood kinship. What Jesus says about himself, he asks of others. "Who are my brothers and sisters and mother?" he asks. It is those who hear the word of God and keep it. Indeed, "Whoever comes to me and does not hate father and mother, wife and children, brothers and sisters, yes, and even life itself, cannot be my disciple" (Luke 14:26). The new "family" is this fellowship of believers, and here a firm line is drawn.

Jesus' preaching of the kingdom abounds in the play of family images. We are to regard God as *Abba* and see ourselves as disciples in this light. The "child" therefore becomes the first image of the disciple, one who trusts God as a child trusts its parents. The disciples are also to regard those who do the will of God and as "brother and sister and mother." In other words, the coming of the kingdom takes the traditional family and redefines its lines. Its membership now extends to all those who respond to the kingdom. Above all, the new family is those who hear the word of God and keep it.

Notable too is how Jesus' own kin, after initial rejection, are easily incorporated into the family of believers. Mary and the brothers and sisters are counted among Jesus' followers in Luke and in Acts. Indeed, it is through an act of discipleship that Jesus himself is conceived in Luke's Gospel. In responding to the angel Gabriel, Mary fulfills the requirements of a disciple. She hears the word of God and keeps it. In John's Gospel, Mary herself becomes a model of discipleship.

The Passion

Why did Jesus go up to Jerusalem on that fateful Passover when he was crucified? Did he go up to provoke the authorities to take action? Did he expect God to intervene on his behalf? Above all, how did Jesus understand his own death? The answer to those questions is contained in the story of Jesus' passion and death. This is the longest continuous narrative in the Synoptic Gospels. The story flows continuously through a series of closely interconnected events: Jesus' entrance into Jerusalem, the "cleansing" of the temple, the final Passover with the Twelve, the agony in the garden, the trial before the high priest and then Pilate, and finally Jesus' crucifixion and death.

The story of Jesus' passion and death in the Gospels is deeply theological. It represents the attempts of Jesus' first followers to interpret why he had to die. Yet this theological narrative stands astride some incontestable historical facts. Indeed, such facts represent the hard data that the passion seeks to interpret. The first and most obvious is that

Jesus was crucified as "King of the Jews." These are the only words that can claim to have been written of him during his lifetime, containing the memory that Jesus was killed as a messianic pretender on political grounds. The easiest and most logical basis of such a charge is that Jesus was considered such during his lifetime. In other words, the title on the cross is not *invention* but rather *confirmation* of a popular view of him.[23] Bartimaeus, a blind beggar, cries out, "Jesus, Son of David, have mercy on me!" (Mark 10:47), and his was probably not a lone voice. On the contrary, preaching the coming of God's kingdom and the restoration of Israel *without* awakening political and messianic expectation is difficult to imagine. The Gospels will later shape such messianic expectation to their own purposes, not least in the account of the passion. They tell of Jesus' entrance into Jerusalem, not on foot as a usual pilgrim but rather riding a mule. Such a description alludes to the oracle of Zechariah and the expectation of a humble messiah who will come in just this way, "riding on a donkey, on a colt, the foal of a donkey." But it is hard to imagine that Jesus conceived of his mission in traditional messianic terms, relatively speaking a comedown from his role as symbol and agent of God's kingdom. Hence, Jesus' demurrals on this score have the ring of truth. "Are you the King of Jews?" Pilate asks in Matthew's Gospel. "You say so," Jesus replies (Matt. 27:11).

The more serious charge concerns the so-called cleansing of the temple. This was no harmless gesture aimed at temple reform; rather, in light of Jesus' preaching of the kingdom and the birth of a new Israel, the gesture seemed to spell the eclipse of the temple in its present form and its replacement by a new temple in which God's presence could more worthily dwell. Indeed, it is difficult to envision a new and restored Israel without imagining in some form a radically renewed temple. It is also surely no accident that these two charges — Jesus' messianic claim and his intentions about the temple — are raised in tandem at his trial before the high priest and Pilate. Kings had been associated with the temple since the beginning of David's dynasty (Nathan's oracle [2 Sam. 7]). The link between a putative messianic claim (the estimation of others) and a radical renewal of the temple (perhaps Jesus' own aim) seems relatively clear.

Yet the combination is lethal. The threat against the temple strikes the nerve center of Second Temple Judaism, the temple establishment that played a central role in a temple-state since the Babylonian exile. It is an easy step for the high priest and the Sadducees to suggest to Pilate that Jesus is a serious troublemaker. It is probably no accident that the Pharisees barely play a role in Jesus' passion. But a public threat against the temple on the part of a popular preacher elevates Jesus from the ranks of a harmless preacher into those of a dangerous troublemaker, meriting the most extreme penalty that the Romans could mete out. And, in truth, Jesus clearly did raise claims about God's kingdom and about himself as its agent. Such claims are never without political ramifications. In this regard, if others in large number thought of Jesus as a possible messiah, in one sense it makes no difference what Jesus himself may have thought. The public expectation was enough to brand him a stormy petrel, worthy of death.

But this was not all. By both his preaching and his actions, Jesus had discounted the social boundaries on which the identities of Pharisees and Sadducees were built. If his preaching intrigued some, it no doubt infuriated others. The double entendres of the parables divided Jesus' listeners along the same lines. In short, Jesus probably was an equal-opportunity offender. If he roused popular support on the one hand, it is hard to imagine that he did not generate opposition in about the same measure.

How did Jesus understand his own death? As people live, so they die, observes John Meier.[24] If Jesus' actions and his preaching reveal insight and acuity, it seems wrong to deny him those same gifts about his own fate. It is certain that Jesus realized that his preaching aroused hostility in influential circles. He had preached a word of judgment on others. It was likely the compliment would be returned at the first opportunity. It is hard to think that such would have escaped Jesus.

As the preaching of the kingdom is the leitmotiv of other aspects of Jesus' life, it should play the same role in regard to his death. If Jesus preached the coming of God's kingdom with confidence and saw himself as its special agent, he hardly would have avoided the consequences of his actions. He knew the fate of John the Baptist. He had the example of the Maccabean martyrs before him. If we credit Jesus with no more insight than John Brown after the incident at Harper's Ferry, then he must have realized that a prophet and his message stand no taller than when they are stamped by the witness of his own death. In this regard, if Jesus' words and deeds coalesce, no better instance of their jointure can be given than Jesus' death. Indeed, Jesus' death was his *last word,* a single gesture at the end that pulled word and deed together into a single, tight bullet-like message. Did Jesus expect his own vindication? Surely, if Jesus was confident about the coming of the kingdom and if his death was a final price, his ultimate witness, then he expected God's vindication. Vindicating the messenger is no more than vindicating the message, especially in this case when the two were inextricably joined together. Speaking of Mark 14:25, John Meier writes, "Jesus is convinced that his cause is God's cause and that therefore, despite Jesus' personal failure and death, God will in the end vindicate his cause and his prophet by bringing in his kingdom and seating Jesus at the final banquet, to drink the festive wine once again."[25]

Some authors go further. At times, it may seem that when striking insights appear in the words of Jesus, the reflex reaction is to attribute them to later Gospel writers and not to Jesus himself. Perhaps, then, Jesus possessed a more complex understanding of his own death. Viewing the event in this light, Peter Stuhlmacher writes, "The earthly Jesus himself understood his witness and his approaching death in the light of the tradition already given to him in Isaiah about the (vicariously suffering) Servant of God. He understood the suffering laid upon him as an event in which God's will was fulfilled."[26]

The Synoptic Gospels record that Jesus ate a final Passover, a "last supper," with the Twelve. John's Gospel has Jesus' washing the feet of his disciples at this climactic moment, "during the supper" (John 13:2). The scene in John is quite deliberately framed; indeed, it plays off the received tradition of a last supper. That tradition comes down to us in two forms, probably reflecting variant liturgical practices (Matt. 26:26–29; Mark 14:22–25; Luke 22:15–29; 1 Cor. 11:23–26). Its importance is clear: this last supper stands as Jesus' interpretation, indeed his anticipation of his own death. The words over the bread stand for Jesus' body: "This is my body"; the words over the cup represent his blood: "This is my blood" (Matt. 26:28; Mark 14:24). "This is the new covenant in my blood," Paul records

(1 Cor. 11:25). In Luke's Gospel Jesus says, "I have eagerly desired to eat this Passover with you before I suffer; for I tell you, I will not eat it until it is fulfilled in the kingdom of God" (Luke 22:15–16). The scene of this last supper is a prime example of history and theology intertwined. It can hardly be doubted that Jesus ate a final supper with his closest disciples. Yet the significance of the event endows its memory and subsequent portrayal with enormous theological importance. The words over the cup — Jesus' blood — look back to the covenant with Moses (Exod. 24:8; Zech. 9:11) as they look forward to a new covenant, the great hope of Jeremiah 31:31, a covenant written not on stone but rather in the human heart. These allusions comprise a tight theological interpretation of Jesus' death. Seeing Jesus' death as a lynchpin reflects the crucial role that it played both in fact and in memory.

Jesus' agony in the garden, trial, and crucifixion carry the identical density as the narrative of the Last Supper. I select one theme that runs through this thickly layered mixture of historical fact and theological interpretation: the motif of the trial. Jesus is brought before the Sanhedrin — the chief priests, the elders, and the scribes. He is questioned about his words against the temple and about his messianic claim: "Are you the Messiah, the Son of the Blessed One?" (Mark 14:61). Then he is handed over to Pilate. "Are you the King of the Jews," Pilate asks (Matt. 27:11; Mark 15:2; Luke 23:3). Luke adds a hearing before Herod (Luke 23:6–16). The scene with the high priest builds up to a dramatic finale, a last exchange between Jesus and his principal accuser. He responds to his own questioning with these words: "You will see the Son of Man seated at the right hand of Power, and coming on the clouds of heaven" (Matt. 26:64; Mark 14:62; Luke 22:69 [Luke deletes the final phrase, "coming on the clouds of heaven"]). Here Jesus alludes to Daniel 7:13, blended with Psalm 110:1, and the effect is striking. At his own trial, Jesus recalls God's higher tribunal before which all people will stand, including the high priest, one that will mete out true justice. No wonder the high priest rends his garments, accusing Jesus of blasphemy!

If this is the trial of Jesus, it becomes the test of his disciples, their trial as well. Thus interspersed between Jesus' hearings are stories about the disciples. Judas betrays Jesus (Matt. 26:47–56; Mark 14:43–52;

Luke 22:47–53). In Matthew's Gospel, Judas hangs himself (Matt. 27:5). Peter denies Jesus three times (Matt. 26:69–75; Mark 14:66–72; Luke 22:56–62). The disciples cannot keep watch with Jesus in the garden, and they flee. Jesus dies alone. The women watch at a distance. It becomes also the trial of those who mock Jesus. In Luke's Gospel, it becomes a test of the thieves who are crucified with Jesus. John's Gospel extends the theme to Pilate. It becomes his trial as well. "What is truth?" Pilate asks as Truth incarnate stands before him, and that is his judgment.

It is amazing that Jesus' last words on earth are recorded differently in the Gospels. Matthew follows Mark with the cry of dereliction, "My God, my God, why have you forsake me?" in Aramaic and Greek (Ps. 22:1). But the gentle Jesus of Luke's Gospel dies with a word of forgiveness on his lips, just as the majestic Jesus of John announces his own departure: "It is finished" (John 19:30). One way or another, these final words echo the portrait of Jesus that the evangelist seeks to sketch.

Around the events of Jesus' trial, the failure of the disciples, his lonely death, and his burial — stubborn facts — theology has woven a dense web of interpretation, not to invent or disguise what has happened but rather to penetrate to the deepest meaning of these invents in light of the resurrection, to which we now turn.

III. The Resurrection of Jesus

Two Ways

As God's special intervention in the fate of Jesus of Nazareth, the resurrection stands at the center of Christian revelation. Here Bultmann was right. The resurrection of Jesus is the object par excellence of Christian faith. But as such, it also contains a message to the human family whose meaning must be discernible in human terms. There are two obvious ways of reading that message.

The first focuses on the *stories about the risen Jesus, especially their visual content*. What was he like, Jesus risen from the dead? However, these stories do not comprise in aggregate a continuous narrative, nor do they offer a description of Jesus' actual egress from the tomb. Rather, they are episodic, often didactic, accounts, with an apologetic aim; at best, they are cameos of the risen Jesus with an enduring lesson. The story of the disciples on the road to Emmaus illustrates the point. On one level, the story tells of Jesus' first encounters with his followers, while on another it offers later believers consoling words: they meet Jesus the same way the very first disciples met him, in the Scriptures and in breaking bread. The story of Thomas in John 20 is similar. His great confession of faith in the risen Christ — "My Lord and My God!" (John 20:28) — is coupled with the lesson: "Blessed are those who have not seen and yet have come to believe" (John 20:29).

The stories are also unanimous in what they report about the appearance of the risen Jesus. On the one hand, the physicality of the event is stressed. Jesus eats. He invites Thomas to touch his wounds and place his hand in his side. The point: it is the same Jesus in the flesh whom they had known. On the other hand, Jesus enters through locked doors. He vanishes from their sight. He is recognized only at his leave. He seems like a ghost. Not the same Jesus at all. Clear in all of this is that no one sees the risen Jesus as one might see a tree across a road. It is a *gifted* experience, one in which sight, insight, and revelation blend. Jesus "appears." It is a gift to see him.

In short, Jesus may have returned to life, but not *this* life. His resurrection is never confused with Lazarus come back from the grave. Rather, Jesus has entered a new dimension of existence that the kingdom of God opens. Human categories do not function well in this new atmosphere beyond this simple statement: *it is the same Jesus, but he is different.* The attempt to parse these events into the *subjective experiences* of the disciples versus their *objective* content gains little ground. The attempt to solve the problem by eliminating the *bodily* aspect of the resurrection misses the point. The *Catechism of the Catholic Church* sets the right perspective. Jesus' risen body is a glorious one with new properties "not limited by space and time."[27]

A more fruitful path opens to understand the risen Jesus within earthly parameters if we turn to the second way, *the proclamation of the resurrection and the impact of the risen Jesus on his followers.* Here one might start not with the appearances of the risen Jesus in the Gospels but rather with the experience of Paul on the road to Damascus. James D. G. Dunn cites these stories as a prime example of oral tradition's reliability.[28] Paul's conversion is narrated three times in the book of

Acts (Acts 9:1–9; 22:6–11; 26:12–18). Although details differ each time, the crucial exchange between the risen Jesus and Paul remains the same: "'Saul, Saul, why are you persecuting me?' I answered, 'Who are you, Lord?' Then he said to me, 'I am Jesus of Nazareth whom you are persecuting.'" The scene is familiar. A light appears. Paul falls to the ground. Then the exchange. Paul is blinded. Not too little light, but rather too much. Jesus *has* risen from the dead as his followers proclaimed, he realizes. Indeed, this is Paul's *second* encounter with him. He had already met Jesus in the followers whom he had persecuted. This flash of insight is blinding. Paul himself now becomes an apostle, one sent by the risen Jesus.

This act of *commissioning* by the risen Jesus steps to the fore when one focuses on the emotive impact of the appearances, and surely this goes back to Jesus' first encounters with his followers after his death. These were not meetings with neutral bystanders; rather, Jesus' closest followers had betrayed, denied, and abandoned him. Thus these first encounters were acts of forgiveness to those who had fled at his crucifixion. As Jesus rises from the dead, his followers rise to new life in *this life*. They now witness and are sent by his spirit to proclaim his resurrection by the witness of their own lives. Reginald Fuller neatly summarizes the relation between these "two ways": "In the early community, the resurrection was not narrated, but proclaimed (e.g., 1 Thess. 1:10)."[29]

The risen Christ sends his disciples to continue his work. They now preach baptism in his name for the forgiveness of sin and the reception of the spirit. Yet this is a unique spirit. If a spirit of violence put Jesus to death by crucifixion, he is raised by a spirit that combines courage with a spirit of peace, forgiveness, and reconciliation. Significantly, Jesus' first followers never seek revenge.[30] Instead, they continue his work in this same spirit. They marvel at the miracle that God wrought by raising Jesus from the dead and the gift of new life that they themselves have experienced. Therefore, the chief outcome of the resurrection experiences is the mission of the disciples.

Dense Experience

As closely as we can tell, what did these encounters with the risen Jesus resemble? Martin Hengel compares them "with the violent force of an explosion."[31] Similarly, we view them here as dense, explosive experiences. Back from the dead, Jesus literally explodes into the lives of his followers. If they are speechless to describe the experience — like Paul, blinded by too much light — that seems natural. The impact of these explosive encounters is reflected in the mission of the apostles as those *sent* to preach the good news of Jesus' resurrection.

Dense, explosive human experience may provide some window into these events. Two examples explore the topic.

> A police officer calls a sleeping husband. After offering an apology for the late call, he relays the news: "Your wife and two daughters were in a serious accident." The husband sputters, "Are they all right? Are they injured?" The officer pauses. The husband waits. But he knows already what the hesitation means. No one has survived the crash.

Note how the cognitive content of the officer's declaration — ten words in all — is immeasurably outweighed by the emotive impact of these few words. The man is literally "struck" by the news. How many months or years will it take for the cognitive dimension, the meaning of a senseless accident, to catch up with these words? The former only unfolds slowly over time. This unfolding could involve a visit to the crash site. But the main thrust of the event is forward. What is the meaning of the event in the lives of the survivors? This is something that cannot be predicted but rather is known only as it plays out in the future in real time.

In an essay on the development of doctrine, Karl Rahner (1904–1984) cites a gentler example of dense experience: a young man who has fallen deeply in love and searches for words to express his feelings.

> Let us suppose that a young man has the genuine and vital experience of a great love, an experience which transforms his whole being. This love may have presuppositions...which are simply unknown to him. His love itself is his "experience"; he is conscious of it, lives through it with the entire fullness and depth of a great love. He "knows" much more about it than he can "state." The clumsy stammerings of his love-letters are paltry and miserable compared to this knowledge. It may even be possible

that the attempt to tell himself and others what he experiences
and "knows" may lead to quite false statements. . . . If he is intelligent, and has at his disposal an adequately differentiated stock
of ideas, he could perhaps make the attempt, slowly and grop-
ingly, approaching the subject in a thousand different ways, to
state what he knows about his love, what he is already aware
of in the consciousness of simply possessing the reality (more
simply but more fully aware), so as finally to "know" (in reflexive
propositions).[32]

Rahner describes the relationship between the original experience and
subsequent reflection this way:

The [original] knowledge is infinitely richer, simpler and denser
than any body of propositions about the love could be. Yet this
knowledge never lacks a certain measure of reflective articulate-
ness: the lover confesses his love at least to himself, "states" at
least to himself something about his love. And it is not a matter
of indifference to the love itself whether or not the lover continues to reflect upon it; this self-reflection is not the subsequent
description of a reality which remains in no way altered by the
description. In this progressive self-achievement, in which love
comprehends itself more and more, in which it goes on to state
something "about" itself and comprehends its own nature more
clearly, the love itself becomes ordered.[33]

Reflection about the original experience necessarily follows, but
the latter never exhausts the former. The experience retains an irreducible surplus of meaning. Subsequent reflection functions best when
it acts as a pathway back to the original. In any case, what is *implicitly communicated*, Rahner observes, always exceeds what can be
explicitly said.

A distinction made by William James (1842–1910) is helpful here,
one for which James claims a broader, linguistic validity. He points to
the double set of verbs for "know" in Latin, German, and French,
respectively. The verbs *noscere, kennen,* and *connaître* denote direct
knowledge of an object — in James's parlance, "knowledge of acquaintance." Another set of verbs — *scire, wissen,* and *savoir* — refer to

more abstract knowing, not direct contact with the object, but rather knowledge *about its meaning.* James calls it "knowledge-about."[34]

When we return to the experience of the resurrection, the emotive impact of the risen Jesus belongs to the more primitive forms of knowing, "knowledge of acquaintance." The outward thrust of this primitive knowledge necessarily propels an exploration of its meaning, "knowledge about" the event. What does it all mean? For the meaning to be valid, it must faithfully unfold the original. In this process, logical consistency is not a first, but a last, requirement. Rather, the first attempts at expression overlap and repeat one another. Such seems normal. Above all, there is a groping search for a set of words that seem to fit and then convey the original experience.

If the foregoing is true in *ordinary* human experience, how much more valid will it be when one tries to grasp the utterly unique experience of someone risen from the dead? How much more will this experience shatter ordinary human categories? How much greater will the challenge be to forge a new language — in the first instance, a new combination of old words — that somehow conveys this unique event? In sum, preaching about the risen Jesus will represent a search for new language to capture this unimaginably singular event: Jesus has risen from the dead.

The process becomes all the more complex and dynamic because these are meetings not simply with individuals — Mary Magdalene, Peter, Paul — but rather with groups. They are *social* encounters. Paul cites Jesus' appearances to "Cephas, then to the twelve. Then he appeared to more than five hundred brothers and sisters at one time" (1 Cor. 15:5–6). The experience of the risen Jesus does not simply change the lives of individuals; it also founds a community. The ancient tradition that the Christian church traces its origin to the feast of Pentecost reflects this memory. The risen Jesus gives birth to a church.

Therefore, as we cross the line between the *experience* of the risen Jesus and the *meaning* of the event, we also enter a *communal* world. Since these experiences were both individual and communal ones, it will have been necessary very early on to establish a basic language and a set of meanings for Jesus' followers to talk among *themselves.* It will have been necessary also in order to preach to *others* about the risen Jesus. His followers will look to the world of Second Temple Judaism and the Scriptures in order to forge an interpretation of Jesus' death and resurrection. Here, religious experience and religious tradition seamlessly merge. The greatest challenge will be to express the uniqueness of Jesus' death and resurrection in language intelligible first to Jews and then to Gentiles.

The experience of the risen Jesus will flow equally into symbolic actions — baptism and Eucharist — as well as into theological reflection on Jesus' death and resurrection. Indeed, the two may often merge. While Christian symbolic actions — baptism and the Eucharist — offer mediated or indirect experiences, they also contain the potential to "flare up" into more direct encounters. A window may open. The resurrected Jesus himself may appear. A powerful dynamic between *witness* and *experience* emerges. The disciples on the road to Emmaus illustrate this link. The story invites believers of every generation to encounter the risen Jesus firsthand in the Scriptures and the breaking of bread. In effect, later believers may duplicate from time to time the encounters of the first disciples and experience firsthand what they normally only know by faith.

Not surprisingly, early Christian worship and the soaring language of hymns are probably the best vehicles to convey this primitive sense of knowing. Here, Jesus' spirit remains alive among his followers. Theology will both lead and follow these experiences of the spirit, seeking to explain the meaning of Jesus' death and resurrection as well this ongoing experience of the spirit.

The ever-present danger in tracing this early development is to seek too much conceptual clarity too early in the fertile seedbed of religious experience. Worse still is to indict the original experience for its lack of such precision. While historical development has its own coherence, its creativity does not consist in conformity to preexisting modes of thought. Indeed, it consists in breaking such. Only in this way can novelty emerge. In sum, the great challenge of the church's preaching is to make Jesus' death and resurrection understandable in known categories, on the one hand, and, on the other, to forge new combinations to capture its uniqueness.

The event of the resurrection affects the subsequent preaching of the early church in five significant ways. First, the resurrection establishes the fundamental meaning of Christology — an interpretation of Jesus' life and, above all, his death *through the perspective* of the resurrection. By doing so, it draws a line between Jesus' *present status* and his actual life and ministry *before* the resurrection. The two dimensions will affect one another and cannot be separated.

Second, the event of the resurrection also means that none of the early Christologies may fairly be described as modest estimates of Jesus. Certainly, the development of Christology will not proceed in a series of graduated steps from a *low* Christology, Jesus as *human,* to a *high* Christology, Jesus as *divine.* Instead, it will consist in the refinement of various elevated estimates of him that go back to the beginning. Jesus always remains the one who rose from the dead.

Third, the resurrection stands as a vindication of Jesus and his preaching. Surely, this will prompt his disciples to be even more faithful to a master whose teachings have been so vindicated. Indeed, the resurrection should highlight Jesus' *aims* in a special way. In other words, if the resurrection represents Jesus' vindication, then the lineaments that are vindicated should stand out all the more clearly. This may prompt the early church to be more consistent than Jesus. In that sense, Jesus' *aims* may be clearer after his death and resurrection than they were before.

Fourth, the resurrection will also act as a powerful filter. Accidental elements about Jesus — details of his facial features — probably will be discarded as scarcely worthy of remembrance. Over time, all-too-human features of Jesus' portrait will be removed. But even here the path is not linear. True, Matthew and Luke edit Mark along these lines. But Luke's portrait is of a gentle Jesus. And John's Gospel, by any reckoning, represents a quantum leap beyond the Synoptic Gospels in showing how Jesus' transcendent glory shines through his earthly life.

Fifth, while the risen Jesus is the first of many brothers and sisters to enter the kingdom, he also becomes, in another sense, *inimitable.* Who can imitate one who rose from the dead? This will have a powerful impact in the forms of presence that the risen Jesus brings to the community of his followers as well as the ways in which his life does and does not represent an exemplar for imitation.

If we described the resurrection as an explosive event, retaining its own *excessus,* its first impact is on the mission of the church, in which the preaching of the kingdom and the story of Jesus are inseparably bound together. Indeed, the mission becomes the principal vehicle for clarifying the meaning of Jesus' death and resurrection. In other words, the explosion gives birth to a shock wave of different effects that will only gain clarity over time but that are contained *in nucleo* from the start in the tight, dense ball of experience — Jesus come back from the dead. The first face to emerge will be the christological one. Who is Jesus?

Chapter Three

CHRIST

This chapter seeks to trace the development of Christology in three stages. The first centers on the simple question "Who is Jesus?" In one sense, this question will remain with us. While the question is answered according to its own first lights, the second stage — the prayer and worship of the early church — provides the creative matrix in which the answer develops and matures. The third stage — the preaching of the early church and the Gospel portraits of Jesus — concludes the first trajectory. As the Gospels confess Jesus as the Son of God, this confession necessarily opens the question of the Trinity for its own completion.

I. Who Is Jesus?

Christology begins in earnest with the resurrection. Through the optic of this event, the question is posed and then answered: "Who is Jesus?" As Jesus' vindication, the resurrection points to the rightness of Jesus' preaching of the kingdom and to his claim to be its special representative. In this regard, it is significant that the resurrection was never considered as an event that happens only to an individual. Rather, as the early kerygma reflects, Jesus risen from the dead is always the first of many brothers and sisters shortly to follow him when the kingdom arrives in its fullness.

This is the context in which the first Christology emerges. Note the straight line that connects Jewish apocalyptic thinking, Jesus' preaching of the kingdom, and the event of the resurrection. Note also how the resurrection fits into Israel's hopes of restoration. Israel's long exile is now ended. The resurrection is proof positive that Yahweh has decided to intervene. Jesus' resurrection is the foretaste and promise of the kingdom in its fullness and of Israel's restoration as well.

Jesus as Judge of the End Time

The resurrection is thus a direct statement about Jesus. God has raised Jesus from the dead. *Jesus lives.* Hence the obvious question "What will he do next?" This context supplies the answer. The resurrection of Jesus becomes, in effect, the first act of a two-act play. Jesus will shortly return as the great judge of the end time to preside over the kingdom when it arrives in its fullness. This is his new action, the second act of the drama. Here it is important to distinguish between *function* and the *various modalities* that can express it. If the function is judgment, it may be expressed by calling Jesus the Son of Man or the Messiah.

First, the Son of Man. The expression occurs eighty-six times in the New Testament. "Striking is the fact that in all four Gospels the phrase appears in effect only on the lips of Jesus."[1] This is the characteristic way Jesus refers to himself. The expression "Son of Man" has various reference points in the Old Testament — Psalms, Ezekiel, and "one like a son of man" in Daniel. Daniel 7 represents a special case in point. Here dominion is taken from the beasts of the sea, the nations that oppressed Israel, and given to one "like a son of man" (Dan. 7:13), the holy ones of Israel. In dispute here is when this *corporate* image for Israel develops into a *single* heavenly figure of judgment. But the expression "Son of Man" never appears in Paul and is not used as a confession of faith, which, all things considered, is understandable enough. Even if some titular use did exist, it would scarcely have acquired sufficient weight in the tradition to function as a good confession of faith.

That difficulty is remedied by confessing Jesus as the Messiah, the Christ. He probably was acclaimed as such during his lifetime. The title on the cross bore the words "King of the Jews." Surely, the coming of the kingdom in its fullness and Israel's restoration includes a messiah. A traditional function of kingship is judgment. So Jesus as the Messiah would return as the great judge of the end time, and the messianic tradition, a millennium long, could bear the full weight of a confession of faith. Jesus *is* the Messiah, the Christ. As messianic judge, he will preside when the kingdom arrives in its fullness. As king, he will spearhead a renewed Israel.

We should note how comfortably Christology to this point fits within a Jewish context. It can hardly have been a point of conflict with the various sects in Jerusalem that one group of Jews began to proclaim Jesus as the Messiah — perhaps odd, but no reason to expel Jesus' followers from the city. The first Christians probably regarded themselves in much the same light. They continued to act as pious Jews who went to the temple to pray, observing other Jewish customs as well.

Jesus as Crucified Messiah

But the stumbling block for Jews and Gentiles alike, the heart of the matter, is Jesus as a *crucified* messiah. This is both a puzzle and even more a scandal on many levels. The core notion of a messiah — an anointed king of the house of David — contains no provision in its long history that this messiah should suffer, much less be crucified. Death by crucifixion adds its own insult. Crucifixion was a widespread punishment in antiquity. The Romans used it for slaves, criminals, and rebellious elements in the provinces, in the latter instance as a public warning to others not to do likewise. Crucifixion was especially offensive to Jews, involving the curse laid on one who hung on a tree (Deut. 21:23).[2]

For many reasons, the death of Jesus as a crucified messiah has no positive meaning at all but rather is a shock and a scandal to his followers themselves. This is surely their first reaction. Or it must come to mean everything. It has to be the center of the message. Therefore the crucifixion can never occupy a secondary role, subordinate to Jesus' role as a teacher of wisdom. For the same reason, it also must be the first conundrum to be solved if the message about the kingdom and Jesus, the crucified messiah, is preached to Jews and Gentiles. It therefore requires a deep anchoring interpretation whose first pillars are set in Jesus' own life and ministry. Are there, then, elements in the preaching of Jesus that helped to interpret his death?

Surely, the theme of reversal that runs so consistently through the parables would come to mind: the first will be last and the last will be first. The kingdom appears where we least expect it — the mustard seed, the smallest of seeds. When God's reign comes, our world is turned upside down. The prodigal is preferred, a Samaritan is termed good, and destitute Lazarus sits in the bosom of Abraham. Certainly, Jesus rising from the dead exemplifies this theme of reversal. Indeed, the notion of a crucified messiah seems to tease out such paradoxes to the breaking point. In death, Jesus may seem an advertisement for his own preaching. This also seems an important step so that his death and then his life themselves can take on a larger-than-life quality, not simply a story told, but a life lived that becomes a parable about God.

As we noted earlier, Jesus doubtless foresaw his suffering and rejection. He knew the fate of John the Baptist. He knew that tribulation and trial would precede the kingdom's climactic finale. Jesus may have drawn upon the theme of the suffering righteous one in Israel's tradition to interpret what was happening. But all such interpretation needs an anchor closer to events. This is the reason why the Last Supper stands as such a convincing witness to Jesus' understanding of his own death.

In this regard, the timing and circumstances of Jesus' death were never regarded as fortuitous but instead as clues that provide a special key. Jesus dies at Passover. In the Synoptic Gospels, the Last Supper is portrayed as a Passover meal in which Jesus himself interprets his passion. In John's Gospel, Jesus is sentenced at the noon hour, when the lambs for Passover are slaughtered. For John, Jesus is the Lamb of God, who dies to take away our sins. Forty years earlier, Paul could write in the same vein, "For our paschal lamb, Christ, has been sacrificed" (1 Cor. 5:7). In other words, almost from the start, Israel's Passover tradition is used to interpret the death of Jesus. He is the lamb of sacrifice whose death takes away our sins. Israel's deliverance from Egypt now becomes a foreshadowing of this deliverance from sin. Indeed, Jesus' blood inaugurates a new covenant. This represents a deep and extensive vein in the tradition that stretches from the Last Supper through Paul and into the Gospel of John and indeed is expanded in the letter to the Hebrews. It is both an anchoring interpretation of Jesus' death and a flowering one.

But it is Paul who thinks through consistently the meaning of Jesus' death. He describes Jesus' death as "a sacrifice of atonement by his blood," put forward by God (Rom. 3:25), thereby tapping into a central vein of Jewish thought and temple practice. But we catch the heart of Paul's thought in Romans 5:6–11; 8:32.

> For while we were still weak, at the right time Christ died for the ungodly. Indeed, rarely will anyone die for a righteous person — though perhaps for a good person someone might actually dare to die. But God proves his love for us in that while we still were sinners Christ died for us. Much more surely then, now that we have been justified by his blood, will we be saved through him from the wrath of God. For if while we were enemies we were reconciled to God through the death of his Son, much more surely, having been reconciled will we be saved by his life. But even more than that, we even boast in God through our Lord Jesus Christ, through whom we have now received reconciliation. (Rom. 5:6–11)

In Romans 8:32 the point is succinctly expressed in a question:

> He who did not withhold his own Son, but gave him up for all of us, will he not with him give us everything else?

Why is Jesus' death so special? Because this is the death of God's own Son. Commenting on Romans 8:32, Jon Levenson writes, "'He who did not spare his own Son' is a transparent reworking of the angel's words to Abraham at the end of the Aqedah: 'since you have not withheld your son, your favored one, from Me' and 'because you have done this and not withheld your son, your favored one' (Gen 22:12, 16)."[3] Thus the crucifixion of Jesus now supplants the binding of Isaac as, in larger terms, God supplants Abraham in the role of the father who did not withhold his own beloved son from death. The death of Jesus reverses the near sacrifice of Isaac. In Genesis 22, a father is willing to sacrifice his son to God the Father; here, God the Father *does* sacrifice his own beloved Son, Jesus, on behalf of the human family. "The father's gift to God has been transformed into the gift of God the Father." The common denominator is a love "greater than even that a Father has for his a beloved son."[4]

Levenson argues that the binding of Isaac, never referred to else-where in the Hebrew Bible, emerges in the Talmud and Second Temple Judaism as the supreme moment in Abraham's life. Indeed, as the near sacrifice of Isaac foreshadows ever more closely the literal slaughter of the Passover lamb, Isaac also becomes more active in his own role. He binds himself, willingly offering his life. The connection of Abraham's "beloved son" with the paschal lamb continues to grow. These asso-ciations, so common among the rabbis, probably also are common among early Christians who came to regard the death of Jesus, the beloved Son, not as a negation of God's love but rather as a manifes-tation of it. "He who did not withhold his own Son, but gave him up for all of us, will he not with him gives us everything else?" "Both the Jewish and Christian systems of sacrifice come to be seen as founded upon a father's willingness to surrender his beloved son and the son's unstinting acceptance of the sacrificial role he has been assigned in the great drama of redemption."[5]

Paul thinks through the momentous implications of the death of God's Son in terms of two representative figures. The first is Abra-ham, and here the focus is Israel and the Torah of Moses. The promise to Abraham, Paul argues, came 430 years before the law and before circumcision (Gal. 3:15–18). This original promise was made to Abra-ham and to his special "descendant" (emphasis on the singular in Paul's exegesis of Gal. 3:16). The special descendant is Christ. With his com-ing, the promise to Abraham is fulfilled. This sheds special light on the status of the law and its function in the past. The law was Israel's guardian or custodian, bringing in its wake a consciousness of sin. Indeed, this heightened consciousness may have rendered sin more at-tractive, turning ordinary desire into fiery lust. But it never guaranteed obedience. If the law is now eclipsed, it is not because it was without meaning but rather because its goal has been reached. In this sense, Christ is the end of the law. Its purpose is fulfilled with his coming. Christ's death for us, the death of God's beloved Son, is God's great and surprising gift. Who could have guessed or predicted it? Who could earn it? Therefore, the only response is one of faith. Here Abra-ham appears once again as the model. Contrary to all odds, he had faith in the promise that God would make him the father of many nations, and so it came to be. We believe in a God who can do the impossible, who has raised Jesus from the dead. The only response to such a God is faith. No earned response on our part can match the extraordinary gift of the death of God's beloved Son.

Adam is a representative figure on an even larger scale. Here the focus is no longer on Israel but instead on the human condition itself. What are the implications of the death of Jesus in this widest of all horizons? In 1 Corinthians 15:45–49, Adam is described as a man of dust from the earth. Through him, death has entered the world. In Romans 5:12–21, Paul expands the thought. Through Adam, sin enters and death follows. In other words, the human condition is contaminated from the start, and this contagion has spread to all of Adam's descendants. It is clear that when Paul speaks of sin and death, he does not mean merely that human life ends at some point or the fact that people do sin. He means, instead, the *power of sin and death,* larger than life, and their dominion over humankind, holding all people in thrall. And not just humanity: all creation groans for redemption. In other words, Adam's sin is a world-historical catastrophe that plants the seed of alienation from God in the center of creation. If sin and death enter through one man, so too salvation comes the same way. Christ's death is equally a world-historical event with cosmic dimensions. This is the reason why God sent his own Son and is the reason why he died. Because in his death, sin and death are destroyed, and their power is broken. Humankind is freed from bondage. Creation is given a new chance. Clearly, too, the message about such an event pertains to Jew and Gentile alike. Indeed, it pertains to everyone who is human, and the message is one of freedom, freedom from the law, freedom from the bondage of sin and death. Rightly in baptism, we are buried into Jesus' death so that we can rise to this kind of new life in his spirit.

The Law and Wisdom

Seen in this world-historical perspective, the revelation of God in Jesus eclipses the Torah of Moses in breadth and scope. By any measure, this represents a momentous turn. The law was God's gift to Israel. After the exile, its significance was captured in the image of personified wisdom. In effect, God's ordering spirit in creation — God's wisdom — has come to fullest expression on earth in the Torah of Moses. This was the clearest expression of God's presence to his people. But, if the revelation in Christ now eclipses all others, then the accolades of wisdom, once given to the Torah, are now transferred to the risen Christ. *An elevated Christology is born in this exchange.* Now Jesus' death reveals God's hidden wisdom, the mysterious purpose of his will.

Another universalizing engine fuels this transfer. If God has raised Jesus from the dead in order to send him once again as the world's final judge, was this not his intention from the start? In other words, at the end of time God fully reveals the hand that he was holding from the beginning. These cards had to be there all along. Therefore, if Jesus is the final judge at the end of time, then he must have been God's Son from the beginning. The inner coherence between eschatology (the end of time) and protology (the beginning of time) demands symmetry. The beginning and end of time must resemble one another. Hence, the conviction that Jesus will return as the great judge will of inner necessity contribute to the insight that he is also the preexistent one from all eternity in the drama of salvation.

Christ's preexistence now enters. However, it enters as *by-product* of the argument. The chief focus of such imagery is not cosmological but rather as a way to describe the unsurpassable finality of God's revelation in Jesus of Nazareth that exceeds even the Torah. But if preexistence enters now as by-product, what can it mean when it becomes a focus of attention in its own right? Answers come only slowly and, at first, on the margin.

Preexistence in Early Pauline Hymns

What does the preexistence mean? Paul writes in capsule form, "Yet for us there is one God, the Father, from whom are all things and for whom we exist, and one Lord Jesus Christ, through whom are all things and through whom we exist" (1 Cor. 8:6). Other passages seem to presuppose Christ's preexistence as well — for example, those that speak of the "sending" of God's Son (Rom. 8:3; Gal. 4:4; see also Rom. 10:6–8; 1 Cor. 10:4). The early hymns in Philippians (Phil. 2:5–11) and Colossians (Col. 1:15–20) give us a better inkling about the possible meaning of preexistence.

> Let the same mind be in you that was in Christ Jesus,
> who, though he was in the form of God,

did not regard equality with God
as something to be exploited,
but emptied himself,
taking the form of a slave,
being born in human likeness.
And being found in human form,
he humbled himself
and became obedience to the point of death,
even death on a cross.
Therefore God also highly exalted him
and gave him the name that is above every name,
so that at the name of Jesus
every knee should bend,
in heaven and on earth and under the earth,
and every tongue should confess
that Jesus Christ is Lord,
to the glory of God the Father. (Phil. 2:5–11)

The hymn is usually reckoned to be pre-Pauline, perhaps one that Paul may have taught the Philippian community on his first visit. Scholars are divided about the interpretation of the phrase "form of God," which begins the hymn. Does it refer to divine preexistence, or is it a reference to Adam, created in the image and likeness of God? The answer makes considerable difference for the subsequent way the hymn is interpreted. In effect, does the hymn begin with the incarnation of a *divine figure* similar to the prologue of John's Gospel? Or does it start with Adam, as part of Paul's speculation about the *first human*? If the former, that represents a significant development. Raymond Brown (1928–1998) comments, "If the hymn is incarnational and was phrased in Aramaic in the 30s, the highest type of Christology was articulated early indeed."[6]

The climax of the hymn is striking. Jesus is given the name that is above all names. He is given God's name. Since God's actual name, "Yahweh," could not be spoken, "Lord" (*Adon* in Hebrew, *Kyrios* in Greek) had become the functional name for God. Because of his death on the cross, this exalted name is now bestowed on Jesus. Striking is the allusion here to the final lines to Isaiah 45:23–25. This is one of the most stridently monotheistic passages in the Hebrew Scriptures. Here, Yahweh boldly proclaims that he is God, and there is no other. "To me every knee shall bow, every tongue shall swear" (Isa. 45:23). Now every knee bends to Jesus, on whom God's own exalted name is bestowed.[7] By any measure, this is an extraordinary turn.

In regard to the letter to the Colossians, the hymn probably predates the letter.

> He is the image of the invisible God, the firstborn of all creation;
> for in him all things in heaven and on earth were created,
> things visible and invisible, whether thrones or dominions or
>   rulers or powers —
> all things have been created through him and for him.
> He himself is before all things, and in him all things hold
>   together.
> He is the head of the body, the church; he is the beginning, the
>   firstborn from the dead,
> so that he might come to have first place in everything.
> For in him all the fullness of God was pleased to dwell,
> and through him God was pleased to reconcile to himself all
>   things,
> whether on earth or in heaven,
> making peace by the blood of his cross. (Col. 1:15–20)

The line of demarcation in the hymn is between "firstborn of creation" and "firstborn from the dead." Noteworthy is the focus on Christ as an agent in creation that almost overshadows his role in redemption. The opening line of the hymn boldly describes Christ as the image of the invisible God, echoing Wisdom 7:26: "a reflection of eternal light, a spotless mirror of the working of God, and an image of his goodness." Creation and redemption in Christ are inseparably intertwined.

What do these passages reveal about the meaning of preexistence? First, the frame of reference of the discussion shifts. Each hymn carries a brief, inchoate narrative about Jesus. The hinge of his work on earth is the crucifixion, Jesus' "death on a cross" in Philippians (Phil. 2:8), the "blood of his cross" in Colossians (Col. 1:20). But the narrative is now placed in a *spatial* framework with *vertical* points of reference.

Every knee bends "in heaven and on earth and under the earth" in Philippians. In other words, the introduction of creation and the wisdom motif ushers in a spatial framework. Historical categories remain. We await Jesus' return. His future coming is our hope. But the story of Jesus' death and resurrection is located in a larger spatial and universal context. God has sent his Son from heaven. His crucifixion is the turning point on earth. He reigns now in heaven. We shortly expect his glorious return from God's right hand.

The frame of reference changes in other ways as well. Originally, Jesus' resurrection was the opening gambit of Israel's national restoration with universal overtones, since the God of Israel was Lord of all peoples. Now the national note recedes as the universal dimension moves to the fore. God's revelation in Jesus becomes instead a message of universal salvation framed in Old Testament categories. The promise to Abraham, the father of all people, is fulfilled in Christ. Through his death, all people are redeemed from the scourge of sin and death.

It is not surprising that the universal dimension of Jesus' life, death, and resurrection is glimpsed by Greek-speaking Jews in the mission. Is the slight distance from Jewish roots necessary to grasp this universal dimension? In turn, does this universal light clarify the "aims" of Jesus' own preaching — for example, his *real* mission, his *real* attitude toward the law and its ritual dimension? The movement is not unlike the one that we noted in chapter 1 in Israel's breakthrough to monotheism at the time of the exile. Were not the fall of Jerusalem, the destruction of the temple, and the collapse of the monarchy — places and institutions that rooted Yahweh in the nation — the precondition for the insight that the God of Israel was also the God of all peoples? Was not a certain deracinating movement necessary? Perhaps here as well.

II. Prayer and Worship
of the Early Christian Community

Significant is the forum in which this early development takes place: hymns, prayers, and community worship. We noted two of the most famous hymns, Philippians 2:5–11 and Colossians 1:15–20. In the same context, one thinks, of course, of the prologue to John's Gospel

(John 1:1–19). Shorter passages may contain the fragments of hymns (Eph. 2:14–16; 5:14; 1 Tim. 3:16; Heb. 1:3; 1 Pet. 3:18–22). The book of Revelation contains hymns and lyrical acclamations to Christ *and* God (see also Rev. 4:8, 11; 5:9–10, 13–14; 7:15–17; 11:15; 15:3–4; 19:1–8). In one sense, these represent a link to Israel. Gerhard von Rad writes, "There were, for Israel, perceptions which could only be expressed, strangely enough to our ears, only in the form of the hymn."[8] Martin Hengel continues in the same vein, "As in ancient Israel in the case of David and the prophets, and also as among the Greeks, the Spirit sought poetical form for the expression of hyperbolic things which were not yet ripe for expression in prose, which could only be expressed in the form of the narrative praise of the song, in divinely inspired singing. Why should this phenomenon not also have applied to earliest Christianity, that movement which more than any other in antiquity was filled the enthusiastic spirit?"[9]

In hymns, prayers, and inspired speech — in the looser, more flexible forms they provide — the spirit soars more easily. With the help of Jesus' spirit, the community ponders and seeks to put into words the meaning of Jesus' death and resurrection, hence the narrative and didactic quality of the hymns. They may fairly be regarded as a search for adequate speech to fit a new experience in which the aesthetic sense leads the way. Early Christian devotional life has been the special focus of Larry Hurtado's study. His conclusion: the highest forms of religious veneration were given to the risen Jesus almost from the start.[10]

Therefore, the hymns should not be seen in isolation. Indeed, it is striking how much of the early tradition handed down to Paul centers on prayer and worship. The distinctive way in which Jesus prayed to God as *Abba* appears in Galatians 4:6 and Romans 8:15. But here the context is unique. It is the work of a double spirit and not merely the imitation of a traditional formula. Rather, *the spirit of Jesus* bears witness in *our spirit*, enabling us to cry out, "Abba, Father!" Such is not a neutral statement but rather a proclamation in prayer. It connects with other traditional prayer proclamations. The Aramaic phrase *Maranatha* or *Marana-tha* occurs in 1 Corinthians 16:22: "Come, O (our) Lord!" The phrase also occurs in Greek in Revelation 22:20: "Come, Lord Jesus!" Here Jesus is addressed in Aramaic as exalted Lord. The prayer is for his swift return. Other prayers to Jesus occur as well. One thinks of Stephen's final words addressed to the risen Jesus: "Lord Jesus, receive my spirit. Lord, do not hold this sin against them" (Acts 7:59–60). Likewise, the great confession of the Pauline mission — Jesus is Lord! — is a proclamation whose home is prayer and worship (Rom. 10:9–10; 1 Cor. 8:5–6). Indeed, in 1 Corinthians, Paul explains that, like the *Abba* prayer, we do not make such an acclamation on our own; rather, it is the work of the Spirit in our spirit. In fact, "No one can say 'Jesus is Lord' except by the Holy Spirit" (1 Cor. 12:3).

We should place in this same context those elements that are characteristic of Paul's preaching. In the first instance, there are prepositional phrases that occur with great frequency in the Pauline letters: "in Christ," "in the Lord," "with Christ," "into Christ," "through Christ," and "of Christ." In turn, they are of a piece with Paul's great image of the church as the body of Christ. Here it is not just the double spirit noted above, the spirit of Jesus working in our individual spirit. Just as prayer and worship are communal activities, so the way the spirit works in one person will relate to the way the spirit works in others. Indeed, the "fellowship" of the Holy Spirit joins believers together, forging them into a community. In other words, in the Pauline mission, the spirit of the risen Jesus becomes a *zone of personal presence* with vertical and horizontal reference points. It is the spirit of the risen Jesus, coming down from on high. But that spirit also encircles his followers, forming them into the body of Christ.

James D. G. Dunn warns against trying to fit these disparate pieces of experience into preformed categories; rather, trust the phenomenon of the spirit as it endeavors to say something new.[11] These early Christians know that Jesus was human, born of a woman, a descendant of David. They know he is expected to return. But God has raised him from the dead. Through his death and resurrection, his spirit has somehow been unleashed in the community. This they know firsthand. If the risen Jesus is alive and well in heaven, his spirit finds itself in similar circumstances on earth. How these pieces fit together remains to be seen. No wonder, then, that the resulting picture is best captured in poetic images!

Summary

Let me draw the elements of this development together. We began with the question "Who is Jesus?" and the answer has drawn us ineluctably along a path that is easier to trace in retrospect than it was to traverse in the first place. The church's confession of Jesus as the one risen from the dead was connected to his expected return as the great judge of the end time. But the great engine that drives the development is Jesus' death. What can it mean? Building on elements in Jesus' own preaching and his expectation of suffering, his fateful death at Passover provides the crucial clue. Here the complex transference of Israel's Passover tradition to Jesus' death begins. Yet it is the apostle Paul who explains why this death is so special and why it can bring salvation to the human family. This is the death of God's beloved Son. Indeed, this is the reason why God has sent him into the world. Paul also thinks through the universal implications of Jesus' death, first to Jews, then to Gentiles. Israel's Torah is fulfilled in Christ's coming, and humanity is renewed in Jesus as the new Adam.

As a corollary of the argument, as Jesus replaces the Torah of Moses, the accolades of preexistent Wisdom are transferred to the risen Christ. God's preexistent Wisdom now finds fullest expression in Jesus of Nazareth, in his life, death, and resurrection. In one sense, this brings us back to Jesus' role at the beginning of the discussion in this chapter: Jesus as judge of the end time. The law of resemblances asks that the first and last times be aligned. Jesus as the great judge of the end time bids us to regard him as God's preexistent Wisdom from all eternity as well.

I sought to locate the discussion of Christology in a twofold context. First, it takes place increasingly in the Pauline mission in which theological and practical questions are entwined at every point. Must Gentile converts be circumcised? How do mixed communities comport themselves at meals, given Jewish food regulations? The overarching question is this: What is the status of the law in light of Jesus' coming? The second context is equally if not more important because it stretches in an unbroken line from the earliest community in Jerusalem to the Gentile mission. The development takes place in the prayer and worship of the church. Here the spirit of Jesus remains alive and available to his followers. Here that original dense knowledge of the risen Jesus becomes the font of prayer, preaching, and teaching.

These two contexts are intertwined. In prayer and worship, Jesus' spirit comes alive. Preaching seeks to translate this experience into words. But it is not as if the preaching comes first and persuades by its logic; rather, the preaching is accompanied by the experience of the Spirit. Indeed, the Spirit may precede the preaching. In other words, the Spirit seems contagious in its own right. And it is the experience of the Spirit that makes the preached word persuasive and believable. Thus, this early preaching may fairly be regarded as a search for words that adequately give voice to what has been experienced first in prayer and worship. If the poetic voice comes first, it is not simply because its forms are more flexible; it is also a more adventuresome voice, better adapted to open new paths. In this regard, the early Christian community did not resemble a traveling study seminar but rather a community of prayer and worship on mission.

I spoke about the original dense experience of the risen Jesus and its impact on his first followers. The experience of the risen Jesus continues most vividly in the prayer and worship of the early church. In the Gentile mission, this experience intensifies. Thus I would draw a straight line connecting the appearances of the risen Jesus to the continuing experience of his Spirit in prayer and worship of the church as the great motivating engine of its mission.

Martin Hengel wrote these bold words: "Thus the christological development from Jesus as far as Paul took place within about eighteen years, a short space of time for such an intellectual process. In essentials more happened in christology within these few years than in the whole subsequent seven hundred years of church history."[12]

Hengel surely is right in this sense. Genius insights do not come piecemeal, the way a plodding student does an algebra problem. They come in a flash all at once. This is probably the way the early church came to understand the death of Jesus as God's beloved Son. But that insight made sense only to believers who had tasted the fruit of the Spirit of the risen Jesus, which had to pass through his death and resurrection to reach them. Ultimately, why God chooses to act this way is beyond them. This is God's secret wisdom, hidden for all ages, now revealed in Jesus' death and resurrection. To their great surprise, they are its beneficiaries. That suffices. On the other hand, it will take considerable time to comprehend the implications of this insight.

In this regard, we have seen Christ's preexistence enter as a by-product of the eclipse of the Torah. This was first a statement about God's intention. In taking on a spatial, universal dimension in the hymns, the insight gains a broader, universal venue. At first in hints and on the margin, it will finally become the context to think through Jesus' own exalted status in its own right. What does it mean to say that Jesus is God's wisdom come down to earth? How are we to understand both God and his Christ together? How are we to understand Jesus' earthly ministry in this heavenly light? But if the breakthrough to Jesus' preexistence comes early and suddenly, it is also a pot that needs to simmer for a long time. For it is one thing to say, as in Sirach 24, that wisdom dwells in Israel in its ancient and venerated tradition, in the Torah, and quite another to say that God's Word has somehow appeared in a young *tekton*, a woodworker, and itinerant preacher from Galilee who was recently crucified. Paul seems aware of the difficulties. He writes with pithy eloquence:

> Brothers and sisters: Jews demand signs and Greeks look for wis-
> dom, but we proclaim Christ crucified, a stumbling block to Jews
> and foolishness to Gentiles, but to those who are called, Jews and
> Greeks alike, Christ the power of God and the wisdom of God.
> For the foolishness of God is wiser than human wisdom, and the
> weakness of God is stronger than human strength.
>
> (1 Cor. 1:22–25)

III. Preaching of the Church and the Gospels

The Gospel of Jesus Christ

The transition from the "gospel" preached by Paul to the four written "Gospels" — stories of Jesus' life, death, and resurrection — represents both an evolutionary and a revolutionary turn, a gradual yet quite original development. The term *gospel* occurs frequently in the letters of Paul.[13] Here it refers to the core of Paul's preaching: the gracious initiative of God, sending his only Son, to redeem all people through Christ's death and resurrection. The *meaning* of the Christ event —

its import for salvation — not the words and actions of Jesus is the principal focus. Paul did not know Jesus in the flesh, only the exalted Christ, whom he encountered on the road to Damascus. But he was far from disinterested in Jesus' human life. We glean from his letters that Jesus was born of woman, a descendant of the house of David. We know that he had relatives, especially James. We know of the Twelve and of Peter, also known as Cephas. We know Jesus' teaching on divorce. Several times Paul refers to "words of the Lord," the teachings of Jesus (1 Cor. 7:10; 9:14; 1 Thess. 4:15; cf. 1 Cor. 14:37). In 1 Corinthians 15:3–5 we learn about an early confession of faith that Paul has received and that he himself will hand on. We also have the words of institution at the Last Supper (1 Cor. 11:23–26), words that would be unintelligible if Paul could not explain in more detail the context of Jesus' passion and death, which these words seek to interpret.

These instances are especially significant given the occasional nature of Paul's letters to communities already in existence. We do not have the content of Paul's preaching to a *new* community that he was founding. But the heart of the matter here is that Paul preached Christ crucified. In other words, he preached the *actual fact* of the hardest, most difficult, and contradictory moment of Jesus' life, his death on a cross. Indeed, Paul's preaching makes sense only if it is grounded in God's initiative in the drama of a single, human life. By one man, Paul insists in Romans, salvation has entered the world. The saving significance of Jesus' death and resurrection — soteriology — is the driving force, but the story of Jesus' human life is its anchor. Paul's preaching simply does not make sense if Jesus were not an actual human being. For the same reason, it seems natural that Paul's preaching of the exalted Christ would ultimately generate interest in the concrete person of Jesus. If salvation comes through the life of this one man, Paul's listeners would be anxious to learn more.

In addition, Paul represents only one strand of missionary preaching. The neat division between a mission to the Gentiles and an entirely separate one to the Jews was, in fact, never so clean. The target audience of missionary preaching in the synagogues of the Diaspora was from the start a mixed group: Greek-speaking Jews and "God-fearing" Gentiles drawn to the synagogues. Clearly, too, those missionaries who *did* know Jesus in the flesh, who had accompanied him during his life, would incorporate more of Jesus' teaching and the events of his life into their preaching.

Christology and, even more, the life of Jesus are topics *implicitly* addressed in the Pauline letters. Now a change takes place. These elements move *explicitly* to the fore, yet no less as a form of preaching. In other words, the story of Jesus now becomes the principal focus of attention with preaching interwoven in the narrative. The two elements — preaching and narrative — remain inseparable, but they are now joined in a different way.[14] The kerygmatic biography of Jesus is born. Portraits of Jesus now appear.

Portraits of Jesus

MARK

The turn takes place in the Gospel of Mark, written around A.D. 70. Such a significant, indeed original, development does not occur in a pure historical ether but rather is propelled by a complex series of events. James, the brother of the Lord, is killed at the hands of Herod Agrippa around A.D. 62. Peter and Paul probably die in the persecutions of Nero two years later in A.D. 64. The founding generation is fading from the scene. Doubtless, the delay of the parousia plays a role. In the book of Acts, the spirit of the risen Jesus spearheads the church's missionary effort, which now takes on a life of its own. From another side, then, a reason appears to set down a record of Jesus' life, his passion and death. The Jewish revolt (A.D. 66–70) and the destruction of the temple and the fall of Jerusalem (A.D. 70) were factors as well. While such cataclysmic events invariably harden the lines between the Jewish community and the fledgling Christian church, they also underscore the need for a permanent record of events, even as they color the record.

Cumulatively, therefore, from many points of view, what once could be reliably passed down by the memory of Jesus' followers now becomes in a more compelling way the object of a formal narrative. Yet the lines between written and oral gospel remain fluid. The Gospel of Mark, at 661 verses, is easily memorized.[15] The style of this Gospel — short, pithy sentences, scenes that cut to the chase, a relentlessly driving story line — lends itself to oral presentation. Countless observers over the centuries have noticed this quality. What Johann Gottfried

Herder (1744–1803) concluded — "His Gospel is written to be read
out aloud" — finds an echo in theater performances to this day.[16] Indeed, it seems likely that the Gospel of Mark was first read aloud,
proclaimed, during the worship of the early church. The first contrast,
then, is not between an oral and written Gospel but rather between
the proclamation of the saving event of Christ's death and resurrection
and the kerygmatic biography of Jesus that tells the story of his life,
culminating in his saving death.

Martin Kähler (1835–1912) characterized the Gospels as passion
narratives with an extended introduction.[17] Nowhere is the remark so
true as in Mark's Gospel. The last week of Jesus' life takes up fully one-
third of the story, and this makes compelling sense. If the death and
resurrection of Jesus formed the core of the earliest church's *preaching,*
this would also be the first and most natural subject of *narration.* Yet
there is nothing in the narrative of the passion that is not proclamation.
Citations from Psalms 22, 69, and 31 guide the story of the passion,
with Psalms 42/43 playing a special role in John's Gospel. Yet, writes
Raymond Brown, "the psalm parallels are to secondary details that fill
in the story (mostly to the incidents involving what other people do
to Jesus); and no psalm offers a parallel to the basic Gospel outline of
Jesus' passion."[18] This is significant. The heart of the matter — Jesus'
passion and death — is original to the tradition and without parallel.
Thus it is easy to see why it must stand at the center of Jesus' life.

Accordingly, the tendrils of this death extend back to the beginning of the ministry. Mark tightly summarizes its key moments. Jesus
teaches with authority, expels demons, heals the sick, forgives sins, and
associates with sinners. Jesus' disciples fail to fast and do what is lawful
on the Sabbath, not least of all because Jesus himself is Lord of the
Sabbath. Later, Jesus places the laws of ritual purity in an entirely new
light, if not, in effect, abolishing them. But enough is said and done
early on in this Gospel for the Pharisees to plot with the Herodians to
destroy Jesus (Mark 3:6).

However, the red thread that holds the story together is a quite explicit reflection on Jesus' identity by way of *heavenly* revelation on the
one hand, in dialogue with *earthly* questions, on the other. The Gospel of Mark opens with a scene of divine revelation to Jesus himself.
"You are my beloved Son" (Mark 1:11; cf. Ps. 2:7; Isa. 42:1). Jesus

is to be a suffering messiah. The revelation is repeated at the transfiguration, now witnessed by Peter, James, and John. Once again, Jesus is identified as God's Son, a suffering messiah. Then the revelation is expanded: "Listen to him" (Mark 9:7). The brief allusion to Deuteronomy 18:15 refers to the promise of a great prophet like Moses, now fulfilled in Jesus of Nazareth. At the transfiguration, as rejection and misunderstanding swirl around Jesus down below, the red velvet curtains are drawn back on the mountaintop to reveal his true identity to his closest followers and to the readers or listeners of the Gospel.

Earthly progress, by contrast, is slower. Jesus himself explicitly raises the question of his own identity at Caesarea Philippi. "Who do people say that I am?" he asks his followers. "Some say John the Baptizer, others Elijah, others one of the prophets," they reply. Then he asks them directly, "Who do you say that I am?" (Mark 8:27–29). Peter confesses Jesus as the Messiah, but here the answer is still a wrong one. At the trial of Jesus, both the high priest and Pilate bluntly question Jesus again about his identity, each from the point of view of his interest. The high priest asks, "Are you the Messiah, the Son of the Blessed One?" "I am," Jesus replies (Mark 14:61–62). Here he confirms his messianic identity, having sufficiently conformed it to this suffering and death. Then he adds a rejoinder that causes the high priest to rend his garments: "And you will see the Son of Man seated at the right hand of the Power, and coming with clouds of heaven" (Mark 14:62; cf. Dan. 7:14; Ps. 110:1). In the face of this earthly trial, Jesus reminds the high priest of the heavenly tribunal at which the Son of Man will preside and true justice will be meted out. Pilate asks what others have said of Jesus and indeed about the crucifying offense. "Are you the King of the Jews?" he asks Jesus (Mark 15:2).

The Gospel underscores the bleakness of Jesus' death. Jesus prays alone in the garden, evoking God as *Abba* (Mark 14:36), the only time this word appears in the Gospels, and the setting is remarkable. In the depth of his agony, Jesus calls to God as a child in distress seeks its parent. Certainly, the death of Jesus in Mark is far removed from the final, composed moments of Socrates, distant as well from the exemplary death of the Maccabean martyrs. Reminiscent of the Lord's Prayer, Jesus prays that this cup might pass from him but also that his Father's will, not his own, be done.

Jesus dies alone — all his disciples have fled — with the desperate cry of Psalm 22:1 on his lips: "My God, my God, why have you forsaken me?" (Mark 15:34). As Jesus dies, the veil of the temple is rent, and the centurion delivers the decisive word: "Truly, this man was God's Son" (Mark 15:39). These events are rejoinders to questions at Jesus' trial. But even more, here the Gospel reaches its climax. The evocation of God as *Abba,* the cry of dereliction, and the confession by the centurion at Jesus' death belong together. Jesus' *Abba* travels with him into the desolation of his own death. The cry of dereliction is resolved not in Psalm 22 but rather in the public confession by the centurion. God's revelation in Jesus has come to clearest expression in his agonized, lonely death for our salvation. As the temple veil is rent, the centurion can see this clearly. Mark places Jesus' death center stage, highlighting it from every side because its meaning is so clear to him. It is also apparent why the disciples have failed to understand. Jesus must first suffer, die, and rise again. And the disciples must suffer too. If the Gospel begins under the banner of Jesus as Son of God, the centurion's words enclose the entire story with the same confession.

According to Mark, Jesus is a suffering messiah. Above all, he is the Son of God. He is also the Son of Man, this title referring less to Jesus' identity than to his all-encompassing *destiny.* Frank Matera comments, "During his earthly ministry Jesus exercises authority to forgive sins and heal on the Sabbath. When the ministry is completed, he must suffer, die and rise so that he can return at the end of the ages to gather God's elect."[19] Certainly, if the heart of the earliest kerygma is the saving death of Jesus, the story of his life according to Mark is true to this emphasis at every point. The success of Mark's Gospel is evident in the speed with which the genre of kerygmatic biography was imitated in the close network of communities between Syria and Rome.[20] Matthew's Gospel follows ten to fifteen years later, A.D. 80–90, and Luke's Gospel arrives around the same time. John's Gospel follows roughly in the mid-90s.

MATTHEW

At 10,681 words, Matthew's Gospel is almost twice as long as Mark's.[21] The sheer infusion of so much new material irrevocably alters the shape of the Gospel genre itself. These additions occur in three places. The

Gospel begins in a different way: Jesus' genealogy is traced back to Abraham, and the story of Jesus' birth recounted. The appearances of the risen Jesus end the Gospel differently as well. In between, Jesus' actions are punctuated by a series of long speeches: the Sermon on the Mount and discourses on mission, parables, the church, and eschatology. If Mark says that Jesus teaches with authority, Matthew takes the insight to the bank, displaying in detail his teaching on a variety of topics. This new infusion also radically alters the portrait of Jesus. If Mark has given us a *charcoal sketch,* each harsh stroke carefully calibrated to highlight contrasting features of Jesus, Matthew has given us something closer to a *portrait in oil,* a much more layered, textured composition. Altogether a more majestic Jesus steps forth in the pages of Matthew's Gospel.

Hence, given the account of Jesus' genealogy and his birth, when the public ministry opens, we already know a great deal about the vaunted personage who submits himself to the rite of baptism in order to fulfill all righteousness. The words of the baptism shift accordingly: "You are my beloved Son," in Mark's Gospel directed to Jesus, becomes "This is my beloved Son." Jesus has been God's Son from birth.

The first of Jesus' discourses, the Sermon on the Mount (Matt. 4:23–7:29), is also a tone-setter. Here Jesus emerges as teacher par excellence. Jesus not only teaches that the entire Torah must be fulfilled, but also he radicalizes the law at successive points. In doing so, he places his own personal authority on the same level as the written Torah. The law of Moses is thereby deepened and sharpened at every point. Likewise, ordinary practices of piety — almsgiving, prayer, fasting — are given a more radical stamp. For those who wish to please God, public fanfare and ostentation are to be avoided at all times.

Perhaps nowhere does the difference between Matthew's and Mark's portraits of Jesus become more pointed than in the great scene at Caesarea Philippi. Here Peter rightly identifies Jesus as Messiah. Jesus says to him, "Blessed are you, Simon son of Jonah! For flesh and blood has not revealed this to you, but my Father in heaven. And I tell you, you are Peter, and on this rock I will build my church, and the gates of Hades will not prevail against it" (Matt. 16:17–18). Now the true confession of Jesus takes place not at his death but during the public ministry. No less a revelation, a work of grace, Peter has recognized Jesus and rightly confessed him as the Messiah. Therefore, Caesarea Philippi becomes a church-founding turning point of the Gospel. Because Simon has recognized Jesus, he is given a new name. He becomes Peter, the rock on which the church is founded, its cornerstone set in Jesus' lifetime.

The words in Matthew 11:25–27 offer an extraordinary insight into Jesus' identity: "At the same time Jesus said, 'I thank you, Father, Lord of heaven and earth, because you have hidden these things from the wise and the intelligent and revealed them to infants; yes, Father, such was your gracious will. All things have been handed over to me by my Father; and no one knows the Son except the Father, and no one knows the Father except the Son and anyone to whom the Son chooses to reveal him." Not only does Jesus emerge more clearly as an actual teacher, but he also appears as wisdom personified. Accordingly, the portrait of Jesus in the Gospel of Matthew becomes thereby a more elevated, majestic one. The inherited likeness from Mark is adjusted. Signs of ignorance or lack of knowledge on Jesus' part are struck. Strong emotions — pity, anger, sorrow — are softened. The passage in which Jesus' family thinks that he is beside himself is deleted. The verse in which Jesus says that no one is good but God is altered. The earlier Jesus may be fine in terms of Mark's Gospel, but when the lines of a stark sketch are transferred to another medium, certain all-too-harsh features no longer fit Matthew's portrait.

This Gospel closes with Jesus the teacher on a mountain, symbolic locus of divine revelation. Jesus sends forth his disciples with this command: "Go therefore and make disciples of all nations, baptizing them in the name of the Father and of the Son and of the Holy Spirit, and teaching them to obey everything that I have commanded you. And remember, I am with you always, to the end of the age" (Matt. 28:19–20). Jesus himself remains with the church, watching over it on the missionary journey that he has initiated with these final words.

LUKE AND THE SERMONS IN THE BOOK OF ACTS

If the way a Gospel begins and ends the story of Jesus contains its signature note, the Gospel of Luke fully qualifies on both scores. Not only is Luke's infancy narrative unique in its own right, but also the

Gospel ends not simply with more elaborate accounts of the resurrection. Instead, Luke begins another, entirely different story. Implicitly
he affirms that it is insufficient to tell the story of Jesus without relating
the story of the church as well, its birth and subsequent growth. These
are the subject of the book of Acts. If we described the other portraits
of Jesus in comparative terms, we might liken Luke's to a *mural* with
Jesus at the center. While each of these books has its own integrity,
they were conceived according to a single design whose connecting
ligatures are strong and simple.

The first are geographic and historic. The central section of this
Gospel (Luke 9–18) is the story of Jesus' journey up to Jerusalem.
This is clearly a theological theme and a narrative structure that carry
Jesus from his ministry in Galilee up to Jerusalem for his passion and
death. The book of Acts picks up the story in Jerusalem and carries it
to Rome. In historical terms, the story of God's action in the Old Testament culminates in Jesus' death and resurrection, and it continues in
the spread of the church. These are chapters in a continuous narrative,
and the whole must be grasped to place the parts in right perspective.

The second theme works at a deeper level. All of this is the work of
the Holy Spirit. The Spirit of God — active in the Old Testament, then
in the life of Jesus, and finally in the spread of the early church — is
not only an organizational theme holding this long narrative together;
it also contributes theological notes that affect the entire story. There is
a profound sense of forgiveness, reconciliation, and providential guidance in Luke-Acts. These themes come to characterize the Gospel's
portrait of Jesus as well.

In this Gospel the Spirit of God rests on Jesus in a unique way.
He is conceived by the Holy Spirit, his human origin being the result
of God's action. That same Spirit descends on him in bodily form
as a dove at his baptism. Full of the Holy Spirit, Jesus launches his
public ministry at the synagogue in Nazareth. He reads from the book
of Isaiah, Isaiah 61:1, proclaiming a year of relief for the oppressed.
These words also constitute a programmatic statement about Jesus'
public ministry in Galilee, describing what is shortly to follow. The
poor have the good news preached to them. The sick are healed and
demons expelled. In effect, these words summarize Jesus' actions in
the next chapters of the Gospel as they clearly identify him at the

beginning of his ministry. Jesus is a *great prophet*. Like the prophets of old, he is filled with the Holy Spirit. Like those prophets, he knows rejection, which begins at once at his home in Nazareth. Jesus quotes fateful words: "Truly, I tell you, no prophet is accepted in the prophet's hometown" (Luke 4:24).

Equally fateful are the words of Luke 9:51: "When the days drew near for him to be taken up, he set his face to go to Jerusalem." Jesus' journey to Jerusalem is fated. He later explains to his disciples on the road to Emmaus, "Was it not necessary that the Messiah should suffer these things and then enter into his glory?" (Luke 24:26). Even more pointedly, "Yet today, tomorrow, and the next day I must be on my way, because it is impossible for a prophet to be killed outside Jerusalem. O Jerusalem, Jerusalem, the city that kills the prophets and stones those who are sent to it!" (Luke 13:33–34). As a great prophet, Jesus turns to face his "exodus" from this life with a sense of acceptance, compassion, and forgiveness, and without a hint of rancor. As Jesus predicts the fall of Jerusalem, he weeps for the city that kills its own prophets.

There is a series of memorable parables, unique to Luke — the good Samaritan, the prodigal son, the rich man and Lazarus — that reflect the tenor of this Gospel and its special portrait of Jesus.

But perhaps Luke's signature note emerges in the way he tells the story of Jesus' passion and death. Like Matthew, he eschews the harsh features of Mark's portrait — the strong emotions, the signs of weakness — the agonized, troubled Jesus, whose soul is sorrowful unto death. Such emotions are replaced by sentiments of compassion, forgiveness, and serenity. Satan has returned and entered into Judas Iscariot (Luke 22:3). Jesus knows that this hour belongs to the power of darkness (Luke 22:53). He remains serene. Just as Jesus' family has been reconciled, so too actions of Jesus' disciples at the passion are treated more kindly. Luke does not describe the flight of the Twelve at Jesus' arrest. Before he predicts Peter's threefold denial, Jesus promises to pray that Peter's faith may not falter. Indeed, he prays that Peter's faith may strengthen his brothers. Poignantly, Jesus looks across the courtyard at him after the third denial. As he has often done during his ministry, Jesus prays in the garden. But only once; only once does he find the disciples sleeping, because of their grief. Jesus' prayers are not in vain. An angel from heaven strengthens him for the ordeal that awaits him. Just as Jesus stops to heal the servant of the high priest whose ear has been severed (Luke 22:50), he later treats with compassion the thieves crucified with him. Three times Pilate proclaims Jesus' innocence, but still he must die. However, the loneliness of Jesus' death is relieved. Simon of Cyrene helps him with the cross. The daughters of Jerusalem weep. A great number of people follow him. Likewise, when Jesus dies, he is surrounded by those sympathetic to him. The rending of the temple veil and the darkness over the land now *precede* Jesus' death. From Luke's point of view, Jesus' death is no less central, and its message should be clearly delivered. Jesus dies with words of forgiveness on his lips that have characterized his life: "Father, forgive them; for they do not know what they are doing" (Luke 23:34). And then, "Father, into your hands I commend my spirit" (Luke 23:46).

The early sermons in the book of Acts deserve a word. These may come from Luke's sources and represent an actual memory of the church's earliest preaching. The stylized quality of Peter's sermons and the Christology of Acts 2–5 may support such a view. However, the striking point here is the obvious one. Here is an author, fifty years after the fact in the midst of *narrative* about Jesus and the early church, who seeks to recreate the church's earliest *kerygma*. And no matter what their origin, these early sermons seem to capture its spirit. They also seem to follow a roughly similar format and theology.

In sum, Luke's differentiated sense of history illumines his entire Christology. In this regard, two benchmark events stand out, largely determining all else. First, Jesus' status is rooted in his miraculous birth. He is literally God's Son from the beginning. Thus, while Jesus remains Israel's messiah throughout Luke-Acts, he is messiah in no ordinary sense. Similarly, if he is a prophet filled with the Holy Spirit, he is different from all other prophets. In Jesus' case, the Holy Spirit is the efficacious principle of his entire life. The second benchmark is Jesus' resurrection from the dead. Luke is keenly aware that Jesus becomes exalted Lord by virtue of the resurrection. Thus, although Jesus may be addressed as Lord on occasion in the Gospel, the title comes into its own in the book of Acts. "The term *kyrios* occurs in Acts 104 times, of which only eighteen are references to God the Father and forty-seven definitely refer to Jesus, with most of the rest referring to Jesus or to God, though it is not always clear which is meant in some of these texts."[22] The fluidity of the title "Lord" is understandable, given Jesus' enthronement in heaven and his own fluid status. Jesus shares in a real but undefined way in God's reign. Similarly, Jesus' role as savior comes into its own after the resurrection when salvation is now preached in his name. On the other hand, the title "Son," which occurs at key moments in the Gospels, all but disappears in Acts. Given the different situation of the Gospel, this is understandable. "Christ" or "Messiah" is used both in a titular and nominal sense in Luke-Acts. It remains, for example, a title for Christ in the early sermons and in discussions with Jewish audiences in the mission. Otherwise, it blends into a name, "Jesus Christ."

JOHN

The Gospel of John represents a special culminating point in the development of Christology. There are other New Testament writings in which Jesus is called God and a differentiated Christology presented. One thinks of the book of Revelation and the letter to the Hebrews. But none can match the seamless way in which Gospel and kerygma are joined in the Fourth Gospel.

This Gospel opens with a hymnic prologue, in one sense reminiscent of early hymns in Philippians 2 and Colossians 1. But those were tentative probes in poetic language into Jesus' exalted status. In John, all such tentativeness has disappeared: "In the beginning was the Word, and the Word was with God, and the Word was God" (John 1:1). The Gospel begins with Jesus as divine. It ends on the same note, with perhaps the clearest confession of Christ's divinity in the New Testament, Thomas's confession: "My Lord and my God" (John 20:28). What two generations ago was poetic probe here becomes deliberate, systematic statement, enclosing the Gospel at its beginning and end and at every point in between. In other words, the prologue establishes a clear point of view that is consistently followed throughout the Gospel. Recalling Sirach 24 and Wisdom 9, God's preexistent Word from all eternity has become flesh in Jesus of Nazareth. This Word is life and light, themes expanded in the Gospel. Still, however, his own people rejected him. The prologue closes on a programmatic note on which the Gospel opens: "From his fullness we have all received, grace upon grace. The law indeed was given through Moses; grace and truth came through Jesus Christ. No one has ever seen God. It is God the Son who is close to the Father's heart, who has made him known" (John 1:16–18).

In the first chapters of this Gospel, John the Baptist and the disciples hail Jesus as Lamb of God, Teacher, Messiah, Son of God, and King of Israel. Jesus himself says they will see "heaven opened and the angels of God ascending and descending upon the Son of Man" (John 1:51). But these traditional ways of regarding Jesus are radically transformed in light of the prologue's perspective. While true, they barely scratch the surface. They comprise, observes Raymond Brown, elementary instruction about Jesus. Indeed, where other Gospels end, the Fourth Gospel begins.[23] In one sense, John subverts the original intent of the Gospel narrative: the desire to tell the story of Jesus in the flesh. Instead, the narrative has become the vehicle of higher revelation. And that revelation centers on a single, sole subject, Jesus himself. Thus there is no need for a transfiguration scene in the Fourth Gospel. Jesus' glory is never hidden. Nor is there any need for resurrection appearances. They have become anticlimactic. Jesus' crucifixion is already his glorification. He is lifted up on the cross to return home to his Father in heaven, from whence he came.

In effect, the prologue has established the point of view of a classic Christology from above. The story of Jesus begins with his divinity. And the Word-made-flesh in his glory remains at center stage throughout the Gospel. Hence, the ministry of Jesus as well as his passion and death become the staging ground on which the preexistent Word is displayed. And in the mouth of Jesus himself are placed the most exalted christological statements. It is Jesus himself who reveals both who he is and what he is about. It is Jesus who preaches the church's kerygma about himself.

Above all, John uses the Gospel tradition of miracle stories — here called "signs" (*semeia*) — as a way to reveals various facets of the preexistent cut diamond, the Word-made-flesh. They also provide the venue for Jesus to deliver extended speeches. At Cana, as Jesus changes water into wine, the miracle reveals that the messianic days have arrived. Wine now flows in abundance. As Jesus multiplies loaves and the fishes, he is revealed as the bread of life. The bread of life signifies both his word as teaching and his actual body and blood. As he cures a man born blind, Jesus is revealed as the light of the world. As he raises Lazarus from the dead, his greatest miracle, Jesus is revealed as the resurrection and the life.

The reason why Jesus is killed is also clearly set forth. Jesus cures a paralytic on the Sabbath. Like God himself, Jesus can work on the Sabbath: "For this reason the Jews were seeking all the more to kill him, because he was not only breaking the Sabbath, but was also calling God his own Father, thereby making himself equal to God" (John 5:18). This becomes the principal reason for Jesus' death at his trial. The Jewish leaders plainly tell Pilate, "We have a law, and according to that law he ought to die because he has claimed to be the Son of God" (John 19:7). And in truth, this is the defining issue of the Gospel. Jesus *is* God's Son. He reveals the Father in every way. He does not do his own will but rather the will of the one who sent him. Father and Son are one. In effect, Father and Son in this Gospel have become synonymous with God and Jesus.

Jesus himself takes the lead in proclaiming this exalted Christology: "Very truly I tell you, before Abraham was, I AM" (John 8:58). On Jesus' lips is placed the great *Ego Eimi,* God's very name. Here the Jewish leaders misunderstand. How can Jesus, not yet fifty years old, have known Abraham? But when Jesus repeats these words later before his arrest, those who hear them step back and fall to the ground (John 18:6). The misunderstanding has disappeared.

Christology also becomes the issue on which the Christian community and the synagogue acrimoniously split apart. Christians are expelled from the synagogue, a fate that the parents of the man born blind wish to avoid. Therefore they deflect questions of the Jewish authorities to their son: "Ask him; he is of age. He will speak for himself" (John 9:21). Many years ago, the confession of Jesus as the Messiah did not separate the Christians from Jewish believers; now the confession of Jesus as God's Son does. Indeed, one might say that the separation from the synagogue and from Judaism is probably the precondition for the clear confession of Christ's divinity in this sense: such a confession moves beyond the limits of what Judaism could tolerate or endorse. It also establishes what is particular and distinguishing to the Christian church. Jesus' identity becomes the defining moment of what it means to be a "Christian."

As Lazarus is raised from the dead, Jesus is condemned to death by the Sanhedrin. Jesus knows his hour has come, the hour "for the Son of Man to be glorified" (John 12:23). If in Mark's Gospel Jesus prays that this hour might pass, here Jesus awaits it with anticipation. His crucifixion is his glorification, his great return to the Father and to his heavenly home.

John's account of Jesus' passion and death follows the logic of this Gospel. Jesus as the preexistent Word of God can hardly fear what the Jewish leaders might do to him. Indeed, Jesus presides at his own trial. The scene before Pilate becomes more elaborate. If Jesus is largely silent in the other passion accounts, here he explains in some detail the nature of his kingship. His kingdom is simply not of this world, he tells Pilate. Pilate's question to Jesus, "What is truth?" is ironic. Incarnate Truth itself stands before Pilate, but he does not recognize him. Likewise, Jesus himself decides the moment of his death. "It is finished," he says and then gives up his spirit (John 19:30). The final confession by Thomas that closes the original Gospel is not without a note of paradox, for on the lips of the doubting Thomas is placed the clearest confession of Christ's divinity.

Looking Back

If the resurrection sets the initial trajectory — *Jesus has been raised from the dead, and he now lives* — then the first answer to the question about Jesus is clear enough: he is the great judge of the last days. But, as we saw, the death of Jesus becomes the special pivot on which the development of Christology turns. In concentrating on Jesus' death, soteriology takes the lead and Christology follows. Capturing this difference, classic theology will later distinguish between the *work* of Christ from the *person* of Christ, the latter called more properly Christology.

The apostle Paul follows the first line of thought. Jesus' death is so special and efficacious because it is the death of God's beloved Son. Were it any other kind of death, it could not accomplish the salvation of the human family. Indeed, Jesus' death in this sense is a manifestation of God's love — and not just God's love, but also his intention.

Therefore, at a relatively early stage, Jesus' preexistence in some sense enters the picture.

The universal implications of Jesus' death and resurrection go hand in hand with the mission to the Gentiles. In Jesus, God has indeed sent a message *to* the Jews, but equally *through* the Jews to Gentiles as well. As the message to the Gentiles comes into its own, Christology enters a new stage. It retains the expectation that Jesus will return as the great judge, but it will also seek to speak about Jesus in fresh language that speaks directly to Gentiles. Although Jesus was called "Lord" in the earliest Aramaic-speaking community, this title comes into its own in the Gentile mission. "Jesus is Lord" becomes its banner cry. The term *Christ* will shortly blend into the tradition as Jesus' family name. Still, its titular sense will remain in the collective memory for a long time. Otherwise, the use of "Messiah" as a title in the Gospels would be inexplicable. And even as Jesus' family name, Jesus as crucified messiah will remain central to the church's preaching.

The Gospels usher in a new moment in the development of Christology. Through the Pauline letters, soteriology — the meaning of Jesus' death — takes the lead with Christology following. In the Synoptic Gospels, the life of Jesus comes into its own, accompanied by his disciples' deeper insight into Jesus' preaching and actions. A different kind of development occurs.

In light of the resurrection and the mission to the Gentiles, for example, Jesus' own deepest *intentions* will become clearer to his followers than they perhaps were in Jesus' lifetime. For although Jesus preached to the lost sheep of the house of Israel, his intention was to seek out the lost sheep of the entire human family. Israel was only the start. Likewise, Jesus' intention toward the Mosaic law and toward Jewish purity regulations will become clearer than the actual memory that Jesus left behind. If the revelation in Jesus is the goal of the law, then at the very least, Gentiles need not be circumcised in order to become Christians. The laws on ritual purity no longer apply at all. Jesus' deepest intention about such matters is revealed in the closing lines of Mark 7. Jesus means to declare all things clean because what comes out of the heart, not what goes into the mouth, is what defiles.

As we noted earlier, in light of the resurrection, all of the Gospel estimates of Jesus are elevated ones. Jesus has come back from the dead as the vindicated messenger of God's kingdom, and that is more than enough to guarantee his exalted status. But granting that, there are differences among the Synoptic Gospels. An obvious one is that Mark begins the story of Jesus and his sonship from the baptism. For Matthew and Luke, Jesus is God's Son from birth. One dare not imply that Mark's Gospel would deny such insight; rather, it is simply not Mark's concern. But having said that, the infancy narratives do make a difference and color, albeit in different ways, the story of Jesus that follows.

But the main significance of the Synoptic Gospels is the simple fact that they display in greater detail what Jesus in the flesh was all about. They relate his teaching, along with their own deeper insight into it. They tell about the way Jesus acted and what he did as a wonder worker and exorcist. The audience gets a genuine sense about Jesus in the flesh who steps forward in these Gospels. One also gets a sense of why four portraits of Jesus were finally deemed necessary to capture this extraordinary personage and the nature of God's intention of sending him into the world. In this regard, the *portraits* that the narratives convey are, in the last analysis, what counts.

I characterized the differences between the Gospels in just such terms. I compared Mark's portrait of Jesus to a *charcoal sketch* in which each hard line is necessary. The compression of this Gospel, at 661 verses, is key. In other words, a tight internal dialectic of sharp contrasts — a tension of opposites — holds the composition together. The brevity of exposition is central and is one reason why any significant departure will require a completely new picture. In this regard, it is easy enough to understand how Matthew might develop from Mark but almost impossible to construe the reverse — that is, how, beginning with Matthew, Mark's Gospel might arise. By contrast, Matthew's Gospel resembles an *oil painting*. It differs from Mark in the way a work in charcoal is different from a more layered composition. Sharp lines now give way to more textured features. A more considered portrait of a more majestic personage emerges. I compared Luke's picture to a *mural*. One can argue that Jesus' atoning death receives less emphasis from Luke, but this is not his chief concern. Luke's concern is to join together a portrait of Jesus with a sketch of the amazing growth of the Christian church from Jerusalem to Rome in the span of a single generation. John's Gospel is comparable to an *El Greco*. Most of Jesus' same features are there, but the dimensions are canted and the perspective is awry. They *seem* right, but they are not. In the same way, John's Gospel *is* different from the Synoptic Gospels. It does represent a more elevated Christology. It is the first of many *Christologies from above* in which the story of Jesus in the flesh begins with his divinity, his status as God's Son from all eternity. Here Jesus' preexistence has been more fully digested and integrated. Jesus emerges as God's Word and, in his own right, as preexistent Son from all eternity, as God himself. Now this has become a quite deliberate statement, and a standpoint, that sheds special light on Jesus' earthly life.

Part Two

The Development of Christian Doctrine: The Center

Chapter Four

HOW DOCTRINES
DEVELOP

We pause at this point in order to inquire about how doctrines develop. To answer the question, we turn once again to Jaroslav Pelikan's definition of doctrine. Christian doctrine, he observes, is what the church *believes* in its devotion, spirituality, and worship; what the church *teaches* in biblical interpretation, catechetical instruction, and theology; and what the church *confesses* in its public professions of faith and its creeds.[1]

But public professions of faith such as the creeds of the Council of Nicea or of Constantinople assume a complex mechanism of interlocking parts for their own development. These parts do not drop from the sky; rather, the conditions of doctrinal growth must themselves develop. Constituent features of the process emerge as answers to distinct, but related, questions. First, what are the sources of doctrine? What comprises the broad playing field that now must be lined for doctrinal play to begin? Second, who or what does the defining, surely an intentional and deliberate act? If creeds do not drop from the sky, who are their makers? Third, what motivates doctrinal development? If creeds are not the fruit of armchair rumination, what are the prompting circumstances that give birth to them? The answers to these questions comprise the subject of this chapter. In brief, the answer to the first is the emergence of the writings that comprise the Old and New Testaments. The answer to the second is the rise of church office and, in the middle of the second century, of apostolic

121

succession. The third factor refers to the disparate challenges of Marcion, of Gnosticism, and of Montanism. In the course of these events the first "rules of faith" appear. They stand as the beginning of more developed creeds. They also introduce a fourth factor, which acts in its own right as a *basso profundo et continuo* in doctrinal development. This is the voice of liturgy and worship, especially in the sacrament of baptism. If the church's worship was the matrix, both creative and conservative, in which Christology evolves, the role continues in the early church, providing its own insight into the growth of doctrine.

I. The Scriptures: Old and New Testaments

The writings of the Old Testament span a history of fifteen hundred years from the Bronze Age to the Roman period. Definitively edited in the middle of the sixth century B.C., the Pentateuch and the historical books down to 2 Kings (early prophets) sketch the broad meaning of Israel's faith in *one* God. Here Yahweh looms as a God set above the rise and fall of nations. As creator, he is the Lord of the universe. As God of Israel, he remains Lord of the Jewish community after the exile. Ezra brought back the "Book of the Torah of Moses" (Neh. 8:1) from the community in Babylon. In a moving ceremony at the square before the Water Gate in Jerusalem, he read the Torah to the assembled community, marking a decisive moment in its own rebirth. The Pentateuch establishes the interpretative cornerstone of Israel's sacred writings.

The writings of the prophets as a distinct literary entity emerge in the third century B.C., if not earlier. They stand as commentary on and interpretation of the Pentateuch. The final, disparate grouping which comprise the Old Testament — the Writings — remains open into the Christian era. For Christians, the Scriptures are, above all, the Greek translation of these sacred writings, called the Septuagint. This becomes for them the Old Testament. But the terms "Old" and "New" for the testaments in the first instance refer not to an authoritative list of books but rather to the two covenants: God's covenant with Israel, and now his new covenant in Jesus Christ with the Christian community (Greek, *diatheke;* Latin, *testamentum*).

The writings that comprise the New Testament begin with Jesus. Jesus assumes the authority of Israel's Scriptures and acts as their authoritative interpreter. In response to the question about which law is preeminent, Jesus quotes the Shema, Deuteronomy 6:4–5, combining it with Leviticus 19:18 (Matt. 22:34–40; Mark 12:28–31; Luke 10:25–28). Love of God and love of neighbor comprise the law's center. Matthew strengthens the point. For him, Jesus came not to abolish the law but rather to fulfill it down to the smallest detail. The antitheses of the Sermon on the Mount belong in the same context. Likewise, the apostle Paul is an interpreter of the Scriptures, framing his argument in its characteristic idiom.

Jesus' own words as teacher are soon taken as authoritative (1 Cor. 10:14; 1 Tim. 5:18); likewise, the writings of Paul are counted on the same footing as "Scripture" (2 Pet. 3:16). Doubtless, the chief factor spurring the development of authoritative Christian writings is the importance of preserving the memory of God's revelation in Jesus of Nazareth. Jesus' words and deeds capped by the story of his death and resurrection comprise the heart of the message. And while it may suffice at first to pass down the nascent gospel orally, the desire to establish a written record follows naturally with the passage of time.

Yet the journey from natural desire to the first significant listing of the actual twenty-seven books of the New Testament is a long one. The thirty-ninth festal letter of Athanasius (ca. 293–373) at Easter of 367 is usually reckoned the first important witness to just these books, although it was far from normative for all churches.[2] In many ways, the twenty-seven books of the New Testament comprise a "collection of collections," in Harry Gamble's phrase.[3] It is a collection of Gospels, a collection of letters with a single apocalypse, the book of Revelation, and a single story of the exploits of Jesus' followers, the book of Acts. Yet if the actual edifice of the twenty-seven books of the New Testament was long in construction, its anchoring pillars were set down in the second century. The letters of Paul represent one pillar. Ten letters of Paul, albeit in truncated form, appear in Marcion's canon (ca. 140). Later, 1–2 Timothy and Titus (the Pastoral Epistles), are attributed to Paul, and much later, the letter to the Hebrews. (Doubts about its Pauline authorship are registered in antiquity.) All together, these fourteen letters attributed to Paul comprise slightly more than half the New Testament.

The more daunting task is the establishment of the four Gospels as we know them. The point of controversy and the counterpositions are clear enough. In one sense, there is only *one* gospel, the good news about Jesus Christ. This is the way Mark's Gospel begins. This may explain and surely forms part of the background for attempts to write a *single Gospel,* harmonizing the various accounts of the life of Jesus. The most famous of these harmonies, the *Diatesseron* of Tatian (170), was long used in the Syrian church. Marcion (110–160) formulates a more radical version of the single Gospel: Luke's Gospel, shorn of the infancy narratives. But the far greater danger lies in the very popularity of the Gospel form itself. Gospels of every kind proliferate in the second century: the *Gospel of Thomas* and the *Gospel of Peter,* the *Gospel of Truth,* the *Protevangelium of James* and the *Infancy Story of Thomas,* the *Gospel of Mary,* the *Gospel of Judas,* and the *Gospel of Philip,* to name but a few. Some of these — the infancy Gospels, for example — reflect the ruminations of pious imagination, seeking to explore the childhood of Jesus and of Mary. Others — the *Gospel of Peter* — relate Jesus' actual departure from the tomb, as tall as a redwood tree. Still others represent radical variants of the gospel message. The *Gospel of Thomas* and the *Gospel of Truth* comprise sayings of Jesus without a mention of his death and resurrection, Gnostic adaptations of the Christian message. Likewise, there is a lush proliferation of written accounts of Jesus' first disciples: not simply of Peter and Paul, but also of John, Paul and Thecla, Thomas, and others. There are also numerous apocalypses. The *Apocalypse of Peter* and the *Shepherd of Hermas* enjoy near canonical status. No simple description suffices to capture the broad gamut of early Christian writings, and this, of course, is the problem.

In this regard, the arguments of Irenaeus (d. ca. 202) for just the four Gospels — Matthew, Mark, Luke, John — are significant. Not content to extol the Gospels as reliable accounts of Jesus' life, death, and resurrection, he anchors them in the numerology of "four": the four winds, the four points of the compass, the four pillars of the world, the four living figures of Revelation 4:7, the four covenants with humankind. In short, the four Gospels are carved into God's plan from all eternity.[4] Hence these four, but no more. The weight that Irenaeus seeks to give his argument remains itself a compelling witness to the force of the vast proliferation of stories and accounts about Jesus.[5] Especially dangerous for Irenaeus is their selective use by Gnostic Christians, shading the teaching of Jesus in esoteric ways. Still, it remains a remarkable fact that the church retained these four quite different renditions of the life of Jesus, rejecting the easier alternative of a pallid harmonization.

Significantly, the Gospels attained their standing as a group, not individually. In other words, they do contain in manageable form a cross-section of the original unity and diversity in their portraits of Jesus' life, death, and resurrection. There is *one* Gospel, yet told *according* to four, sometimes quite different, accounts.[6] They also collectively block Gnostic adaptations — the practical side of Irenaeus's arguments. At roughly the same time, Irenaeus and Tertullian (ca. 155–230) in the West and Clement of Alexandria (d. ca. 215) in the East witness to the emergence of the core New Testament canon ca. 200. The sources of doctrine are beginning to coalesce.

Still, it is significant that the canon of the New Testament has to follow its own meandering process of filtration. True, Athanasius's Easter letter of 367 represented a significant milestone, but the canon of Scriptures was not a topic addressed by the great ecumenical councils of antiquity. It first appears on the agenda of the Council of Laodicea (363) and the regional North African Councils of Hippo (393) and Carthage (397.)[7] The truth is that those writings that sustain and guide the church in its worship, teaching, and preaching come to be regarded as authoritative and then are formally recognized as such.

The interpretation of the Scriptures is also significant. The Old and New Testaments are regarded as multilayered sacred writings. The Scriptures as a whole are seen as inspired, as well as every detail they contain. We have already seen an instance of the latter in Paul's exegesis in Galatians 3:16, which hinges on the use of "seed" in the singular as a reference to Christ. We will see it again in the Arian controversy in the interpretation of Proverbs 8:22, which is taken as a precise indicator of the Son's status as a creature.[8]

II. The Bishop's Office

The rise of church leadership is decisive in its own right in the development of Christian doctrine. The course of its growth is no less surprising. The starting point is Paul's description of church leaders in 1 Corinthians 12:28: "And God has appointed in the church first apostles, second prophets, third teachers, then deeds of power, then gifts of healing, forms of assistance, forms of leadership, various kinds of tongues." Charismatic leaders guide the Corinthian church. Jesus' return is nigh. The spirit directly guides the community through the gifts and charisms of its members.

But by the time of the Pastoral Epistles (1–2 Timothy and Titus) and the book of Acts, the situation has changed dramatically. The missionary thrust has been successful. Now the challenge is to consolidate its gains. Here one catches a glimpse of a community in transition — the church of the 80s — which calls for new kinds of leaders. Accordingly, the tasks of charismatic missionaries gives way to those of community-builders, to the duties of pastors. There is little distinction between "overseers" (*episkopoi*) of the Pastoral Epistles and "elders" (*presbyteroi*) mentioned in the book of Acts. Deacons round out the roster of early ministers. In all cases, the rationale for these ministries is *functional*. The church may have been founded on apostles and prophets, but now it needs other kinds of leaders. It needs people who are sober, reliable, and dependable who can be faithful stewards of the deposit of faith. The model is the father of a stable family. The flavor of the new breed is captured in 1 Timothy 3:2–5: "Now a bishop must be above reproach, married only once, temperate, sensible, respectable, hospitable, an apt teacher, not a drunkard, not violent but gentle, not quarrelsome, and not a lover of money. He must manage his own household well, keeping his children submissive and respectful in every way — for if someone does not know now to manage his own household, how can he take care of God's church?" In modern terms, the leader of a community in Ephesus or Crete in the 80s seems more like the president of the local Rotary than the spirited pastor of a Pentecostal church!

Yet twenty years later, the signs of the time have changed again. The early second-century bishop Ignatius of Antioch (ca. 50–117) represents a bishop who steps decisively to the fore in the guidance of his local church. In this regard, he certainly is not typical of all churches — not, for example, of the leadership of the church of Rome. But he represents a template for the future that other churches will shortly follow. First, in Antioch under Ignatius's leadership, the *three-tiered order* of church ministers — bishop, priest, deacon — emerges clearly. Ignatius is a single bishop, presiding over the local church, surrounded by a group of presbyters who, in turn, are assisted by a cadre of deacons.[9] Second, and even more striking, is the rationale that Ignatius gives for the office of bishop. It is not functional at all. Instead, he says, there can be no legitimate baptism or Eucharist without the bishop.[10]

Does Ignatius of Antioch represent a significant step toward a hierarchical church and a "routinization" of the spirit? Or does Ignatius perhaps represent a recovery at another level of the charismatic element of the early Pauline churches? Ignatius is a *martyr.* Is there more eloquent testimony to charismatic sanctity? Yves Congar warns against dichotomizing charismatic and hierarchical ministries in the early church: "Ignatius of Antioch, for example, claimed that he called out his essential message under the action of the Spirit, Polycarp of Smyrna was called a 'teacher who was both an apostle and a prophet' and Melito of Sardis was said to 'live entirely in the Holy Spirit.'"[11] If Ignatius of Antioch represents the template of the future as a bishop, he is also a martyr who resisted all attempts to dissuade him from his bloody fate. Indeed, it is probably in some measure through such personal witness that the office of bishop itself is established. Congar notes that the first bishops of the church were often martyrs; the second group was the great monastic bishops of late antiquity.[12] In both cases, personal charism contributed to the consolidation of ecclesiastical office. If there is another close link between the church of the Pastoral Epistles and that of Ignatius of Antioch, it is the duty to defend the faith and combat false teaching. This becomes a characteristic task of church leadership.

Apostolic Succession

The notion of apostolic succession fits hand in glove with the emerging office of bishop. It appears in the first letter from Clement of Rome to the church of Corinth. Here, church leaders in Rome rebuke those in Corinth for deposing their legitimate local leaders who had been appointed as successors of the apostles.[13] The notion here is not yet focused on the office of bishop, nor is it fully formalized. But surely it was a custom that pastors trace their lineage back to earliest times. Irenaeus recalls that the aged bishop Polycarp of Smyrna (ca. 69–155) was taught by the apostles, mentioning John "the Lord's disciple" by name.[14] Now particular circumstances crystallize this custom in more formal terms. This development seeks to counter the claims of Gnostic Christians who appeal to a *secret* tradition for their interpretation of the gospel. By contrast, bishops appeal to a *public* tradition, available in every church. Each bishop received his teaching from his predecessor, tracing their lineage back to Jesus and the first apostles. And this public succession can better anchor a claim to authority. In this regard, Gnostics have set the rules of the game. They appeal to personal experience in light of a secret tradition. Such a claim cannot be answered by a reasoned argument, for it does not rest on one in the first place. It is not an argued position. It can only be countered by a more credible claim to authority, in this case, the public authority of a known succession of bishops who trace their teaching back to Jesus and the apostles. And these are not church functionaries. Bishops are often "witnesses" themselves, like the aged Polycarp, whose personal testimony strengthens not just his office but also the claim that bishops are the true successors of the apostles.

Hence, Irenaeus's classic refutation of Gnostic teaching rests on a double basis. It rests on the authority of a public tradition, the succession of bishops in the principal cities of the empire, to which the community can testify firsthand. Irenaeus cites the church of Rome, with its double apostolic foundation of Peter and Paul, as a prime example.[15] As this argument from authority slips into place, Irenaeus launches his theological refutation of Gnostic teaching. He reformulates the teaching of John and Paul in light of Gnostic attacks on the doctrine of creation. Creation, Irenaeus argues, is the work of the one God, the only God, not of a lesser deity. Thus creation cannot constitute the fall. True, the world enters a dark valley through Adam's sin. But in Christ, the new Adam, creation is given a second chance and a new start, literally recapitulated, "headed up" anew in the person of Jesus Christ.[16]

The Starting Point

We now return to our starting point, the experience of the resurrection. The proclamation that God has revealed himself in a unique way in the fate of Jesus of Nazareth may be fairly compared to a stone hurled into a pool of still water. The effects of this proclamation spread in ever-widening circles; first, there are the reactions of Jesus' disciples, deep, diffuse, and powerful. Here Walter Bauer (1877–1960) surely was right. No unitary message came forth from the mouth of Jesus to his followers. Rather, powerful surges of dense experience — first of the risen Jesus, then of the Spirit alive in the church's worship — are the bearers of the proclamation. These experiences contain in compressed form a series of questions that only slowly separate themselves from one another.

If we were to try to convey a sense of this condensed mass, we might think of the following questions without punctuation or separation, a single question whose parts overlap and interrelate at every point: *Was Jesus a human being like ourselves? Or was he a heavenly personage who briefly descended to earth? And what of the divine realm itself? Is there one God, as Judaism claims, or many gods? Are there levels of divinity, tiers of gods? Was the Logos in Jesus created, as Yahweh created the rest of the world? Or was he begotten as the ancient pagan gods created their progeny? And then what kind of God does Jesus reveal? Why has he come into this world? Does salvation in Christ touch the whole world or just the soul? Is this world in its material aspect beyond redemption? If the world was created, was it the work of a lesser God? Was perhaps creation itself, so riddled with flaws, the original mistake? Does salvation consist in our escape from it or is the world's salvation included in our own?*

If the Christian message possesses an *internal gyroscope,* the foregoing questions represent the choppy waters that it must now navigate in order to find its own sense of direction in an extended voyage of self-discovery.

Looking backward toward Judaism as the point of departure, we see that the lines of continuity and discontinuity are both profound. The Christian church carries with it a belief in *one* God, who has definitively revealed himself in Jesus' death and resurrection. It absorbs from Judaism a substantial ethical dimension as well. The first tablet of the

Decalogue leads to the second, which regulates the life of Yahweh's followers. The Christian message continues, indeed radicalizes, these ethical demands in the antitheses of the Sermon on the Mount. Jesus' imminent return as judge of the end time adds an additional note of urgency to all ethical obligations.

Jewish beliefs about Yahweh as creator also shape Christian attitudes. If the world is God's creation, then it must be good, for it comes forth from Yahweh's hands. Therefore, salvation must encompass this world as well. The apocalyptic vision of God's final intervention means nothing less than a new heaven and a new earth, including the resurrection of the body. God has raised Jesus bodily from the dead, the first of many brothers and sisters shortly to follow him into the kingdom.

Other factors play a role as well. While the Old Testament describes Yahweh in human terms with all the qualities of a unique personality, it sees his role in creation in a different light. By contrast, the gods of ancient Greece procreate in quite human terms, producing creatures quite like themselves. This is one of the reasons they seem like human projections.[17] Yahweh, on the other hand, creates in the manner of an artisan. This is how Wisdom is described in Proverbs 8:30, as Yahweh's "master workman." The difference here is considerable. If God procreates in human terms, then he will produce a world like himself, but if he creates as a skilled artisan, then he can create a world quite unlike himself, and indeed the latter is how the Old Testament envisions creation. Therefore, the genius of the Hebrew Scriptures is to describe God in quite human terms yet nevertheless to see him as author of a world very different world from himself. Yahweh remains unlike "anything that is in heaven above, or that is in the earth beneath, or that is in the water under the earth" (Exod. 20:4; cf. Deut. 4:39; 5:8).[18]

But the lines of discontinuity are equally profound. If Christ's coming fulfills the law and the promise of salvation is now opened to Jews and Gentiles alike, then the church replaces Israel as the vehicle of salvation. In effect, the church becomes the new people of God, the new Israel. But the disagreement goes still deeper. In Christian terms, the revelation of God in Jesus Christ is so ultimate that Jesus himself is confessed as divine. First in the Pauline and deutero-Pauline letters and then in the Gospel of John, Jesus' divinity is expressed in ever more explicit terms. From a Christian point of view, this confession never contradicts or compromises Israel's faith in *one* God. But from a Jewish point of view, such a claim is not simply contradictory but rather is blasphemous and offensive.

Looking forward to the Greco-Roman world that the gospel now enters, we see that the contrasts are different. Christianity and Judaism relate as blood relatives within the same family. While the lines of continuity are strong, in the same measure, the parting is often bitter and acrimonious. In regard to the religions of the empire, there is almost a *species gap* between them and the nascent Christian gospel. These religions are largely matters of practice, the *cultus* (= "care") of the gods. Such *cultus* consists of prayers and sacrifice. The gods make no internal claims, certainly no demand for faith, and generally they require nothing by way of conduct. The cult of the gods of Rome, largely an amalgam of Greek and Roman deities, is a matter of public conduct, a civic duty performed to ensure the welfare of the state.

Traditional religions are also polytheistic — a world of many gods — whose cults are compatible and inclusive of one another. Indeed, each city or region has its own god, intimately linked to its history.[19] By contrast, Christianity from the start includes as essential something foreign to those religions: *faith*. Like Judaism, it is an exclusive religion. Faith in Jesus Christ forbids the worship or cult of other gods. Indeed, the Christian God demands an absolute allegiance without compromise. In sum, Christianity from the start makes deep personal claims about faith and about personal conduct. As the element of sacrifice is so essential to other religions, for Christians Jesus' death is the sacrifice par excellence. What is required of his followers is faith in its efficacy.

But perhaps most strikingly, the religions of antiquity in their origins are precursors to the birth of philosophy.[20] In effect, the turn toward reason effectively banishes the gods to the neighboring realm of mythology as a way of explaining the world. The worship of the gods continues, but on a separate track. In Christianity, this pattern is reversed. Because it centers so much on a single historical event — the life, death, and resurrection of Jesus of Nazareth — the banishment of Christian faith to the realm of mythology would effectively sever its historical link and destroy its claim to uniqueness at its most critical point. On the contrary, the specific and exclusive demands of Christian faith require that its own central object be continuously fine-tuned.

Who is Jesus? What did he teach? Was he really a human being? For many reasons, the followers of Jesus reverse a long-standing relationship between philosophy and religion, because the claims of Christian faith require extensive explanation almost from the start.

Hence, Christianity will use the tools of reason to define its exclusive and universal claims; it will use them also to guard and explain its special historical origins. Thus the relation between faith and reason, envisioned in different ways, will be central from the start. Indeed, the tools of both are required to illumine the audacious Christian claim that God's Word had come to unique expression in Jesus of Nazareth. Given this unique combination of circumstances, it is not difficult to grasp why the early Christians were called "atheists." In effect, Christianity also breaks the mold in the ancient world on what religions are about, its universal and exclusive claim setting new canons here as well. This may also explain its appeal to a world grown weary of its familiar forms of religion.[21]

The foregoing factors also explain the nature of the challenge that the church faces in the second century. The Greco-Roman world will require, above all, apologetics, explanation about the nature of this new religion. The clash with Judaism, while still on the horizon, is fading into the past. Thus these first challenges are *internal* to the Christian message itself: variant interpretations of the gospel. They therefore bear characteristic family features. They often involve quarrels about Christian writings. Which writings are authoritative and which are not? They also involve claims to authority. In the last analysis, whose voice in disputed questions will cast the final vote?

These internal disputes also serve to introduce the gospel to the surrounding world, external to its message. In this sense, they are adventitious, historical events that mark the beginning of an extended voyage of discovery in new territory. They also bring together the formal conditions of doctrinal development that we have thus far examined separately. These elements now enter into dynamic interaction with one another as they seek to explain and defend the Christian message. In effect, the *conditions* of doctrinal development evolve along with the *doctrines* that they seek to articulate. Thus far we have set the stage. Now the action of the play begins. Three challenges stand out

in this first leg of the journey: the claims of Marcion and his followers, the Gnostic interpretations of Jesus, and the special burst of the
prophetic spirit called Montanism.

III. Marcion, Gnosticism, and Montanism

In the mid-second century, Marcion offers the first canon of the New
Testament: a truncated version of Luke's Gospel, plus ten Pauline letters.[22] However, Marcion's canon is only one part of a much larger
scenario. He also proposes a method of interpretation. In his view, the
Scriptures should be interpreted literally. But such an approach takes
the *contrasting* elements of the Christian message and makes them into
outright *contradictions,* either-or choices. In this regard, the Pauline
contrast between law and gospel does not go far enough. In stark and
literal terms, the Old Testament is rejected because it fundamentally reveals a different God. The wrathful deity of the old covenant is totally
different from the God of love, whom Jesus proclaims. This same God
of the Old Testament is also the creator of our flawed universe. This
means, in turn, that Jesus could not have actually taken on human flesh,
contaminating himself by entering a fallen world. He only appears to
do so. Likewise, salvation must mean escape from and abandonment
of this world.

Marcion's enduring contribution is to pose so many questions so
sharply without compromise. In effect, he is a classic *divider.* He seeks
to divide Paul from the other apostles, Luke from the other Gospels,
the literal sense of Scripture from the figurative, creation from redemption, and finally to *divide* the God of the Old Testament from the God
of the New Testament. In every case, the tradition decides against
Marcion; yet it is forced to present more compelling answers under
the prodding of his single-minded questions. The leading ones surely
are these: Is the God of Israel the one whom Jesus Christ comes to
reveal? Does Jesus fully take on human flesh to save this fallen world
and not to abandon it? Marcion came to Rome from Asia Minor about
139. After his views were rejected by the church of Rome around
144, he returned home, where his message met with greater success.
Marcionite churches sprang up in Asia Minor.

If the challenge of Marcion is pointed and specific, by contrast, the challenge of Gnosticism is connected to its diffuse character.[23] Gnosticism represents less a series of differing theoretical positions about God and the universe than a gaseous effluvium given off by a broad-based, second-century *cultural climate*. What W. H. C. Frend writes of Alexandria is, then, more generally characteristic: "The Gnostics caught the tide of religious feeling."[24] Conceivably, it may have sprung from Christianity itself. Gnosticism's typical feature is an almost endless capacity to morph into different versions of essentially the same doctrine, better, *the same series of questions*. The word *gnosis* means "knowledge"; this is the common denominator. Gnostic systems usually involve elaborate theories about the cosmos, the realm of the gods, and how our fallen world is the creation of a lesser deity. But beneath these cosmological dramas pulse simple human questions. This is its strength. To those who feel alienated and estranged in this world, they offer compelling answers to ordinary human dilemmas. Where do I truly belong? How did I find myself in a world that seems so foreign to me? What is my destiny and what may I hope for? In effect, *gnosis* represents knowledge, *answers,* to such questions.

Although the words may differ, the music remains largely the same in these answers. A typical melody line goes something like this: The highest and best parts of the human spirit do *not* belong in this world. Thus the feeling of alienation is fully justified. The soul or spirit — shards of divinity — are doubly trapped here below, first in human flesh, then in a fallen world. They yearn for release. This becomes the message of Jesus. He does not save us by his death and resurrection. He comes instead to bring us Christian *gnosis,* knowledge, of our true origin. And he comes to lead us out of this world to a higher and better one in which the best part of the human spirit can finally feel at home. In this sense, the incarnation is only apparent. The Word does not take flesh. The Word only grazes this surface of the world to gather the shards of divinity, human souls of the better kind, and return them to that higher world from which they came and in which they truly belong.

What characterizes Gnosticism in its many forms is the ease with which elaborate cosmological dramas sit astride basic human dilemmas. Gnostic Christians also claim their own authoritative writings, among the most famous, the *Gospel of Thomas* and the *Gospel of Truth*. They thereby also raise the question of the canon. They could also appeal selectively to one of the four Gospels. Irenaeus's argument in favor of the four Gospels is that they collectively block and cancel Gnostic selectivity. Gnostics also claim a secret tradition in which this esoteric information is passed down to chosen, elite Christians. What constitutes the potency of the Gnostic challenge is its unerring capacity to find and then speak so directly to such deeply felt, widespread feelings of alienation. In doing so, it presents an exact mirror reflection of the Christian message. All the pieces are there. But the perspective is reversed, thereby producing a distorted reflection of the Gospel. Jesus only appears to take flesh. In reality, he is on a rescue mission. He brings us knowledge of our heavenly home to aid in our escape. John's Gospel lends itself in a special way to such renditions.

The third challenge is posed by the early Christian preacher Montanus (mid-second century).[25] He probably was a convert to Christianity from the cult of Cybele, the mother-goddess of fertility. He appears in Phyrgia in the west of the Anatolian plateau (in modern Turkey) about 170 (the date uncertain), accompanied by two prophets, Maximilla and Prisca (or Priscilla). Above all, Montanus claims to be a special apparition of the Paraclete. Such a propitious messenger would only come to announce equally momentous news about a great and final outpouring of the Holy Spirit and Jesus' imminent return as the Son of Man, the judge of the end time. Montanus also makes connections. He links the flagging prophetic voice in the church to its growing worldliness, evident in its lax moral preaching. The church offers the forgiveness of sins too freely and easily to Christians who fall after baptism. It allows widows and widowers to remarry. It relaxes the discipline of fasting. No wonder the prophetic voice has waned! With the full authority of a prophet, Montanus preaches against all such tendencies. Instead, he issues a stern call to reform, a return to strict moral and ascetic discipline in expectation of Jesus' return. The message of Montanus spread westward from Asia Minor, making its most notable convert in a great theologian of the African church, Tertullian. In one sense, Montanism represents a stubbornly recurring version of the gospel: a radical, prophetic call for moral reform in the face of the worldliness of the church, linked to the expectation of the second coming of Christ.

In another sense, its appearance in the late second century is notable and unique in its own right. Jaroslav Pelikan reckons it as a turning point, the close of one era and the opening of another. And the pivotal question on which the era turns is one of authority. Whose voice rings with final authority in the church? Is it the voice of the prophet in the assembly? Is it the voice of Christ, judge of the end time, whose imminent return is expected? Or is it the voice of Jesus whose memory is preserved in the church, the Jesus of Christian origins? In the clash with Montanus, this latter voice now rings with final authority above all other contenders.[26] And although the question will reappear, the answer given here is decisive for the future. Henceforth, the authoritative voice in deciding the meaning of the Christian faith belongs to the church's apostolic origins. Here the memory of Jesus has been faithfully preserved and transmitted in oral and then written form, the latter comprising a "New Testament." A way of interpreting those writings also emerges in which literal, allegorical, and moral voices are distinguished and then blended. The public tradition about *what* is handed down is also marked by a clear sense of *who* the guardians of the tradition are. These are the bishops, successors of the apostles. Their task is to guard and interpret the deposit of faith.

Now expressions such as "the rule of faith" and "the canon of truth" appear in the writings of Irenaeus, Tertullian, Clement of Alexandria, Origen (185–254), and others.[27] They refer to the objective content of the Christian faith in condensed form, the source of the church's unity and a bulwark against heretical views. Although the wording of these "rules of faith" may vary, even within the same author, the content is firmly fixed around two points: faith in God as Father, Son, and Holy Spirit, and faith in Jesus Christ, his life, death, and resurrection. Such "rules of faith" provide a key to interpret the Scriptures. The Scriptures, in turn, illumine the "rule of faith." In all cases, they provide a compelling witness to the apostolic tradition, on which the church is founded. If the "rule of faith" provides the *content* of the message, apostolic succession provides the *means* of assuring that it has been faithfully transmitted from the first generation of Jesus' followers to later believers. Such "rules of faith" represent a significant milestone on the way to more fixed declaratory creeds.[28]

IV. The Role of Liturgy and Worship

These topics — the "rule of faith" and creeds — also introduce the role of liturgy and worship in the development of Christian doctrine. I described this voice as a *basso profundo et continuo* in the evolution of Christian belief. In one sense, this only continues the role of the church's liturgy that we have observed in the development of Christology. Christ was first venerated in the church's prayer and devotional life before his divinity was confessed in more explicit and formal terms.

That role, no less important, now takes another form, above all, in the sacrament of baptism. While in the book of Acts and other New Testament writings baptism is described as performed in the name of Jesus, the great missionary command of Matthew 28:19 soon sets the standard: "Go therefore and make disciples of all nations, baptizing them in the name of the Father and of the Son and of the Holy Spirit and teaching them to obey everything that I have commanded you."[29] From the start, a confession of faith is required as baptism is administered. This now takes the form of a question-and-answer exchange around the confession of faith in God as Father, Son, and Holy Spirit, becoming a central feature of the ceremony of baptism: a threefold question, a threefold confession of faith, and a threefold immersion in the waters of baptism.

In turn, this threefold confession of faith will require further elaboration. What does it mean to confess God as Father, Son, and Holy Spirit? The individual articles are now explained in greater detail. Naturally enough, the second article, belief in the Son, will require extended elaboration from the start: Christ is born of the Virgin Mary, suffered, died, and rose on the third day. Belief in the Holy Spirit is soon coupled with the topic church and the resurrection of the flesh. From these *interrogatory* confessions of faith, more elaborate *declaratory* creeds evolve as their natural complement. These longer confessions of faith will play an important role in the *preparation* of candidates for baptism. Indeed, they become a mainstay of the catechumenate. These features are evident in the creed of Hippolytus of Rome, around 215.[30]

The role of liturgy in the context of doctrinal development is important for several reasons. Certainly, a motivating factor in the development of creeds is the refutation of heresy. Heretical views must be effectively countered. Such emphases appear in different ways in Tertullian and Irenaeus.[31] In addition, some traditional articles of faith have a natural polemical thrust. Belief in one God, creator of heaven and earth, rebuts the claims of those who see this world as a fallen one. Yet, one way or another, while the refutation of heresy is a factor, it is not the primary one.

The primary motivating factor in the development of creeds is quite simply the importance of explaining the faith to those who wish to be baptized. If the liturgy represents a lead agent in the development of doctrine, that role belongs in a special way to the preparation of candidates for baptism and its threefold confession of faith in God as Father, Son, and Holy Spirit. In other words, the transmission of the faith in its integrity to new members provides the natural and positive context in which doctrines expand and develop so that catechumens may fully understand the faith that they confess in receiving baptism. This factor also adds balance and perspective to our own discussion. If the Christian faith contains an *internal gyroscope* in its own development, it is probably best located in this context.

Chapter Five

THE TRINITY

In turning now to the doctrine of the Trinity, our previous discussion of development continues. Certainly, the doctrine of the Trinity, a classic example of doctrinal development, sheds considerable light on the process by which doctrines evolve. But the principal focus of the chapter is the Trinity itself. We will seek to trace the development of this doctrine through four stages toward its emergence at the Councils of Nicea (325) and Constantinople (381).

Experience. We begin with the experience of the Trinity. Here we seek to answer the question about the origins of the doctrine. How does the Trinity begin in human experience, and what does it mean in simplest terms?

The Scriptures. We then turn to the scriptural witness to belief in a Triune God. We examine the scriptural source for our understanding of God as Father, Son, and Holy Spirit as well as the first beginning of a threefold confession of faith. Our subject here in classical theological terms is the *economic Trinity,* the Triune God in human experience and in the history of salvation.

Theology. We examine the development of the Trinity in the first four centuries of the church's life down to 381. Here the experience of the Trinity seeks to express itself in a series of theological visions. It thereby enters the domain of apologetics, rational thought, and artistic expression. This initial transition seems clear enough. The experience of the Trinity in human experience and in the Scriptures generates a series of questions of its own. The persons of the Trinity, singly and together, are described in different ways in the biblical text. Not all such descriptions are consistent or compatible. The need for greater clarity of thought follows. Unacceptable interpretations of the Trinity are also identified. Thus a movement toward a more consistent, explanatory framework follows, once again, naturally enough. Such a framework must eliminate possible inconsistencies and contradictions as it seeks to explain the faith of the church. Above all, the experience of the Trinity gives birth to a series of visions of the Trinity in piety and thought. The foregoing suffices to explain the various *theologies* of the Trinity that emerge in the first three centuries of the church's life.

Doctrine. But these factors do not suffice to explain the emergence of trinitarian *doctrine.* In 275, the Christian community tolerates a wide spectrum of opinions about the Triune God. By bold strokes in 325 and 381, decisions are made about which of those theologies are acceptable and which are not. Doctrine is the fruit of those decisions, and the spectrum is considerably narrowed. What prompts such decisions?

Here we turn to factors beyond theology, concerning the fortunes of the Christian community. As a small community in the first century, the church poses no significant public threat to the order of the empire and is not the object of official persecution. The advice of the emperor Trajan (98–117) to Pliny (63–ca. 113), provincial governor of Bithynia in Asia Minor, reflects as much: tolerate, with some prejudice, members of this sect.[1] However, the situation changes dramatically by the late third century. The most serious persecution of Christians takes place under the emperor Diocletian (284–305) because the Christian community is now a force to be reckoned with and, in his view, a possible threat to the welfare of the empire. Then the emperor Constantine converts to Christianity in 312.[2] This means that in the course of a single generation, the Christian community experiences an almost unimaginable reversal of fortune: from persecuted sect, to the religion of the emperor, then, with time, of the empire itself. Suddenly theological differences matter in a new way. Yet it would be wrong to underestimate the tensions already *within* these competing theological visions about the Trinity prior to 312. A combination of internal and external factors form the cauldron in which *theology* about the Trinity is forged into *doctrine,* decisions about what is acceptable and what is not in the Christian understanding of God.

As a result of those decisions, the Logos is identified as divine and then the Holy Spirit too. Our main subject thereby shifts. Here we approach what classical theology calls the *immanent Trinity*, the Triune Godhead in and of itself. While our knowledge of the Trinity obviously begins in human experience, the other end of such experience offers a rare insight into the very nature of the Godhead. In other words, the Trinity abuts human history on one end. Otherwise, how would we know about it in the first place? The other end touches the nature of God. In other words, we can use this experience as a lens in order to look into God's very nature. But in doing so our powers of sight are strained to the limit. All Christian thinkers acknowledge the inadequacy of human language to capture a true insight into the heart of God. And in truth, the immanent Trinity represents a deep but dim insight. By faith, we confess it as a true one, not simply a creature of human thought. At this limit of human thought, in negative (*apophatic*) theology, the human spirit seeks to reach beyond itself. In doing so, it does not seek to encapsulate divine truth in human terms; rather, it simply seeks to "touch" or, better, "be touched" by divine realities that are above it. Here the language of experience once again enters, but at a higher power in the so-called spiritual senses and mystical experience. But the translation of such experience back into usual human discourse best occurs in metaphoric speech, not in speculative thought.

I. Experience

We begin with the original dense ball of experience: Jesus risen from the dead. As we have seen, the explosive impact of this experience demands articulation. For Jesus' followers, what can it mean? This experience becomes the epicenter and driving force in the church's confession of faith as it expands outward, seeking more and more layers of intelligible speech. Only then can such faith be "confessed"; only then can it be passed down.

We have already traced one leg of this journey. The experience of the resurrection raises enormous questions about Jesus' own identity. Who *is* Jesus? What is his next move? Looking back, who *was* Jesus in the flesh, and how do we interpret his life and, above all, his death and resurrection? These questions give birth to Christology as they seek to answer this question: In light of the resurrection, who is Jesus?

But as Christology develops, as Jesus is identified in some sense as God, another question moves from the periphery to the center. Indeed, another cycle of questions appears. If we confess that Jesus is God, our focus of attention has thereby shifted. Indeed, we continue to ask questions about Jesus. But does not a second question emerge as well? *Who, in light of Jesus, is God?* This is the question of the Trinity, and it arises in a special way for Christians. There is every reason to assume that the confession of Christ's divinity took place rather seamlessly. In giving religious veneration to Jesus, the early Christians never felt that they were compromising their belief in the *one* God of Israel. As we saw, the hymn in Philippians 2 alludes to a stridently monotheistic passage in the Old Testament (Isa. 45) in order to finally bestow on Jesus "the name that is above all names, so that at the name of Jesus every knee should bend in heaven and on earth and under the earth and every tongue should confess that Jesus Christ is Lord, to the glory of God the Father" (Phil. 2:9–11). "To the glory of God the Father!" For these Christians, this confession does not compromise but rather enhances their confession of the *one* God of Israel. But such was not the view of Jews or of others. In other words, the confession of Christ's divinity seems to assume a special way in which the risen Jesus was experienced and interpreted *within* the Christian community. There is no evidence that Jesus was regarded by early Christians as a lesser deity; rather, he was understood as a special revelation of the *one* God of Israel. In this sense, Christology quite naturally points beyond itself to the Trinity. In light of the resurrection of Jesus and the gift of his spirit, God is *experienced* in a fresh way and then subsequently *rethought* in new ways as well.

We need to make a distinction here. If we look for the *doctrine* of the Trinity in the New Testament, we search in vain. True, there are triadic confessions of faith, notably the baptismal formula in Matthew 28:19 and the closing words of 2 Corinthians 13:13. But if we seek a clearly articulated doctrine of the Trinity, we must wait until 381 and the Council of Constantinople before such appears. And key elements — the status of the Holy Spirit — were unclear until almost the end. What one finds in the early church is a new *experience* of God. But it will take almost four hundred years for this experience to develop into explicit doctrine, and that, in turn, will represent only a beginning. But the *experience* of a Triune God — of God known in a new way in light of Jesus' resurrection and the gift of his spirit — goes back to the resurrection itself, part and parcel of that dense ball of explosive force of Jesus come back from the dead. For those within the community, it *illumines* their confession of one God. For those outside, it seems perplexing at best.

How would we describe this new experience of God, and why is it illuminating? The starting point once again is Jesus risen from the dead. By virtue of his resurrection, Jesus' entire life, including (above all) his death, becomes a sustained story about the God of Israel. Jesus spoke in parables. Now, by virtue of his resurrection, Jesus himself becomes a parable, a metaphor about God's nature. In this light, I will speak of a new experience of God with three points of reference, or, better, a tripartite experience in which individual elements are inseparable because they are mutually illuminating.

God as *Father* refers to the God of the Old Testament, who has himself acquired a considerable history in dialogue first with Israel and then, after the exile, with the Jewish community. In this sense, God as Father is both a known and unknown quantum. This is the God of Abraham, Isaac, and Jacob, who revealed his name to Moses at Sinai in the desert. By revealing his name, Yahweh discloses his *personality* as he simultaneously displays his *otherness* or transcendence. There is nothing in heaven or on earth like the God who has chosen to reveal himself. The subsequent history of the tribes of Israel, then of the nation, and finally of the Jewish community becomes commentary and expansion of Israel's original revelation. Yahweh's power grows in the process. In the prophets, especially Second Isaiah, it becomes clear that there is only one God, creator of heaven and earth. His personality also takes on new contours. He cares for Israel as a mother for her infant child. After the exile, Yahweh is present to Israel in a special way in the law. But this all-powerful God remains equally mysterious and elusive. He is the God of Job as well. Indeed, as he abides with Israel and draws closer, the nearness of God only serves to underscore his mysterious, incalculable nature. Hence, deep from within that nature, a question arises: *What is God like?* This is not a new question, but it is posed in an urgent way when Jesus proclaims the coming of God's kingdom.

God as *Son* refers to Jesus. He proclaims the coming of God's kingdom and testifies to it finally by his death on the cross. Then God raised Jesus from the dead as an extraordinary gesture of vindication of message and messenger together. God's kingdom is indeed appearing. Jesus' proclamation was true, and Jesus himself is its agent and messenger. Indeed, the messenger becomes the message. If God reveals his *personality* to Moses at Mount Sinai, through Jesus God himself takes on a *human person* who can give a definitive answer to the question "What is God like?"[3] The meaning of *persona* in Latin and *propospon* in Greek is "face," and so in the person of Jesus, the God of Israel reveals his face. This is what God is like. And this is not just an informational item; God intervenes to save Israel and indeed all humankind from the burden of sin and death.

Thus Jesus' life, death, and resurrection answer a perennial question about God. They reveal God's nature. But this does not relieve the mystery of God's nature. Indeed, in many ways, it intensifies it. It seemed a scandal to Jews and to others to say that *this Jesus* was God's Son. In this sense, the *scandal of particularity,* inseparable from Christian revelation, deepens the hiddenness of God. Yet if this mysterious God chooses to reveal himself to the human family, what better way could there be than through the grammar of a single, individual human life? What message is better suited to its recipients than the life of the messenger itself?

God as *Spirit* refers to Jesus' spirit and God's spirit too. The significant point is that through the resurrection, Jesus has given this Spirit to his followers. The New Testament describes this gift in several ways that we will consider later. I underscore two points here. Passing through his death and resurrection, Jesus marks the Spirit as his own, and this becomes its defining moment. Yet the spirit of Jesus also gains momentum on its own after the resurrection. This experience of the Spirit becomes powerful and dynamic, a force in its own right. Yes, it is the spirit of God; yes, it is the spirit of Jesus too. But also the Holy Spirit. This part of Jesus, remaining in the heart of his followers, takes on a certain independence. "Because you are children,

God has sent the Spirit of his Son into our hearts, crying 'Abba! Father!'" (Gal. 4:6). Indeed, when we pray, this Spirit, bearing witness in our own spirit, allows us to call God "Abba, Father."

That the Spirit emerges in time as a *person* in its own right is testimony to the strength, endurance, and unique character of this experience. Therefore, the Spirit also provides an answer to the question "What is God like?" God is revealed in the life, death, and resurrection of Jesus. Here God reveals his face. But we also look to the living presence of Jesus in the hearts of his followers. This is the most *intimate* form of presence; this Spirit comingling with our own spirit enables us to pray as Jesus taught us. At the same time, it is also a great providential force, a *world-historical force,* impelling the mission of the church. This is also what God is like. Yet, again, as the movement of the Spirit reveals God, it also conceals his nature.

This tripartite experience of God as Father, now revealed in Jesus as Son, remaining with us in his Spirit, is basic to Christian faith. It represents no contradiction with belief in one God; rather, it seeks to enhance such faith. But it will take a long time before this experience can be translated into articulate speech, and even longer until it finds adequate expression in theology and doctrine. Still, this represents the Trinity in its liveliest form.

II. Scriptural Witness

We begin by examining the way the Scripture treats the three persons of the Trinity individually as Father, Son, and Holy Spirit.

Father

Perhaps the challenge is most straightforward in regard to God as Father. This dimension of God had already acquired a long history, and even if that history was often puzzling and mysterious, it nevertheless was *known.* Karl Rahner's classic "Theos in the New Testament" (1954) examines the use of the word *God* (*ho theos*) in the Christian Scriptures.[4] His conclusion has general validity. With few exceptions, when the New Testament speaks of God, the reference is to God the Father. However, this should not be interpreted as identical with a later Western confession of faith in three coequal persons sharing one nature; rather, the so-called Greek conception of the Trinity remains closer to New Testament usage. Here "Father" is seen as origin and source of the Godhead and the starting point for all subsequent discussion. Thus when Jesus prays to God as *Abba*, Father, he prays to the God of Israel. His disciples in Luke's Gospel ask for a prayer of their own. They seek to pray as Jesus did. Their request also assumes an identity with Israel's faith. The surprise that the term *God* is used of Jesus at all makes sense only against the prior assumption that the reference is to the God of Israel, to God the Father in Christian terms.

Son

Therefore, the force of its use in regard to Jesus lies in its exceptional quality. Since the normal referent is the God of Israel, its use in regard to Jesus is startling. We begin with the point of arrival, the *terminus ad quem* of the question, those cases in which the New Testament explicitly refers to Jesus as God. Raymond Brown examines such passages from an exegetical point of view, carefully weighing the manuscript evidence and grammatical syntax for the most reliable textual readings.[5] He concludes that three passages in the New Testament *clearly* call Jesus God: Hebrews 1:8–9; John 1:1; 20:28. There are five others, in his judgment, in which the use is *probable:* John 1:18; Romans 9:5; Titus 2:13; 2 Peter 1:1; 1 John 5:20. But if these are the most certain instances, this development represents a point of arrival of a deliberate and consistent trajectory.

The crucial issue is the nature of this trajectory. Its starting point is prayer and worship. Representative is the acclamation of 1 Corinthians 16:22: *Maranatha,* "Our (O) Lord, come!" This is one of the earliest examples of Christian prayer, an Aramaic version of what came to be the banner cry of the Gentile mission: "Jesus is Lord." Here the exalted title "Lord," reserved to the God of Israel, is bestowed on Jesus himself. Brown notes that the majority of cases in which Jesus is referred to as God occur in the context of worship and liturgy.[6] This reinforces Larry Hurtado's conclusion that Jesus was given prayerful veneration in the Christian community from its earliest days. Significantly, the earliest outside witness to the Christian community, Pliny's letter to Trajan (ca. 112), describes Christians in just the same way as singing "hymns to Christ as to a god."[7]

These factors give us powerful clues as to the nature of the trajectory that led to the explicit confession of Jesus as God. The path did not go from a modest estimate of Jesus to an exalted one; rather, it went from an *experience* of worshipful veneration of Jesus to an *articulate confession* of him as divine. Here the experience was able to find adequate words to express itself in a more formal way. In one sense, it may seem a small and consistent step from the worshipful prayer to the narrative confession by Thomas in John 20:28: "My Lord and my God!" In another sense, the step is momentous. Perhaps one of the reasons it took so long and was made so sparingly is that Christians realized intuitively what was at stake in the confession of Christ's divinity. Such a confession opens still another, larger question: *What can it mean to call Jesus God?* Here the answer cannot be simple. In other words, those few instances in the New Testament in which Jesus is referred to as God bring one trajectory to a close as they open an equally large one.

Spirit

Like the Father, the Spirit has a long history in the Old Testament, stretching back to the book of Genesis. The Spirit of God, literally his breath (*ruah*), moves over the primeval waters (Gen. 1:2), and creation follows. In Genesis 2, God breathes his spirit into Adam, and he comes to life as well.

God's Spirit comes upon all of Israel's leaders. In Israel's early years, the Spirit chooses the judges. When the Spirit calls David, a covenant with his house or dynasty follows (2 Sam. 7:8–16); the call is institutionalized, what sociology calls a "routinization" of the Spirit ensues. Henceforth the Spirit comes upon Israel's kings of the house of David in dynastic succession. After the breakup of the monarchy, the northern kingdom reverts to the older pattern reminiscent of the judges. The institutionalized form continues in Judah, the southern kingdom over which the house of David presides. The Spirit calls the prophets, granting to each a special vision at their calling. Prophets act as a counterpoint to kings. The dialectic between them turns on the Spirit's independence from all institutional forms.

The Spirit of the Lord comes upon Israel as a whole. It leads Ezekiel into the valley of dry bones (Ezek. 37), promising national restoration, a new spirit poured into Israel's dead bones. After the exile, the sense of the Spirit's presence to the Jewish community waxes and wanes. For long periods the Spirit seems silent. Apocalyptic expectations about the last days are intimately linked to a renewed outpouring of the Spirit.

The Spirit is also not confined to Israel or humankind. And not all spirits are of God. There are evil spirits that can inhabit individuals, impelling them to evil deeds. Not all spirits are earthly ones. There are angelic spirits, sometimes good and beneficent, but also malign.

The word *spirit* (*pneuma*) occurs 380 times in the New Testament, reflecting the wide-ranging Old Testament usage that we have reviewed. What sets the New Testament apart are different *trajectories* in which the Spirit's activity is framed. The Spirit is intimately linked to Jesus' calling, bestowing on him his unique status. In Mark, the Spirit comes upon Jesus at his baptism, announcing, "You are my Son, the Beloved; with you I am well pleased" (Mark 1:11). In Matthew and Luke, the Spirit's activity begins with his conception; Jesus is God's Son from birth. The trajectory is carried further in John, but without the motif of the Spirit. Jesus is God's Son, his Word, from all eternity.

Luke's Gospel is unique in the way it combines personal and impersonal features of the Spirit. The Spirit of God, active in Israel, becomes the responsible agent of Jesus' birth. Then the Spirit comes on him in bodily form as a dove at his baptism. At the synagogue in Nazareth, Jesus begins his public ministry using the proclamation of Isaiah 61:1: "The Spirit of the Lord is upon me" (Luke 4:18). As a Spirit-filled prophet, Jesus goes up to Jerusalem to die. His last words are about the Spirit, which he returns to the Father. At Pentecost, this Spirit is poured out on the apostles, fulfilling the prophetic words of Joel 2:28–32. Now Jesus' spirit becomes a world-historical force leading the church's mission. We can see Luke's simple but ingenuous strategy. The great Holy Spirit of Israel, siphoned through the life, death, and resurrection of Jesus, is poured out once again as a world-historical force, leading the church's missionary effort from Jerusalem to Rome in the course of a single generation.

But Luke's theology comes into perspective only when we place it over against the radically different notion of the Spirit in the apostle Paul. Here we come closer to the primitive experience of the Spirit in all its diversity. If the Spirit is a world-historical force, on the one hand, it appears in Paul as the most intimate, personal experience, on the other. Paul mentions twice the special way of praying that goes back to Jesus, his use of the word *Abba,* "Father" (Rom. 8:15–16; Gal. 4:6). When we pray to God as *Abba,* this is the work of the Holy Spirit, comingling with our spirit, bearing witness that we are children of God. Paul tells us in 1 Corinthians 12:3 that no one can say "Jesus is Lord" except by the Holy Spirit. Could the Spirit be portrayed in a more intimate or personal way? All the gifts and charisms are the work of one Spirit bestowed on members of the community for the common good to build up the body of Christ. Significantly, among these gifts and charisms mentioned here, prophets are mentioned in the second position, after apostles and before teachers (1 Cor. 12:27–31).

But the larger-than-life quality of the Spirit is equally present. Paul speaks of Jesus' followers as existing "in Christ," "of Christ," "through Christ"; they are brought "into Christ." The experience of Christ and the Spirit often simply overlap, impossible to separate one from another. "At best," comments James D. G. Dunn, "we may speak of Christ as the context and the Spirit as the power."[8] Christ is mystically present to the community. Christ becomes a special kind of corporate presence in Colossians and Ephesians. The world-historical dimension of the Holy Spirit in the book of Acts is here translated into universal, cosmic terms. The body of Christ is the earthly extension of Christ, its heavenly head.

The Spirit in the Gospel of John is different again. Called the Paraclete, literally "advocate" (*parakletos*), the Spirit is Jesus' lawyer-like presence among his followers when Jesus himself is absent. The Paraclete will remind them of all that Jesus said (John 14:26–27). He will prove the world wrong about sin, righteousness, and judgment (John 16:8–11). And if Jesus does not return to the Father, he cannot send the Paraclete.

What are we to make of all these diverse manifestations of the Spirit? Dunn indicates the starting point: "Something happened in the lives of Gentiles who heard the gospel, whether it was initially preached to them directly, or they overhead it as adherents in diaspora synagogues when the Nazarene missionaries began to preach there. The manifestations were such that the missionaries could only conclude: 'the gift of the Spirit has been poured out even on the Gentiles'

(Acts 10:45)."[9] The experience of Jesus' spirit after the resurrection is the great driving force of the church's mission. There are two irreducible elements in the development that follows. All experiences are seen as the manifestation of the *one Spirit of Jesus*. Equally, the *diversity* of the phenomenon remains a stubborn fact. By turns, this Spirit is intimate and personal, comingling with our spirit; then the corporate bond in the Pauline church, making members into the body of Christ; finally the great cosmic connection between the church on earth and Christ, its heavenly head. If there is *one* Spirit, its *diverse* manifestations are also an irreducible given. This side of the equation does not fit easily into conventional patterns of thought. It is not difficult to grasp why the experience of the Spirit, so fresh, alive, and diverse, will be difficult to adequately capture in conceptual terms. The Spirit therefore remains the most concrete yet the most elusive element in the Christian doctrine of God.

Consequently, Son and Spirit play different roles in the subsequent development of the Trinity. Translating the experience of the Triune God into conceptual terms, the Son takes the lead, and then the Spirit follows. But in general terms, what is decided about the status of the Son is, with time, accorded to the Spirit as well. It is the voice of prayer and devotion that often leads the way in this latter step. In the church's prayer and worship, the Spirit is invoked together with the Father and the Son, and this is a strong factor in theological argumentation. This also means that trinitarian development is never the bloodless child of abstract thought but rather is the fruit of prayer and worship as an independent factor in its own right that seeks its own adequate forms of expression.

III. Theology

The Logos and the Son

The most pressing question that the Scriptures bequeath to us is the one that closes our examination of the Son: *What can it mean to refer to Jesus as God?* Significantly, two of the three New Testament passages that clearly do so belong to the Gospel of John. They comprise the beginning (John 1:1) and original ending of the Gospel (John

20:28), rendering the whole into a deliberate statement about Christ's divinity as God's Word. The Old Testament discussion on preexistent Wisdom, which we examined earlier, stands as the source of John's use of the Greek word *logos*.[10] Here a vivid family of different but related metaphors about God's immanence crosses the line between *metaphoric description* and *factual statement*. The Gospel proclaims with great deliberation that the Word has become flesh in Jesus of Nazareth. It also shifts the operative word. The words for *wisdom* in Hebrew (*hokma*) and Greek (*sophia*) are feminine — Woman Wisdom. The word *logos* is masculine, and so is Jesus. But the background for John's description of Jesus as God's Logos in the Gospel is this Old Testament Sophia speculation. If John's Gospel brings the Old Testament discussion of Wisdom to a certain culminating point, it also opens the door to Greek speculation on the Logos.

The Logos

The door to Greek speculation on the Logos opens almost on its own. Philo (d. ca. 50) has already explored the similarities between Old Testament speculation on Wisdom and other surrogates of God's presence (the angel of God) and their Greek counterparts, tracing the latter to biblical inspiration. But the use of Greek speculation on the Logos represents a momentous turn in its own right. The turn touches a deep vein of classical thought with a distinguished pedigree. The notion of Logos first appears in Heraclitus. In an ever-changing world captured in the metaphor of fire, Logos provides an immanent dialectic that holds a restless universe together and a society as well whose first law is strife. Stoic thought makes extended use of the Logos concept as a mainstay of its understanding of the universe, society, and the human person, exploring the immanent *potential of the notion.*[11] *There is rational order, a Logos, that pervades the universe, giving it a sense of purpose and design. Seeds of this Logos are present in creation, preeminently in human reason. That is what allows us to perceive order in the cosmos. The same sense of rational order pervades society, providing the basis for natural law that all human beings can recognize. Stoic thought also contributes an important distinction to trinitarian thought in its first stages, between God's immanent Logos, within God from all eternity, and his expressed Logos, extended for the purpose of creation and redemption. As noted, Stoic thought explores the immanent potential of Logos, different ways of describing the Word's rational, ordering presence to this world.*

By contrast, Platonic thought in its middle and later stages explores the transcendent *potential of the Logos concept. Here the Logos relates first to God, the Good or the One. According to Platonic lights, the world of ordinary human experience is a reflection of a higher, ideal world that is perfect, changeless, and eternal. This transcendent reality looms above our natural world as truly real and relates to us as reality to appearance. In middle- and neo-Platonic systems, this highest level of reality descends by stages to our own world, a layered sense of divinity marking the cosmos. The Logos becomes God's first expression, the locus of ideal multiplicity, of Plato's world of forms. Plotinus will use the notion of mind* (nous) *to express the same idea. It should be clear how much natural attraction this Platonic worldview will have for Christians, an outlook in which that which is most spiritual is most real, in which our world is a reflection of a higher, ideal one.*

Thus the use of the Logos concept represents a flexible universal joint *of enormous usefulness and importance for subsequent Christian thought. It connects Old Testament speculation on preexistent Wisdom to Greek speculation on the Logos. In doing so, it opens the door to Christian apologists to explain the gospel to the wider culture. Later, it will provide the framework for the Christian message to understand itself more clearly in these same patterns of thought. It therefore helps to weld together the Christian faith with the world of classical antiquity.*

It also helps to answer the question with which this section began: What can it mean to call Jesus God? The Gospel of John gives us two sets of parallel terms that hereafter will be linked at every point. God is Father. Jesus is Son. God the Father is the one God; the divine in Jesus is the Logos. The notion of Logos, drawing on multiple sources in Old Testament thought and Greek antiquity, will explain what it means to refer to Jesus as God's Son. A root meaning lies in the simple identity-in-difference between a person and his or her word. The word is one with the speaker. Yet once uttered, it takes on an independence of its own. In the same way, the Son is one with the Father, yet different and independent too. Four layers of meaning can be derived from this basic analogy.[12]

First, Logos means **revelation**. *Just as a word reveals the person's inner life, just as the two are one yet distinct, so too revelation in the Logos reveals the nature of the Father, yet is independent too. Indeed, God's Logos had revealed himself in the Old Testament in the prophets and in Greek thought as well, according to Justin Martyr. Such revelations now culminate in Jesus Christ, who provides the key to other manifestations of the Logos.*

Second, Logos means **reason**. *The Logos reveals God's plan for the universe and for human history. In other words, the key to these wider dimensions of purpose is revealed in the Logos in Christ. Human rationality also becomes a privileged instance of God's presence, sown into the fabric of human nature. Reason allows humankind to recognize God's presence, his Logos in the world. Reason and revelation are intimately connected.*

Third, Logos means **will**. *God speaks, and the world is created. God's Word is not simply revelatory; it is creative and dynamic. Thus God does not simply reveal himself in Jesus of Nazareth as an informational item; instead, he does so as an action and part of a plan. God's word was the responsible agent in the act of creation and now acts in the same way in redemption. Thus the Logos reveals the Father, who chooses now to save the human family from the shackles of sin and death in the death and resurrection of Jesus of Nazareth. Here Logos acquires a soteriological face.*

Fourth, the Logos means the **divine in Jesus of Nazareth**. *The Word becomes flesh. Jesus' origins by virtue of the Spirit are left to sediment in the text, overshadowed by this larger truth. The divine in Christ is inseparably joined to Jesus' humanity, the Logos responsible for the latter, sometimes conceived as the work of the Spirit as well.*

If the language of Logos serves to explain what it means to call Jesus God, the terms Father *and* Son *remain more concrete and personal. This is the language of prayer and worship in a tradition that stretches back to Jesus' prayer to God as* Abba, Father. *These family relationships of Father and Son also enclose and explain the relationship between God and his Logos. Together, these terms set forth what it mean to call Christ divine and see him as God's Son in the special way that does not prejudice but rather enhances Israel's belief in one God.*

However, this answer finally turns on another question in two parts: What is the status of the Logos, and then of the Holy Spirit? The definitive answer here comes only after protracted debate and discussion and ultimately by the deliberate decisions of the first two ecumenical councils.

The Development of Trinitarian Thought

The Apologists — Justin Martyr (ca. 100–165), his disciple Tatian (ca. 110–180), Theophilus of Antioch (d. ca. 180–185), Athenagoras (late second century), and others — are the first to undertake a rational exposition of the Trinity. For Justin, the seminal *logos* in the human spirit allows Jews and Greeks alike to grasp facets of truth in the world around them and to read the Old Testament in a new way.[13] Indeed, God's Logos and his Spirit have appeared in a hidden but threefold way many times in Israel's history. Witness the visit of the three angels to Abraham at Mamre (Gen. 18:2) Was this not a divine visitation in angelic form?[14] The words of creation — "Let us make humankind in our image, according to our likeness" (Gen. 1:26) — also reflect the divine persons at work, present but hidden, too.[15] Justin is one of many to read Proverbs 8:22 as proof that God put forth his Word for the purpose of creation and revelation.[16] He is also representative of those who trace the truth in Greek philosophy to its biblical inspiration. For Justin, Moses is the source for Plato's ideas in the *Timaeus*.[17] So if the Logos allows the human spirit to recognize God's presence in diverse times and place, God's Logos from the other side has appeared in different forms on earth before the time of Christ.

This Logos now becomes flesh in Jesus of Nazareth to reveal the Father and accomplish the work of salvation. Compared to the Father, Justin may hold the Logos in "second" place and the Spirit in "third," but in another sense, this means no diminishment.[18] One fire is not lessened when it enkindles another, nor is a word diminished by its utterance. The sun in heaven is not any less for the light it sheds on earth.[19]

The Stoic distinctions that we noted earlier are used by the apologists and others. The Logos is *immanent* to God from all eternity but is put forth at a later point first for the purpose of creation, then redemption. Theophilus of Antioch (later second century) and Hippolytus (d. ca. 236) use the technical terms for this two-stage Logos, immanent in God (*endiathetos*) and then expressed (*prophorikos*) for creation and redemption. The reasoning here is easy to grasp and seems an obvious first line of explanation. We only learn about the Logos from creation and then redemption. It makes sense to assume that the

Logos originates in a new way at the same point as well. It may have a shadowy existence in God from all eternity, just as an unspoken word may quietly slumber within a person. But only when the word is uttered does it enter the public arena. In short, a *functional* explanation of the Logos seems a natural starting point. It remains to be seen whether such an approach can do justice to the relationship between Father and Son, God and his Logos. It also seems to suggest that the Logos in its active phase has a temporal origin. A correlate of the *functional* explanation of the persons is the clear *monarchy* of the Father, the origin and source of the Godhead.

The latter point is clear in the work of Irenaeus, whose trinitarian thought is both representative and original. His image of the Trinity is famous. God the Father is compared to a "Man with Two Hands."

The Father's "hands" are his *Wisdom* (the Spirit) and his *Word* (the Logos).[20] The image echoes Job 10:8 and Psalm 119:73, underscoring "the indissoluble unity between the creative Father and the organs of His activity."[21] God the Father has no need for the ministry of angels in the work of creation or its adornment. He has his built-in tools, his two hands to accomplish such tasks. The image of the Man with Two Hands also endows God's Wisdom and his Word with greater permanence. Like a person's two hands, they are with the Father from the start.

Tertullian, as a theologian, has a strong sense of the *inner logic* of the Trinity. Father, Son, and Spirit, he argues, represent a unique way of expressing the oneness of God. Far from imperiling the unity of the Godhead, Father, Son, and Spirit display what is unique to trinitarian monotheism, belief in one God as Father, Son, and Spirit.

Tertullian brings clear distinctions and significant images to his exposition of the Trinity. In his treatise *Against Praxeas,* he carefully argues that the Trinity is *one* in substance, condition, and power yet *three* in degree, form, and aspect. Such distinctions enable him to explain the special unity of the Trinity in which the three persons become the key to God's oneness. Tertullian bequeaths to the West its basic terms to describe the Trinity: *one substance, three persons*. These terms do not possess here their later philosophical precision. However, as Eric Osborn notes, Tertullian "has given contours for the use of the new terms. Both refer to the inner life of God. *Persona* points to what characterizes and distinguishes that inner life. *Substantia* refers to what joins and unifies it."[22]

Tertullian's trinitarian images are striking. Justin's images argued that the persons of the Trinity do not *diminish* the Godhead. Tertullian turns the argument around. His images illumine in a *positive* way God's special kind of unity as Father, Son, and Spirit. God and his Word are distinct but related, as a root is to a tree, a fountain to a river, the sun to its rays. When the Spirit is added, the images expand: "Now the Spirit indeed is third from God and the Son; just as the fruit of the tree is third from the root, or as the stream out of the river is third from the fountain, or as the apex of the ray is third from sun. Nothing, however, is alien from that original source whence it derives its own properties. In like manner the Trinity, flowing down from the Father through intertwined and connected steps, does not at all disturb the *Monarchy*, whilst it at the same time guards the state of the *Economy*."[23] Tertullian also argues that a ruler's authority is not diminished by delegation. In the same way, the Father's authority is not lessened in the economy of divine persons.

What is significant here is the search for an *organic* unity that is not easily grasped in abstract categories because the dynamic element is invariably omitted. Here, on the other hand, deceptively simple images — fruit, tree, root; stream, river, fountain — are better able to convey a sense of organic unity in which the parts derive from one another but at the same time comprise an encompassing whole.

We have taken Justin, Irenaeus, and Tertullian as representative of trinitarian thought in these beginning stages. Here the fixed poles of later discussion emerge. The first is the *monarchy* of God the Father. He is the origin and source of divinity and the anchor of the three persons. He is the sun, the root, the fountain, or, in Irenaeus's image, the Man with Two Hands. "The *Principatus* of the Father," wrote John Henry Newman, "is a great Catholic truth, and was taught in the church after the Nicene Council as well as before."[24] This is a fixed assumption of subsequent discussion: God is *one,* rooted in the Father as its source. The other fixed pole emerges in the functional explanation of the Son and the Spirit. It is best expressed in images and in temporal categories which describe creation and redemption. But what is central is the way in which Son and Spirit are *derived* from the Father without imperiling his *Principatus*. The persons themselves in these first stages may seem lesser creatures, the hands of the Father, the tools of his will. But the *logic of derivation* is the second fixed pole of trinitarian thought, here first explored in functional terms: God is *three*, as the persons of the Son and Holy Spirit flow from the Father as their source.

This also seems a good place to say a word about the role of "images" in the development of trinitarian thought. They may appear as lesser vehicles in disentangling a complex logical problem, of one God and three persons. But the Trinity must also satisfy the impulses of prayer and devotion. Here images play a better role because they speak more directly to the devotional and aesthetic sense. Significantly, several Roman sarcophagi from the fourth century represent the Trinity in bas relief.[25] Here the Trinity is portrayed as three consoling figures, close enough to popular piety to decorate a tomb. The images often center on themes from creation with the persons of the Trinity pictured above and Adam and Eve below, sounding the hope of resurrection. In this regard, funeral art is invariably conservative. Indeed, it is difficult to imagine lively trinitarian faith that does not find expression in the language of images.

On the other hand, the theological discussion will take a sharp turn when it leaves the domain of functional explanations of Son and Spirit. It will increasingly realize that when it seeks to speak about the inner life of God, human words fail. A negative (*apophatic*) approach is better equipped to speak about what is ineffable and beyond the normal range of human speech. These diverse paths — images in their concrete, familiar forms and human thought straining to convey the ineffable — will remain companions on the road.

Modalism and Subordinationism

The standard classification of failed paths in the development of trinitarian thought founder on the fixed poles of trinitarian thought that we have identified. In reacting against any distinction between the persons of the Trinity, *modalism* in various forms argues that Father, Son, and Spirit are simply different names for the same reality. In effect, the differences between persons are nominal, not real. Sabellius (early third century) proposed a more nuanced version of the same theory. Here Father, Son, and Spirit are seen as *successive manifestations* of the one God, who appears first as Father, then as Son, and finally as Spirit. Modalism represents a certain understandable tendency to cut the Gordian knot in regard to the Trinity — to protect the unity of God by reducing the difference between the persons to only a matter of words. But, by the same token, it fails to do justice to the second pole of trinitarian thought: God as three persons.

And in this regard, there is simply too much evidence in Scripture, tradition, and Christian life that witnesses to the distinct reality of the three persons. Jesus prays to God as *Abba,* Father, distinct from himself. And if Father and Son are one in John's Gospel, the Son has come to do the Father's will, which makes sense only if Father and Son are *one yet different.* And what to do with the crucifixion of Jesus if Father and Son are one? It is difficult enough to associate Jesus' death with the Son. Connecting it to the Father violates all canons that surround and protect God's eternal impassiblility. The crux of the matter is how to adequately capture the differences of the person, an issue that modalism seeks to avoid. Hence, while it is easy to understand the *motivation* behind modalist thought, the resulting trinitarian solutions never prove satisfactory.

Subordinationism is quite another matter. The term is a catchall one for different systems of thought, but it is fair to characterize them as ranking Father, Son, and Spirit as subordinate divine beings in hierarchical order. The Father, the monarch, stands in first place, the Son in second, and the Spirit as the lowest rank of divinity. The dangers of this kind of schema, when applied to the Trinity, are serious. First, the pattern of thought quite matches the tenor of the age. In the populated universe of antiquity, it is simply the common assumption that there are different kinds and grades of divine beings and that the upper story of the cosmos is home to them all. "The gods were not airy abstractions," observes Peter Brown. "They were vibrant beings, who hovered rank after rank above and around the human race."[26]

However, this heavenly realm, a more perfect one than our own, displays a rational order. Thus a natural, rational subordination exists between higher and lower levels of divinity. Such assumptions are reflected in the eclectic systems of Middle Platonism. Here are also philosophies sensitive to religious concerns. But J. Rebecca Lyman argues that it is wrong to conclude too quickly that the *cosmological* categories of Middle Platonism subvert the *religious* concerns of the Christian faith.[27] On the contrary, the Gospels portray Jesus as one who seeks to do the will of the Father and is subordinate to him as both Son and Savior. In other words, the Gospels seek on their own for a way to phrase the subordination of Son to Father. It is also a mistake to underestimate the independence of Christian thinkers in freely adapting from contemporary philosophic systems yet knowing where to draw the line. And sometimes the line is clear and sharp. The coeternity of matter, for example, is simply incompatible with the Christian God of creation. Where to draw the line between creator and the level of creatures looms now as especially crucial. All the more so as the line becomes sharper.

The great catechetical school of Alexandria represents the preeminent crossroads between philosophical thought, sympathetic to religious concerns, and Christian impulses to use such tools to explain the truth of the Gospels. Clement is the first great teacher whom tradition associates with the school. The great theologian Origen belongs in a class by himself by virtue of his Christian piety, the originality and boldness of his thought, and his prolific output across the entire spectrum of theology. Origen literally supplies arguments, in effect ammunition, to all sides in the theological battles that break out after the Council of Nicea. Lyman captures his legacy this way: "His Christian commitment was unquestionable, but his theological conclusions stimulated passionate apologetic or repudiation; he was too right to be wrong, or too attractively wrong to be ignored."[28]

I wish to pick out only two points in his complex legacy. Origen is the first to propose the eternal generation of the Son from the Father, an event with no temporal starting point, rather a process of everlasting continuance without beginning or end. Yet, by the same token, the Son is eternally subordinate to the Father and the Spirit as well. However, Origen draws a sharp line between these levels of divinity and the lower orders of creation. Still, this question remains: Are the Son and Holy Spirit ranked as lower levels of divinity or are they placed on the same plane with the Father? Origen can be read both ways, depending on how the question is posed.

This ambiguity is a bellwether. Let us sum up the crucial issue before the Council of Nicea on this note. We began this section with a question of the status of the Logos. We conclude it on the same score with the following options. Is the Logos the first of God's creatures through whom the rest of creation takes place? This seems a fair reading of Proverbs 8:22, the touchstone opening the Arian controversy. In simplest terms, is the Logos a creature, albeit the highest and most exalted of creatures? Or is the Logos, eternally begotten before all ages, of the same rank as the Father but derived as a perfect Son originates from his Father? And what words do we use to describe this latter process? Is the Logos "begotten," "generated," "made," or "created"? There is simply no accepted vocabulary to express the Son's origin from the Father, for there is no one standard way of interpreting God's relation to the Logos. Clearly, both his status and the manner of his coming forth from the Father are related. An equally significant question looms: Why are a series of somewhat differing theological visions of the Trinity incompatible with one another? Why must the broad spectrum of views about Father and Son from around 275 be narrowed in 325? Certainly, the spectrum is not narrowed by debate, for each of these *is* a different vision, perhaps tolerant of one another but not identical. The field is narrowed by decisions. Here also our topic changes from theology to doctrine and to the decisions first of the Council of Nicea in 325, then of the Council of Constantinople in 381.

IV. Doctrine

The Arian Controversy

In regard to the Arian controversy,[29] the first and most critical task is locating the right categories to understand the events that now unfold. In regard to the traditional ones, Rowan Williams comments, "The textbook picture of an Arian system, defended by self-conscious doctrinal dissidents, inspired by the teaching of the Alexandrian presbyter, is the invention of Athanasius' polemic; most non-Nicenes would probably have been as little likely to call themselves Arians as Nicenes were to call themselves Athanasians."[30] In other words, the received picture of the Arian controversy stems in large measure from Athanasius (296–373), who establishes the narrative of record.[31] This version of events then glides into the annals of history, becoming the standard account. According to its lights, the Arian controversy is the first self-conscious clash between heresy and the orthodox faith. Both sides are clearly defined. So too are the villain and hero of the piece. Arius (ca. 250–336) becomes the archetypal heretic; Athanasius, close to the hero. Likewise, Arianism is portrayed as the archetypal heresy in which later ages will glimpse a reflection of the church crises of their own day.

The traditional interpretation suffers largely as a result of the categories through which it views the controversy. In reality, Arius is best seen as the man who fires the first shot, then disappears. The watchword of Nicea, *homoousios,* and the authority of the Council of Nicea hardly play a role in much of Athanasius's writings, their most ardent defender in the traditional picture. Likewise, if Jerome can write in 360 that "the whole world groaned and marveled that it was Arian," then the teachings of a minor figure in Alexandria must have struck a deeply resonant chord in many other churches, especially those in the East, a fact that requires some explanation.[32]

But first, how did the Arian controversy begin? And then the crucial question: If "Arian" and "Nicene" are no longer adequate ways of describing the parties that clash here, what are better ones that allow us to grasp the depth and magnitude of the crisis facing the ancient church?

The controversy begins about 318 because of a dispute that arose between Arius, a presbyter of Alexandria, and Alexander, his bishop, about the correct interpretation of Proverbs 8:22: "The LORD created me at the beginning of his work, the first of his acts long ago." In effect, the question, and the passage, are about the status of the Logos. Arius's answer tilts in one direction, the Logos being a creature, and Alexander's in another, the Logos not being a creature. Then the controversy spreads. The emperor Constantine calls a Council at Nicea in 325 to settle the dispute. He also supplies the crucial word that becomes the council's watchword, *homoousios.*[33] The Son is *of the same substance* as the Father. The word has its own doubtful history. It is used here because it is wholly unacceptable to Arius who is excommunicated (but later reconciled.) *Homoousios* therefore begins its long career as a decisive word whose chief function is to condemn

Arius and vindicate Alexander. It draws a line between the contending parties.

The word *homoousios* is soon followed by other words: *homoiousios* ("similar substance") and *hypostasis* (eventually, "person") to mention just two. What these new words have in common is that they are not scriptural. In modern terms, they seek to create a metalanguage — a framework above the Scriptures — to interpret disputed texts such as Proverbs 8:22. They share another quality of new terminology. Their meaning is unclear and often confusing. But it would be a serious error to regard the controversy as a quibble about words. Rather, these terms represent the search for a public vocabulary to set down the meaning of issues that are difficult and sharply controverted. For the same reason, they now must be defined for the sake of decisions on which the welfare of the church depends. R. P. C. Hanson describes the ensuing process of development as one of trial and error, and this seems close to the facts.[34]

What is the heart of the matter? If traditional categories falter, what are more adequate ways of describing these events that now unfold? Joseph Lienhard suggests that the clash is better characterized as one between two deeply rooted theological traditions. He terms the first a "theology of one substance," and the second "a theology of two substances."[35] If one compares them as ideal types, differences emerge that illumine the depth of the crisis facing the ancient church. As we grasp the strength of each viewpoint, we can also understand why they drew large numbers to their banner almost from the start. We grasp as well what it means for the orthodox faith to emerge, not at the beginning but rather at the end of the clash between these rival traditions.

The "theology of two substances," of which Arius's thought represents a variation,[36] begins with the absolute singularity of God, utterly transcendent, beyond all distinctions and ultimately unknowable in himself. The Son cannot be of the same substance as the Father, for God the Father is one, simple and undivided. The Son therefore must comprise a "second substance." Although the Son is a creature, he is no ordinary one. The Logos is the first of God's works through whom the rest of creation takes place, much in the plain sense of Proverbs 8:22. A slogan of the day captures his status: "There was a then when he did not exist."[37] The Son was not always with God, nor was God always a Father. A degree of subordinationism has been a standard part of trinitarian theology up to this time. Here it is spun out to an extreme in the explicitly argued creaturely status of the Son.

The Son is divine, but in a lesser sense. This suffices for his role in creation and redemption. The Logos is the mediator of creation, the revealer of the Father in so far as that is possible, the teacher of all truths, and the role model in virtue for humankind. The Logos, so conceived, becomes incarnate in Jesus of Nazareth. Although the incarnation is important, it does not represent a world-historical turning point; rather, the traditional roles of the Logos as revealer, teacher, and role model are displayed in a new and more prominent way in the life of Jesus. Aspects of the gospel come into sharper focus. If the Logos is not of the same substance as the Father, he can change. He can display moral progress and grow in virtue. Above all, the Logos can suffer. He can truly become the crucified Son of God.

If the Logos as a second god is accorded greater freedom in his earthly ministry, so too the understanding of redemption that follows assigns a more substantial role to human cooperation. If the Logos stands as teacher and role model, it follows that human freedom in the work of redemption takes on great prominence. If the issue is one between divine initiative and human response in the work of salvation, the theology of two substances emphasizes the importance of human cooperation to God's initiative.

If the Son is given a certain derivative divine status, this tradition is open to the charge of polytheism in the eyes of its opponents. It will also blend more easily into the systems of the day that envision a great chain of being between God and creation. It should also be noted that there is little room for the Holy Spirit in this schema. And if the question of the Spirit's status is raised at all, the answer is predictable. If the Son is a creature, then, *a fortiori*, the Spirit is a creature as well.

The "theology of one substance" reflects the views of Athanasius and others in East and West. It begins with a strict monotheism and with a pronounced soteriological bent. The great concern is human salvation. For this tradition, the incarnation does represent a world-historical turning point that sets it apart from other appearances of the Logos. A famous dictum of Athanasius catches the logic: "For He was made man that we might be made God."[38] God takes on human flesh so that humankind might become like God, and no lesser deity could accomplish this task. Hence, if the Son is not of the same substance as the Father, if he is not creator as well, then he cannot fulfill his role in redemption, which is nothing less than the work of re-creation, the deification of humankind.

Therefore, powerful religious concerns drive the argument that Father and Son must share the same nature. The generation of the Son from the Father must represent an eternal process within the Godhead that means no lessening of the divine nature as it passes from Father to Son. A certain priority of the Father is retained to which the tradition attests. The words *Father* and *Son* also come to us from the Scriptures. But such terms are shorn of all temporal associations and any sense of earthly dependence. The Father is eternally God, and the Son is eternally God. Nothing less suffices to accomplish the work of salvation.

Just as religious concerns drive the argument, so too does the role of liturgy and worship of the church. The church has always venerated Jesus as divine and worshiped him as God. In a special way, the baptismal formula — faith in Father, Son, and Holy Spirit — is significant. Can the continuous practice of the church have been wrong? Rather, the church's worship acts as a compass, pointing in the right direction. It therefore follows that when the status of the Holy Spirit arises, the same arguments will be used, leading to the same conclusion. If the Holy Spirit performs the work of sanctification, then he must share from all eternity the Father's nature. The Holy Spirit must be God as well.

If the choice is between divine initiative and human response, this theology will come down decisively on the importance of God's initiative. The elevation and deification of the human race cannot hinge on our response but rather only on God's gracious action, which takes the lead. This theology will also draw a sharper line between creator and all of creation. God the Father and the Logos Son are counted on the side of the creator. All other beings belong to the realm of created reality. These accents also explain why in the arguments of Athanasius, the one nature of God plays such a prominent role, while the Trinity, as such, enters only later in his thought. The chief concern is the oneness of God's nature, which must be shared equally between Father and

Son in order to accomplish the great work of salvation, the deification of humankind.

A New Moment: the Holy Spirit and the Trinity

What makes a difference is the entrance of a *new* factor: the role of the Holy Spirit. Heretofore in both traditions, the focus was on the relation between the Father and the Son. Hence, for Athanasius, the cogent answer was to emphasize the *one* nature of God, which both persons share. The Holy Spirit plays no role in the discussion. The Nicene Creed accords the Spirit a brief mention: "and in the Holy Spirit." In effect, we also believe in the Holy Spirit. The topic is not on the horizon in 325, but the situation changes considerably by the 360s. Now Athanasius argues for the coequal divinity of the Holy Spirit based on many of the same arguments that he used to establish the status of the Logos.

But there are differences here. The scriptural witness to the Holy Spirit is diffuse and sometimes ambiguous. The Spirit's role in worship is different too. Whereas Jesus is venerated from the start and prayers are directed *to* him, there is almost no tradition of prayers *to* the Holy Spirit. Rather one prays *for* and *in* the Spirit.[39] On the other hand, the doxologies and the baptismal formula witness to the Spirit's coequality with the Father and the Son, and these play a powerful role. Still, uncertainty reigns until the opening of the Council of Constantinople in 381. One year earlier, Gregory of Nazianzus made this astonishing statement: "Some members of our own intelligentsia suppose the Holy Spirit to be an 'activity,' other a 'creature'; others think of him as God; yet others fail to come to a decision, allegedly through reverence for the Scriptures, on the ground they give no clear revelation on the question."[40]

What the topic of the Holy Spirit does is to shift the *focus of attention*. While heretofore when the spotlight was on the relation between Father and Son, it sufficed for Athanasius to stress the oneness of God as his opponents emphasized the duality of divine substances. Now both traditions are superseded. Instead, a new point of view must be sought that, in transcending those alternatives, introduces a reconciling moment as well. The entrance of not *two* but rather of *three persons* establishes an essential plural moment. Ultimately, then, the topic of the Spirit serves to shift the focus of attention to the Godhead itself. The question now becomes one of how to explain the distinguishing marks of the three persons without impairing the unity of the Godhead. Better, the real solution lies in grasping the character of Father, Son, and Spirit in a way that *enhances* the oneness of God. The mystery of the Trinity is now directly broached, one God in three persons. The turn to the Godhead, one and three, occurs in a relatively brief period of time. This comprises a genius turn, not unlike the swift grasp of Christ's divinity. It also points to answers to older problems as previous alternatives are taken up in this new perspective.

The architects of the doctrine of the Trinity in these first stages are the Cappadocians: Basil the Great (330–379), Gregory of Nazianzus (329–389), and Basil's younger brother, Gregory of Nyssa (330–395), and their elder sister, Marcrina (327–379). The so-called Cappadocian Settlement "finally fixed the statement of Trinitarian orthodoxy in the formula of one *ousia* and three *hypostaseis*. It was worked out largely by Basil...preached by the inspired populariser, Gregory of Nazianzus and elaborated by the acute and speculative mind of Gregory of Nyssa."[41] But the settlement should not be fixed too closely to the formula of one essence and three persons, a phrase rare in the writings of the Cappadocians.[42] It also narrows their contribution. In this regard, Lienhard sets the right perspective: "The Church prays to almighty God through Jesus Christ his Son in the Holy Spirit. The formula 'one *ousia* in three *hypostaseis*' was crafted on the workbench of theologians; and even for them, it is more of a convenient abbreviation than the last word that might be uttered."[43]

The Cappadocians differ among themselves in considerable ways, but of interest to us here are the qualities that join them.[44] The first is surely the negative (*apophatic*) method. The Cappadocians are keenly aware of the limitations of human language in describing the ineffable mystery of God. This awareness runs throughout their entire theological endeavor. And revelation does not lessen but instead only increases the *apophatic* quality of theological discourse. Only by revelation do we truly know God as Father, Son, and Holy Spirit. We receive such revelation by faith, which the letter to the Hebrews describes as "the assurance of things hoped for, and the conviction of things not seen" (Heb. 11:1). If such a definition applies at all, it must first apply to the Trinity. Thus the point of theological discourse about this holy mystery is not to increase the content of our knowledge, as if the revelation of the Trinity resolved the mystery of God's nature, making it more comprehendible in human terms. The effect is just the opposite. This knowledge in faith based on revelation gives us confidence in the *upward aim* of words such as *Father, Son,* and *Holy Spirit.* But they do not work as earthly analogues projected onto heavenly realities to bring them down to human size; rather, human language consciously aims beyond itself, seeking to touch the ineffable mystery of God. Through revelation, these heavenly realities become the exemplars of their earthly counterparts.

Revelation, faith, and the *apophatic* method work together, providing their own kind of insight. In human terms, for example, no son is ever identical to his father; no light is equal to the source of its radiance; no image is perfectly true to the object that it seeks to mirror. But such examples display human limitation at every point. By revelation, we grasp the possibility of other kinds of relationships in which such limits are overcome and they are exemplified in the mystery of God as Father, Son, and Holy Spirit. Such terms apply to but do not encompass this divine mystery; they *touch* but do not *grasp* their heavenly object. Rather, they point beyond themselves to the three persons who share one nature from all eternity, each of them equally God. However, they share this one divine nature in different ways that do not sunder but rather enhance the oneness of God. Thus the Trinity represents the summit of Christian revelation, an insight by faith and through revelation into the *dynamic unity* of God. Here Jewish monotheism on the one hand and pagan polytheism on the other are overcome in the mystery of one God in three persons. In effect, the three persons become the key to the oneness of God. The oneness of God's nature only exists as it passes from Father to Son and through the Son to the Holy Spirit. This dynamic quality of God's oneness is proper to a God of the living, not the dead, who reveals himself to Moses as the mystery of Being, according to Exodus 3:14.

Two trajectories run through the work of the Cappadocians. The first concerns terminology. One can trace the gradual evolution of the term *person* (*hypostasis*) as it begins to take on something close to a technical sense as distinct from *essence* (*ousia*).[45] But other terms are used as well to describe what is *one* in God and what is *three*.[46] Key is the distinctiveness of Father, Son, and Holy Spirit. The issue becomes not one of words but rather of the realities that they signify — the second trajectory. How do we explain the distinguishing characteristics of Father, Son, and Holy Spirit?[47] The Cappadocian turn to causal language is, in one sense, old and familiar: the language of derivation, used to describe how the Son and Spirit come forth from the Father for the purpose of creation and salvation. But now such language is shorn of all time-bound earthly association of change and dependence. Instead, it is transferred to the eternal realm in order to describe a continual divine process within the Godhead without beginning or end.[48] Father and Son — clearly relational terms — are divested of earthly limitations as well and used to illumine this eternal relatedness between a divine Father and his perfect Son, which includes the Holy Spirit as an essential moment.

Hence, the Father is described as *ungenerated* and *unbegotten*. He is the source and principle of the Son and Holy Spirit to which the tradition has consistently witnessed. This is his distinguishing characteristic. Yet all trace of earthly subordination is removed. The Son is *begotten* or *generated* from the Father. This is his distinguishing mark. As in John 15:26, the Spirit is described as *proceeding* from the Father. Since he completes the work of the Son, he may be said to proceed from the Father through the Son. This is the Holy Spirit's special characteristic. If generation and procession are "action" words, they now describe a continuing eternal process by which the Father begets the Son and the Holy Spirit proceeds from the Father through the Son. Theology will describe the particularities of each person in terms of their *mode of origin,* which per force is their *mode of existence* as well.

It should also be clear that while dogmatic formulas, crafted on the workbenches of theologians, are important, the deeper insight into the Trinity is often carried by metaphors in which human language reaches beyond itself. Hence the analogies of the spring from which water continually gushes and of the rainbow with its arc of light better illumine how Father, Son, and Holy Spirit comingle, forming a single God. What Sarah Coakley writes of Gregory of Nyssa captures the point: "What we are presented with is the idea of a unified *flow* of divine will and love, catching us up reflexively toward the light of the

'Father,' and allowing to the 'persons' only the minimally distinctive features of their different internal causal relations."[49]

All such theological discourse gives way to a profound sense of mystery that enshrouds the Trinity at every point. If Israel bequeathed to the Christian church a belief in one God, the doctrine of the Trinity seeks to rephrase that faith in dynamic terms in light of the revelation in Jesus and the gift of the Spirit. God is one, yet the key to this oneness is a dynamic, eternal process between Father, Son, and Holy Spirit. Hence, Father, Son, and Holy Spirit are distinct moments of a single God. It is the *paradox* of three persons in one God that is at the heart of the mystery. But if we are at the limits of human language straining to speak about what is beyond itself, it will also be important for just the same reason to fix the *public vocabulary* for describing the mystery of the Trinity.

This is the work of the Council of Constantinople.[50] This second ecumenical council translates these *theological* developments, however inchoately, into *doctrinal* terms, in effect, into *decisions* about the doctrine of the Trinity. The reserve about the Holy Spirit continues. The creed confesses, "And in the Holy Spirit, the Lord and Life-Giver, who proceeds from the Father, who is worshiped and glorified together with the Father and Son, who spoke by the prophets." The Spirit's divinity is clearly confessed, yet with a certain indirection. A letter of the Synod of Constantinople to Western bishops employs the actual vocabulary of *person* (*hypostasis*) and *substance* (*ousia*.)[51] What George Prestige writes about ancient creeds sets the right perspective: they "might be compared to accurate sign-posts rather than to exhaustive charts."[52] They point to the future but do not settle all details. Still, this is the way doctrines are forged. Yet the entire process — all terms and distinctions — is still "settling," gaining in density of meaning.

What do we learn about doctrinal development in the course of these earliest councils? Indeed the Councils of Nicea and Constantinople are meetings of bishops, but the emperor's presence is decisive. The emperors call the councils. Constantine attends. Theodosius follows the proceedings of Constantinople closely. By virtue of the emperor's authority, the creeds of the councils also have the force of civil law, compelling adherence and banishing opponents. But even here they function largely as signposts. Arian Christianity still finds a home among the Gothic tribes.

The cumulative impact of these first two councils is considerable. If they establish a public vocabulary about the Trinity, they also draw a sharp line between the world of the creator and those of all creatures below. Father, Son, and Spirit belong to the realm of the creator, the three persons signifying this continuous eternal process between these three coequal sharers in one divine nature. Theology will call this the *immanent* Trinity. The layered world of antiquity is thereby cut more sharply in two. In this sense, the decisions of these councils represent not a Hellenizing of Christianity but rather a departure from the regnant worldview of antiquity. This sharp line between creator and creatures will stand as a hallmark of the Christian faith.

But *within* the world of creatures there are considerable differences. Here the Christian cosmos is repopulated with another cast of characters. Some old faces appear with some new ones added as well. Although clearly creatures, the angels continue to act as God's messengers and lesser mediators for Christians in the world. Christian saints appear in heaven. Indeed, the church in heaven ceaselessly prays and intercedes for the church on earth.

Augustine and the West

Augustine's great work *On the Trinity,* written over a span of seventeen years, becomes the source of the standard Western interpretation of the Trinity, but for Augustine, it is "neither his last nor his only work on the Trinity."[53] Thomas Aquinas follows and sharpens Augustine's insights, thereby establishing this trinitarian theology as normative.

Augustine's contributions to trinitarian thought are innumerable. He realizes clearly that the *internal, invisible processions* within the Trinity manifest themselves in the *visible external missions* of the three persons in the world. He uses the category of relation to distinguish the three persons from one another. The Father is unbegotten, and the Son begotten. The Spirit proceeds from the Father *and* the Son. This becomes the distinguishing mark of Western trinitarian theology — *filioque* ("and the Son") — later inserted into the creed in the West. The persons are distinctive ways in which the one common nature is possessed. Hence, all actions of the Trinity in the world are the work of one God, attributed to one nature. By the same token, each person by the language of appropriation has its own proper role in this common work.

Augustine offers numerous analogies of the Trinity, twenty in *On the Trinity* alone. The most accessible is the triad of lover, beloved, and the bond of love that joins them together. Yet if the human person is made in the image and likeness of God (Gen. 1:26), the apex of the human mind offers a better basis for analogy. Thus the *psychological analogy* provides the best hint of how the three persons relate. Memory, understanding, and will in their mutual yet their distinctive roles give some sense of the restless unity of Father, Son, and Holy Spirit. If this is the best and highest analogy, Augustine nevertheless is aware of its limitations.[54] He also explicitly warns against identifying memory, understanding, and will with particular persons of the Trinity.[55] Such identification is too redolent of earthly, not heavenly, realities.

Yet it would be wrong to separate these analogies from one another. Indeed, they gain strength cumulatively. Their common purpose also becomes clear. By the use of analogies, Augustine does not offer a speculative exploration of the mystery of the Trinity, even less a theological explanation of the doctrine. His purpose is more modest and more spiritual. Rather, the psychological analogy, George Tavard writes, "explains how we, as human beings, can experience the Trinity in the exercise of our spiritual faculties. It provides a scale of ascent to God up to more and more adequate formulations of the image of God in us."[56]

Trinity in the East and West

The standard way of contrasting Greek and Latin thought on the Trinity usually follows this paradigm. Eastern thought — the Cappadocians are taken as a prime example — begins with the reality of the *three persons,* the "social Trinity." Unity becomes the derived category. This approach is said to be closer to Scripture and to human experience. By contrast, the West begins with the *unity* of the divine nature. Here Augustine is the exemplar. This approach is said to be more abstract and philosophical, closer to the later scholastic model of the Trinity.

Such a paradigm stems in large measure from an influential study on the Trinity by Théodore de Régnon (1831–1893) in the 1890s.[57]

In schematized form, it becomes the trinitarian gospel for much of twentieth-century theology. But, as Michael Barnes observes, "A belief in the existence of this Greek/Latin paradigm is a unique property of modern trinitarian theology."[58] In truth, de Regnon's paradigm of schematic contrasts as they hardened and were further simplified often became "misleading caricatures," according to Yves Congar.[59] This is not to say that there are not significant differences between East and West that were consciously recognized in antiquity, beginning with language. Gregory of Nazianzus and Basil regarded Latin language as an inferior vehicle to convey the subtleties of Greek thought.[60] But there are similarities too. The larger truth is that larger-than-life polar contrasts often steamroll historical truth, cloaking false assumptions. It is wrong to classify Gregory of Nyssa as a "social" trinitarian at all, argues Coakley.[61] Nor can Augustine's trinitarian thought be shoehorned into a single model without change or development, argues Barnes.[62]

Still, if the doctrine of the Trinity is finally formulated in simple terms — three persons in one God — there is probably a kernel of truth to some generalizations. Maurice Wiles may fairly capture the point:

> It is not possible for the human mind to hold its view of the three and the one in equal focus. One can give them equal value on the written page, but the mind needs to make its approach from one side or the other. The East (with the important exception of Athanasius) tends to approach from the side of the three, the West from the side of the one. When an Easterner spoke of God he thought most naturally of the Father, with whom the Son and the Spirit must somehow be joined in one coequal godhead. When a Westerner spoke of God he thought most naturally of the one Triune God, within whose being real distinctions of persons must somehow be admitted.[63]

The deeper truth may be that it is ultimately a matter of secondary importance whether the mystery of the Trinity is approached from the side of one or of three. Such approaches are comparable to different routes of ascent in scaling a tall mountain peak. The heart of the mystery is three-persons-in-one-God, all parts inseparably bound together. Although the route of ascent may be different, the *ineffable mystery* of the Triune God is the paramount issue. The mystery probably can be equally appreciated from either side of the mountain.

Recent Trinitarian Theology

Interest in the Trinity has flourished in recent years. Anne Hunt traces the course of the various streams of modern trinitarian thought under the heading of "interconnection."[64] *The Trinity can be linked to Christology, church, ecology, world religions, ministry, spirituality and worship, grace and the moral life, human liberation, and eschatology. A common thread running through these burgeoning theologies is a movement away from the classical* psychological analogy *of Augustine and Thomas Aquinas.* The social-interpersonal model *of the Trinity has now moved to the fore. The social model is also closer to Eastern trinitarian thought. Hunt explains its contemporary appeal: "The social model is attractive and well suited to the theological goals of liberation theology of various kinds — for example Latin American theology (Leonardo Boff), feminist theology (Catherine LaCugna), eco-theology (Dennis Edwards) — and to ecclesiology (John Zizioulas.)"*[65]

Our interest here is in terms of doctrine, *the movement away from the psychological analogy, in effect, the break with the normative treatment of the Trinity in the scholastic tradition. If trinitarian theology now flourishes, it may be because a particular* doctrinal logjam *was broken. In this regard, we focus on the first third of Karl Rahner's 1967 essay "The Trinity."*[66] *The section represents nothing less than a stinging indictment of the scholastic treatment of the doctrine. The standard treatment on the Trinity was divided into two parts, "God as One"* (de Deo Uno), *then "God as Three"* (de Deo Trino). *Everything essential about God was said in the first part. The actual section on the Trinity became a compendium of abstract terms about the inner workings of the three divine persons, its five notions, four properties, three persons, and two missions.*

The core of the problem was that the traditional trinitarian dictum — all actions of the Trinity in the world (ad extra) *are attributable to the nature, not the persons — had the effect of making the Trinity's action in creation and redemption appear not tripersonal but rather impersonal. These were the actions of the common nature. Hence the accent on "God as One." The missions of the Trinity in the world seemed reduced to almost nominal designations, honorary flags flown by Father, Son, and Spirit. Conclusion: the trinitarian God in the scholastic tradition had become a unitarian deity. It was also puzzling why the series of internal trinitarian distinctions were revealed to us in the first place. They surely were mysteries in the strict sense. What was the purpose of this strange message that sailed so far over our heads? It certainly touched no one's salvation. Instead of the Trinity's role in the drama of salvation, we were offered a rarified description of the inner workings of the Godhead, which seemed abstract and arcane.*

In effect, the economic Trinity seemed to have been reabsorbed back into the immanent one, the three persons becoming vestigial organs whose actual functions had shriveled. In truth, the doctrine of the Trinity in the Scholastic tradition represented an atrophied version of the original, which had lost its voice to speak. Instead, a unitarian God was proclaimed whose persons were diminished, if not at times subject to outright replacement. In this regard, the working Catholic Trinity often became God, Christ, and the Blessed Virgin Mary, who had absorbed the duties of the Holy Spirit as consoler and advocate.

But Catholics were not alone. The great reformulation of Protestant dogmatics by Friedrich Schleiermacher (1768–1834), The Christian Faith, *relegated the Trinity to a concluding postscript. The Trinity, he maintained, "is not an immediate utterance concerning Christian self-consciousness, but only a combination of several such utterances."[67] The Trinity has been taken more seriously in twentieth-century Protestant and Catholic thought. Karl Barth (1886–1968) proposes "mode of being"[68] and Karl Rahner "manner of subsisting"[69] as clarifications of the traditional trinitarian term* person. *But George Tavard surely is correct when he comments, "It is certainly no improvement to replace the relatively clear term, person, which is rich in human and spiritual experience, by obscure paraphrases."[70]*

Finally, the Trinity in Roman Catholic circles has become in recent years a lynchpin of a "theology of communion," which emerged at Vatican II. In turn, this "theology of communion" has become a master-concept for understanding many forms of church life and ministry from a fresh perspective.

Chapter Six

CHRIST
AND THE CHURCH

Although the focus of this chapter is the church, I have entitled it "Christ and the Church." This is to underscore from the start the intimate relationship between the risen Christ and the community of his followers. In the first chapter, "God in the Old Testament," I sought to emphasize the close relationship between Yahweh and the community brought into existence by the revelation of God's name. Then I followed the subsequent interplay between Israel's understanding of God and the tribe, then the nation, and finally the religious community in which this faith was nourished. This relationship becomes even closer in the Christian community. In this chapter, I trace the relationship between Christ and the church in three stages.

First, I explore the experience of the resurrection and the origins of the church, building on Jesus' call of the Twelve. In this context, I will indicate also how each subsequent Christology contains its own inchoate vision of the church.

Second, I note the various images of the church that remain remarkably stable throughout the first centuries of the community's life. These are largely compatible, not competitive, visions.

Third, the doctrinal turning point occurs at the third and fourth ecumenical councils, the Councils of Ephesus and Chalcedon, in which the person of Christ becomes the object of dogmatic definition: one person in two natures, human and divine. These *christological* definitions have a direct *ecclesiological* impact, thereafter dividing the Christian

175

community on the basis of incompatible visions of the person of Christ and salvation in his name.

I. Experience and the Scriptures

We begin once again with that dense ball of experience, the risen Jesus come back from the dead. As we have seen, the experience of the risen Jesus generates a series of interlocking questions. Certainly among the first is this: *Who is Jesus and what will he do now?* We pursued this question as we traced the development of Christology. But implicit in this first question, *Who is Jesus?* is a second one: *Who, in light of Jesus, is God?* As the revelation of Jesus comes into focus, as Jesus is confessed as divine, it becomes clear that the community is in the process of thinking about God in a radically new way. Yet this is not first a thought experiment. God is *experienced* in a new way in light of Jesus' resurrection and the gift of the Spirit. It will take four centuries for this experience to give a satisfactory account of itself so that God can be confessed in a new way. The Councils of Nicea and Constantinople lay down the markers of this Triune confession of faith — one God in three persons — the subject of the preceding chapter.

Yet the initial question is still more layered, and in this section we return to separate another strand of this complex experience of the risen Christ, come back from the dead: *Who, in light of Jesus, are we?* In other words, the experience of the risen Jesus also defines the role of his followers, both *individually* and as a *community*. The way one understands the risen Lord determines also what it means to be his follower. In pursuing this line of thought, the disciples follow a path that Jesus himself had opened. He taught his disciples to call God *Abba,* and so to see themselves as God's children. So we receive from Jesus the first and enduring image of what it means to be his disciple — *a child* — to whom God is Father.

Discipleship

Now this image is given special focus in light of Jesus' death and resurrection. We begin with Mark's Gospel, where this point is made most sharply. After the pivotal scene at Caesarea Philippi (Mark 8:27–30), in which Peter misunderstands Jesus' identity (Mark 8:32–33), three predictions of the passion follow (Mark 9:30–10:45). Each time as Jesus predicts his passion, the disciples misunderstand their own role, prompting Jesus to instruct them on what it means to follow him. He holds before them children, and says, "Truly, I tell you, whoever does not receive the kingdom as a little child will never enter it" (Mark 10:15). But the overarching teaching about discipleship is plainly stated directly after Caesarea Philippi: "If any want to become my followers, let them deny themselves and take up their cross and follow me" (Mark 8:34). Jesus is a crucified messiah. Those who follow him must be willing to take up their cross as well.

The entire section is enclosed by two stories about the cure of blind men (Mark 8:22–26; 10:46–52). These stories become bookends, as it were, enclosing the tale of the spiritual blindness of Jesus' disciples. They fail to recognize Jesus as a suffering messiah. They also fail to understand their own role as his followers. Indeed, the blindness of the disciples in Mark's Gospel becomes a foil to develop two themes that are intertwined: Jesus' own identity and what it means to be the follower of a crucified messiah. Conclusion: as disciples define Jesus, they define what it means to follow him.

The role of Jesus' followers is treated more favorably in the other Gospels. So too Jesus' natural family. Luke includes them among his followers, and this how they appear at Pentecost in the book of Acts (Acts 1:14). The role of women deserves special mention both during his lifetime and among the first generation of his followers.[1]

Images of the Church as Community

The images of the church as a *community* also begin with Jesus himself. Jesus calls the Twelve. As we noted, the number *twelve* is significant, hearkening back to the twelve patriarchs and the twelve tribes of Israel. In Jesus' usage, it also looks forward to the coming of the kingdom. When the kingdom arrives in its fullness, the Twelve — starter shoots of new growth — will expand in every way. They are described as eschatological judges of this new Israel (Matt. 19:28; Luke 22:30). Thus the earliest vision of the church as a whole is born. The church is a new Israel, a new people of God. We can also see how this vision connects with the Christology of the earliest community. Recall that Jesus' resurrection is the first act of a two-act play. The disciples wait for

him to return as the *Son of Man* to complete his work and inaugurate
the kingdom in its fullness. They consequently see themselves as a *new
people of God,* awaiting this momentous event. They look to the East in
expectation of the Son of Man's return. The future note in the church's
prayer and worship comes from this earliest vision. The disciples pray,
"Our Lord, come!" (1 Cor. 16:22). They celebrate the Eucharist as an
anticipation of the banquet feast of heaven: "For as often as you eat
this bread and drink this cup, you proclaim the Lord's death until he
come" (1 Cor. 11:26). Noteworthy is that both these earliest images —
Jesus as the Son of Man and the church as the new Israel — function
within the limits of inherited Jewish beliefs. In other words, the early
church stands within Judaism of the day, awaiting Jesus' return as the
Messiah, understanding the community itself as the beginning of a
new people of God, shortly to grow into full stature.

The church as the new Israel also establishes a series of trajectories
of interpretation as the image is adapted to new situations. It appears
in Paul's letter to the Galatians (Gal. 3:6–29). Here it is used to explain
how the children of Abraham, Gentiles and Jews alike, can comprise a
new people of God, heirs to the promise made to their common father
in faith. The image appears again in 1 Peter. Here the community is
told explicitly, "Now you are God's people" (1 Pet. 2:10). Thus the
titles given to Israel on Mount Sinai (Exod. 19:1–6) are now transferred to the church: "a chosen race, a royal priesthood, a holy nation,
God's own people" (1 Pet. 2:9).

The Mission

Just as Christology changes in the Gentile mission, so too its accom-
panying vision of the church will grow. It was in Antioch that "the
disciples were first called Christians" (Acts 11:26). Now the church's
self-understanding begins to chart a course beyond the boundaries
of Judaism. But it does not do this in a single, unitary way; rather,
the Gentile mission itself produces a series of differing visions of
the church. Such visions are always connected to an understanding
of Christ as the highest angle of the community's aspirations, but
they also display traces of the differing ways communities have separated themselves from Judaism. Some remain close to their Jewish
roots (Matthew, James, 1 Peter). For others, the parting is bitter

and acrimonious (John, Hebrews, Revelation). For still others, some reconciliation between Jews and Gentiles is envisioned (Romans, Ephesians). If the elevated vision of Christ is one point of reference, practical concerns in the parting of ways also play a role.

In what follows, we begin by examining the Pauline vision of the church and its expansion in the letters to the Colossians and the Ephesians. Here the community takes the precedence, and the individual's role comes into focus in these larger communal terms. The vision of the church in the Gospel of John is different. Here the relationship of the individual believer to Christ is the primary focus. The community is the resulting group of individual believers. Each of these visions also contains inchoate attitudes toward church structure. We will close this section by considering the Gospel of Matthew because the church occupies a special place in that Gospel. In the same context, we will examine Peter's role as bridge builder in the early Christian community.

The Body of Christ

The great cry of the Pauline mission — "Jesus is Lord!" — becomes in capsule form its leading vision of Christ. Jesus remains, of course, the Son of Man, who is expected to return, and the church remains the new Israel. But above all now, Jesus is Lord! This exultant cry will later swell into an expanded vision of the risen Christ as Lord of the cosmos (Col. 1:15–20). But first, Jesus is Lord of the community. His rule is experienced firsthand in the gifts and charisms showered on his followers. A great vision is born. The church is the body of Christ. A luminous example of how Christ and the church are joined together is 1 Corinthians 12:1–27.

The passage is remarkable, first of all, because of its impromptu character. Here we catch Paul preaching to a live audience whose problems remain palpable. The community seems to suffer from an overabundance of charismatic gifts — too much spirit. Therefore Paul faces the delicate task of affirming individual gifts while encouraging members of the community to work together harmoniously. Toward that end, he holds up the image of a *coordinated body* in which each member plays a part in a common endeavor. Each is irreplaceable. None are interchangeable. Ultimately, no member is more important than any other.

But Paul's impromptu instruction contains, on another level, striking insights. Josiah Royce writes, "A community is not a mere collection of individuals. It is a sort of live unit, that has organs as the body of an individual has organs.... Not only does the community live, it has a mind of its own — a mind whose psychology is not the same as the psychology of an individual human being."[2] Later Royce writes specifically about the body of Christ: "The risen Lord dwells in it, and is its life. It is as much a person as he was when he walked the earth. And he is as much the spirit of the community as he is a person."[3]

In just this way, Jesus' indwelling spirit makes the community into the body of Christ, whose members are likened to limbs of a single organism. The body of Christ also seems to have a life of its own. This is the point of harmonious cooperation. Certainly, belonging to it is not like membership in a club. The relationship is more intimate and organic because the animating force is the spirit of the risen Jesus. This spirit manifests itself in the gifts and charism of the members. But gifts are never individually bestowed. They are given for the common good, not for individual adornment or pleasure.

The image of the body of Christ in 1 Corinthians 12 surely stands on the basis of a widespread experience of community in the Pauline mission. In its suggestiveness, it also represents the starting point for subsequent trajectories. Within the Pauline letters, the image is quickly universalized, taking on cosmic dimensions. In the hymn in Colossians, Jesus is called "the image of the invisible God, the firstborn of all creation" (Col. 1:15); "he is head of the body, the church" (Col. 1:18); "for in him all the fullness of God was pleased to dwell to reconcile to himself all things, whether on earth or in heaven through the blood of his cross" (Col. 1:19–20). By this reckoning, the church as Christ's body contains angelic spirits as well. The letter to the Ephesians expands the contrast between Christ as *head* and the church as his *body:* "We must grow up in every way into him who is the head, into Christ, from whom the whole body, joined and knit together by every ligament with which it is equipped, as each part is working properly, promotes the body's growth in building itself up in love" (Eph. 4:15–16).

The earlier image of the body of Christ uses the analogy of a *coordinated body* whose limbs work harmoniously together (Rom. 12:4–5;

1 Cor. 12–14). Here the focus is on the local community. As the image is universalized, the analogy shifts. Now the contrast is between Christ, who is the heavenly *head* of the church, which is his *body*, his earthly extension. Thus the image becomes a way of understanding the universal church. The church also becomes *the* church in a more exalted sense. The book of Acts refers to the church (*ekklesia*) both as the local congregation (Acts 1:13; 2:42; 12:12) and as the universal church (Acts 9:31; 15:14).

But the common denominator is what interests us. Jesus, a single individual, becomes in his risen life a *zone of personal presence*. He becomes a *social* reality, animating the community of his followers from within. He is present in the gifts and charisms that enliven members from within. These are all workings of his Spirit. In this sense, the communal dimension of the church takes precedence. In terms of individual discipleship in Mark's Gospel, Jesus himself is a model of how the disciples should act: "If any want to become my followers, let them deny themselves and take up their cross and follow me" (Mark 8:34). But in the community, his spirit enters the lives of his followers and comingles with their own spirit. In this sense, Jesus' spirit *enables* them from within to act as they should. It surely enables them to pray as Jesus did, to call God *Abba*, Father (Rom. 8:16). And if it does that, what else can it fail to do? In Colossians and Ephesians, Christ is not simply a social reality; he is a *cosmic* one. He is present in all churches, and here the church universal becomes an overarching zone of presence, linking heaven and earth.

The community, so understood, also receives its defining marks. The church is where the spirit of Jesus dwells. Hence the church is a *community of presence*. The church also becomes a *community of interpretation* in which Jesus' memory is preserved and the meaning of his death and resurrection is interpreted.[4]

In this sense, the church stands in a unique relationship to the other questions that we have examined: *Who is Jesus? Who, in light of Jesus, is God?* The church is the community that asks and then answers these questions. This also means that the church does not first speak about itself. It may seem odd that the first explicit tracts on the church date from the early 1300s. In another sense, it is not odd at all. The church is that community in which Jesus' spirit continues to live, that interprets for its members and for all who would listen what God has done in the life, death, and resurrection of Jesus and in the gift of his spirit. The church speaks first about God and Christ, their presence and their work. In Colossians and Ephesians, it also receives another mark of Christ's presence: the church is *holy*. It is significant that in his letter to the Romans, Paul holds up the image of an olive tree to represent the eventual reconciliation of Jews and Gentiles. The wild olive branch (the Gentiles) will finally grow together with the natural shoot (the Jewish people). The two will be reconciled. Ephesians strikes a similar note. Christ's blood will break down the dividing wall, the hostility between Jew and Gentile. The church is described here as the "household of God, built on the foundation of the apostles and prophets, with Christ Jesus himself as the cornerstone" (Eph. 2:20).

The Vine and the Branches, the Shepherd and the Sheepfold

Nowhere is the link between Jesus and his followers closer than in the Gospel of John, but in a quite unique way. In the other Gospels, Jesus preaches about God's kingdom, present in his ministry, awaited in its fullness. All such language of the kingdom now disappears, with a single exception (John 3:3, 5). It is replaced by characteristic self-identifying statements from Jesus — for example, "I am the bread of life" (John 6:35, 41, 51); "I am the light of the world" (John 8:12; 9:5); "I am the resurrection and the life" (John 11:25). For John, Jesus represents the Father's presence fully realized here and now and available to his disciples. All such statements are expressed in the present tense because they describe Jesus' presence to each of his followers as well.

But these followers have been expelled from the synagogue (John 9:22; 16:2). They regard Judaism not just as another religion but rather as a hostile force. Jewish rituals are not reinterpreted for Christian use; they are replaced. Jesus himself refers to the Torah as "their law" (John 15:25). In sum, the rupture with Judaism is now complete and tinged with bitterness. Its source: the community's estimation of Jesus as God's preexistent Word — as God (John 1:1; 20:29). It seems clear that the precondition — the price — of this piercing insight into

Christ's divinity is in the first instance a rupture with the community's Jewish coreligionists. This is how the Jews regarded it. In an analogous way, the breakthrough to a pure monotheism at the time of the exile — Yahweh as the one God, the only God — was connected to the disappearance of the visible symbols of Israel's special election: the destruction of the temple, the collapse of the monarchy, the fall of Jerusalem. Here some severance with Judaism seems a precondition of the clear confession of Christ's divinity that animates the Gospel of John from start to finish. Perhaps an insight of such high-voltage shocks and electrifies before it consoles and brings a community together.

The insight certainly animates John's two images of the church. Jesus is the shepherd. "I am the good shepherd" (John 10:11), and his followers are the sheep of his flock. He knows each one by name and he lays down his life for them. In John 15, the image shifts but the logic remains the same: "I am the vine, you are the branches" (John 15:5). Each of the branches is individually connected to the Christ, the life-giving vine. This is why they can bear much fruit. But how are the branches connected to one another? How do the individual sheep comprise a flock? They know their Lord as shepherd and as vine in an ongoing personal relationship that is the source of their life. This is the only answer that the Gospel offers. In a positive sense, these images underscore the unique and mysterious way that each follower of Jesus is joined to the risen Lord. But that very uniqueness has a splintering potential.

The way Raymond Brown describes the Fourth Gospel surely applies to its portrait of Jesus: a diamond whose brilliant facets glitter because they have been cut sharp and polished by the chisel and hammer blows of controversy and opposition. But the ultimate danger, he observes, is "that the final blow splits the diamond itself because of an internal flaw."[5]

The combination of this Gospel's exalted Christology with the highly personal and individualized relationship of every believer to Christ carries a considerable potential to splinter a community. This is the flaw. The combination is made all the more volatile because of the Gospel's single-minded, consistent vision. No surprise, then, that the rupture with Judaism is followed by divisions within the community with about the same degree of bitterness. Once again, the source is an estimate of Jesus. Some in the community have now discounted Jesus' humanity (1 John 4:2; 2 John 7). But it could be argued that such views are consistent with several facets of the diamond, with the portrait of Jesus who displays not only no human weakness, but not even a simple lack of knowledge. Sectarians also seem to regard as the only sin a refusal to believe in Jesus (1 John 1:8, 10). The relationship of the believer to Christ becomes all the closer.

If the language of the kingdom is absent from John's Gospel, so too is the notion of "apostle," as it is also from the Johannine Epistles. The operative term in John is *disciple,* followers who are coequal with one another. Thus there is no reason in this community to have teachers who are especially charged with passing down the traditions. Jesus will send the Paraclete. The Spirit is teacher enough. The individual relationship with Jesus continues in the gift of the Paraclete — lawyer, teacher, prosecutor. In a community of coequal disciples, women occupy a special role. This was in general the case in the Gospel tradition and for Paul. Now the emphasis is heightened. The conversion of the Samaritan woman brings an entire village to believe in Jesus (John 4:39). Peter's confession in Matthew 16:17 is placed on the lips of Martha: "You are the Christ, the Son of God" (John 11:27). Mary Magdalene, not Peter, is the first to see the risen Christ (John 20:14). At the cross, Mary, the mother of the Lord, becomes the model for all disciples.

In one sense, the highly individual character of each disciple in John's community — each one with a special channel to the Paraclete — will not make community members receptive to church structure. The Pauline churches, with the steady emphasis on community, will adopt more positive attitudes. Cast as directive from a dying Paul to Timothy and Titus, the Pastoral Epistles indicate as much. The role of women in those letters is also more traditional. By contrast, the sectarian dynamic of John's community means that while it may act as a critique of the church's life, it is not a source of the community's abiding identity.

Indicative of such shift in emphasis is the addition of a final chapter, John 21, to the already completed Gospel. In effect, it appears that John's community has gone into ecclesiastical receivership to the larger church, whose representative figure is Peter. In that chapter, Peter appears first as fisherman or missionary, then as shepherd or pastor. Yet Jesus questions him three times about his care for the sheep of this flock. Peter must pass the test set down by Jesus himself as the measure of a good shepherd. He must lay down his life for his flock.

Matthew's Gospel and the Figure of Peter

The Gospel of Matthew is the only Gospel to use the word *church* (Matt. 16:17), and this is entirely fitting. Matthew inserts the church into the very center of Jesus' public ministry. The scene at Caesarea Philippi about Jesus' identity is transformed in this Gospel into a church-founding event. Here Peter *rightly* identifies Jesus as the Messiah: "You are the Messiah, the Son of the Living God" (Matt. 16:17). Jesus answers, "Blessed are you, Simon son of Jonah! For flesh and blood has not revealed this to you, but my Father in heaven. And I tell you, you are Peter, and on this rock I will build my church and the gates of Hades will not prevail against it" (Matt. 16:17–18). Therefore, in the midst of the public ministry, on the basis of Peter's confession, Jesus himself founds the church, which will last until the end of time.

There is a balance and solidity to the picture of the church that Matthew presents. Jesus has not come to abolish the law and the prophets but rather to fulfill them (Matt. 5:17). He has come to preach a radicalized Torah. Hence, Jewish ethical teaching combines with an openness to Gentile converts. The final command of Jesus in the Gospel contains Matthew's vision of the church's mission: "Go therefore and makes disciples of all nations" (Matt. 28:19). The Gospel also envisions that authority will be exercised decisively. Peter is given the "keys of the kingdom of heaven" (Matt. 16:19), reminiscent of Isaiah 22:22, the powers given to a prime minister. Yet the Gospel displays considerable nuance in the way it deals with pastoral problems within the community (Matt. 18).

Part of the solidity of the Gospel is linked to the figure of Peter. Peter is a historical personage, but he also quickly becomes a symbolic one as well. We noted the latter quality in John 21. The development is natural and understandable. Peter is the leader of the Twelve, whom Jesus calls during his lifetime. He is also the first witness to the resurrection (1 Cor. 15:5). He then becomes the leader of the early community in Jerusalem. Peter is also the only one of the Twelve who subsequently becomes a missionary. We are informed about his career from the Pauline letters, the book of Acts, and the letters in the Petrine tradition. As a missionary, Peter is mentioned in the Corinthian community (1 Cor. 1:12). His encounter with Paul in Antioch is related at some length (Gal. 2:11–14). He dies in Rome in the 60s. By the time of Clement of Rome, Peter and Paul are regarded as pillars of the church of Rome.[6] From Jesus in Galilee to Jerusalem represents step one in his career. Step two takes Peter from Jerusalem via Corinth and Antioch to Rome. This single historical figure who traverses not only geographic distances but also differing symbolic epochs in the church's life acquires for himself a considerable symbolic valence — Peter as a bridge builder between churches and generations.

Images of the Church

Other exalted Christologies refer to Jesus' followers in different ways. The letter to the Hebrews begins by describing Christ as "the reflection of God's glory and the exact imprint of God's very being, sustaining all things by his powerful word" (Heb. 1:3). Here this exalted Christology is used to develop a traditional theme: the meaning of Jesus' sacrificial death. Hebrews describes Jesus as a great high priest "according to the order of Melchizedek" (Heb. 5:6). Melchizedek is without forebears or progeny. Therefore, he can act as precursor and model of Christ, the eternal high priest, who offers a unique sacrifice of his own blood. In Christ, priest and victim become one. But ultimately, Christ as the great high priest enters the heavenly sanctuary so that he can intercede more effectively for his followers on earth. He also becomes the mediator of a new covenant on the basis of his sacrifice (Rev. 8:6; cf. Jer. 31:31–34). The letter to the Hebrews is notable in the way it combines an exalted Christology with generous admission of Jesus' humanity as one who can "sympathize with our weakness" (Heb. 4:15) and who, though without sin, has been tested in every way.

The book of Revelation combines an elevated Christology with reference to the church in another way. Certainly the Christology of Revelation is sophisticated. God is described as "the Alpha and the Omega" (Rev. 1:8). Christ, the slain Lamb, speaks of himself as "the first and the last" (Rev. 1:17; 2:8), with a clear allusion to Isaiah 44:6.

In other words, God and Christ are described in the same language, and the intent is evident: Jesus, the slain Lamb, is divine. But here the exalted Christ in heaven shows solicitude for seven particular churches on earth, sending each one a message tailored to its special needs. In some cases, the message warns of false teaching; in others, the danger is complacency; in still others, encouragement in the face of persecution is primacy. But, above all, the book of Revelation delivers a great vision of consolation to all of Jesus' followers. In the final, great battle, the slain Lamb conquers all adversaries, dragons and beasts (Rome and the worship of the emperor), establishing an earthly reign of one thousand years (and a conundrum for Christians ever since).

The New Testament contains many other images of the church. In this regard, the treatment given here is representative, not exhaustive. Many images contain the note of mutuality that we have seen elsewhere. The letter to the Ephesians compares Christ's love of the church to the relationship between a husband and wife (Eph. 5:31–33). The church is also described as "a cultivated field" (1 Cor. 3:9). Jesus' parable of the wheat and the weeds seems to refer to the church as the "kingdom" of the Son (Matt. 13:24–30, 36–43). The church as the "God's building" (1 Cor. 3:9) elicits extended trajectories. Christ is the "stone which the builders rejected which has become the cornerstone" (Matt. 21:42; cf. Acts 4:11; 1 Pet. 2:7; Ps. 118:22). The apostles and prophets are said to be the church's foundation with Christ as the cornerstone (Eph. 2:20–21), the building's foundation (1 Cor. 3:11). The church's members are described as "living stones" (1 Pet. 2:5). The church is also called the "household of God" (1 Tim. 3:15). Finally, the church is called the "new Jerusalem" (Rev. 21:2), "Jerusalem which is above" (Gal. 4:26), "the city of the living God, the heavenly Jerusalem" (Heb. 12:22–23). Here the church's "preexistence" enters. That is, the church was envisioned in some sense as part of God's plan from all eternity. Hence, the new Israel was contained in the old, antedating creation itself. This theme is developed by the church fathers, appearing already in Clement of Rome and the *Shepherd of Hermas.*[7] In the Shepherd of Hermas, the church appears as an old woman, created before the world began, who becomes progressively younger.

II. Theology

We have proceeded on the assumption that the way a community envisions the risen Christ contains its own self-definition as a church and
of what it means to be a follower of Jesus individually. This is the
community's angle of aspiration. But other practical concerns also determine the nature of the church. As we noted, a leading one is the
nature of each community's departure from its Jewish forebears in the
first generation. Did it remain close to its Jewish roots? Was the rupture with Judaism bitter and complete? Did it envision an eventual
reconciliation between Jews and Gentiles?

However, with the passage of time, these circumstances of departure
fade. On the one hand, the decision against Marcion establishes Christianity's essential link to the Old Testament; on the other hand, interaction with the Jewish synagogue is no longer an event of the daily life.
This means that the great visions of the church created by the New Testament shed the vicissitudes of origin the way a series of rockets, once
launched, jettison the engines that fueled them into orbit. Consequently,
different images of the church are interpreted as largely compatible.
Perhaps John's Gospel never fully distances itself from its origins, its
bitter polemic against the Jews regarded as fuel for anti-Semitic sentiments over the centuries. Still, the first and most obvious point is that
the images of the church in the New Testament, though they differ in
accent, usually are interpreted as compatible with one another.

Still, the underlying tensions among these images are important.
They remain, giving the Christian vision of the church torque or
counterpoint, source of both creativity and tension in the future. The
difference between the Pauline emphasis on the *community* and the Johannine emphasis on the *individual* is clear enough. But within the
Pauline orbit itself, which takes precedence, the *local* church or the
church *universal*? And how does the mystical notion of the church as
the new Jerusalem, its preexistence in God's plan from all eternity, relate to the church's historical existence, a church of saints and sinners?
All of these images underscore the fact that the church from the start
is envisioned in diverse ways. Each of them captures and magnifies
an angle of the whole. Nothing less than the entire ensemble can do
justice to the reality of the church.

Differing Paths of Developments

We trace in this section two lines of development in the church's subsequent understanding of itself. An image from Paul's first letter to the Corinthians captures the first of these paths, the way different but related limbs grow from a single body. I term these elements of *continuous growth,* ligatures that tie the church together. The emergence of ecclesiastical office and the growth of sacramental life illustrate this side of the ledger. The second line of development relates to elements of *discontinuity,* the way the churches grow apart on significant matters of faith. This is how I will describe the great christological controversies of the fifth century. Their effect on the ancient churches is to split them asunder on the basis of differing visions of Christ and the meaning of salvation in his name. Together, these lines of development also underscore that the empirical unity of the church in this world is never more than partial; the true oneness of the church remains an eschatological gift, bestowed by Christ of the end time.

Church Office

I described the beginnings of church office in an earlier chapter, how the church's missionary effort in the first generation gave way to the need for stable pastors in each local church in the second. In the process, a two-tiered structure of church office appears: presbyter-bishops and deacons. Such is the church of the 80s, reflected in 1 Peter, the book of Acts, and the Pastoral Epistles. We also noted the special qualities called for in these local leaders: they should be dependable men who are able to manage their own households; not recent converts, not lovers of money, and not overly fond of drink. If a special talent is needed, it is the quality of a teacher. These leaders must teach "sound doctrine," refute error, and hold the community together. In sum, they should embody the best of institutional virtues. In this sense, the rationale of office in the second generation is functional. There is no connection of these presbyter-bishops and deacons with the Eucharist or baptism. Although charismatic elements do not disappear in these churches, they are no longer the tone-setters in this generation.[8]

In one sense, the development of church office to this point seems to represent a prime example of the routinization of the spirit in the face of the practical needs of the community. The picture is also quite self-contained and makes sense. And so it spreads. In the last decades of the first century, similar structures appear in the churches descended from the three great apostolic figures, Paul, James, and Peter, and perhaps, a while later and reluctantly, in the churches of John as well.

Against this background, the turn that church office takes in Ignatius of Antioch is striking. We saw earlier that the threefold structure of bishop-priest-deacon emerges here, reflecting the churches of Antioch and of Western Asia minor, not of Philippi, Corinth, or Rome. But Ignatius's threefold template was a harbinger of the future. I also described Ignatius as a charismatic, a martyr, setting him apart from the stolid presbyter-bishops of the Pastoral Epistles. But what is notable, above all, is the identification of the bishop with the Eucharist.

Ignatius writes, "Take care, therefore, to participate in one Eucharist (for there is one flesh of our Lord Jesus Christ, and one cup which leads to unity through his blood; there is one altar, just as there is one bishop, together with the presbytery and the deacons, my fellow servants), in order that whatever you do, you do in accordance with God."[9] Francis Sullivan comments, "The sequence 'one Eucharist, one altar, one bishop' shows that for Ignatius the unity of the church is profoundly rooted in the 'one flesh and one cup' of the Eucharist and in the person of the bishop who presided at it."[10]

There are two intersecting poles of church office that emerge here with clarity for the first time. A single bishop presiding over a church guarantees stability. Strong leadership assures that true doctrine is taught and error confounded. This comprises the *functional* rationale of church office that emerges in the Pastoral Epistles and the church of the 80s. Ignatius adds a second note: the bishop's practical duties must be anchored in a deeper, spiritual source. This is the significance of the bishop's connection to baptism and, above all, the Eucharist. Here a striking identification is made and a template for the future is forged. The church's deepest *inner* source of unity, the Eucharist, is connected to its most visible, *external* symbol, the office of bishop. The community then needs a personified symbol of its encompassing unity that goes from *inner* source to *outer* expression. This emerges first in regard to the office of bishop. But as the various levels of unity in the church appear, the same need for a personified symbol will be felt. In other words, the assumption in faith and in fact is that the church is *one*. The bishop is symbol and agent of this unity in the local church. As the church becomes aware of itself as *one* regional church, the office of metropolitan appears. As the church becomes aware of itself as *one* church universal, the office of pope emerges as its symbol and center. But on every level, the connection with the Eucharist, the church's deepest source of unity, is essential to the actual function of church office as its symbol and agent in the world.[11]

Sacramental Life

The church's sacramental life emerges from the interaction between the sacrament's *inner* meaning and the *external* rites that seek to express it as the church's life grows and develops. For the Eucharist and baptism, the scriptural sources lay down clear markers. In regard to the Eucharist, the words of institution in the Gospels and 1 Corinthians, although in two variant forms, establish both symbols and their meaning in rather explicit terms: bread and wine, Jesus' body and blood. They look back to Jesus' sacrificial death and make it present in the liturgy. They also look forward to the banquet feast of heaven. In all cases, a *symbolic* dimension (bread and wine) and a *real* one (Jesus' body and blood) are inseparably intertwined. However, these notes allow for considerable difference in emphasis. The symbolic dimension of the Eucharist resonates more strongly with the Alexandrians, Clement and Origen. In the West, for Hippolytus and Tertullian, the identification of the consecrated elements with Christ's body and blood seems more straightforward. But both *real* and *symbolic* dimensions of the Eucharist are original, essential, and inseparable parts of the sacrament.

By contrast, baptism is an exfoliating sacrament that will split off in different directions in succeeding centuries. From the start, the sacrament has distinct moments. Tertullian summarizes the gifts of baptism under four headings: remission of sins, deliverance from death, regeneration, and the gift of the Holy Spirit.[12] Therefore, on the one hand, baptism means the remission of sins and deliverance from death. In Paul's words, we are baptized into the death and resurrection of Christ (Rom. 6:1–11). The symbolism of washing captures the dimension of deliverance. On the other hand, baptism also means the gift of the spirit and regeneration, which can also be called enlightenment or illumination. Here the spirit imprints a seal, making a person into a member of the church. It is not surprising that this second moment will seek its own symbolic expression. A rite of anointing and the laying on of hands are soon joined to the rite of washing. In the West, there is a growing tendency to focus the gift of the Spirit on these later rites.[13]

The baptism of adults is the earliest practice of the church, but the baptism of infants becomes the norm in subsequent centuries, mandatory in the West in light of Augustine's doctrine of original sin, since even an infant who dies without baptism can incur eternal damnation.

In later centuries, the laying on of hands and the rite of anointing take on a life of their own, becoming a separate sacrament. In the West, these rites were reserved to the bishop and given to children between the ages of seven and twelve, considered the age of discretion. This rite was regarded as a "strengthening" of the gift of the Spirit given in baptism, hence the name "confirmation." The name first appears in the second canon of the First Council of Orange (441).[14]

The remission of sins given in baptism also has a second life in subsequent centuries. However, the course of its development is difficult and complex. It focuses on the forgiveness of sins committed *after* baptism, especially the so-called irremissable sins: apostasy, adultery, fornication, and murder. Could they be forgiven at all? And if so, how? The discussion takes place against the continuing strain of rigorist Christianity that appears in different forms and under diverse names: Montanism, Novatianism, and Donatism. But the rigorists represent a consistent point of view. Grave sins committed after baptism should not be forgiven. The issue becomes more pressing under the persecutions by the emperors Decius (249–251) and Diocletian (284–305). These are widespread public persecutions, turning Christians, especially bishops and priests, literally into "traitors" (*traditores*), those who "hand over" the sacred symbols of the church in the face of persecution. Now other questions arise. Must those who were baptized by such apostate ministers be rebaptized by those who remained faithful? Were the sacraments performed by apostate ministers valid? At the heart of the discussion, what constitutes a sacrament?

In spite of this rigorist strain, another, equally persistent point of view emerges in favor of "second penance" after baptism. Such appears in Clement of Alexandria.[15] Origen also speaks of a "way" of penance for the forgiveness of sins.[16] Tertullian not only witnesses to this second penance but also indicates the process that it involves.[17] In practice, austere Hippolytus upbraids Pope Callistus (217–222) for his lenient attitude toward sins of the flesh.[18] Callistus is said to have justified his action by appeal to the parable of the wheat and the tares (Matt. 13:30) and the story of Noah's ark, which contained both clean and unclean animals. In effect, the church on earth remains a community of saints and sinners. By the time of Basil and Gregory of Nyssa in the East and Ambrose (339–397) in the West, penitential systems have emerged. But sinners can have recourse to the discipline only once. The process itself is extended, rigorous, and public. It involves a confession of sin, exclusion from the community, the performance of a lengthy penance, and finally public reception back into the community, usually reserved to the bishop, and readmission to the Eucharist.

An answer also emerges about the nature of the sacraments and their validity. Augustine delivers the normative response for the Western church down to the Reformation. Sacraments do not depend on the holiness of the minister, for Christ himself is their author. Hence, baptism performed by an unworthy minister remains true and valid baptism because it is Christ himself who baptizes.

In sum, we have traced two elements essential to the life of the church through the first course of their development as examples of continuous development: the sacraments and the nature of church office. Both will continue to evolve in subsequent centuries, but they will do so in ways consistent with what we have seen. In the Western church, this note of continuity continues down to the time of the Reformation. Then discontinuity, indeed an element of rupture, enters in regard to the understanding both of the sacraments and of church office.

The Christological Controversies and the Unity of the Church

The note of discontinuity enters with the Councils of Ephesus (431) and of Chalcedon (451). I have described the church as a community of interpretation whose great task is to describe what God has accomplished in the death and resurrection of Jesus of Nazareth. Now differing interpretations on this score split the ancient church asunder. Such differences constitute the heart of the "christological controversies."

To grasp the nature of these events, a sense of the larger context is important. If we compare the christological controversies with those over the Trinity that precede them by about a century, the differences become clear. At the Council of Nicea, different religious and theological traditions clash on the relation between God the Father and his Son the Logos. The doctrine of the Trinity — one God in three persons — transcends these alternatives, and Christian doctrine of Triune God eventually establishes itself. This is not to say that the alternative of "Arianism" simply disappears or that the road ahead did not contain difficulties. Indeed, the christological controversies will reopen the question of the Trinity. Still, the trinitarian settlement represents the wave of the future that, with time, becomes normative doctrine, albeit with differing interpretations in East and West. By contrast, the christological controversies represent the clash of traditions that is as sharp, if not sharper. These are embattled positions from the start. And there is no viewpoint that eventually emerges to transcend these differences. And, if not superseded, these traditions fall back on themselves, becoming all the more antagonistic to one another. In effect, a protracted conflict now begins with no sign of future resolution. When I spoke of the doctrine of the Trinity, I compared the differences between East and West to differing routes of ascent on a single mountain peak. Here we seem to be left with two peaks in a range of related mountains but with a considerable valley between them.

The Clash of Traditions

The condemnation of Apollinarius (ca. 310–390) at the Council of Constantinople in 381 signals the change in focus from the doctrine of the Trinity to the person of Christ. Apollinarus, a staunch defender of trinitarian orthodoxy and ardent opponent of the "two substances" tradition, teaches that the Logos takes the place of the highest rational element in Christ, thus impairing his integral humanity. This is the focus of the council's condemnation.

Once this shift occurs, the differences between these rival Chris-tologies become ever sharper and more pronounced. For these are not just differences of theological interpretation at the surface; rather, they involve the choice of particular scriptural texts, differing methods of interpreting these texts, and preferred philosophical tools to explain them. In effect, they are considered theologies from the start. In turn, these theological differences are fraught with political consequences. They are espoused by the rival sees of Alexandria and of Antioch, theologies emblematic of these different churches and their piety. The situation is made more complex still by the ambitions of the see of Constantinople, the "new Rome" of the East versus the prerogatives of "old Rome" of the West, both sides caught up in the maelstrom of imperial politics. And, as if on cue, a remarkable cast of charac-ters appears: John Chrysostom (347–407), Theodore of Mopsuestia (350–428), Cyril of Alexandria (d. 444), Nestorius (d. ca. 451), the archimandrite Eutyches (378–454), and Leo the Great (d. 461), to name only a few. The full brunt of the conflict is borne by the church of the East. The church of the West is, by turns, participant and ob-server. In sum, a christological drama now begins on the well-lit stage of world-historical events with the full panoply that belongs to de-liberate conflict in which few concessions are made by one side to the other.

For just the same reason, it is important to identify the *thread* that we will follow as we seek to trace a single line through this maze of complex events. The issue that finally emerges from the Council of Chalcedon in 451 is a definition of the person of Christ: one person in two natures, human and divine. Yet if the *person* of Christ is the focus, it is the *work* of Christ that leads the way. In many respects, the nature of the incarnation remains as inscrutable after the decisions of Chalcedon as the mystery of the Trinity does after the Council of Constantinople. *Why* and *how* God chose to enter human history in the person of Jesus of Nazareth remains a mystery in the strictest sense and the proper object of faith. But given our belief in this mystery, the *meaning of the incarnation for our salvation* is clearer and more ac-cessible. It is on this score that the clash begins. Around two different poles on the meaning of salvation rival Christologies crystallize.

The tradition of the Alexandria church is perhaps the older one of the two, and its central contention is simply put. Athanasius quotes Irenaeus, making the latter's dictum his own: "He [the Logos] became man that man might become God."[19] In a word, salvation in Christ means the *deification* of humankind. The Logos became flesh in order to elevate and divinize the human family. We have already seen this point of view in a trinitarian setting.

Its consistent application in a christological context reveals both the strengths and weaknesses of Alexandrian theology. Certainly, the great strength of this tradition is the dynamic sense of a single acting person — the God-man — at the center of the Scriptures and in the life of the church. This is achieved at every point by stressing the inseparable union of humanity and divinity in the person of Christ. Indeed, the closeness of this union cannot be emphasized enough. This is the reason why Mary as *Theotokos*, God-bearer, captures the heart of this theology in a single word. In this sense, the title makes a clear christological statement.[20] There never was a time, not even a moment, when Jesus' humanity was not indissolubly connected to his divine nature. Hence, it is not just possible, it is necessary, to call Mary "the Mother of God" because human and divine natures were inseparably linked from the moment of Jesus' conception.

Alexandrian theology coalesces in the fourth century, coming together by way of these kinds of assumptions about the person of Christ. Apollinarus is representative in his generation. The replacement of the highest part of Jesus' human soul by the person of the Word as its animating principle certainly delivers a dynamic sense of union associated with this tradition. The theology of Word/Flesh (*Logos/Sarx*) looks to John 1:14, welding the God-man into a single acting person but, in the case of Apollinarus, at too high a price, according to the lights of the Council of Constantinople. In the next generation, Cyril of Alexandria seeks to energize this theology of union in a new but no less dynamic way. Granted a human body and soul in Christ, the person of the Word takes over the function of a human *person* in other individuals. In other words, what person does to human nature in other cases is to surround and encapsulate it, making it into just *this* one person with its own distinctive characteristics. In regard to Jesus, the person of the Word individualizes his human nature, body and soul. The resulting theology of "hypostatic union" — the union of divine and human natures in the person of the Word — now becomes representative of the Alexandrian tradition.

The great strength of this tradition is to bring a single, acting person to the fore. Like the Logos in John's Gospel, the divine Word is always center stage. The theology revels in paradox — Mary as the Mother of God, the suffering Logos — but it does not integrate well passages of Scripture that describe Jesus' moral development (e.g., Luke 2:52). How can the divine Logos, already perfect, be said to grow and develop? In other words, there is a strong tendency in this theology to see human and divine natures fuse into one after the incarnation, so completely does the divine person penetrate Jesus' human nature. Therefore, from an Alexandrian point of view, there is a world of difference between the description of Christ as "out of two natures" and "in two natures." In theory, one can distinguish the natures after the incarnation, but in practice, they fuse into one. For Cyril, this theology is also closely related to the Eucharist. The eucharistic body of Christ must contain both humanity and divinity in one to accomplish its purpose of sanctifying the faithful. The eucharistic link also illustrates how closely this theology is joined to piety, especially the piety of countless monks who surround these controversies as audience-participants.

The dangers of the theology are also evident. If the point of salvation is deification, then Christ's own human nature should be its first exemplar. Therefore, one nature after the incarnation of Christ (= monophysitism) follows easily. But if the high-voltage current of divinity directly touches human nature without proper insulation, will it not reduce the latter to ashes, burned away by a divine fire too fierce to contain? Thus the closeness of the union can attenuate Christ' humanity. It can also endanger Christ's divinity as unchanging and impassible. How can God be said to suffer even in an extended sense without that statement raising a host of other questions? And if Jesus' humanity and divinity fuse into one nature, does this not reopen the question of the Trinity, of the single nature shared by three coequal divine persons?

The theology of Antioch is seen to best advantage in the writings of its foremost expositor, Theodore of Mopsuestia.[21] Once again, the *work* of Christ is the natural point of entry in determining how the *person* of Christ is configured. For Theodore, Jesus' full and integral

humanity is the key to the meaning of salvation. Theodore turns here
to ancient wisdom, with deep roots in classical thought and in other
religions as well. The controlling insight is that the human person,
body and soul, is the *middle creature* in all of creation. Through mind
and soul, he is related to the realms of creation above us, to the sphere
of angels and archangels, principalities and powers. By virtue of his
body, the human person is related to what is below us, to the earthly
world of plants and animals. As middle creature, the human person
becomes the natural bond, indeed the lynchpin, in the drama of salvation. In effect, his fate will determine the outcome of the entire
universe.[22] For special insight, Theodore turns to the hymn of Colossians 1:15–20: Christ, the image of the invisible God, the firstborn
of all creation. The figure of Adam becomes a type who foreshadows
Christ, the primal archetype. Therefore, the key to the world's salvation
is the full restoration of Christ's humanity, body and soul. In this light,
it is preferable to describe the incarnation as the action of the Word
"assuming" a human person (Word/Man [*Logos/Anthropos*]). In doing
so, the Word seeks to bring creation's archetypal image to perfection,
thereby accomplishing the world's salvation in the way the Lord has
specially intended.

Strengths and weaknesses of Antiochene theology follow. The complete human nature of Christ, the key to salvation, dare not be
jeopardized. The Word is also conceived as a separate divine agent
whose impassibility dare not be endangered either. Thus this theology
will highlight the two natures of Christ after the incarnation. From
a theoretical point of view, the theology of Antioch presents a clear
schema with firm edges. However, from the point of view of piety,
the result is often less satisfying. It is not one but rather two players —
"two sons" — who seem to appear on the biblical page. In a typical
phrase, "the man Jesus" undergoes moral development, suffering, and
death. The divine Logos performs miracles, raising Lazarus from the
dead. Such distinctions also allow this theology to be caricatured as the
approach of intellectuals who split hairs about the sacred page instead
of entering more deeply into its mystery.

The Achilles' heel of the theology is explaining the unique union
between the divine Logos and the man Jesus who is assumed. This theology also speaks of a union in the "person," but it uses another word,

prosopon, with a different meaning. Here "person" connotes countenance, the outward appearance of an individual. "When Theodore speaks of Christ as one *propsopon,* he means that, because of the union between the Word and the assumed Man, the Lord presents himself to the world and to the believer as a single object of knowledge and faith and a single agent of reconciliation with God."[23] In other words, Christ is perceived on the world-historical stage as a single person. But the theology tackles less adequately the *inner dynamics* of the union between human and divine in Christ. Theodore of Mopsuestia rejects both a substantial and an accidental union of the two natures. Instead, he describes the union in Christ as an especially "graced indwelling of good pleasure," taking his inspiration from Colossians 1–2, especially Colossians 2:9, which describes Christ as the one "in whom the whole fullness of deity dwells bodily."[24] But such a distinction fits no standard categories. What can it mean in common parlance? In the eyes of its opponents, it confirms the suspicion that the theology of Antioch is unable to explain the unique union of human and divine in Christ, which sets him apart from God's indwelling in Moses or one of the prophets.

III. Doctrine

The Councils of Ephesus and Chalcedon

The theologies that I have described come into conflict first at the Council of Ephesus in 431 and again at the Council of Chalcedon in 451. These councils, as well as many others synods and councils in between, may be likened to chapters in an ongoing saga whose final outcome aggrieves many more than it pleases. Indeed, in the eyes of some participants, the outcome only exacerbates the problems the councils set out to solve.

The controversies begin on a matter of piety. In one sense, it is hardly a surprise that a clash of piety would ignite the tinderbox of accumulated differences in theology, politics, and culture into a blaze that will not be easily contained, much less extinguished. Nestorius, newly elected Antiochene patriarch of Constantinople, is called upon to pronounce on the suitability of the title of Mary as *Theotokos,* Mother of God. The gesture is calculated to draw out the new patriarch. He responds according to his own theological lights: it is better to understand Mary as the Mother of Christ rather than the Mother of God or Mother of the man Jesus. His response, taken as a caricature, pleases no one, especially the monks of the capital who planned the encounter. This adverse reaction produces a ripple effect, setting in motion a full-scale controversy. Nestorius offends popular piety at home and abroad, news that travels swiftly through the network of monasteries in the empire. His response also offends an established tradition of the Alexandrian church, which has long venerated Mary in just this way as the Mother of God. Nestorius thereby creates for himself a formidable opponent in Cyril, patriarch of Alexandria. Cyril is not only a theologian of the highest caliber, the gold standard for Eastern thought; he is also politically astute. As he responds to Nestorius in a series of careful letters, he also consolidates his support, indeed his alliance, with Celestine, bishop of Rome (422–432). The conflict bubbles to the surface at the Council of Ephesus.

We narrow our focus here to the final decision of the council and its symbolic import. The Council of Ephesus accepts Cyril's second letter to Nestorius as fully in accord with the faith of Nicea, endorsing the title *Theotokos,* Mary as the Mother of God. The deposition of Nestorius as patriarch of Constantinople follows.[25] Symbolically, the Council of Ephesus stands as a clear vindication of the theology of Alexandria as it disparages the traditions of Antioch, however inadequately represented by Nestorius. But the victory is too one-sided. At the emperor's prompting, a "Formulary of Reunion" is composed two years later in 433 that gives a better account of the Antiochene position to which Cyril himself agrees. But such an adjustment, a scant two years after the council, testifies firsthand to the widespread impression that Ephesus had given the palm too decidedly to one of the disputing parties.

Therefore, far from resolving the conflict, this one-sided outcome only emboldens the winning side to press its case more forcefully and more publicly. Eutyches, a cleric (archimandrite) of Constantinople, now openly preaches the one nature of Christ after the incarnation, and his views are upheld by a second council at Ephesus in 449, which enters the annals of history with the title of "Robber Council" (*Latrocinium*). The controversy between opposing sides moves from a simmer to a boil. With the death of one emperor and the accession of a successor, the new emperor Marcian calls a new council at Chalcedon in 451 to establish order in an ever more rancorous situation.

Once again our focus here is a narrow one, the final statement of the council and its symbolic import. The Chalcedonian Creed is a "mosaic of excerpts from Cyril's two Letters, Leo's Tome, the Union Symbol and Flavian's profession of faith."[26] Both Eutyches and Nestorius are condemned. But the letter (tome) of Pope Leo the Great to Flavian, patriarch of Constantinople, is the tone-setter. Certainly, this is the way the issue is viewed in the immediate wake of the council. Here, as well, its symbolic significance is anchored. In the long run, Chalcedon establishes the classic dogmatic definition of the person of Christ, normative without question for the Western church: *one person in two natures;* the unity is grounded in the person, duality in the natures. Four fateful adverbs describe how the natures relate. Divine and human natures in Christ exist together "unconfusedly, unchangeably, indivisibly and inseparably."[27]

However, Leo's letter represents the theology of the Western church, which is separate and distinct from the traditions of either Antioch or Alexandria. Its insertion into the heart of a conflict between *other viewpoints* can scarcely guarantee that it will be interpreted according to its own lights. Rather a wildcard is thrown into the game, with the law of unforeseen consequences at play. W. H. C. Frend captures how it is read by many at the time: "The Tome of Leo seemed to consecrate the doctrine of Nestorius while condemning Nestorius by name."[28] Egyptian bishops understand it this way: they exclaim, "We shall all be killed if we subscribe to Leo's epistle. Every district in Egypt will rise against us. We would rather be put to death by you here than there (in Alexandria). Have pity on us."[29] Subsequent events confirm their fears. In March 457, Proterius, patriarch of Alexandria, is lynched by an angry mob because of his views of Christ.

Thus the aggrieved party after the Council of Chalcedon is the Alexandrian church and its traditions. In effect, the Chalcedonian definition of Christ has different faces. As it looks to the West, it appears a model of balance. The oneness of the person of Christ is acknowledged as well as the duality of natures. But from an Eastern perspective, the creed can seem less coherent and more often, as favoring the traditions of Antioch at the expense of Alexandria. And although the council condemns both Eutyches and Nestorius, the latter seems to gain the better portion. Peter Brown describes the effect of the Council of Chalcedon on the subsequent life of the church: "Much as modern European Christianity has taken centuries to transcend the issues raised, 300 years ago, at the Reformation, so late antique Christianity remained locked in the issues brought together and, fatefully, left unresolved at the Council of Chalcedon"; Christians were "left to struggle with the manner in which this High God had joined humanity in the person of Jesus Christ."[30]

The neuralgic issue for the Eastern church is clear enough. Can the decisions of Chalcedon be modified in an Alexandrian direction without, in effect, disavowing them? The condemnation of the "three chapters," works of significant theologians of Antioch at the Second Council of Constantinople in 553, tilts in this direction.[31] But the council provides only a brief respite in an impacted controversy that erupts again at the Third Council of Constantinople in 680–681.[32] And although these controversies occur in the East, they are known in all parts of the Christian world: "Up to as late as the end of the seventh century, the Christological debates which took place in the eastern Churches were constantly discussed in Rome. But they were also known in northern Gaul and even in Britain."[33]

In effect, the christological controversies open a suppurating wound in the Eastern churches that will not heal. And the final result of so much extended, unresolved conflict is to separate these churches progressively from one another. The Nestorian church slips out of the empire into Persia, establishing a renowned center of learning at Nisibis. Here the traditions of Antioch are nourished, as well as those of Greek antiquity. Persian Christians also prove intrepid missionaries, carrying the gospel to China.[34] By contrast, in setting up its own hierarchy in the mid-sixth century, the Monophysite church of Egypt and Syria embarks on a collision course with the empire. At first, this church is not unhappy to exchange old Christian overlords for new Islamic ones, but such proves short-term gain.

The larger truth is that the Christian church becomes increasingly a family of related churches. Perhaps in one sense, they always were. They share a patrimony of belief in the God of Jesus Christ. They share sacraments, the episcopate, and the priesthood. But they differ in significant ways as well. Now culture and history will shape this common patrimony and these specific differences in still other ways. Like many closely related families, these churches do not always regard one another with equal fondness. Separation often emphasizes the distinguishing characteristics, removing the perspective that other commonly held traditions might bring. Yet with all their differences, they continue to confess that the church is *one* — holy, catholic, and apostolic.

The Definition of Chalcedon

The definition of Chalcedon is fascinating in its own right. Although a collection of statements, it has its own integrity. Otherwise, it would not have provoked such fierce opposition in some quarters. Note how it begins: "We **teach** *that it should be* **confessed.**" *The council is highly deliberate in what it wants to say and equally in what it chooses not to say. A certain distance is also registered between "teaching" and "confessing." The definition assumes the creeds of Nicea and Constantinople as a given. Salvation is the known quantum. The definition of Christ in modern terms takes on the structure of a transcendental argument.[35] What is the condition of the possibility of a definition of Christ that assures the basis of our salvation? The council's response: Christ is one person in two natures, a definition completed at the Second Council of Constantinople in 553.[36] Its obvious purpose is to mediate between the rival schools of Alexandria and Antioch. It therefore seeks to establish social conventions about how to rightly speak about the person of Christ. It also indicates positions that are wrong (Nestorius and Eutyches).*

But significantly, the bishops resist pressure from the emperor for greater precision. They deliberately do not define their prime terms, nature *and* person. *These remain open. After the definition points to wrong solutions, it encloses the mystery of the two natures in a riddle of negatives, "without confusion or change, without division or separation." The two natures never intermingle, yet they are inseparably joined for all eternity. The definition will beg for theologians to follow these tantalizing clues to explain the double helix strands of intertwined divinity and humanity. What Karl Rahner said about this definition surely is true: of necessity, it represents both an end and a beginning.*[37] *Yet, did the definition only seek to regulate the way we speak about Christ, the human rules of social discourse? No. The Chalcedonian definition of one person in two natures never* "explains or grasps *the reality toward which it points,"* observes Sarah Coakley, because *"it is an 'apophatic' document."*[38] *The words* person *and* nature, *themselves undefined, stretch beyond human usage, in the confidence based on faith, though while they do not "grasp" divine realities, they "touch" them or, better, "are touched by them."*

Part Three

The Development of Catholic Doctrine: Closing the Circle

Chapter Seven

THE WESTERN CHURCH

We turn in this chapter to the development of the Western church. First, we examine representative figures in Latin patristic thought: Tertullian (ca. 155–230), Cyprian of Carthage (d. 258), Augustine (354–430), Leo the Great (d. 461), and Gregory the Great (ca. 540–604). We observe how the great themes of Latin patristic thought emerge to form what I will call the Western template on the nature of the church.

Second, we trace the history of the church from the end of the patristic era, the time of Gregory the Great, to the first beginnings of a formal theology of the church in the 1300s. The *connecting thread* in a historical glissando over this long period is the story of the papacy in the last centuries of the first millennium and the first centuries of the second.

Third, we follow the development of the theology of the church through its various permutations in the neo-Scholastic synthesis down to the beginning of the Second Vatican Council in 1962.

Fourth, the concluding section of the chapter examines the vision of the church that emerges at Vatican II. In this regard, this chapter is quite different from preceding ones. Here we seek to follow the development of the Roman Catholic Church into the modern era. We will do the same in the next chapter when we turn to the person of the Virgin Mary and the particular accents that Vatican II sets in interpreting her role theologically.

I. The Church in Latin Patristic Thought

The conclusion of the preceding chapter brings us to view the church of the West in a new light. The great themes of Eastern patristic thought, as we have seen, are the nature of the Trinity and the person of Christ. The churches of the West are participants in these debates, but they are not always lead agents in the discussions. Robert Evans selects representative figures for the patristic era in East and in West, Origen and Augustine respectively.[1] He takes characteristic writings of each: for Origen, *On First Principles,* for Augustine, *The City of God.* Then he argues that whereas the doctrines of Christ and the Trinity stand at the center of the Eastern Church's meditation, for the West, the great theme is the nature of the church. Augustine's *City of God* is indeed a book about the church. Other characteristic features follow. Whereas Origen envisions the universal salvation of all creation (*apokatastasis*), Augustine sees duality between the heavenly and earthly cities, between sin and grace, those predestined to persevere and those denied this final grace.

Two threads run through the representative Western theologians whom we will examine in this chapter: the church as *one* and as *holy.* The challenge will be to hold these themes together against the backdrop of the actual life of the church. Accordingly, the task will change over time as the threads are woven together in different ways. We catch the interplay in its first stages in Tertullian of Carthage.

Against the Gnostic threat, Tertullian argues that the unity of the church is grounded in the Scriptures, the rule of faith, and the role of bishops in apostolic successions as interpreters of the faith. These are characteristic features of actual church life, and where they are found, the church is one. But all such characteristics are empirical realities, easily identified parts of church order.

The challenge will be to combine these *external* criteria of the church's unity with the *internal* quality of its holiness. In Tertullian's Montanist phase, the church as one by traditional standards and the church as holy split apart. The witness of the Spirit proves too strong and the immanent return of Christ too certain to tolerate the presence of sinners in the church. Tertullian is aware of "second penance," which does not lead to full restoration to the church but rather gives penitents virtual assurance that God in the end will forgive them. Now he is not so sure.

In the last analysis for Tertullian, the holiness of the church must be palpable in the rigorous asceticism of its members in their daily lives. This is not their *doing* but rather their *cooperation* with the action of the Spirit that allows them to live extraordinary lives. The model of the Christian life remains the martyr. While others may not share that crown, they must come as close as possible in upright, sinless lives. In effect, the church as holy becomes the key to the church as one. Only those elect few, filled with the Spirit, belong to it. The church as one by apostolic standards and the church as holy by the presence of the Spirit split asunder.

Tertullian fails to hold these threads together, but his situation lays out the challenges that others will face in the future as they confront new situations. Three of those situations stand out, each posing its own challenge to the church's unity and its holiness. The first, the persecutions by the emperors Decian and of Diocletian, pose acute questions on both scores. In the face of these persecutions, some succumb while others persevere. What is the church to do in the midst of persecution, and, equally important, what is the church to do in the aftermath to put the community back together? Here we look to the witness of Cyprian of Carthage. The second situation is different again. Constantine converts to the Christian faith, and later Christianity virtually becomes the established religion of the empire. How do these events affect the way the church's unity and its holiness are understood? Hereafter it will become a *given* that the church is composed of saints and sinners, sheep and goats. How, then, is its holiness described? We look to Augustine to interpret this turn of events. The third challenge arises as the center of gravity of the empire shifts from West to East, from Rome to Constantinople. A growing power vacuum in the West follows. What do these events portend for the unity of the church? How do they affect its holiness? This is the challenge facing the great popes of antiquity, Leo the Great and Gregory the Great.

Cyprian of Carthage

Cyprian of Carthage dies a martyr's death in 258 and is regarded as a patron by the Donatist churches in North Africa. In the midst of persecution, he adapts an older solution to a new situation, seeking to balance unity and holiness under the duress of persecution. For Cyprian, the unity of the church is guaranteed by its worldwide episcopate. This is how he interprets Christ's promise to Peter in Matthew 16:18.[2] Christ establishes the episcopate as a worldwide order of coequal bishops, successors of the apostles, as a visible guarantee that the church will remain one. But bishops are equally central to the church's holiness. Indeed, the holiness of the church must be displayed, above all, in the lives of the clergy. True, there may be sinners in the church, those who have surrendered in the face of persecution, but it cannot be so among bishops and priests. For Cyprian, the apostasy in their ranks is equivalent to ritual profanation. Thus an apostate bishop cannot perform valid sacraments. He can only spread the contagion that he himself embodies. Clergy in serious sin are living examples that the corruption of the best is the worst of all. Therefore, those who are baptized at the hands of apostate clergy must be baptized again. And this is not a case of *rebaptism,* since they were not rightly baptized in the first place.

Whether Cyprian's solution will stand up over the long haul remains to be seen. He does unabashedly connect the validity of the sacraments to the holiness of the minister. Does this concede too much power over the sacraments to those who are themselves only servants of God's grace? Still, Cyprian does point to a way of reconciling the church's unity and its holiness by connecting them to the office of bishop in a worldwide episcopate.

Augustine

Among the prompting circumstances for the composition of *The City of God,* Augustine tells, is the sack of Rome in 410. Has Rome been plundered because it abandoned its old protector gods? Will the God of the Christians bring prosperity and benefaction to the empire and to its citizens who have embraced the true faith? Augustine swiftly dispatches all such questions. The fate of the church and the fortunes of the empire are completely separate questions, however praiseworthy the conversion of its individual citizens.

Augustine's solution is to transpose all such earthly questions about the church's unity and its holiness to a completely new context, thereby transforming the discussion that we have followed to this point. The church is primarily a heavenly reality, and its first citizens are the good angels who persevere. They are the first members of the church. But the fallen angels have left a gap in the heavenly ranks. God "thus fills up and repairs the blank made by the fallen angels" so that the "beloved and heavenly city is not defrauded of its full number of its citizens, but perhaps may even rejoice in a still more overflowing population."[3] In other words, God has made a place in heaven for those here on earth whom he predestines for citizenship in the heavenly city of God.

This dramatically broadened context provides Augustine with a new venue on traditional questions. The contest between the heavenly Jerusalem and the earthly Babylon is literally as old as creation itself. Adam's sin, passed on through conception, is on full display in his son Cain, who slays his brother, Abel. Fittingly, Cain builds the first city. The laws of this earthly city are ever the same: domination and self-love. The Roman Empire is only its latest example. The heavenly church begins with Cain's slain brother, Abel. The heavenly Jerusalem manifests itself only fleetingly and by shadow-traces in this world. In other words, it belongs to the nature of the church in a fallen world to be visible yet hidden. It certainly is visible yet hidden in the history of Israel, clearly visible in Christ. In the church on earth, the city of God is visible yet hidden too. The signs of the visible church are evident enough: the Scriptures, the creeds, the role of bishops, and, above all, the sacraments as channels of grace. In regard to the latter, Augustine argues that in a fallen world the validity of the sacraments cannot depend on the frail, earthly ciphers of their ministers. The sacraments are valid because Christ is their author. It is Christ who baptizes through the action of his ministers. In the sacraments, Augustine firmly anchors the holiness of the church.

In this world, the true church remains visible yet hidden among its members. Therefore, the church is made up of sheep and goats, wheat and tares, the net full of good and bad fish. And they must continue to live side by side until God's reaping angel comes to separate them at the final judgment. Here on earth, it is impossible to discern the true elect in the visible church. It was naive on the part of the Donatists to think otherwise.

The overarching mystery for Augustine is God's election. God gives grace to all who seek it, but not to all the grace of perseverance. Why he gives it to some and not to others is an inscrutable mystery, hidden in the deeper mystery of God's free choice. In this sense, the parable of wheat and the tares brings no consolation to sinners, even less to the righteous. What apparently upright and moral life is not tainted by sin? And although the sacraments are always channels of grace, that does not guarantee their fruitful reception. There is a fixed number of the elect destined for the heavenly Jerusalem. God's reasons here remain hidden in the mystery of his free decision. Augustine is fond of Romans 11:33 because it summarizes succinctly his own final answer to the deepest of human questions: "O the depth of the riches and wisdom of God! How unsearchable are his judgments and how inscrutable are his ways!"[4]

But, in truth, the mystery of God's will predestining some and not others is only part of the larger mystery that surrounds the church and the Christian at every point. The holiness of the church is indeed grounded in the sacraments. The unity of the visible church in this world is important. Yet the church as fully one and as fully holy comprises eschatological gifts that will manifest themselves only when the city of God arrives in its fullness.

Leo the Great and Gregory the Great

We regard Leo and Gregory as related figures on a historical continuum as the papacy progressively stakes out its claim to jurisdictional and doctrinal primacy. This occurs as Rome's actual independence from the Eastern empire grows in the face of an increasingly chaotic situation in the West.

Leo is the chief strategist of papal primacy who puts forth its central arguments for universal jurisdiction. In doing so, he takes a quite different view of the Roman Empire than does Augustine. Indeed, he draws a parallel between the structures of civil society and those of the church. In his providence, God has established the empire and chosen its rulers. In the same way, God endows the church with a symbol and agents of its own universality, and such is the nature of the papal office. In making this argument, Leo is fully aware of the claims of "new Rome," Constantinople, endorsed first by the Council of Constantinople in 381 and then again in the hated twenty-eighth canon of the Council of Chalcedon.[5] Leo will have none of such claims. Since this is a matter of law, Leo will take a legal approach to Rome's claim for a primacy not only of honor but also of jurisdiction.

His argument rests on his interpretation of Christ' promise to Peter in Matthew 16:18, which becomes normative in the West and the key to a series of other passages (Luke 22:31; John 21:17). Christ's intention at Caesarea Philippi is not simply to appoint Peter as the first of the apostles; rather, the Lord appoints him the *prince* of the apostles, and, by right of legal inheritance, this princely office is passed down to Peter's successors.[6] Therefore, the popes have jurisdiction not simply over the churches of the West but over all churches, a prerogative that is legally theirs by inheritance. Thus the pope is rightly called the "vicar of Peter" because through his mouth, the voice of Peter rings in the church.[7] There are other reasons for Rome's importance. The see rests on the blood of two martyrs, Peter and Paul, and this is where the bones of Peter are buried. But while true, such facts are secondary. The centerpiece for Leo is Peter's position as prince of the apostles, according to Christ's dictates, an office passed down to his successors by the laws of inheritance. The argument is finely honed. Walter Ullmann comments, "In working out the function of the pope Leo displayed a mastery of Roman law as well as of biblical exegesis which was second to none."[8] Therefore, the pope as bishop of Rome is a unique symbol and agent of the church's worldwide unity. Of course, it is one thing to stake such a claim and quite another to make good on it. We can be sure that Leo was fully conscious of the difference. But for its future exercise, the claim needs to be made, and Leo's contribution consists in performing this task.

Gregory assumes the papal office 130 years after Leo in a situation that has deteriorated in every way. Gregory is a monk who has fled the world for a life of contemplation. But true to his family's tradition of clerical service, he returns to public life, first as legate to the court at Constantinople and then as pope (590–604). Gregory fully shares Leo's view of papal prerogatives. Indeed, he extends them. The actions of synods or councils, he contends, are not binding without the approval of the bishop of Rome.[9] Theologically, Gregory plays an important role in passing down the Augustinian synthesis that emerges after the Council of Orange in 529. He adds his own contribution as well, notably in regard to the doctrine of purgatory and the Mass as a sacrifice. His "Pastoral Rule" (*Regula Pastoralis*) becomes a virtual guidebook for centuries of higher clerics.[10] "The *Regula Pastoralis* was to be Gregory's equivalent of Benedict's *Rule*. It was a *Rule for Bishops*."[11] It becomes a reliable guide for the exercise of the pastoral office in a myriad of practical settings, not least in discharging the duties of preaching.

Doubtless Gregory's "Pastoral Rule" was influential because it carried the stamp of lessons learned by dint of his own hard experience as bishop of Rome. Here Gregory is beset by problems on every side. Italy lies devastated in the wake of the emperor Justinian's campaign to reconquer it. The Lombards enter Italy from the north. Schism grows in northern Italy and Gaul. The patriarch of Constantinople continues to make his claims. The population of Rome has plummeted. There is no effective central authority in the city to administer basic services. From a life of contemplation, Gregory is plunged into this vortex of near intractable problems. If a person's stature in office is measured by the challenge of the age in which that person serves, then in the forthright way that he faced a multiplicity of thorny problems, Gregory justly earned the cognomen "the Great."

Perhaps the most remarkable feature of this problem-driven situation is Gregory's own skillful ability to manage the complex affairs of the church. Eamon Duffy observes that Gregory exemplifies "all the Roman virtues — practicality, realism, a passion for order."[12] If Leo has staked out wide-ranging claims of papal authority, the power vacuum in the West provides Gregory with ample opportunity to exercise vast authority on multiple fronts. He defends the city of Rome, negotiates with invaders, deals with the emperor in Constantinople, and manages the lassitude of his representatives in Ravenna. He also carefully tends the patrimony of Peter. The church by now is the largest landowner in the West, with vast estates in Italy and elsewhere; those in Sicily are of special importance because they had been spared the devastation of invasion. Gregory manages this patrimony to feed the city of Rome. He hires and fires administrators, carefully supervising those whom he appoints. He must deal so nakedly with issues of power and authority that he wonders if he will reach his heavenly home.[13] And he can have no illusions about the church itself, knowing that the flock is filled with sheep and goats on every tier.

Yet despite the reactive mode forced on him by events, despite his palpable expectation of Christ's imminent return, Gregory plans for the future. He does what no pope before him has done: he sends missionaries to territories beyond the empire.[14] Gregory sends a party of forty Roman monks, led by another Augustine, to evangelize distant England.

The Western Template

We have been following Robert Evans's thesis that the church is the great theme of Latin patristic thought, and that its connecting threads are the church as *one* and as *holy*. Certainly, the church as one in this world makes it a visible community with all the marks of an earthly institution. The question naturally arises as to whether such a visible institution can be the true church. Clearly, the church as *one* and as *holy* is never coextensive in this world. The church of the elect is *invisibly* present in the wider community of saints and sinners. The church on earth is finally *one* with the church in heaven. Indeed, this is the source of its unity and its final goal. Yet the notes of *one* and *holy* dare not be played out against one another in the earthly church, struggling to display these qualities through creeds, sacraments, and structure. Here, Augustine's great contribution is to rightly frame this discussion. As first a heavenly reality, it belongs to the nature of the church in this world to be both manifest and hidden, a community of sheep and goats, only to be separated at the end of time. Augustine also firmly anchors the holiness of the church in the sacraments. With Christ as their author, these heavenly sources of grace continue to flow in a fallen world to a church of saints and sinners.

The contribution of Leo and Gregory is to endow the papal structure of the church with overarching significance. The church of Rome is the inheritor of the fallen Western empire and must make a convincing case for its own visible, autonomous authority. Leo argues that the princely office of pope as vicar of Peter is passed down by inheritance to Peter's successors as bishops of Rome, and Gregory expands the argument. In effect, the sword of disciplinary and doctrinal authority is enclosed in a scabbard of heavenly authority. The pope as the vicar of Peter shares in the holiness of the church by virtue of the exalted origin of his authority.

We now face another question: Does the Western church in the patristic era develop a genetic template of lasting qualities that will show themselves again in the future? The answer is yes, and two characteristics stand out. There is an ironic twist to the first. For all the exalted claims that Leo and Gregory raise for the papal office, the translation of these high claims into practice results in mundane, indeed quite ordinary virtues in one sense. In this regard, what Eamon Duffy writes about Gregory the Great might characterize the Western church as a whole: practicality, realism, and a passion for order. These are qualities for the long haul that make the Roman church in the patristic era a *survivor.* The church of Rome survives the dissolution of the Western Roman Empire, and this gives it a range of enduring qualities — above all, a penchant for *law and administration.* If the Roman church claims a primacy in doctrine and discipline, then it must have a talent for the exercise of such authority. These gifts seem clear in Leo and Gregory. The bishops of Rome also display the ability to pursue the issue of their own authority with consistency through the reign of successive popes. Such qualities belong to the genetic template of the Western church, closely connected to the papal office, and they will show themselves even more decisively in the future.

The second quality appears in nascent form in the patristic era: a penchant for *rational thought.* Jaroslav Pelikan selects two representative figures of the Western tradition at the close of the era, Gregory the Great and Boethius.[15] The choice of Boethius looks to the future and to his role as a bridge to medieval thought. In regard to an actual penchant for philosophy in the patristic era, it appears first in the church of the East. One issue, not a minor one, is that of language, of Greek, the tongue of the Eastern church and of ancient philosophy. John O'Malley observes that Origen's *First Principles* displays all the elements of the Aristotelian ideal of a science. Knowledge of Aristotle is a feature of Alexandrian theology in the late patristic era as well.[16]

Boethius is important for the future on two scores. He is the translator of Aristotle's *Logic,* the only part of Aristotle's great corpus known to the early medieval world and, even in fragment, deeply influential. His translation also supplies the *known* piece of the puzzle when the great body of Aristotle's works appears in the West in the thirteenth century. Of equal importance are his short works on trinitarian and christological dogmas. Key here is his method. Boethius uses rational argumentation to unlock the riches of doctrinal truth. In effect, reason is applied to faith in a new and more extensive way. Boethius's efforts are reckoned the precursor of the scholastic method that will blossom in the great summae of the Middle Ages. Hence, he becomes mentor and pioneer for this era in which faith and reason are blended in different ways in theologians such as Aquinas, Albert, Bonaventure, Scotus, and others. But the seeds of this development are sown in the patristic era.

The Roman Catholic Church

I wish to focus the final section of this chapter on the Roman Catholic Church. The ultimate goal here is to compare official Catholic teaching about the church before the Second Vatican Council with the views which emerges at the council itself — in brief, the Roman Catholic Church before and after Vatican II. The purpose of the immediate section before us is to connect the discussion of the church in Western patristic thought to the first beginnings of treatises on the church in the early 1300s. I do so by means of a *historical glissando,* a great slide through history, highlighting those moments in subsequent centuries that pertain to our topic and our goal.

II. Historical Glissando

We take as the leitmotiv in this section the fate of the papacy in subsequent centuries after Gregory the Great. First, we note the slow divorce that occurs between the Greek empire at Constantinople and the popes in Rome. Ironically, this takes place largely under Greek-speaking popes.[17] Henceforth, Rome will look to the West, not to the East. In this regard, the coronation of Charlemagne by Pope Leo III (795–816) on Christmas day in 800 represents a symbolic turning point. Second, less known but thoroughly documented, is the collapse of the papacy itself. The papacy implodes, becoming a pawn in the local politics of competing Roman families. The rule of popes in this era has been called a "pornocracy," the rule of pigs, and unruly pigs at that.[18] "A third of the popes elected between 872 and 1012 dies in suspicious circumstances."[19] From the lofty heights of Leo and Gregory, the papal office in the 900s falls into a state of disrepute. One thing is clear at the turn of the millennium: the papacy is badly in need of reform.

The German emperors take the lead, appointing reform-minded popes. What follows is a series of symbolic gestures and practical steps that indicate that the reforming impulse has caught fire at Rome. The reforming initiative thereby shifts from German emperors to Roman Popes. Significantly, the pope who straddles the millennium, Sylvester II (999–1003), takes the name of an ancient pope and friend of Constantine. Hereafter, the pope's name becomes a weapon in the struggle. "From 1047 to 1146 the popes chose to be 'Seconds' to imitate the time of the fathers of the Church, by singling out venerable names from the first centuries. Never was there a more deliberate 'Renaissance' than in this century of renaming the popes."[20] In 1059, the election of the pope is placed in the hands of the cardinal-bishops. Initial difficulties are remedied by the Third Lateran Council in 1179.[21] More significantly, the Roman aristocracy and populace as well as the emperor are excluded from the process.

In retrospect, these steps seem only preparatory ones for the pontificate of Gregory VII, Hildebrand (1073–1085). His choice of name is symbolic. He confirms the legitimacy of Gregory VI. Above all, he looks back to Gregory the Great. He becomes aware of earlier legislation, indicating that, contrary to the present custom, bishops and abbots had not always been installed by laity.[22] He concludes that the practice should be stopped. Investiture should be an affair of the church.

Subsequent European revolutions involve more and more people, culminating in the great Russian revolution of 1917. The first of those revolutions, the Gregorian, takes place in one man, Gregory VII, indeed *nel petto del papa,* "in the pope's breast."[23] This seems clear from the remarkable document that he composes, "the dictates of the pope" (*dictatus papae*). Although the circumstances of its compilation remain enigmatic, its revolutionary content is not.[24] The dictates comprise twenty-seven trenchant statements that, even as an exploratory probe, set down claims to papal authority far exceeding those of previous popes. John O'Malley puts his finger on a key point about Gregory and his exalted claims.[25] In Gregory VII, at the pinnacle of church office, so recently in dire straits, a prophetic monk appears. In political terms, Gregory is nothing less than a revolutionary, a clerical Trotskyite. His reforms fit into a neat package, indeed a program: the rejection of lay investiture, the condemnation of the sale of church office (simony), and clerical celibacy. The program is captured in a single slogan: "the Freedom of the Church." But here Gregory is the innovator and lay investiture a long-standing custom. If his reforms succeed, they will involve far more than the church. They will mean a vast restructuring of Western society on every level. They also mean a secularization of the role of the emperor, himself regarded as a sacral figure, the successor of St. Paul. Gregory claims for the popes Paul's legacy as well. Significantly, "Gregory VII was the first to put Paul together with Peter on his coins and later popes put them on their seals."[26]

If Gregory formulates the program, successive popes carry it through in a quite distinctive style. Richard Southern observes, "There is one fact which more than any other sums up this period of papal history: every notable pope from 1159 to 1303 was a lawyer. At a time when the traditions of ancient law had been almost completely obliterated in Europe, the popes retained the elements of a legal system on which they could build. Besides this they could claim a legislative authority to which no other ruler in the West could aspire."[27] The reign of Innocent III (1198–1216) and the Fourth Lateran Council are culminating moments in the era. Walter Ullmann comments, "Innocent III was the man who came nearer to accomplishing the task begun by Gregory VII — that is, the translation of abstract papal ideology into reality."[28] The Fourth Lateran Council is attended by seventy patriarchs and archbishops, nearly four hundred bishops, and more than eight hundred abbots. The legislation of this council in its breadth, practicality, and moderation determines the face of the Western church down to our time.

The plain fact is that the papacy and its curia had devised a sophisticated and efficient system of canon law for peacefully settling disputes of every kind. In effect, the pope presides as chief justice of Christendom in a court not of last resort but rather of first instance for those who seek its services. The preferred title of the pope also changes: no longer vicar of Peter, now vicar of Christ.[29] However, the title does not refer back to the historical Jesus but rather forward to Christ, the judge of the end time. Indeed, in the judgments of the pope, Christ's vicar on earth, one comes as close as possible to such higher judgments. And the system works. If the pope claims a "plentitude of power" — for Innocent, the pope stood between God and humankind, less than God but more than a mere human — such claims are vindicated at its zenith by the balanced and fair way it deals with those who seek its judgments.

But if the papacy rockets to its zenith in the thirteenth century, its decline is equally swift in the fourteenth century. In fact, the years of exaltation (1200–1269) and humiliation (1309–1377) are of about equal length. A key factor here: the papacy had taken the measure of the Holy Roman emperors whom they crown, the pope's secular vicar in temporal affairs. But they were at a disadvantage with nation-states whose rulers they had scorned as "kinglets" (*reguli*).[30] This becomes clear in the confrontation between Boniface VIII (1294–1303) and Philip the Fair of France (1268–1314), culminating in the bull *Unam Sanctam* (1302). Here Boniface only repeats and does not expand papal claims. But times have changed, and the opponent has changed as well.

What follows in the decline of the papal office is close to what Polybius describes as the rotation of government.[31] What begins as the papal monarchy gives way in the Avignon years (1309–1377) to the de facto rule of cardinals, as the papal office remains vacant for sustained periods. In turn, the rule of cardinal-factions produces the multiple popes of the Great Western Schism (1377–1409). These multiple popes call for an era of clerical democracy to solve the schism, the Councils of Pisa (1409), Constance (1414–1418), and Basel (1431–1439). The councils themselves finally give way to an era of papal despots. In regard to the latter, Eugen Rosenstock-Huessy writes, "Any institution in its senility goes back to a kind of primitive restoration; all the detail and refinement of subtle forms are given up. The papal government of 1460 was more brutal and primitive than that of

Gregory, Innocent or Boniface had been."[32] The popes now become regional Italian despots, anxious about their own fortunes. The Fifth Lateran Council (1512–1517) and the Concordat of Bologna (1516) are harbingers of the future. The latter grants to the French king authority to appoint archbishops, bishops, and virtually all abbots and priors in France.[33] The papacy is willing to bargain away local appointments for the support of its claims over those of a general council. It seems like the investiture controversy has come full circle.

I bring this historical survey to a close and to a single conclusion. At the "tipping point" in the early 1300s, between steep ascent and sharp decline of the papacy, the first treatises on the church appear. They carry all the characteristic marks of their birth at this auspicious moment.

III. The Theology of the Church

The first book exclusively devoted to the church, *De regimini christiano*, is written by James of Viterbo (ca. 1255–1308) in 1302. In this regard, Walter Ullmann observes, "The obvious conclusion to be drawn is that until then there was no need to devote a whole book to this subject, but that this need was now clearly felt."[34] And this is indeed the point. The thinking of Giles of Rome (1247–1316) undergirds Boniface VIII's bull *Unam Sanctam* (1302). John of Paris (d. 1306) devotes a treatise to royal and papal authority, favoring the king's side. But the larger fact is that papal power is not simply challenged in its *exercise*; now, the *theory* is under attack, and this by some of the best minds of the age. Marsilius of Padua (ca. 1270–1342) launches an assault, using arguments from Aristotelian philosophy and Roman law. In his *Defender of Peace* (1324), the papacy is portrayed as the disturber of the peace. William of Occam (1280–1349) attacks the papacy from a theological angle, criticizing as well the personalities of the popes.[35]

In the midst of these disputes, certain continuing trajectories are set in the treatise on the church. First, the discussion for and against the church's authority is conducted in the categories of Aristotelian thought and Roman law. These generally are arguments about jurisdiction. Such are the appropriate terms of the discussion. Second, these treatises invariably see the institutional church in a defensive posture, faced with an *enemy*. In the future, the enemies will change, but henceforth there will always be one. I list future opponents without claiming that the list is exhaustive: first, the French monarchy and the temporal authority of kings; then, the great councils and the claim that the pope is subject to the authority of a general council. At the Reformation, another kind of opponent enters the list. Now it is a matter of the claims of Reformation churches against those of the church of Rome, a theological conflict about doctrine and a practical one about property and jurisdiction. In the eighteenth century, the enemy is a rationalist Enlightenment. In the nineteenth century, it becomes secular European culture, hostile to the traditional piety of Roman Catholics and later to the claims of papal infallibility. The American variation features an immigrant Catholic Church facing an unfriendly Protestant culture. Although the names, faces, and challenge change, this ecclesiology is a *defensive* one. So it was at the beginning, and so it continues.

It should also be clear that the treatise on the church, so conceived, almost never reflects the actual life of the church. Such actualities — the birth of religious orders, movements of renewal, the vitality of intellectual life and grassroots spirituality — move on a parallel track and are simply not reflected in official or nearly official treatments of the church. In other words, the thread that we are following here is a narrow one, and that belongs to its character too.

The Neo-Scholastic Synthesis

Each of these opponents will also leave a mark on neo-Scholastic theology and its treatment of the church. Hence, the foundation and style of this theology will differ considerably from its medieval counterpart. The Reformation calls into question the interpretation of Scripture. In doing so, it renders problematic the incontestable foundation on which Thomas Aquinas built his *Summa theologiae*. For Thomas, sacred doctrine is based on the authority of divine revelation, found in the Scriptures.[36] Now this basis becomes ambiguous. Scripture is open to competing interpretations. The neo-Scholastic method solves the dilemma by making church teaching the *immediate rule* of faith. Scripture and tradition recede, becoming the *remote rule* of faith. Dennis Petau contributes the characteristic style. Theology becomes a deductive science that proceeds by syllogistic reasoning. A premium is thereby placed on clear and distinct ideas.

These factors come together in the neo-Scholastic synthesis of the Baroque era.[37] The "question" — the building block — of the medieval summae is now replaced by the neo-Scholastic "thesis." These "theses" about theology become the brick and mortar of a new deductive system of clear and distinct propositions. A distinctly rationalist tone is set. Indeed, neo-Scholastic theology seeks to refute Enlightenment objections to revelation and to the possibility of miracles by adopting the rational argumentation of its opponent. By doing so, it becomes thoroughly impregnated with the same rationalism. This is particularly true in regard to the discipline of "fundamental" theology as distinct from "dogmatic" theology.

I might illumine these differences here and provide an overall sense of the neo-Scholastic "project" by comparing these elements to a house with its foundation and its upper stories. Fundamental theology — apologetics, revelation, and faith — comprises the foundation of the building, the *horizontal* planks on which the upper stories will rest. Here the methodology is different too. *Rational* argumentation is used to prove the existence of God and to establish the nature of religion. Reason also sets forth the claims to credibility of Christ and the church. Fundamental theology introduces the teaching office of the church at this point as the guarantor and authoritative interpreter of the sources of revelation, Scripture, and tradition. The argument is capped by the discussion of faith and the assent to God's revelation as it has been explained. Now that the church and its authority are established, *vertical* construction may commence on this secure foundation. "Dogmatic" theology thus proceeds on its agenda of topics: God, one and three, creation, incarnation, redemption, church, grace, sacraments, Mary, and the last things. But in these upper stories, the methodology has shifted. The decisive appeal is not to reason but rather to church teaching as the immediate rule of faith and to Scripture and tradition as the remote rule. A speculative exposition may follow, but only to illumine by reason what faith and authority have already established. The decisive instance is church teaching, but the church's authority is engaged on a sliding scale. Here the system displays its subtlety in the moderate engagement of authority on a case-by-case basis.

Thomas Aquinas as Official Catholic Thinker

The next chapter in this story centers on the establishment of Thomism as the official philosophy of the Roman Catholic Church by virtue of Pope Leo XIII's 1879 encyclical *Aeterni Patris* (*Eternal Father*). This policy is written into the 1917 Code of Canon law and is widely followed and strictly enforced. But in adopting Thomism, no distinction is made between Thomas himself and his later commentators. Nor is much distinction made between medieval thinkers such as Thomas and Bonaventure. In effect, the encyclical endorses that version of Thomism closest to the neo-Scholastic synthesis. This is apparent in the fact that, although quite different in origin, the terms *neo-Scholasticism* and *neo-Thomism* are often used interchangeably.[38] In other words, it is fair to regard the Thomist renewal as an updating and strengthening of the neo-Scholastic synthesis in new circumstances.

As we saw, the neo-Scholastic synthesis arose in the eighteenth century when the enemy was a rationalist Enlightenment. It becomes official policy of the Catholic Church in the nineteenth century in a different setting. Bernhard Welte (1906–1983) characterizes the cultural climate of the second half of the nineteenth century as one that is especially hostile to religious faith.[39] An optimistic belief in scientific and technological progress casts a baleful eye on religious traditions and, after the definition of papal infallibility, on the Catholic Church in particular. What the church needs at this critical juncture is a way of establishing a single, unified system in which all parts of philosophy and theology fit tightly together. It needs a *pugnacious rationality* to meet dissension within and the ever-sharper questions of its critics outside. In this regard, neo-Scholastic thought has little time for emotions and sentiment in religious matters. Two generations ago, Romantic thinkers in Catholic Germany prized sentiment and feeling; but now, in the harsher climate of late nineteenth century, emotion seems too close to subjectivism, which robs theology of its objective content, dissolving substance in a wash of feeling. Thus neo-Thomism of the first generation prefers hard edges and sharp dichotomies: between nature and supernature, thought and feeling, church and society.

Beginning in the fourteenth century, this ecclesiology reaches a culminating point — an apogee, as it were — in the closing decades of the nineteenth century. The adoption of Thomism is only one factor among many in this regard. The hammer blows of the surrounding cultures bring the surface of this defensive ecclesiology to a burnished finish. If visibility was an important component of the church, it now becomes all the more critical. In this regard, who could be more visible than the person of the pope, the symbol and agent of the church's unity? The simultaneous definition of papal infallibility, coupled with the loss of the papal states, makes the pope an ever more visible and dramatic symbol of the church in a way that utterly captures the imagination. The pope is now *the prisoner of the Vatican* on earth, as he presides over a worldwide church as its *infallible, spiritual teacher.* No sharper line could be drawn between the church and the world than the one that the pope himself embodies: earthly captive, yet teacher of universal spiritual truth.

Here the church also regains elements of its medieval universality, but in an entirely different way. In the opening decades of the thirteenth century, Innocent III and the church stood at the actual center of Western society. Now the pope stands at the center of an *alternative society* outside the mainstream but with universal spiritual claims. The embrace of Thomism should be seen in this light. If the pope is the prisoner of the Vatican, the church itself comes into focus as an *embattled citadel* in a hostile world. Therefore, the church needs its own philosophy, Thomism. It already has its own language, Latin. But it also needs its own schools, universities, hospitals, orphanages, newspapers, magazines, and its own political parties in many countries. If the church finds itself in a defensive posture, it has also become a skilled counterpuncher with considerable resources at its disposal, able to land telling blows on the surrounding culture. And it attracts notable converts because it stands in marked contrast to and in proud defiance of the surrounding culture. If there was a single ethos that ran through the church, it is captured in the motto of the last prefect of the Holy Office, Cardinal Alfredo Ottaviani (1890–1979): *Semper idem,* "Always the same." The world changes; the church does not. It represents the one point in this changing world where eternal and enduring truth may be found. For the same reason, neo-Scholastic theology has an innate aversion to all notions of historical development. The church is the unchanging home of unchanging truths that drop down vertically from above and are the same in every age. The church is above history, just as the world is immersed in it.

The Church

As we noted, each of the church's opponents leaves its mark on the church's own self-understanding. Thus Robert Bellarmine's (1542–1621) famous definition of the church — a single society with the same faith, the same sacraments, and the same pastors, above all the Roman pontiff[40] — seeks to counter the Reformation notion of two churches, one visible and one invisible. Bellarmine is also aware that this definition supplies only the *minimum* in order to identify those who belong to the church and those who do not.

The treatment of the church in the neo-Scholastic synthesis begins with a variation of Bellarmine's definition. The church is described as a visible, hierarchical society with the same teaching, the same sacraments, and the same pastors, above all, the Roman pontiff. The church is characterized as a *perfect society* in Aristotelian terms. This means that the church has all the means at its disposal to achieve its appointed goals. These are the same faith, the life of the sacraments, and the governance of legitimate pastors. It is therefore dependent on no other society but rather is self-contained — perfect in this sense — in order to achieve its purposes.

If the accent on visibility is understandable, so too are its inherent dangers. The differences with the churches of the Reformation are about doctrine but also about tangible, visible assets — property and official state affiliation. The danger of identifying the true church with its spiritual, invisible elements only — Bellarmine's concern — reinforces the importance of a visible church. The principal weakness, of course, is the identification of the church with its most prominent, external features to the detriment of its interior life.

This accent on visibility had its own effect within the church. Certainly, Catholics should know what is expected of them to be members in good standing. They should know the rules for Mass attendance, Easter duty, fasting, and other duties. The rules on the sacraments — the matter and form of each — should be clear. Such matters are all the more important because the church is in hostile territory. The opponents outside are visible. Dependable troops within should be recognizable as well. The church may be fairly described as a *pyramid* in which its most visible member is also its most important, the pope. Given its imperiled status, obedience is a high virtue.

Yet the church in the neo-Scholastic synthesis is also more than Robert Bellarmine's *perfect society*. Recall that the subject of the church first appears in "fundamental" theology as the guardian of the deposit of faith. The appeal to church teaching is the decisive decision-making instance in regard to the "theses" of neo-Scholastic thought. That means that while the church will be a topic for itself in theology, it will also be *the all-encompassing authoritative presence* that holds the entire neo-Scholastic synthesis together.

For this reason, the various parts of this synthesis fit tightly together as interlocking pieces of a single system. Revelation and faith form a unit. The doctrines of the Trinity, of Christ, the church, sacraments, grace, and the last things fit together as well. They may often appear desiccated, caught in the amber of old disputes, but that is secondary. The objective content of each doctrine is sharply defined in conceptual terms, and that is important. If the neo-Scholastic theology in its construction comprises a tight package, the 1928 encyclical *The Souls of Mortals* (*Mortalium Animos*) ties the pieces even closer together.[41] This encyclical rejects any Catholic participation in the ecumenical movement. It argues that the authority of the church stands behind all doctrine of the faith, equally behind the Trinity, the Immaculate Conception, papal infallibility, and other teachings. Hence, the denial of any truth constitutes a formal attack on the church's authority. Accordingly, for Catholics, there is no hierarchy of truths and therefore no basis for dialogue with other Christians. The encyclical makes Catholic doctrine into a very tightly woven garment. Pull out a thread here, and a sleeve may fall off. Pull out two threads, and the garment may unravel. Question the authority of the church, and the garment comes apart at the seams. Although a 1949 Instruction of the Holy Office adopts a cautiously positive attitude toward the ecumenical movement — a turning point in one sense — it does not fundamentally alter this picture.[42]

The 1943 encyclical *The Mystical Body of Christ* (*Mystici Corporis*) of Pope Pius XII seeks to remedy a largely juridical understanding of the church by a return to biblical sources. In the Pauline notion of the body of Christ, especially as it appears in Colossians and Ephesians, a biblical metaphor is found that aptly describes the church. The image turns on a vision of Christ as the heavenly head of the church, which is his body, his earthly extension, here identified with the visible Roman Catholic Church. Perhaps the encyclical's most notable contribution is the identification of the Holy Spirit with the soul or unifying principle of the church. The encyclical quotes Pope Leo XIII making his thought its own: "Let it suffice to say that, as Christ is the head of the Church, so the Holy Spirit is its soul."[43]

Yet the identification of the mystical body of Christ with the visible Roman Catholic Church, repeated again in 1951 in *Humani Generis*, creates its own problematic. If there is no salvation outside the church, then membership in the church must be understood in a nuanced way to accommodate, as it were, the salvation of countless non-Catholic Christians as well as non-Christians, and this is what the encyclical seeks to do.

This issue comes to a head six years after *Mystici Corporis*. In 1949, the Holy Office sends a letter to Archbishop Richard Cushing (1895– 1970) of Boston regarding the teaching of Jesuit Leonard Feeney (1897–1978).[44] The letter is significant because it reveals the weakness of the older ecclesiology at its own most enlightened point. Feeney takes the traditional axiom "outside the Church, no salvation" quite literally. He therefore preaches that Protestants, all non-Catholics, are denied salvation unless they convert to the visible Roman Catholic Church. No, the Holy Office tartly replies. Instead, it is Feeney who finds himself outside the visible Catholic Church. The letter recalls the teaching of the 1943 encyclical about membership in the Roman Catholic Church. True, there is no salvation outside the church. But there are different kinds of baptism, hence different ways of belonging to the church. There is traditional baptism by water (*in re*). There is also baptism of desire (*in voto*), which may be an *explicit* or *implicit* desire. Therefore, through implicit baptism of desire, millions of Protestants, Jews, Muslim, Hindus, and others are able to be saved. They are counted in this way as members of the visible Roman Catholic Church. Through this complex reasoning and really by this loophole clause, the salvation of the great majority of the human race is made possible.

The weakness of the traditional ecclesiology, here on display, is its exclusive focus on the visible Roman Catholic Church. It also forgets its *own other lessons and practices.* Catholics recognize the baptism of other Christian churches if the baptismal formula is correct. By doing so, it recognizes a basic link to other churches. It also recognizes the hierarchy and the validity of sacraments in Eastern Orthodox churches. Here the connection becomes stronger. Yet in terms of *Mystici Corporis,* people are saved not *because of* but rather *in spite of* their membership in other Christian churches or religions. The latter cannot function as vehicles of salvation for their members. It also follows that people are saved *one by one.* Membership in the Roman Catholic Church by virtue of implicit baptism of desire is an individual affair, not a group affair. Likewise, little distinction is made between other Christians and non-Christians.

Two final comments on this traditional ecclesiology are in order. First, because we view it now across a *species gap,* on the far side of an unbridgeable divide, there may be a tendency to treat this theology disparagingly. This is a mistake. As a defensive ecclesiology, it was highly effective in the nineteenth century and then again in the twentieth century toward even more formidable opponents. Nazism and communism were themselves quasi-religious ideologies, promising their own secular version of salvation. They wanted no peace or compromise with the Roman Catholic Church but only its destruction or, at least, its full submission to their authority. The only option was a defensive ecclesiology. And the enemies were real, not imagined.

Second, the older ecclesiology was not undone by any of its outside opponents. It collapsed because of forces within the church. Welte observes that the same positivist spirit that motivated "progressive" opposition to the church in the late nineteenth century also found a fruitful outlet within the church.[45] The same spirit spurred groundbreaking historical research in Scripture, church history, archeology, patristics, liturgy, and medieval studies. These were the years, for example, in which the great Berlin and Vienna editions of the Fathers appeared. But such research found expression either in individual monographs or in extended collections such as the editions of the Fathers. Although the material begged for incorporation into a larger theology, a *synthetic moment,* such was lacking. Welte speaks of a *disso-ciation* between the mounds of accumulating discrete research and an analysis of their meaning for Catholic theology. But this was precisely the kind of historical material the neo-Scholastic synthesis could not absorb. Consequently, Catholic theology from the nineteenth century to the middle of the twentieth century moved on parallel tracks. The neo-Scholastic manual tradition continued to be taught in seminaries, updated by *Mystici Corporis* of 1943, reflecting as well the cautions of *Humani Generis* of 1950. But all around this official theology, move-ment of renewal swirled. Invariably, *renewal* meant *retrieval,* a return to the sources. Research into the fathers of the church that could hardly be suspect had wide-ranging ramifications for the modern church. Like-wise, research into Thomas Aquinas revealed him to be quite different from the hard-edged Thomism of the first generation. He was simply much more original, balanced, and optimistic about the capacity of human reason than the first neo-Thomists. The recovery of Thomas himself spontaneously prompted dialogue with modern streams of thought.

Hence, outside neo-Scholastic theology and official circles, renewal movements in Scripture, patristics, liturgy, medieval thought, and Mar-iology were steadily gaining momentum. The official church observed these developments, at times registering approval, at other times cau-tion and disapproval. Thus in a larger sense, the notion of the church as an institution outside history that receives its teaching directly from above becomes increasingly implausible. If such functioned at first as a useful fiction, it becomes increasingly an untenable conceit.

IV. Vatican II and the Church

Looking back on the Second Vatican Council, church historian John O'Malley writes, "From the viewpoint of Church history, it can be categorically asserted that never before in the history of Catholicism had so many and such sudden changes been implemented, often with-out adequate explanation, that immediately touched the lives of all the faithful, and never before had such a radical adjustment of attitude been required of them."[46] Such an event, now almost two genera-tions distant from us, gains an air of inevitability. The Second Vatican

Council had to happen. Vatican II had to be. Theologians who were widely suspect ten years before the council — Yves Congar (1904–1995), Henri de Lubac (1896–1991), Karl Rahner (1904–1984), John Courtney Murray (1904–1967) — were now engaged in fashioning council documents. The vindication of the council reflected in the lives of individual theologians reinforces the aura of inevitability. But such a perspective is false. The council occurs at an optimistic moment, a window of opportunity, in the early 1960s, in an otherwise bleak and tragic century. The decision to convene the council rests with one man, truly *nel petto del papa,* in the breast of Pope John XXIII. As unexpected as his unlikely name, the decision to call a council is his own. There is no reason why Catholic theology could not have continued on its uncomfortable parallel tracks for the foreseeable future. But once the decision is made to call a council, what is *inevitable* is that these two tracks had to be brought together, no matter what the consequences.

O'Malley seeks to identify what is particular to Vatican II, comparing this event to other great turning points in church history, the Reformation and the Gregorian revolution. Those movements had a strong element of reversal. Simply put, they were closer to revolutions in the usual sense. The banner cry of Vatican II — *aggiornamento* — is different, although it represents no less a momentous turning point. O'Malley seeks to characterize the difference: "Whereas, in those reformations the paradigm flew in the face of convention, in this instance it represents a belated recognition of the already established reality of the new historical consciousness. There are other realities to which it relates as well: the emergence of democracy as a favored political form, the world as a global village, a new religious and cultural pluralism, and similar phenomena."[47]

Aggiornamento, in John XXIII's word, pastoral updating, might be described as the church's effort to update its message in a way that speaks more effectively in the modern era. It is significant that such a seemingly benign and modest goal could involve so many stark changes. The fact is all the more significant given the style of the council documents. Vatican II consciously avoided the legal language of earlier councils with their terse, closing anathemas, the language of commands and prohibitions. Instead, it chose a style close to those patristic sources that inspired the renewal in the first place. The documents are exhortatory. Their language is one of persuasion. The documents set forth an ideal in a consistently magnanimous and high-minded tone.[48]

The documents are also committee statements, seeking to forge consensus by blending different, sometimes conflicting, points of view. But they are fair and even-handed in doing so. Much like the intent of the documents themselves, consensus is sought by persuasion and fair compromise. Given the same factors, the documents are wordy, not easy to read, and difficult to interpret for the uninitiated without a commentary in hand. Yet, with all these difficulties, at two generations' distance, the documents of Vatican II stand up well. In fact, the closer the scrutiny, the better they look.

But given the seemingly modest goals and the diffuse style of compromise documents, the council was nevertheless able to strike out boldly in new directions whose lineaments are clear and unmistakable. One might compare the broad goal of *aggiornamento* to the wheeling movement of an entire army that seeks to change the direction it faces. If *aggiornamento* was as diffuse as the style of the documents of Vatican II, it was also very broadly based. Because Vatican II was not prompted by specific aggravating problems, it could review and update the church's life as a whole, and therein lay its revolutionary character. I will seek to trace these changes on five fronts: the church and the churches, the church itself, the liturgy, revelation, and the church in the modern world. These five topics do not exhaust the teaching of Vatican II on the church, but they do give us a fair sense of it.

The Church and the Churches

It is significant that Vatican II's dogmatic constitution on the church, *Lumen Gentium* (*Light of the Peoples*), begins with the mystery of the church. Here the church is described as the sacrament that reveals the mystery of the Trinity and the incarnation. Here as well the church returns to its ancient starting point. The church does not speak about itself first. It speaks about what God has chosen to reveal about himself by sending His Son into the world for the sake of our salvation. Only in this perspective does the church itself come into proper focus. It is notable that few official statements about the church since the commencement of the genre in the early 1300s had begun in quite this way.

The starting point yields a fresh perspective and it appears at once in *Lumen Gentium* §8: "This Church (the sole Church of Christ), constituted and organized as a society in the present world, subsists in the Catholic Church which is governed by the successor of Peter and by the bishops in communion with him. Nevertheless, many elements of sanctification and of truth are found outside its visible confines. Since these are gifts belonging to the Church of Christ, they are forces impelling towards Catholic unity." The text departs from a rather substantial tradition of the Ordinary Magisterium, which simply identifies the church of Christ with the visible Roman Catholic Church.[49] Doubtless the words on which the text turns are perhaps the most famous in the council's vocabulary: *subsist in.*[50] In otherwise diffuse documents, these two words are deliberately chosen and, after still further deliberation, consciously reaffirmed. The church of Christ *subsists in* — is concretely found — in its fullness in the visible Roman Catholic Church; however, elements are also found outside of it in other Christian churches and in a still broader sense in other religions as well.

The text makes two points. First, the "fullness" of the elements that comprise the church of Christ is concretely found in the visible Catholic Church. The church is not a spiritual entity that hovers above space and time; it exists as an institution in this world. Second, elements or endowments of the church of Christ exist outside the Roman Catholic Church in other Christian churches. Insofar as these elements are found in other churches, they are vehicles of salvation for their members. Gone is the language of baptism of desire, except for Roman Catholics. Instead, the documents speak of "full or partial" incorporation into the church of Christ. The larger point is that, according to Vatican II, people are saved *not in spite of* but rather *because of* their membership in other Christian churches. This *social* recognition of other Christian churches and ecclesial communities represents a signal contribution of Vatican II. Such may have been implicit in some sense before. Here it becomes explicit and central.

What are these elements of sanctification and truth that comprise the church of Christ? *Lumen Gentium* §15 lists them without attempting to be exhaustive or even systematic: "For there are many who hold sacred scripture in honor as a rule of faith and of life, who have a sincere religious zeal, who lovingly believe in God the Father Almighty and in Christ, the Son of God, and the Savior, who are sealed by baptism which unites them to Christ, and who indeed recognize and receive other sacraments in their own Churches or ecclesiastical communities. Many of them possess the episcopate, celebrate the holy Eucharist and cultivate devotion to the Virgin Mother of God. There is a further sharing in prayer and spiritual benefits."[51]

This paragraph introduces the so-called "ecclesiology of elements," which needs to be properly contextualized. The approach does not itself represent a formal doctrine but rather a practical tool to gain some sense of how the church of Christ is present in other Christian "Churches and ecclesiastical communities." The latter two terms are used in tandem for a variety of reasons.[52] The approach is also helpful because it avoids a one-size-fits-all approach to other Christian churches. However, the dangers are also apparent. It simply is impossible to tabulate these elements in a mathematical formula and so arrive at a *quantitative measure* of closeness to the church of Christ. What is absent in an "ecclesiology of elements" taken by itself is a sense of the larger *whole* in which those elements receive a context and find their meaning.

This sense of the whole is supplied in several ways. First, all elements or endowments spring from the church of Christ and are the action of *one* Spirit. They have a common origin. They also look forward to a future fulfillment when the church of Christ is present not just in its fullness but also in its perfection. In other words, the goal of church unity is not envisioned as the return of other churches to the visible Roman Catholic Church as errant children returning home; rather, the goal looks to the future, first to the gradual growth together of Christian churches and finally to their eschatological union in the kingdom. Indeed, the point of the recognizing these elements is that they comprise forces that impel toward Christian unity. In regard to the distinctive unity of other Christian churches and ecclesial communities, Vatican II's decree on ecumenism *Unitatis Redintegratio* (*Restoration of Unity*) specifies that dialogue between churches is only possible if one appreciates the "spirit" or the unique character of other churches.[53]

Here the "endowments" of the church of Christ receive their context and meaning in terms of the ethos of other churches and communities.

Likewise, it should be noted that the *fullness* does not mean their *perfection* of these elements. If elements of the church of Christ are found in other churches and communities outside the visible Catholic Church, they may have been better preserved there. This would be true of the Scriptures in the church of the Reformation, for whom the Word of God is paramount. Liturgy and spirituality seem especially lustrous endowments of the Eastern churches.

In regard to other religions, those close to Christianity, Judaism, and Islam and those distant, here *Lumen Gentium* reveals its widest aperture of good will: "Those who, through no fault of their own, do not know the Gospel of Christ or his Church, but nevertheless seek God with a sincere heart, and, moved by grace, try in their actions to do his will as they know it through the dictates of their conscience — those too may achieve eternal salvation. Nor shall divine providence deny the assistance necessary for salvation to those who, without any fault of theirs, have not yet arrived at an explicit knowledge of God, and who, not without grace, strive to lead a good life. Whatever good or truth is found among them is considered by the Church to be a preparation."[54]

I wish to present this central insight of Vatican II in its simplicity and its boldness, but this is also a complex insight with wide-ranging implications. In other words, the bold opening of *Lumen Gentium* requires further expansion and careful elaborations that I can only briefly sketch. This elaboration takes place in concentric circles of cross-references *within Lumen Gentium* and then *with other* decrees and declarations of Vatican II. Within *Lumen Gentium,* §§14–16 treat successively the situation of Catholics, other Christians, and non-Christians. These sections are cross-referenced to the decree *Unitatis Redintegratio.* That decree's first chapter continues to unfold the doctrinal implications of the new position before moving on to the practice of ecumenism. Chapter 3 of *Unitatis Redintegratio* treats with special sensitivity the nature of the separation with the Eastern churches and then with the churches of the Reformation. The constitution on the church must also take account of Eastern churches already within the Catholic fold (the decree *Orientalium Ecclesiarum* [*Of the Eastern*

Churches]). The broadest implication of *Lumen Gentium* §16 toward
non-Christian religions is unfolded in the declaration *Nostra Aetate* (*In
Our Time*). The declaration mentions Buddhism, Hinduism, Islam,
and, above all, Judaism. "Other religions which are found throughout
the world attempt in their own way to calm the hearts of men by out-
lining a program of life covering doctrine, moral precepts and sacred
rites. The Catholic Church rejects nothing of what is true and holy in
these religions."[55] Noteworthy is that the church formally dissociates
itself from all forms of anti-Semitism that seek to implicate Jews, past
or present, in the crucifixion of Jesus.

Vatican II

Our focus now shifts to the Catholic Church itself. We return to *Lumen
Gentium* §8 as our starting point. It is significant that the section describes the Catholic Church as "governed by the successor of Peter and
by other bishops in communion with him." Respecting the sensitivi-
ties of Eastern Catholics, *Roman* Catholic in an earlier draft becomes
simply *Catholic* Church in the official text. Similarly, *Roman Pontiff* in
an earlier draft becomes in the final version "the successor of Peter."[56]

These changes signal another significant shift in the church's self-
understanding. The first meaning of the church is the *local* church.
Here the church dissociates itself from the view, often a caricature, of
the Roman Catholic Church as an international religious conglomer-
ate with the local churches as branch offices and bishops as appointed
branch managers. On the contrary, every local church is a full em-
bodiment of the church as one, holy, catholic, and apostolic. Each
local church realizes the fullness of the church when it celebrates the
Eucharist.

In other words, the Catholic Church itself is a union of local
churches, reflecting wide ethnic and cultural diversity. The bishop of
Rome is the head of the local church of Rome. As successor of Peter,
he presides over the whole church. But the local church is where the
Catholic Church lives and breathes in its most lively and natural way.
In one sense, this notion of the Catholic Church as a union of diverse local churches that share *full* communion dovetails with the view
of the *partial* communion of the Catholic churches with other Christian churches and communities. The church of its nature represents

unity in diversity.[57] In regard to other Christian churches, the accent on diversity is strong enough to make the union only a partial one.

This accent on the local church is inseparable from Vatican II's renewed emphasis on the role of the bishop. This was by far the most controversial topic on the council's agenda, the neuralgic flashpoint of conflict between progressive and traditional viewpoints. The issue is a complex one. First, it has to do with the role of the bishop's office *individually* in terms of the Sacrament of Orders. Does the episcopacy belong to the Sacrament of Orders? Does the episcopacy represent the *fullness* of the priesthood? The theological consensus before Vatican II was affirmative on both scores. The council takes a further step and makes a doctrinal decision in their favor. In other words, at Vatican II those *theological opinions* become *official Catholic teaching*. But in taking this step, the Catholic Church departs from a roughly 850–year-old Western tradition that saw the fullness of the Sacrament of Orders in the ordinary priesthood, inseparable from the moment when a man received the power to change bread and wine into the body and blood of Christ. What could be higher than this endowment? This decision will prove a fateful one with the law of unforeseen consequences fully engaged.

But the real nub of the controversy lies elsewhere. It was the bishops' *communal* status if they comprise an officially separate order within the priesthood. Branch managers have no independent status. They are merely appointees. But if the bishops are successors of the apostles in their own right, if they comprise the fullness of the priesthood, then the bishops' collective status — the college of bishops — becomes a force to be reckoned with in the church. Here the issue of collegiality enters and a new torque is given to the teaching of Vatican I. Without denying the doctrine of papal infallibility, is the college of bishops with the successor of Peter as its head collegially responsible not just for the local churches but also for the universal church? Does such represent a collegial responsibility of the bishops with the pope, a duty that they collaboratively discharge? Here the periphery, the local church and its bishop, seeks to play a larger role at the center in the life of the universal church.

The fear, of course, was that the teaching of Vatican I on papal infallibility could be played off against the teaching of Vatican II on episcopal collegiality.[58] Or are these complementary insights? And if so, how could they be implemented in order to highlight the role of the bishops in the overall guidance of the Catholic Church? It is not difficult to see why this issue comprised the most serious and thorny one facing the Second Vatican Council.

The Liturgy

The constitution on the liturgy, *Sacrosanctum Concilium* (*Sacred Council*), is the first major document approved by Vatican II.[59] The action was taken on December 3, 1963, and the vote was 2,147 in favor, 4 opposed. Given the firestorm that this constitution ignites, its passage through the council is placid. The only source of controversy is whether the council should lay down general principles, leaving more specific implementation to others later on. The council decides otherwise. It chooses instead to undertake a major overhaul of the Western rite. Here, in spite of the favored language of persuasion, the velvet glove is removed, revealing a steely iron fist. By any measure, *Sacrosanctum Concilium* is a draconian document, setting down a series of master commands. Most constitutions or decrees of Vatican II have only a few follow-up documents, some none. *Sacrosanctum Concilium* required twenty-four follow-up documents. What makes the reform all the more effective is that it is specifically focused. The focus is boldly proclaimed in §14. The "aim" of reform "to be considered before all else" is the "full, active participation of all the people." Here the favored metaphor of the Vatican II church — the people of God — seems fully on display.

These reforms are swiftly implemented. A new book of rites is issued in 1976, completing the sacramental overhaul. The new Mass appears almost at once. Little matter that importance changes are introduced by loophole clauses — for example, the vernacular, communion under both kinds, and concelebration. The centerpiece of the reform is the new Mass. Two elements in its composition dovetail exactly: the vernacular liturgy and Mass facing the people. Together, they establish an *interactive moment* between celebrant and congregation. An electric spark arcs between these poles. New roles for priest and people come to life. A new ethos is born almost at once. The Mass of Pius V of

1570 virtually disappears overnight. It was not that Catholics disliked the Latin Mass; they simply like the vernacular liturgy more.

By any measure, a revolution now begins that may be channeled but cannot be stopped until it runs it course. The council fathers could hardly have intended this when they approved so overwhelmingly *Sacrosanctum Concilium* on December 3, 1963. But who intends a revolution? Later on, the lament is often heard that the people were unprepared for the new liturgy. Can anyone ever be prepared for a revolutionary turn?

Revelation

The dogmatic constitution on divine revelation, *Dei Verbum* (*Word of God*), addresses the most fundamental category of Catholic theology: the nature of divine revelation, establishing a new starting point on this topic. God reveals himself not in theological proposition (as it may have seemed in the neo-Scholastic synthesis) but rather in word and deed in salvation history. God's words and deeds mutually interpret one another as complementary moments of divine revelation.

This new starting point sheds fresh light on the traditional discussion of Scripture and tradition. How are they understood? Together, Scripture and tradition are compared to a "mirror, in which the Church during its pilgrim journey on earth, contemplates God."[60] The Scripture is the Word of God in written form. Tradition is the way in which the Scriptures are handed on in the "doctrine, life and worship" of the church. The question of the *material* sufficiency of the Scriptures (whether all doctrines are contained in the Scriptures) is left open, but the emphasis shifts. Tradition is regarded no longer as an additional source of doctrinal information but rather as a locus of the church's *certitude*. "The Church does not draw her certainty about all revealed truths from the Holy Scriptures alone."[61] The task of authentic interpretation is entrusted to the teaching office of the church alone. However, "this Magisterium is not above the Word of God but is its servant." Indeed, "sacred Tradition, sacred Scripture and the Magisterium of the Church are so connected and associated that one of them cannot stand with the others."[62]

Dei Verbum considers basic questions about the Scriptures as a whole: the meaning of biblical authorship, inspiration, and inerrancy.

In regard to the latter, the Scriptures are without error in light of their purpose. They contain the truth that God seeks to convey for the sake of our salvation; they do not seek to teach natural science. The text turns first to the Old Testament, endorsing the teaching of Pius XII's 1943 encyclical *Divino Afflante Spiritu*. Then it moves to the New Testament, carefully endorsing a form-critical approach to the Gospels. This passage captures the most sensitive issue about the Gospels' historical character: "The sacred authors, in writing the four Gospels, selected certain of the many elements which had been handed on, either orally or already in written form; others they synthesized or explained with an eye to the situation of the churches, the while sustaining the form of preaching, but always in such a fashion that they have told us the honest truth about Jesus."[63]

When we add these factors together, we see that *Dei Verbum* establishes a new place for the Bible in Catholic life. It also points to a new, more biblical orientation for Catholic theology as a whole. Therefore, when *Dei Verbum* endorses Leo XIII's pithy saying "The study of the sacred page should be the soul of theology," it gives the maxim new meaning.[64] Yves Congar describes *Dei Verbum* on the day of its promulgation, November 18, 1965, as "a great document that provides theology with the *means* to become fully evangelical."[65] Henri de Lubac sees progress first and foremost in the area of "fundamental theology — which is also theology of the Bible."[66]

It was noted early on in *Dei Verbum* that if the nature of revelation shifts in meaning, the meaning of faith must change as well. And so it does. Faith is first described as a commitment of the "entire self."[67] Only in this larger existential context does the traditional intellectual definition of faith make sense. But small changes of this kind presage larger ones shortly to follow. Revelation and faith as correlative notions fit together. They comprise the heart of fundamental theology. But if fundamental theology — the horizontal foundation of the theological superstructure — changes, can the upper stories remain the same? To return to our image: pull out one thread of the neo-Scholastic synthesis, and a sleeve may fall off; pull out more, and the entire garment may come apart. This is what we now see. On the one hand, a more biblically oriented Catholic theology struggles to find its way on the basis of *Dei Verbum*; on the other hand, the neo-Scholastic manual disappears virtually overnight. What is a usable textbook in a semi-nary classroom in 1963 becomes a dinosaur bone by 1965. This is the second such disappearance we have seen.

The Church in the Modern World

The constitution on the church in the modern world adds the final piece to the new conception of the church. The first two words of this pastoral constitution say it all: *Gaudium et Spes (Joy and Hope)*. What would the first two words have been had such a document been issued twenty-five or fifty years earlier, "Sadness and Suspicion"? But there was no document like this before. If those had been the sentiments, better to say nothing. Yet here the church seeks to speak not just to Catholics or Christians but rather to all people. Here Vatican II breaks new ground. There simply is no prior model for this kind of council document.

The church speaks to all people of the age because it acknowledges the world's concrete problems as its own: the protection and promo-tion of human rights, the question of war and peace, the problems of hunger and disease, the condition of the family and the workplace. In other words, the right ordering of the economic and social order is a first concern of the church. *Gaudium et Spes* uses biblical perspectives to frame its social teaching without renouncing the appeal to natural law. But biblical teaching is the special light that it has to shed on the world's problems.

Gaudium et Spes is approved in the final session of Vatican II on December 7, 1965. It is the subject of debate and withering criticism both from within and from outside the council.[68] Its weaknesses are well known. But despite all such limitations, a beginning is made. New ground must be broken, no matter how incomplete the effort; therein lies the special significance of *Gaudium et Spes*. This constitution also has an immediate effect. Peter Hünermann observes, "In the post-conciliar period there has been almost no great ecclesial controversy that has not been closely connected with what is said in *Gaudium et Spes*." He tabulates the count from birth control to liberation theology and other problem areas, drawing this conclusion: "All these questions were occasioned by and had roots in *Gaudium et Spes*."[69]

Summary

When we add these factors together — the church and the churches, the church itself, the liturgy, revelation, the church in the modern world — we see that they comprise a coherent new theology of the church. The difficulty comes when we place them against an equally coherent but quite different theology that this new conception replaces. If the older view regarded the world with suspicion, the newer one greets it with hope and joy, extending a hand of friendship. If the older theology viewed other churches and religions with hesitation, once again the newer one extends a hand of friendship. If biblical scholarship was formerly viewed with caution, it is now embraced. If the old liturgy was in Latin, it is now consistent with the newer conception that the Catholic liturgy speaks the world's vernacular languages.

Taken one by one, these changes are hardly extreme, but in the aggregate they comprise a momentous turn, indeed a revolutionary one but of a special kind. It was not as if the battle cry went out against entrenched positions with the ensuing theological and doctrinal battles stretching over generations. The council's debates were often heated, but high-minded consensus invariably won the day on even the most hotly contested questions. It was rather that there was *so little flexibility* in the older conception of the church. The church had prided itself on its changeless character in the face of an ever-changing world. Now the church changes. It was as if air from outside reached a hermetically sealed building, a fresh breeze penetrating the mummy's tomb, old bones turning to ashes on the spot. Hence, a characteristic feature of the changes of Vatican II are a series of virtual *disappearances*. The Latin Mass virtually disappears as a normal experience for the average Catholic. Many old devotions disappear as well. The neo-Scholastic manual becomes an outright relic. The seminary system, emblematic of the Tridentine church, totters briefly on its foundations, and then, like a tall brick building in an earthquake, it collapses.

The law of unforeseen consequences is everywhere at play in changes of this magnitude, especially when they are coherent. And Vatican II's consistency was the key to its effectiveness. It literally sucked the air out of the older view of the church. The virtual disappearances also had the effect of presenting a conservative viewpoint with a series of *faits accomplis,* chief of which was the new liturgy.

We are still too close to Vatican II to have an accurate perspective about its lasting significance. Such will require the experience of several generations because it will take that long to implement the council's initiatives, much less assess their outcome. But it does seem that John O'Malley's article "Vatican II: Did Anything Happen?" is a bellwether of the current moment. Perhaps only when the changes of the council, at two generations remove, loom so large do they prompt the rejoinder that, in reality, nothing much happened, that "the council was in all important regards continuous with the Catholic past."[70] That may be true. The Catholic past is broad and capacious.

But this much is now clear: there is no turning back from the paths that Vatican II has opened, although the road may stretch far into the future with challenges that are arduous. One may retrieve lost items. Some traditional devotions are returning — for example, eucharistic adoration, Marian devotion, the stations of the cross — but turning back the clock is not an option. It is also impossible to predict the future. We note but one ironic consequence, an unforeseen consequence, of the enhanced role of the episcopate and the importance of the local church. Regular synods of bishops with the pope occur now every three years. Regional gatherings of bishops take on greater importance, as do national episcopal conferences. But who could have guessed that the papacy, which on one level some might view as a somewhat diminished player in the new scheme of things, would see the accession in 1978 of Pope John Paul II, who grasped the new situation as an opportunity for the papacy? If a new relation between center and periphery was introduced by Vatican II, John Paul II had an affection for and a mission to local churches. During his pontificate of almost twenty-seven years, this pope tirelessly visited every region of the globe, bringing the luster of the papal office to the life of the local church. At his death in 2005, one sitting American president and two former ones were happy to bask in the bright afterglow of this heroic pope at his funeral. Who could have guessed at such a turn? Who can know what lies ahead?

Chapter Eight

MARY

Our attention turns in this chapter to the Blessed Virgin Mary, historical person, the mother of Jesus, and symbolic figure, important to all Christians, especially to Eastern Orthodox and Roman Catholics. This chapter seeks to trace the role of Mary in Catholic tradition through seven stages.

First, we begin with the role of Mary in the Gospels and the kind of trajectory that emerges when we place the Gospels side by side. Here the basic viewpoint about Mary's role is established. Here as well the torque, a counterpoint, is set that gives later development both its dynamism and originality with its own negative potential.

Second, we trace in broad strokes the development of the church's understanding of Mary in the patristic era. This development reaches a significant moment and a new starting point at the Council of Ephesus in 431, when Mary is declared *Theotokos,* Mother of God, the touchstone of the council's teaching. *Theotokos* is, of course, a christological statement about the close union of the two natures of Christ, humanity never existing apart from divinity. We examined this side of the ledger in an earlier chapter. But *Theotokos* is equally a statement about Mary. This is the focus in the present one.

Third, this chapter resembles the previous one on the church in that it seeks to examine what is unique to Mary's role in the Western tradition. We begin this section with Anselm and Eadmer of Canterbury and trace the emergence of Western medieval Mariology with its characteristic features. This discussion comes to a head in the debate about the doctrine of the Immaculate Conception, proclaimed a dogma by the Council of Basel in 1439, but after the council's official mandate had expired.

Fourth, the doctrine of the Immaculate Conception represents the *historical glissando* in this chapter just as the section on the papacy did in the previous chapter on the Western Church. It provides us here with a double link. The Immaculate Conception serves to introduce the modern discussion of the Virgin's role in the Western Church. It also connects us with the final section of the chapter on Marian apparitions. Recall that Mary introduces herself at Lourdes as the Immaculate Conception.

Fifth, the Immaculate Conception, the Reformation debates about the Virgin, and the controversy as well as the devotional exuberance of the seventeenth century each add a touch to a new vision of Mary. Now the Virgin is transformed from a single person or doctrine into a series of *personifications* about the post-Reformation Catholic Church. We examine here these various symbolic personifications that cluster around the figure of Mary.

Sixth, the Second Vatican Council represents a turning point and watershed moment in Roman Catholic understanding of Mary. Vatican II was faced with two quite different approaches to the person and role of the Virgin. Although the text of *Lumen Gentium* seeks to balance opposing views, this is not how the outcome of the council's deliberations was read at the time or is read now. Rather, Vatican II made a *decision* about Mary's role and how it should be interpreted. We will examine this decision and the way it was received in the church after Vatican II.

Seventh, we will examine the role of Mary as she appears in modern apparitions that represent the most active tectonic plate in Marian devotion and perhaps in doctrine as well. New perspectives emerge in the nineteenth and twentieth centuries that complete the story.

I believe that two basic trajectories stretch throughout the development of Mary's role in Christian tradition. Rooted in the New Testament, the first envisions Mary as *disciple* par excellence, the model of what it means to be a follower of Jesus. This trajectory emerges on the basis of a plain reading of the Gospels. The second may be particular to the Western church. Here Mary becomes the *receptacle for recessive traits* of the Deity that are essential to God or Christ but are difficult for an age to envision. Such qualities migrate to the person of Mary. For the medieval era, the element is mercy, hence the special quality that the title "Mother of Mercies" takes on — Mary as the special source of human succor and consolation. In the modern era, the quality may be justice. Here Mary, especially as she appears in modern apparitions, becomes an apocalyptic figure, proclaiming God's judgment on the world. This occurs in an era in which divine judgment envisioned in graphic terms is not a favored topic of enlightened theological discourse.

I. Mary in the Scriptures

The apostle Paul mentions that Jesus was "born of a woman" (Gal. 4:4), but the figure of Mary emerges more clearly from the pages of the Gospels. Here the starting point is Mark 3:31–35. And the first note struck is one of rejection. Jesus' family — his mother and his brothers and sisters — come to restrain him because people are saying, "He has gone out of his mind" (Mark 3:21). The remark sets the context for the following exchange. Jesus is told, "Your mother and your brothers and sisters are outside, asking for you." He replies, "Who are my mother and my brothers?" And, then, looking at those sitting around him, he says, "Here are my mother and my brothers! Whoever does the will of God is my brother and sister and mother" (Mark 3:32–35).

One thinks of a similar moment in the puzzling dialogue at the wedding feast in Cana in the Gospel of John: "Woman, what concern is that to you and to me? My hour has not yet come" (John 2:4). This may not be a note of rejection, but it is, at least, one of distance, not unlike the words of the child Jesus in the temple in Luke's Gospel. Also recall the proverb that Jesus quotes in Nazareth: "A prophet is not without honor except in his own country, and among his own kin, and in his own house" (Luke 4:4; cf. Mark 6:4; Matt. 13:57). The Gospel of Luke captures the point: "A woman in the crowd raised her voice and said to him, 'Blessed is the womb that bore you and the breasts that nursed you!' But he said, 'Blessed rather are those who hear the word of God and obey it!'" (Luke 11:27–28).

The Gospels display here rare unanimity, surely an indication that the teaching goes back to Jesus himself. The first family is not established by the claims of blood kinship; rather, Jesus' family comprises those who hear the word of God and keep it. These are his true family, mother and sister and brother to him. This is what it means to be a follower of Jesus.

When Mark 3:21–35 is taken over by Matthew and Luke, all hint of Jesus' "gone out of his mind" is struck. Indeed, Luke suggests that Jesus' natural family may be included among the family of believers. The suggestion is confirmed in Acts 1:14 when they are, in fact, counted among his followers. But they are included because they have met the test of discipleship. Jesus' natural family has heard the word of God and kept it. Indeed, such obedience becomes the key to interpreting Jesus' own conception according to Luke. The angel announces to Mary that she will bear a son and is to name him Jesus (Luke 1:30–31). Mary's response echoes the words of a disciple: "Let it be with me according to your word" (Luke 1:38). Mary has heard the word and kept it. Through her obedient response, Jesus himself is conceived.

These accents on discipleship culminate in the great scene under the cross in the Gospel of John. Mary is never called by her proper name in this Gospel; rather she is the "mother" of Jesus, underscoring her symbolic role in the drama that unfolds. Recall that in the earliest tradition, Jesus dies alone, abandoned by his followers. But in John's Gospel, some remain faithful: Jesus' mother, his mother's sister, Mary the wife of Clopas, Mary Magdalene (shortly to be the first witness to Jesus' resurrection), and the unnamed "beloved disciple." The dialogue under the cross is striking: "When Jesus saw his mother and the disciple whom he loved standing beside her, he said to his mother, 'Woman, here is your son.' Then he said to the disciple, 'Here is your mother.' And from that hour the disciple took her into his own home" (John 19:26–27). The dialogue represents Jesus' last will and testament on discipleship. Under the cross, Mary, his mother, remains a faithful disciple. But at this climactic moment, she also becomes mother of the beloved disciple, heretofore the model of discipleship. Now Mary herself becomes that model. She becomes *disciple* par excellence.

John understands the paradoxical logic of the Gospels, set by Jesus himself, the crucified Messiah who rises from the dead. Mary is now ranged among the stunning figures of reversal who exemplify in different ways what it means to follow Jesus. They begin with Peter, who denies Jesus three times and abandons him at the moment of testing. In light of the resurrection, he becomes chief shepherd who tends Jesus' flock. Likewise, Paul, who persecutes the first mission of the fledgling church, becomes its chief missionary. In the same vein, John places on the lips of Thomas, who doubts, one of the clearest confessions of Christ's divinity: "My Lord and my God!" (John 20:28).

Mary's role should be seen in this light. The image of the disciple in the Gospel is the child who regards God as Father and receives the kingdom as a little one (Mark 10:15; Matt. 18:2–5; Luke 9:46–48). Now Mary the mother becomes offspring to her own Son's preaching. Hence, this most natural and basic relationship, that of a mother to a son, is subordinated to and derived from Mary's role as disciple. In other words, discipleship establishes a stronger bond than natural motherhood. Indeed, discipleship has determined the very nature of Mary's motherhood. This is not the usual way that mothers and sons relate, not the usual way that the fierce, primordial bond of motherhood is understood. Indeed, the subordination of *motherhood to discipleship* establishes the torque, or counterpoint, that later gives the development of the doctrine of Mary its dynamism and special quality.

But for now, Mary is disciple par excellence, mother of the beloved disciple. Here she also becomes mother of many other sons and daughters who aspire to discipleship in Jesus' name in the centuries that follow. We noted in earlier chapters that in light of the resurrection of Jesus, certain questions are asked and then answered. Here this question is posed: *In light of Jesus' resurrection, what does it mean to be a disciple of Jesus?* The figure of Mary provides the answer. It means to hear the word of God and keep it. It means to subordinate that deepest of human relationships, that of a mother to a son, to the demands of discipleship.

The infancy narrative of Matthew's Gospel sees the birth of Jesus and the motherhood of Mary in continuity with Israel's past and its earliest ancestors. The genealogy of Matthew begins the story of Jesus with Abraham, tracing the paradoxical places in which the seed of the messiah has slumbered. The genealogy passes through the best of Israel's kings, David and Solomon, as well as the worst, Manasseh. It travels through the faceless Jews after the exile of whom only a name remains. But nowhere is the genealogy more paradoxical than in the four women it reckons as ancestors of Jesus. Not the traditional heroines of the Old Testament — Sarah, Rachel, Rebecca. Instead, it names four women — Rahab, Tamar, Ruth, Bathsheba — who are either foreigners or, in the case of Bathsheba, married to a foreigner. They are outsiders, women out of the mainstream. Rahab, told of in the book of Joshua, is the prostitute in Jericho who hides Israelite spies as they reconnoiter the city. If they are joined by a single characteristic, it is the irregular marital unions in which these women are enmeshed. They therefore foreshadow the embarrassment of Mary, who finds herself with child before she lives with her husband, Joseph. So it may seem to worldly eyes. Through the eyes of faith, Joseph learns in a dream that all of this takes place to fulfill the words of the prophet Isaiah in the (Greek) Old Testament that a virgin will conceive and bear a son, "and they shall name him Emmanuel" (Isa. 7:14; Matt. 1:22–25). Clearly, the hero of the story in Matthew is Joseph, through whom Jesus' messianic lineage is established, his descent from the house of David.

Not so in Luke. Here Mary is the commanding figure. Luke ranges the births of John the Baptist and of Jesus with similar births in Israel's tradition that tell a single lesson. The child of the promise enters the world through a difficult, indeed a miraculous, passage. So it was with Sarah, who, at age eighty, bears Isaac. Samson is the son of a barren woman. Similarly, Hannah is childless before the birth of Samuel. In the same light, John the Baptist is the child of Mary's elderly cousin, and Mary herself is a virgin, whose status witnesses to the special, miraculous intervention of the Holy Spirit.

If, as the infancy narratives argue, Mary's virginal conception of Jesus was part of God's plan from the start, then her role should extend into the future as well. The Gospels have established this trajectory. Here the figure of Mary under the cross in the Gospel of John represents the culminating point of the tradition: Mary is the disciple par excellence, not simply mother, but model as well of what it means to be a follower of Jesus. But the Gospels leave us with a paradox.

Mary is *symbolically important, but historically her portrait is not fully contoured*. She is quite different from Jesus, whose words and deeds are remembered in detail. But does this not fit her role exactly? Because her portrait is not fully detailed, she can function more easily as a mirror in which future generations will glimpse their own portrait as they seek to understand what it means to be a follower of Jesus. Her face will blend with theirs to form a single image. But Jesus' words and attitudes about Mary and his natural family will be remembered as well.

II. Mary in the Patristic Tradition

The figure of Mary, symbolically important but historically not fully contoured, provides natural impetus for later generations to fill in the features of her portrait. The task begins almost at once in the second-century *Protevangelium of James,* which tells the story of Mary's own childhood. Not surprisingly, at key points, it resembles Jesus' own. Here as well the cast of characters around Mary expands. Mary's parents, Anna and Joachim, now appear.[1] We also glean important information about Joseph. He is an elderly widower with children from his first marriage, a fact that helps to explain the mention of Jesus' brothers and sisters in the Gospels.[2]

The particulars about Mary herself are precise and detailed. The child of elderly parents, she takes seven steps at six months of age. Her feet do not touch the ground again until she is presented in the temple at the age of three. Then she sits on the third step of the altar and dances to the delight of the priests.[3] Henceforth she remains in the temple, fed by angels, until she is placed under Joseph's protection at the age of twelve. Mary is also assigned the role of weaving the purple and scarlet threads for the temple veil.[4] If the narrative delivers an overall impression, it is that Mary, herself an angelic creature, is a perpetual virgin, untainted by even a hint human imperfection. Her own immaculate conception is strongly implied. Joachim learns that Anna is with child at a time and in circumstances when he could not have been the father. Not surprisingly, *Protevangelium of James* will provide a veritable feast for artistic and devotional life as it intrigues pious imagination in the centuries that follow.

The earliest *theological* reflection on Mary aligns her role with that of Jesus, seeking Old Testament parallels that illumine the beginning of salvation. The oldest, and perhaps the richest, theological vein sees Mary as the *new Eve*. The theme appears first in Justin Martyr, in the mid-second century, and is developed at length by Irenaeus. If Christ is the new Adam, then Mary is the new Eve. Just as Eve by her disobedience was the cause of death for herself and her descendants, so Mary becomes "the cause of salvation for herself and the whole human race."[5] "And thus it was that the knot of Eve's disobedience was loosed by the obedience of Mary. For what the virgin Eve had bound fast through unbelief, this did the Virgin Mary set free through faith."[6] The theme of Mary as the new Eve is often echoed in the patristic era by Tertullian, Origen, John Chrysostom, and many others.

Other themes coalesce. The consensus about Mary's perpetual virginity grows in both East and West, despite dissenting voices.[7] Nor are Mary's faults overlooked. An Alexandrian tradition interprets Simeon's prophecy (Luke 2:35) of the sword piercing Mary's heart as a prediction of her doubts at Jesus passion. If the apostles doubted and fled, Origen asks, why should Mary be exempt from such temptations?[8]

However, the major factor determining Mary's role in the patristic era is the differing views of the person of Christ in terms of which her own role will come into a different light. Here, three theological trajectories stand out, each one quite distinct from the other. For Alexandrian theologians, the description of Mary as *Theotokos*, Godbearer, becomes the watchword that exactly captures their view of the person of Christ. It therefore becomes a touchstone of orthodoxy. Antiochene theologians, in rejecting the Alexandrian view of Christ, necessarily object to this characterization of Mary, preferring a more modest title, *Christotokos*, the Mother of Christ. It is not surprising that they are also sensitive to Gospel passages that treat Mary in a less flattering light. For example, John Chrysostom sees faults and imperfection in Mary on the basis of the scene in Mark 3:31–35 and her intervention at the wedding feast of Cana before Jesus' hour had arrived.[9] But certainly the more modest view of Mary, stressing her role as the human mother of Christ, will supply less motivation to speculate on her exalted role in salvation. Christ is an integral human being. Mary is his mother, and so the story tends to end.

The third variant belongs to the church of the West. Just as its view of Christ is different from both Eastern variants, so too its way of characterizing Mary differs. Local issues may also play a role. The term *Mother of God* (*Mater Dei*) is rarely used, perhaps because of fear of confusion with the cult of Cybele, the mother goddess. Both Ambrose (339–397) and Augustine combat the heretical views that dispute Mary's perpetual virginity.[10] Ambrose sets the characteristic notes of this Western theology that remains close to its biblical roots. The first is christological. Christ is the Son of God, born of the Virgin Mary, fully human and divine, in order to accomplish the work of salvation. Mary is the gate through which Christ passes, but his virginal birth does not open it.[11] His views on Mary are also anchored in the church. In conceiving Christ, Mary brings forth the followers of Christ, who find new life in his name. Mary is therefore a type of the church and a model for his followers.[12] But Jesus had no need of a "helper" in the work of redemption.[13] Ambrose is aware of possible excess: "Mary was the temple of God, not God of the temple."[14]

Augustine is the first of the Latin Fathers to assume that Mary has made a vow of virginity.[15] He focuses in a special way on Mary's personal response, reflecting the emphases of the Gospels: "It means more for her, an altogether greater blessing to have been Christ's disciple, than to have been Christ's Mother. That is why Mary was blessed, because even before she gave birth to him, she bore her teacher in her womb."[16] Mary is first of Jesus' disciples, and her motherhood is understood as a response in faith to the angel's words. In bringing forth Christ, she also brings forth those who are reborn in Christ. She is the mother of all believers but remains a member of the church. Within such a context, Mary's role comes into focus. In regard to Mary's own conception, Augustine's response is unclear.[17] Later commentators interpret his response as negative, thereby establishing a significant precedent against the doctrine of the Immaculate Conception. For both Ambrose and Augustine, Mary's perpetual virginity is central, although they differ somewhat on its symbolic meaning.[18]

These various trajectories come together at the Council of Ephesus. It therefore represents a culminating moment and a new starting point. The declaration of Mary as *Theotokos* by the council in 431 is, in the first instance, a vindication of Alexandrian teaching about the person of Christ. But when the Council of Ephesus is placed together with the Council of Chalcedon in 451, the title *Theotokos* comes into a slightly different light. If Alexandrian in origin, it now becomes the teaching of the universal church, balanced by the teaching of Chalcedon on the two natures of Christ. But the title also takes on a life of its own. It certainly is understood in the context of antiquity's estimate of the "bond of the womb." Peter Brown comments,

> Mary came to be shown, in art of the late fifth and sixth centuries as holding Christ enthroned on her lap, as if he were still tied to her womb. Christ was spoken of, in hymns sung by whole congregations, as drawing his human flesh from sucking the breasts of Mary. For a mother's milk, to ancient persons, was interchangeable with her blood: it was liquid flesh, transferred to the child by suckling. Christ must listen to those who prayed to his mother; for it was she who had rendered him fully human. Only she could remind him, with the authority of a mother, of what he shared with the afflicted human flesh of those who turned to him.[19]

In the wake of the Council of Ephesus and the declaration of Mary as *Theotokos,* devotion to the Virgin flourishes. Churches are built in her honor. In the sixth century, the "Assumption" or "Dormition" or "Passing" of Mary is celebrated. These different names reflect differing views of her last days on earth. Did Mary die, or did she simply fall asleep? They unite in celebrating her triumphant arrival in heaven. In 600, the emperor Maurice declares the celebration of the feast of the Assumption throughout the empire on August 15. Likewise, the feast of Mary's nativity is celebrated in the second half of the sixth century, and toward the end of the seventh century, the feast of her conception and her presentation in the temple.[20] But it should be noted, in regard to the latter, that the celebration of the Immaculate Conception carries a different connotation in the East because the Eastern doctrine of original sin is more fluid and not as sharply defined as its Western counterpart. For the same reason, the introduction of this feast into the West will be controversial.

Prayers to Mary are equally significant. Perhaps the oldest, the *Sub Tuum,* dates from the third or fourth century. This short prayer invokes Mary's intercessory power under the title "Mother of God," applying the words "deliver us," reminiscent of the Lord's Prayer (Matt. 6:13).[21] The most famous Marian hymn of the Eastern Church, the *Akathistos*, was composed for the feast of the Annunciation. The hymn is highly elaborate, lyrically beautiful, filled with the sentiments of exalted piety. Michael O'Carroll observes, "It unites liturgical form, doctrinal content and popular piety in a way until now unequaled."[22] When we add to these kinds of prayers to the special devotion shown to the icons of the *Theotokos* — not representations in the Western sense, but closer to sacramental symbols of grace — we enter the special world of Byzantine piety.

Larry Hurtado has studied devotion to Jesus in the first centuries of the church, the tendency to treat him in prayer "as a 'divine' figure or, at least a figure of unique significance in God's plan."[23] It is clear from his analysis that long before Jesus is *explicitly* confessed as divine, he is *practically* treated as such in prayer. If one views Marian devotion in the same light, the extraordinary intercessory powers with which Mary is endowed early on are striking. Even allowing for the free form of hymns and prayers, this objective content seems undeniable. But the best interpreters of this tradition are the theologians who bring the golden age of Greek patristic thought to a close in the eighth century.

Germanus of Constantinople (643–733) may be regarded as the "high-water-mark of Marian devotion in the Church of the Fathers."[24] Along with Andrew of Crete (660–740) and John of Damascus (675–749), they reflect the mind of the Eastern church at the close of the era. John of Damascus, in particular, stands as the measure of orthodoxy in the Byzantine tradition. Two related themes surface in Germanus that will reappear repeatedly in later Western thought.[25] Mary is the one who averts the wrath of God, which imperils the sinner at every turn. And she can act as such a powerful mediatrix because the Son not only listens to, but also obeys, the voice of his mother.

Here the torque in the New Testament picture of Mary begins to show itself. In the Lukan annunciation scene and the Gospel of John, claims of discipleship are stronger than even the deepest human bonds, those between a mother and a child. But now a parental voice, the voice of a mother, is heard in its own right. And even in heaven, later commentators will say, the fourth commandment — to honor one's father and mother — still obtains. These themes are like melodies that will be developed in symphonic variations in later centuries, played in both major and minor keys. But the signature chords of the piece are now sounded.

Meanwhile, Mary's human portrait will shift as the meaning of discipleship changes in different cultures. As the church is established and martyrdom gives way to asceticism as the mark of a disciple, Mary is portrayed as the ideal, consecrated virgin.[26] Epiphanius the Monk (d. ca. 800) describes her in some detail according to Byzantine standards of beauty. Mary is a woman with a light complexion, golden hair, blue eyes, black eyebrows, a strait nose, a long face, and with long hands and fingers.[27] Still others see her as the Stoic ideal of *apatheia*, freedom from passion. Not only is she without faults, but also she is without passion, embodying a Stoic version of what it means to be a disciple.[28] When the gospel is preached to Germanic tribes, Mary will appear as the ideal civilizing maiden with blond hair and blue eyes.[29]

III. Mary in Western Medieval Thought

The Mary of Western medieval thought and piety is a child of the scholastic method. We noted in an earlier chapter that a characteristic feature of the Western Christian template is an inclination to rational thought. Nowhere is this trait on better display that in the heady mixture of piety and speculation that characterizes the development of medieval Mariology. Perhaps the best starting point to grasp this unique combination is with two famous and characteristic remarks of Anselm of Canterbury (1033–1109). He writes, "It was fitting that the Virgin should be radiant with a purity so great than that a greater purity cannot be conceived (other than the purity of God Himself)."[30] In a prayer to Mary, Anselm puts the matter more simply: "Nothing is equal to Mary, nothing save God is greater than Mary."[31]

What is significant in these remarks is the beginnings of a *method*. Anselm's *ontological argument* asks us to regard God as that being greater than which no being can be conceived. Hence, God must exist. (Our conception is not exalted enough if it omits God's existence.) We see here the beginnings of a similar argument about Mary. She is that creature greater than which no creature can be conceived. The argument turns on the question of suitability. What perfections, if suitable or fitting, should not be showered on the Virgin, since nothing is greater than her, save the Lord God? Perhaps more to the point, the argument is an aesthetic one, a question of taste and proportion. Here, piety quietly enters with its own subjective perspectives. It would hardly seem suitable to image Mary as the queen of hairstylists. Such a quality seems ordinary and not exalted. But in regard to intelligence, virtue, and purity, the matter is different. These are worthy perfections, suitable to the Mother of God.

This methodological insight is elaborated in a standard three-word adage that becomes a staple of medieval argumentation: *potuit, voluit* (or *decuit*), *fecit*. The first words contain questions; the last, a statement. Could God give Mary a particular perfection, say, superior intelligence (*potuit*)? Would God wish to do it (*voluit*)? Would it be fitting or worthy of her (*decuit*)? If yes on these counts, then the deed is done (*fecit*). Mary is endowed with superior intelligence. In effect, the method becomes a way of showering rational perfections on the Virgin that brings her person into new perspective.

Anselm's close associate and biographer, Eadmer of Canterbury (1055–1124), uses this line of reasoning to argue for Mary's Immaculate Conception.[32] Could God exempt the Virgin from original sin? Indeed he could. Would it be worthy or fitting to do so?[33] Indeed it would. Therefore we may move from *possibility* to *fact* and conclude that Mary herself is conceived without original sin. In advancing this argument, Eadmer argues not for a minor perfection but rather for the ultimate one. He thereby sets down a controversial marker that will affect medieval Mariology in every way. Henceforth, the doctrine of the Immaculate Conception will spark controversy and split successive schools of theology for the next seven hundred years, finally involving the intervention of the great powers. No point about Mary will be as controversial as her Immaculate Conception. The celebration of the feast, imported from the East, spreads quietly enough into England before the Norman Conquest. But when it is introduced into Southern France around 1150, the celebration of the feast prompts stormy fulminations from Bernard of Clairvaux (1090–1153): "The royal virgin has no need of false honor."[34]

The doctrine of the Immaculate Conception is opposed by Anselm, Bernard, Peter Lombard (1100–1160), Albert the Great (1200–1280), Thomas Aquinas, Bonaventure (1221–1274), and others.[35] This vast array of different theologians would not form a consensus if the issue were minor. It is not. The tradition knows various instances of redemption in the womb, as in the case of Jeremiah or John the Baptist. But to argue for the Immaculate Conception without qualification seems to say that Mary herself does not need redemption, generating an even more serious question: Is Mary to be counted on the side of humanity in need of redemption, or is she now reckoned on the side of the Redeemer, his helpmate in the work of salvation? We will return to the question of the Immaculate Conception later, for it provides a running thread of continuity, of piety and controversy, into the 1700s. We pause here to examine the new portrait of Mary that is emerging. As the adage *potuit, voluit, fecit* is deployed, a series of *rational possibilities become actual perfections* is generated. Soon they outflank the biblical and patristic picture of the Virgin on every side. A new portrait of Mary — her humanity stretched to the limit — begins to emerge.

If we were to draw a pencil-line sketch of the new portrait, it would begin, of course, with Mary's Immaculate Conception. She is conceived without original sin, perhaps herself a creature higher than all the angels and saints. Hermann of Tournai (ca. 1090–1147) adds a metaphor destined for a long shelf life.[36] Mary is the neck of the church (later the mystical body) because she is the mediatrix between God and humankind. When Mary is assumed into heaven, she takes on her proper role as Queen of Heaven, above all, as Mother of Mercies.

To the fertile medieval mind, heaven is pictured as a joint stock venture in which a division of labor obtains. God the Father and Christ are in charge of justice and judgment. Mary is the mother and dispenser of mercy and forgiveness. Piety prompts further steps. Mary remains, even in heaven, a mother. Hence, the Son will listen with special attentiveness to her voice. More practical advice follows. Do not go first to God the Father or Christ, for they will ask you for a full bill of particulars, the detailed arguments that favor your petition. Go instead to Mary, who will not ask the whys and wherefores of your prayers. She will listen as a mother and then simply speak to her son on your behalf. Bernard describes the situations this way. With this mediator one needs a mediator, and "there is no one more efficacious than Mary."[37] These words of his are often quoted: "God willed us to have everything through Mary."[38] In a famous sermon, Bernard likens her to an aqueduct that brings us the fruits of paradise.[39] This portrait of Mary remains remarkably stable, fueled by piety and imagination, shared by those who might otherwise disagree theologically.

If we pick up the portrait some three hundred years later with Gabriel Biel (1420–1495), we note developments. The methodological considerations have become more elaborate.[40] The starting point changes as well. Biel begins with the eternal predestination of Mary. If she is to play such an important role at the end of time, then she must have been the Mother of God by divine intention from all eternity. But the essentials of the story remain the same. Mary is immaculately conceived. She cooperates not only in Christ's incarnation but also in his *passion* through her own *compassion*. But her great intercessory work begins with her assumption into heaven. "In his welcoming speech Christ announces that he will share the kingdom of his father with her; of its two parts Christ will give his mother the responsibility for compassion. He himself will be responsible for justice and truth."[41] But she will rule not by command (*imperare*) but rather by virtue of her intercessory power on behalf of sinners (*impetrare*). "The righteous God could not possibly hear the prayers of a sinner; what is needed is therefore a mediator with the mediator. From eternity God has provided one, thus erecting a new Trinitarian hierarchy: the Virgin Mary hears the sinners, the Son hears his Mother, and the Father his Son."[42]

In the transition from doctrinal discussion to homiletic application, a significant shift of emphasis occurs in Biel's thought. While Christ is God-man (*homo deus*), only Mary is fully human (*homo purus*). If she is more accessible, it is because she is truly one of us. Thus Mary is better able to understand the human condition, with all its weaknesses, than does Christ, the exalted God-man. Her Assumption is therefore a better measure of our hope for the future. Her entrance into heaven gives us a more realistic hope of future glory.

The tendency to treat Christ as distant and Mary as closer to the human condition, accentuated in a homiletic context, is not unique or original to Biel. Heiko Oberman comments, "All the primary and secondary sources consulted suggest that Biel's views represent on most points an emerging late medieval piety which draws on a long medieval tradition which transcends narrow school boundaries."[43]

If Gabriel Biel represents the mean, it also seems important to give some sense of the extremes. Popular Franciscan preacher Bernardine of Siena (1380–1444) provides a good example.[44] "From the time she conceived God in her womb, she has had, if I may express it, a certain jurisdiction or authority in every temporal procession of the Holy Spirit, so that no creature receives any grace save through the distribution of the same Virgin."[45] The influence of Bernardine of Siena appears clearly in Pope Leo XIII's 1894 encyclical *Iucunda semper expectatione* (*Always with Joyful Expectation*) on the rosary: "Every grace granted to man has three degrees in order; for by God it is communicated to Christ, from Christ it passes to the Virgin, and from the Virgin it descends to us."[46]

We pause here to observe that such portraits of Mary carry a significant negative potential. For if Mary has become the Mother of Mercies, what does this say about the role of God the Father or of Christ the Son? Are they not cast, at best, in the role of just judge and, at worst, in the role of irate husband, angry potentate whose hand of vengeance is stayed only by Mary's intercession? And if Mary intercedes more effectively on our behalf, what does that say about the mediatorship of Christ? Does he who was Lord and brother now become Lord and no longer brother, exalted above the human condition? And what of the Holy Spirit, whose role Mary as advocate par excellence has effectively absorbed?

In effect, Mary now becomes the receptacle in which those qualities of God were kept that the medievals could no longer easily find in God or in Christ: mercy and forgiveness. Similarly, the tendency to divinize her, far from consistent, represents the primitive reflection that somehow mercy, not simply justice, must stand within the Deity. And if it does not, then that creature in whom mercy finds a home must herself be raised close to divinity. It is therefore in Mary, above all, that the medievals see the mercy and the forgiveness of God, and so, understandably, they elevate her role, speaking of her preexistence, her special mediatorship, and of Mary as a separate order of creation between God and the world.

IV. The Immaculate Conception

John Duns Scotus (1274–1308) proposes an argument in favor of the Immaculate Conception that is nothing less than a tour de force. He takes the strongest argument of his opponents, Mary's seeming exemption from redemption, and turns it against them, in effect, hoisting them on their own petard. Far from exempting Mary, he argues, the Immaculate Conception exemplifies the most perfect form of redemption. The Virgin is not freed from original sin; rather, she is *preserved* from it. And preservative redemption is the most perfect way of being saved, which Christ, fittingly enough, reserves for his mother, the most perfect of creatures. Her preservative redemption is the exemplar of our own. Mary is preserved from original sin. We, although tainted, are subsequently freed from its stain.[47]

Scotus gives those who favor the Immaculate Conception a formidable new weapon for their theological arsenal, one that quite fits the tenor of contemporary argumentation. But it also has the air of sleight of hand, and it does not persuade the doctrine's opponents. So theological polemics continue with Dominicans ranged with Thomas Aquinas against the Immaculate Conception. Encouraged by Scotus, the Franciscans, joined by the Carmelites, become its public defenders. The terms of the fourteenth century debate about the Immaculate Conception are set.

The doctrine of the Immaculate Conception bubbles to the surface at the Council of Basel (1431–1449). A decision is made at the thrity-sixth session on September 15, 1439 and announced two days later. The council publicly declares in favor of the Immaculate Conception.[48] But its official mandate extends only through the first twenty-two sessions. The decision is not official. Still, the unofficial declaration of the Council of Basel encourages those who favor the doctrine as it enrages those who opposes it. The lines harden. Franciscan Pope Sixtus IV (1414–1484), on February 27, 1476, approves a Mass and office in honor of the Immaculate Conception, investing it with indulgences.[49] The ensuing reaction is bitter and acrimonious. Further debate is prohibited in 1482 and 1483.[50] Neither side is allowed to brand the other as heretical. The prohibition is repeated in 1503. Typical of the time, the University of Paris in 1497 requires all degree candidates to take an oath to defend the Immaculate Conception, an example followed by other universities.[51]

The Protestant Reformation opens a new chapter on the role of Mary. The Reformers — Luther, Calvin, Zwingli, Bullinger, and others — differ somewhat in their estimation of Mary. Generally, they stay within the parameters of the New Testament and the early councils. But as the Reformation moves into its second and third generation, it becomes apparent that the underlying principles of the reform — Christ alone, faith alone, Scripture alone — leave no room for an exalted role for Mary either in salvation or in the dispensation of grace.

As time progresses, the lines between Catholics and Protestants harden. Indeed, it is as if, at the time of the Reformation, the old family homestead of the Christian faith is broken up after a death in the family and then divided among not always happy children. The Reformers inherit full right to the Scriptures, a modest conception of church office, and two sacraments — baptism and eucharist. Catholics retain the papacy, the traditional priesthood, seven sacraments, and devotion to Mary and the saints. Subsequently, devotion to Mary and the saints becomes emblematic of post-Reformation Catholicism.

Just as Protestants reject Mary's special role, so it seems incumbent upon Catholics after the Reformation to defend it in the strongest terms. Old battles break out anew. A new chapter opens on the Immaculate Conception. New faces appear. The Society of Jesus generally enters the list as defender of the doctrine. Passions run high. So-called blood vows are taken to defend the Immaculate Conception at the cost of life and limb.[52] The Holy See attempts to referee the debate. Between 1627 and 1644 the actual phrase "Immaculate Conception" is disallowed. Supporters must speak instead of the "conception of the immaculate Virgin." Public actions against the doctrine are forbidden in 1617. The prohibition is extended to private actions in 1622. But in neither case are such measures to be taken as statements against the opposing views.[53]

In response to King Philip IV of Spain (1605–1665), Pope Alexander VII (1599–1667) in 1661 publicly commits the Holy See to support the Immaculate Conception without, however, condemning the opposing view.[54] The tide turns. In 1695, Pope Innocent XII

(1615–1700) imposes on the whole church the office and Mass of the Conception of the Immaculate Virgin Mary. In 1708, the feast becomes a holy day of obligation.[55] But the Immaculate Conception becomes defined doctrine only 145 years later in 1854. Between the death of Eadmer of Canterbury around 1124 and Pope Pius IX's *Ineffabilis Deus* in 1854 defining the dogma of the Immaculate Conception, roughly 730 years have passed. The doctrine of the Immaculate Conception has required a long, often difficult gestation. And the story is not over.

V. Mary in the Life of the Church after the Reformation

I wish to draw a single conclusion from this discussion of the Immaculate Conception. As Mary is *drawn through* three sets of polemical discussions, first in the fourteenth century, then at the Reformation, and subsequently in the seventeenth century, she is *ground into* the very fabric of the Roman Catholic Church. She thereby becomes not simply a person or a single doctrine; rather, in the post-Reformation era, she becomes a series of *personifications* that broadly characterize Roman Catholic Christianity.

First, she becomes a statement about the Catholic conception of the church, set now in sharp relief against the churches of the Reformation. Christ stands to the church in the same degree of closeness as he stands to his mother. In the face of Protestant criticism, the figure of Mary affirms that the church has not betrayed Christ, because it cannot. Despite human weakness, the church is as organically linked to its Savior as a mother to a son. Mary increasingly becomes the symbol par excellence of the Catholic system — devotion to and intercession of the saints, a particular understanding of the sacraments and of church order.

Second, Mary personifies a particular understanding of redemption, of how God desires to save the human family. Her response, her *fiat,* to the angel Gabriel is taken as a more general statement about human capacities. It means that men and women are not passive or helpless in their own salvation. On the contrary, redemption is the result of a synergism between God's initiative and human cooperation with men and women as active agents in the process. Mary personifies human activity in the work of redemption. In the words of the apostle Paul, we make up what is lacking in the sufferings of Christ as God has intended (Col. 1:24). This means yes to faith as the Reformation taught, but yes to good works as well. It also means that the sole mediatorship of Christ must be understood not in exclusive terms but rather in *inclusive* ones. In other words, Christ never appears alone but rather is always surrounded by the angels and the saints, by Mary and Joseph, who join him in the great work of redemption.

Third, devotion to Mary comes to personify Catholic spirituality in general. Devotion to the Sacred Heart is emblematic of the seventeenth-century French school of spirituality. "Heart" in this context, writes Hans Urs von Balthasar, "means the personal center that sustains the whole reality of the Redeemer."[56] It therefore aptly symbolizes an interiorized piety, of Christ's heart entering the heart of his followers. Devotion to the Sacred Heart of Jesus extends easily to the Sacred Heart of Mary, introducing a hallmark of the French school: the closeness between Christ and his mother, exemplified by special devotion to the Christ child in the womb. The lovely prayer "O Jesus, Living in Mary" (*O Jesu, Vivens in Maria*) is framed in these terms. According to Jean Jacques Olier (1608–1657), Jesus' sojourn in the womb represents a privileged moment in his earthly life.[57]

Indeed, this impassioned devotion to the Virgin is the positive reflection of the negative polemics around the Immaculate Conception. Just as the heart symbolizes a radical interiorized piety surmounting all boundaries, so it often becomes difficult to separate the hearts of Jesus and Mary, just as their names are invoked together. In the devotional exuberance of the French school, devotion to Jesus and to Mary tends to meld into one, symbolized by the child in the womb.

Fourth, Mary becomes increasingly in the Enlightenment and then in the nineteenth century a personification of higher human aspirations. One thinks here of Mary and a series of Mary-like figures, of Bernadette Soubirous (1844–1879), of Thérèse of Lisieux (1873–1897), of Mary of the Immaculate Conception of 1854 and of the Assumption of 1950. Are they not anthropological countertypes? In an increasingly secular age that extols Goethe's "Faust," Marx's "economic man," and Nietzsche's "superman," the church raises up the figure not of a man at all, but rather of a woman, actually a series of them. These women are not justified in terms of functional rationality or personal autonomy. Their status is not based on acquisition or conquest. Their level of aspiration is not measured in socioeconomic terms. Instead, Mary is justified by her assent to the angel Gabriel. Her status is based on surrender to God's will. And she is raised up as a model for men and women, for all people who ask about human nature and the nature of human aspirations. What may we hope for? It is significant that the two modern Marian dogmas — the Immaculate Conception and the Assumption — have nothing to do with Mary's life on earth. Instead, they speak of her origin and her destiny, and, as the model of discipleship, they raise the level of human aspiration beyond the limits of this world. They also underscore how low the bar is set on human aspirations in a secular world. In this regard, they carry with them a judgment on such standards and what they say about what men and women may ultimately hope for.

Fifth, we should not fail to note in this same context that Mary has long personified the national dignity of many peoples. It is hard to imagine Poland apart from Our Lady of Czestochowa, of the Catalan people separate from Our Lady of Montserrat, of the Mexican people distinct from our Lady of Guadalupe. These images are almost always born in the struggle for a nation's birth. In such circumstances, a people often catches a first glimpse of its dignity and identity in the face of the Virgin. For the same reason, these images of Mary are not interchangeable. Instead, they stand as unique symbols of the corporate identity of successive peoples. They certainly speak as Catholic images, but they extend beyond these limits too. They stand as national symbols of dignity and solidarity. For the same reason, devotion to Mary will vary in nature and intensity from one culture to another. In all cases, devotion to the Virgin reflects the features of grassroots piety.

VI. Vatican II and Mary

In his letter to E. B. Pusey (1800–1882), Cardinal Newman makes a distinction between *devotion* to Mary, which he concedes has grown over the centuries, compared to Marian *doctrine,* which has remained the same.[58] In regard to the devotions that we have reviewed, what is striking is the paucity of new features about the exalted status of

Mary since the late 1400s. What marks the French school is devotional exuberance. The idea, however, such as Louis-Marie Grignon de Mont-fort's (1673–1716) — it is preferable to have an intercessor intercede for us, much as we would scarce approach an earthly king without an introduction — is essentially an old notion recycled against the back-drop of French court life.[59] If something new is added, it is not in the arsenal of novel features but rather in the cultural climate against which they are presented. Thus Alfonso Maria de Liguori's (1696–1787) *Glories of Mary* (1786) contains little that is original, even in devotional literature.[60] What has changed is the Enlightenment back-drop, which makes the figure of Mary stand out all the more starkly by virtue of the contrast.

This is also what makes Vatican II's treatment of Mary unique. It *does* add something new to the doctrinal discussion, both by way of addition and, equally, by way of subtraction. Balthasar writes of "the ebb and flow, through history, of Mariology's tides," observing that "a flood of lofty attributes, titles and veneration is almost necessarily followed by an ebb that restores the level; but the ebb-tide can also seep away, leading to a forgetfulness that is unworthy of theology."[61] Perhaps. But it has been a long time since the tide has ebbed in the West and the humble Virgin of the Gospels has appeared on the scene. This certainly was not a result that one might have predicted before Vatican II. But it is its outcome. Hence, the council does represent a turning point in a story that has gone from exaltation to exaltation, finally to a high-altitude plateau of Marian glory. The reversal of such a tendency is remarkable, and this is the development to which we turn.

The immediate background is provided by "the return to the sources" that marks the movements of renewal in the first half of the twentieth century. The biblical renewal recovers once again the paradoxical but highly coherent portrait of Mary as mother-become-disciple contained in the Gospels. The patristic renewal reveals the sober Mariology of Ambrose and Augustine and its consistency with the biblical portrait. Such research is reflected in a series of high-level books on the Virgin Mary by premier Catholic theologians, many of whom are destined to play important roles at Vatican II: Hugo Rahner,[62] Karl Rahner,[63] Edward Schillebeeckx,[64] Otto Semmelroth,[65] Rene Laurentin,[66] and others. Without denying her singularity, this emerging tendency seeks to locate Mary's role *within* the context of the church. It is also more ecumenically aware, sensitive to the views of other Christian churches.

Quite the opposite tendency is strengthened as well. The year 1900 marks the beginning of the era of Marian congresses, which reaches a high point at midcentury with the proclamation of the dogma of the Assumption in 1950, then the celebration of the centenary of the Immaculate Conception in 1954 and of the apparition at Lourdes in 1958. They represent a movement to carry forward the impulses of post-Reformation Mariology, seeking to increase the privileges of the Virgin that mark her singularity. Three commissions are also established in 1921 in Spain, Belgium, and Rome to study the feasibility of a dogmatic pronouncement on Mary's universal mediation. At Lourdes in 1958, the question is raised about Mary's role in the drama of salvation. Does she stand on the side of Christ as redeemer, perhaps as his helpmate? Or does she stand on the side of humanity in need of redemption? Other considerations follow. In what sense may Mary be considered mediatrix of all graces or coredemptrix? Are such titles merely fittingly (*de congruo*) given to the Virgin? Or are they hers by right (*de condigno*)? Such questions hang in the air in Catholic circles in the 1950s. Not surprisingly, in the preliminary consultation in preparation for Vatican II, the topic of Mary stands first in the list. There are 570 respondents who ask that Mary be a subject on the council's agenda; 382 seek a statement on her mediation; 266 desire a dogmatic definition.[67]

Thus the discussion of Mary at Vatican II must seek to chart a course in choppy waters between divided viewpoints. The final text is the result of a series of confrontations and then decisions, always with a sizable, unhappy minority. The first and most notable occurs on October 29, 1963. The question is whether a separate document should be devoted to the Virgin or whether the council should keep to its original intention and include its discussion of Mary in the document on the church. The vote is 1,114 in favor of inclusion; 1,074 against, favoring instead a separate document. The vote carries by a scant 17 votes (a majority being 1,097).[68] This is the closest vote at Vatican II, the narrowest majority by which any significant decision is made. And in a council that seeks resolutely for compromise, this is an up-and-down vote with no return. By the same token, the vote is indicative that the discussion is far from over. The battle lines are now drawn on two titles in the proposed text: "Mediatrix" and "Mother of the Church." Pope Paul VI is actively involved in the discussion. The decision in regard to "Mediatrix" is to include it among a series of other related titles, "Advocate," "Helper," "Benefactress," and "Mediatrix."[69] The intent is to shift the title from a dogmatic to a devotional context, somewhat like the way the Eastern church might use the term. "Mother of the Church," not an ancient but rather a medieval title, is judged too open to misunderstanding and not appropriate from an ecumenical point of view. It is not used at all. Instead, the text says that the church honors Mary "as a most beloved mother."[70] On November 18, 1964, Pope Paul VI, as a personal, not as a conciliar, act, declares Mary the Mother of the Church.[71] Among the reasons prompting his decision, the desire to assuage a grieved, but sizable minority on the subject of Mary plays a role.

The final text on Mary, the concluding chapter of *Lumen Gentium,* emerges as a battle-scarred veteran in the third session of Vatican II in 1964. This is evident in the way the title of the chapter changes from one session to the next. The final one is the lengthiest: "The Role of the Blessed Virgin Mary in the Mystery of Christ and the Church."[72] Gerard Philips, himself an active participant in the discussion, describes the final reaction of the council to the text as "general agreement without enthusiasm"; many still reproach the draft for "minimizing tendencies."[73]

All the same, a clear portrait of Mary emerges. The Virgin is first placed in a biblical context. The foreshadowing of her role in the Old Testament is considered, then her role in the New Testament with special attention given to the scene of the annunciation and to Mary's *fiat.* Here Mary unties the knot of Eve's disobedience and becomes herself, in the words of Irenaeus, "the cause of salvation." The text follows Mary's role through the Gospels, ending with the scene of Pentecost (Acts 1:14). It also becomes clear how the present context as the concluding chapter of the document on the church preempts a discussion of Mary's singularity. The sole mediatorship of Christ is clearly emphasized, just as Mary's subordinate role is plainly professed. In explaining her role in the church, the chapter goes back to the teaching of Ambrose. Mary is an archetype of the church. Just as the church is called "virgin" and "mother," the Virgin "stands out in eminent and singular fashion as exemplar" on both scores.[74] As a type of the church, she brings forth new sons and daughters in Christ. By the same token, Mary of the Assumption stands as fitting symbol to close *Lumen Gentium,* the constitution on the church. She stands as a sign of hope and comfort to the pilgrim church on earth. From her place in heaven as the first to follow Christ, she represents the goal for the rest of humanity, who one day, like Mary, hope to reach their heavenly home.

Equally significant is what the chapter on Mary omits. It brackets any discussion of Mary's role as mediatrix, even less of her role as coredemptrix.[75] The latter word never appears at all. This has also been part of the journey of the text through successive drafts. If anything, the chapter relentlessly emphasizes Christ's role as sole mediator. Balthasar speaks of the "limits of Vatican II's Mariology," and surely he is correct.[76] Post-Reformation developments play almost no role. Still, on such a hotly contested subject, the portrait of Mary is coherent and consistent. It has the merit of scriptural and patristic grounding, with a steady focus on the larger topic of the church. Again, Balthasar: "In deciding to make its teaching on Mary part of the Constitution on the Church, as the latter's conclusion, the Council has set a landmark that will not easily be moved."[77] From a historical perspective, this treatment of Mary has the effect of pruning back the lush growth of Mariology in order to give room for other doctrines and devotions to grow, especially those surrounding the Holy Spirit.

The reception of Vatican II's treatment of Mary is also significant. Elizabeth Johnson's observation surely is correct: "The post-Vatican II church in North America is marked by noticeable diminishment of private devotion and public reflection regarding Mary."[78] In progressive circles in the decade following Vatican II, theological discussion of Mary virtually ceases. But this is not a normal silence but rather an awkward one, like the stillness that surrounds a missing person whose voice had only recently rung so clearly. In Latin as well as Slavic countries such as Poland, Vatican II's discussion of Mary barely has an effect on the thick native piety surrounding the Virgin. Paul VI's 1974 exhortation *Cultus Marialis* probably had a larger impact by keeping Marian devotion within acceptable theological and liturgical limits.

But devotion to Mary is a sturdy plant in Catholic soil. It is not surprising that Paul VI's successor, once removed, John Paul II, would select a motto, *Totus Tuus* (*Totally Yours*), that echoes the French school and Louis de Montfort.[79] The apparition at Medjugorje in 1981 wins worldwide attention, seamlessly picking up the threads of traditional Mariology. Feminist retrievals pick up other threads.[80] One is persuaded of the wisdom of Balthasar's observation that no single principle or point of view can encompass the many-sided figure of the Virgin Mary in Catholic thought and piety.[81]

VII. Mary of the Apparitions

The final word on Mary in the modern era belongs to the story of her apparitions. Their number is legion. The list of approved apparitions is short. The following were sanctioned by a local bishop and "went to win international attention: Rue de Bac (Paris, France, 1830), La Salette (France, 1846), Lourdes (France, 1858), Pontmain (France, 1870), Fatima (Portugal, 1917), Beauraing (Belgium, 1932–1933) and Banneux (Belgium, 1933)."[82] An appearance at Knock in Ireland (1879) enjoys informal approval. The most recent apparition occurred at Medjugorje in 1981 and still continues. It enjoys a status somewhere between benign tolerance and informal recognition.

The appearance of the Virgin to Catherine Labouré (1806–1875) at the convent of the Sisters of Charity on the Rue de Bac in Paris in November 1830 is reckoned the modern starting point. Here the Virgin instructs Sister Catherine to have a medal struck in her honor. The image on the medal depicts Mary with outstretched arms, crushing the head of a serpent. She wears a crown of stars, evoking the woman of the book of Revelation who is clothed with the sun and wears a crown of stars (Rev. 12:1). There is no Christ child in the image. The following words surround it: "O Mary, conceived without sin, pray for us who have recourse to you." The first such medal is minted in 1832. It is called the "Miraculous Medal," the source of worldwide Marian devotion for the next century. It was a rare Roman Catholic growing up in America in the twentieth century who did not have a Miraculous Medal. This first modern apparition is connected to the doctrine of the Immaculate Conception, a tie that continues into the next generation of Marian appearances. In another sense, the apparition to Catherine Labouré marks a close. This is the only one to a professional religious, priest or nun. It is also the last one to take place in a convent or chapel. Hereafter the recipients of visions are children or adolescents. The appearances occur out of doors. They also involve secrets. Some secrets pertain to the personal lives of the recipients. Others contain a public message whose contents may be communicated at once or, just as often, only slowly later on. Church authorities are invariably cautious, if not skeptical, about apparitions and their messages.

These features begin to emerge at the apparition of the Virgin to two children, Melanie Calvat (1831–1904) and Maximin Giraud (1835–1875), at La Salette near Grenoble in 1846. The Virgin visits the children a single time in a field as cattle are grazing nearby. Her words have a querulous tone; her message to the children, an admonition: "If the potatoes rot, it is your fault. I made you see it would happen a year ago, and you did nothing about it. If you have wheat, do not sow it, the animals will eat all that you sow, and anything that ripens will turn into dust. There will be great famine."[83] Mary's son has been offended by those who have taken his name in vain. They also work on Sunday and miss Mass. They eat meat during Lent. This recent failure of the potato crop should stand as a sign of things to come if people do not repent. Although the offending sins change, such admonitions become a staple of Marian apparitions in the future. A spring is discovered near the scene of the apparition at La Salette. Cures follow.

The appearances to Bernadette Soubirous at Lourdes in 1858 unfold still other features. The apparitions are now no longer a private experience as they were at La Salette. Instead, they become public events. The estimated crowd for the appearance on March 4, 1858, ranges from five to twenty thousand.[84] Lourdes also involves more than a single visit of the Virgin as at La Salette. Now there are serial apparitions from February 11 to July 16, 1858, the feast of Our Lady of Mount Carmel. A high point occurs on March 25, the feast of the Annunciation. Thus far, Bernadette refers to the Lady in the vision as "Aquero," *That One* in the local dialect. On the March 25, she asks the Lady her name. The Virgin responds, "I am the Immaculate Conception." The child is confused. Some years later, Bernadette writes to Pope Pius IX,

"I did not know what that meant. I had never heard the words."[85] The Virgin asks that a chapel be built. There is a grotto and a miraculous spring. Lourdes soon becomes a pilgrimage site for those who wish to drink the water or wash in the spring. There are no words of admonition, no public secrets connected to the apparition meant for broader public consumption. But the connection to the Immaculate Conception "fits well into the rather apocalyptic Marian piety of French Catholics during this period and was to contribute a great deal toward making Lourdes the most popular devotion in France within a very few years."[86] A shrine is established with the miraculous spring as a sign that Mary, the provident mother, continues to look after her children in need. It quickly becomes a magnet for pilgrimages from all of France and in the next century from all over the world.

The apparition of the Virgin at Fatima in Portugal in 1917 is different. Fatima is the fifth of the so-called approved appearances, surrounded by many more of lesser provenance. From the beginning, these apparitions blend together, establishing possible lines of interpretation and shaping the message of individual appearances. But the chief question looms: Why has the Virgin decided to appear on earth with such frequency at this time? A note of urgency is conveyed by the frequency of the apparitions. What can they mean?

The appearances at Fatima in 1917 to three children, Lucia Santos (1907–2005) and her cousins Jacinta (1910–1920) and Francisco Marto (1908–1919), seem to provide an answer. Once again, these are serial appearances. Mary appears to the children often in 1917 and apparently before then as well and after that year to Lucia. The apparitions are also major public events. A crowd estimated at seventy thousand is said to have witnessed a great miracle on October 13, 1917, when the sun is said to have danced in the sky.[87] The year of the apparition, 1917, is crucial for its interpretation. This is late in the year before the terrible First World War draws to a close. It is also the year of the Russian Revolution. How do these events connect? What do they portend? The usual surfeit of answers to such questions, secular and religious, have long since run their course.

The core of the apparitions at Fatima is the secrets given to the children. On the one hand, the journey of the secrets is itself long and protracted. Lucia records the first parts of the secret conveyed by the Virgin on July 13, 1917, in a memorandum in August of 1941. The famous third secret is recorded in late 1943 or early 1944. The secrets are sent to Rome in the spring of 1957. On the other hand, the chief content of the message is soon revealed, with the famous "third secret" of Fatima, the tantalizing trump card, remaining face down. This mixture of public yet secret revelations makes the impact of Fatima enormous. These secrets can also be connected to the Virgin's warnings at La Salette in 1846, which have not been heeded. But now it is no longer a matter of a failed potato crop, but rather one of a worldwide social order in ruins.

A series of world events occur just as the apparitions of Fatima have predicted. World War I draws to a close. This was foretold. Then another great war is predicted in the pontificate of Pius XI. This is fulfilled by the outbreak of World War II. Because these events have actually happened, the Virgin's concern about Russia is taken as an accurate prediction of the rise of the Soviet Union. The message of Fatima blends seamlessly into concerns about the Cold War. Prayers to the Virgin for the conversion of Russia seem the only bulwark against the inroads of militantly atheistic communism.

Fatima gives birth to a series of related visions elsewhere in the world. In the spring of 1950, a forty-one-year-old housewife, Mary Ann von Hoof (1909–1984), announces that the Virgin has appeared to her in Necedah, Wisconsin. An estimated crowd of one hundred thousand gathers around her on August 15, 1950. Her announcement strikes a resonant chord in rural Wisconsin. In effect, her visions repeat and apply the message of Fatima close to home. The Virgin also appears to be an ally in the Cold War. She warns of miniature submarines entering the Saint Lawrence Seaway. She warns of chemical poisons in water, soil, air, and livestock feed that may sap the resolve of Americans to fight the demon of communism. The messages are also laced with racial and anti-Semitic overtones.[88] The apparition is subsequently condemned by the local bishop in 1955. However, it is worth mentioning because it typifies the extreme of this phenomenon, one that remains a recurrent feature of these apparitions. The voice of Mary also becomes more shrill as the admonitions grow sharper, a far cry from the gentle Mother of Mercies of an earlier era. A generation later, Virginia Lueken (1923–1995), the "seer of Bay Side, Long

Island," hears the Virgin speak in the same cadence. The enemy has changed. The foe is no longer communist Russia. Now it is the evil of abortion. But the thunder of the Virgin's voice is the same. A message from August 5, 1971, proclaims, "The Eternal Father commands you stop these murders at once! You will not destroy the life of the unborn. Human life is sacred in the eyes of God. No man has the right to destroy a life."[89] The Bayside apparitions are condemned by the local bishop in 1986.

The year 1981 is a fateful one in this story. On May 13, 1981, an attempt is made on the life of Pope John Paul II. This is the feast of Our Lady of Fatima. The following year, John Paul II returns to Fatima on May 13 to place in Mary's crown the bullet that struck him. "One hand fired," he writes, "and another guided the bullet."[90] He attributes his survival to the intercession of our Lady of Fatima. He also interprets the third secret of Fatima as a prediction of an attempt on the pope's life.

Less than a month after the assassination attempt, the apparitions of the Virgin at Medjugorje commence, returning the story to calmer waters. The appearances begin in June of 1981, with almost daily visits of the Virgin to six children. Each is to receive ten secrets. Then the visits cease, except perhaps for a later one on a birthday or in a time of crisis. Although secrets of different kinds, personal and public, are involved, the apocalyptic note of the message seems to have receded over time as personal and devotional elements have grown. Perhaps the simple continuance of the appearances over a number of years moderates the note of eschatological urgency. Medjugorje seems to blend into Catholic piety. It becomes a pilgrimage site for those who seek healing and guidance in traditional terms.

To summarize: We have briefly surveyed a cross-section of Marian apparitions in order to finally establish what they contribute to our understanding of Mary's role in the Catholic tradition. First, they represent a new form of international Mariology. Apparitions in one place give birth to lesser, satellite appearances elsewhere that easily cross national boundaries. The 1917 apparition in Portugal flows into rural Wisconsin in the 1950s. The Medjugorje apparition of 1981 spins off similar events in Melleray in Ireland in 1985 and Lubbock, Texas, in 1988. The apparition sites also become a magnet for national, then international, pilgrimages. Catholics from all over the globe flock to these shrines for a variety of reasons. Lourdes was visited by four to five million pilgrims in recent years.[91] This represents a new turn in an old devotion. Heretofore, devotion to May was a fiercely regional, national piety. In the modern era, aided by the ease of world travel, it becomes an international devotion as well. Pilgrimages, whether to Jerusalem or to Santiago de Compostela, have always crossed national boundaries. Perhaps these international Marian devotions revive an old tradition.

Second, these heavenly apparitions occur in the West against the backdrop of ever more secularized societies. The contrast is both a source of skepticism as well as a stimulus to faith. The low ceiling of modern aspirations makes such events all the more attractive. There is no simple formula that captures how religion and modernity affect one another from one culture to another. To attempt such is far beyond the scope of this book. Thomas Kselman has studied the role of miracles and prophecies in nineteenth-century France. His concluding words bear repetition. In regard to the ability to deal with problems of individual illness and social and political disorder, he writes, "There is nothing inherent in the process of modernization which makes such crises less frightening. Miracles and prophecies persisted in France because they offered meaning and order to people when a secular perspective failed them."[92] Much the same could be said of Marian apparitions.

Third, Mary in an apocalyptic context takes on a new role. She remains ever the mother of mercy, but she also becomes a figure of judgment. Louis de Montfort predicted that the second coming of Christ would be preceded by an age of Mary.[93] In the last days, God the Father does not send the Son of Man; he first sends the Virgin Mary because she is the devil's most formidable opponent. De Montfort's words have struck resonant chords in the nineteenth and twentieth centuries, and they fit her roles in the apparitions. When Mary appears, she pronounces words of judgment: about Russia, about the evils of abortion, sometimes about the reforms of Vatican II. The common denominator is judgment. This is not traditionally a quality associated with the mother of mercies, the last refuge of sinners who flee from judgment. But it is her characteristic in the modern era.

The contrast is especially stark against the backdrop of American civil religion. Here God is simultaneously evoked but domesticated. God is still accorded a public role in civic ceremonies, but only as long as his conduct is up to modern standards. No more angry fulminations and no more slaughtering of enemies, as Yahweh of the Old Testament was wont to do. The words of H. Richard Niebuhr (1894–1962) some seventy years ago still ring true of aspects of such civil religion: "A God without wrath brought man without sin into a kingdom without judgment through the ministrations of Christ without a cross."[94] Mary of the apparitions in apocalyptic mode flies directly in the face of such assumptions. In doing so, she also finds herself in the company of fundamentalist and evangelical Christians. Perhaps she reminds us of the judgment of God in a society that either denies or is forgetful of such judgment. The particularity of her targets may offend a modern sensibility, and often the judgments are not balanced. But that is not the significant point.

In a society in which the social consensus about God's existence is precarious, there is a temptation to avoid the topic of God's judgment or of divine justice. Are we not perhaps, in our own way, as blind as the medievals? They lost touch with the mercy of God. Have we not lost touch with the justice of God? And do not mercy and justice imply one another? Is not the existence of one unintelligible without the other? Is not their unimaginable jointure central to the mystery of God? In an odd way, the field may be reversed these days. Mary now becomes the figure in whom the vestiges of God's judgment are kept. She reminds us, in a way vastly different from that of the medieval picture, that Christ will return as the Son of Man, and much like the great scene of the sheep and the goats in Matthew 25, it will not be a matter of indifference whether we recognized his presence in the hungry men and women who pass our way.

Fourth, apparitions belong to what is called in Catholic terms "private revelation," the object of human, not divine, faith. The endorsement of the church obliges no one to believe in the authenticity of an apparition. This also means that in regard to their credibility, the apparitions must carry their own weight. They must seem credible in ordinary human terms. Sometimes they are found wanting. Marina Warner was put off by the shabby commercialization of Lourdes; the pilgrimage site became a vast cottage industry for a poor section of France.[95] But Sandra Zimdars-Swartz represents perhaps a more typical voice. She went to Lourdes "on a whim." She writes, "The impression that I had of the *malades* and those who accompanied and cared for them, however, was that under the ever-present image of Mary at Lourdes these people had achieved some kind of peace with themselves and their situation and that their suffering, if not physically alleviated, was at least being transformed into something meaningful."[96]

Chapter Nine

THE LAST THINGS AND FAITH

We turn in this final chapter to the last things: death, heaven, hell, and judgment. They bring this discussion of doctrine to a conclusion in its own terms, and this topic comprises the first half of this chapter. I acknowledge the lively debate about eschatology, perhaps the foremost topic of twentieth-century theology, as the context for our own discussion. Then I turn to the meaning of resurrection in the Old Testament as the origin and source of the New Testament understanding of these realities. Finally, I seek to state as simply as possible the *enduring meaning* of the last things as the pivot to the subject of faith.

Then I ask what it means to believe in the long tradition whose winding paths I have sought to trace: faith in Christ, the Trinity, the church, and Mary. Although such do not exhaust the articles of the creed, they do touch the heart of what it means to be a believing Christian. And while it is one thing to peruse long stretches of history, seeking traces of meaning as an outsider looking in, it is quite another to enter the family of believers and view the world from inside the house looking out. The latter perspective is the focus in the second half of this chapter.

I. The Last Things

Eschatology in the Twentieth Century

The last things — death, judgment, heaven, and hell — comprise the final topics of traditional theology textbooks. For centuries, these are somnolent topics that quietly close the door of theology. They focus largely on the fate of the individual after death, with a vague nod to a general judgment and Christ's return, as distant and mythic as the world's beginning. This scene changes dramatically with the pioneering work of Johannes Weiss (1863–1914) and Albert Schweitzer (1875–1965). They argue persuasively that Jesus' proclamation of the kingdom is, in effect, an announcement that the world is soon to end. In other words, eschatology — the last things — stands at the heart of Jesus' preaching. At first, this discovery seems to consign the preaching of Jesus irrevocably to the dustbin of old and irrelevant ideas. But after the cataclysmic events of World War I, when the Western world comes close to the brink of destruction, the sharp edge of eschatology seems to capture the mood of the postwar era. Thereafter, eschatology becomes a dominant theme in the great theologies of the twentieth century, of Karl Barth (1886–1968), Rudolph Bultmann (1884–1976), Oscar Cullmann (1902–1999), and others.

The movement seems to gain new momentum at midcentury from the future-oriented Marxism of Ernst Bloch (1885–1977).[1] Adapted by Jürgen Moltmann, God as the power of the future, ever new, breaking into the present, becomes the lynchpin of a "theology of hope."[2] If theology has to do with the future, that future is, in part, the result of our making. In this sense, eschatology now acquires a social and political dimension. It means a critique of the structures of society that produce poverty and injustice. It also includes positive planning for the kind of future that brings about a more just and equitable society. And theologians, indeed all Christian, are not just spectators to the process; they are called to be active participants. Such sentiments can claim validation in Vatican II's pastoral constitution on the church in the modern world, *Gaudium et Spes* (*Joy and Hope*). In this vein, eschatology is an important factor in the "political theology" of Johannes Baptist Metz as the basis of fundamental theology.[3] Various kinds of "liberation theologies" focus an even sharper critique, largely in Marxist terms, on the social structures of societies, advocating active involvement on the part of Christians in the process of changing society for the better. On a completely different tack, Pierre Teilhard de Chardin (1881–1955) develops a vision of natural evolution that reaches its culmination in a supernatural "Omega" point, the coming of Christ.[4] Finally, in terms of individual eschatology, some now argue for a resurrection-in-stages, beginning immediately after death.[5] Language about the immortality of the soul is avoided. People are confused. What can resurrection-in-stages mean?

The Holy See follows these developments with varying degrees of concern. An Instruction of the Congregation for the Doctrine of the Faith in 1979 focuses on seven theses on the question of the "intermediate state" after death.[6] In 1984, the congregation warns of one-sided tendencies in liberation theology. In 1986, it returns to the same topic in a critical but also a more positive vein.[7]

In sum, the often-quoted words that Hans Urs von Balthasar wrote about eschatology in 1957 characterize the twentieth century as a whole, first Protestant and then Catholic thought: "If Troeltsch, speaking in behalf of nineteenth-century liberalism, could say that 'the eschatological office is usually closed,' we can now say that it is working overtime." Balthasar describes eschatology as theology's "storm center": "It is here that those thunderstorms begin which threaten the whole country-side of contemporary theology with the havoc of hail or the refreshing shower of gentle rain."[8]

A Single Conclusion

I wish to draw a single conclusion from the contemporary discussion of eschatology: no doctrine is complete unless and until it is viewed in light of the last things. The Christian understanding of the human person is incomplete without a sense of humankind's ultimate fate. The doctrine of Christ stands open until his return in glory. Likewise, creation and human history are not complete until they reach their final goal. In other words, all the topics discussed in previous chapters remain both unfinished and not fully intelligible without some sense of their own *denouement*. The play is not over until the last act is complete and the curtain has fallen. The last act is about the last things: death, judgment, heaven, and hell.

The connection here to faith is twofold. How can we speak about faith's object until that object is fully in sight? Therefore, the last things not only complete this discussion of God, Christ, the Trinity, and the church individually, but also pull these topics *together* into a single object of faith. And in the last analysis, faith's object is simple, not complex.

We also return to the beginning of this discussion. The creeds originate in the great missionary command of Matthew 28:19: "Go therefore and make disciples of all nations, baptizing them in the name of the Father and of the Son and of the Holy Spirit." They begin as the baptismal formula is expanded in order to prepare candidates for the reception of the sacrament. This threefold confession of faith is also linked to a threefold renunciation of the devil and all his works.[9] In other words, baptism involves personal conversion, a *turning away from sin toward God as Father, Son, and Spirit*. Here the second link to faith becomes clear. The content of the act of faith (*fides quae*) and the actual act itself (*fides qua*) are inseparably linked.[10] The object of faith must be fully before us. But it does not appear as an informational item that is now rounded out. Rather, it becomes the goal of a personal act of faith because we are convinced that our salvation can be accomplished only by entering the community of believes. The ecclesial context is therefore paramount. A person is baptized into the faith of the church, which is consciously confessed before baptism takes place. Christian beliefs are not, then, a set of private ideas. Instead, the faith of the church comes to a person from outside, as it were, and is consciously confessed and then handed on to others. And the last things close the creed because they articulate the ultimate gift of salvation toward which the act of faith aims.

The Last Things Together

When we view the last things *together* — death, judgment, heaven, and hell — they comprise an asymmetrical set of topics. They hover between the unimaginable and barely conceivable on the one hand — heaven and hell — and the bluntly factual on the other hand — the reality of death. Death is the first of these topics, the brutal eventuality that faces us all. We witness the death of family and friends and experience the irreparable sense of loss that their passing means to us.

Our own death, like our birth, is an event that we *experience* but do not consciously *know*. We may be fully aware of ourselves in the process of dying but not in the actual passing. At the other end of the spectrum, the end of the world as we know it becomes, in a nuclear age, not just a distant possibility but rather a possible actuality with, some might argue, a certain probability of its occurrence. One way or another, death serves as the opening door to the last things. Does it open on a blank wall or does it lead to a higher life? Surely it is no accident that the bedrock and starting point of Christian faith is Jesus' resurrection, his conquest of death. Christians have always connected death to sin because the Scriptures identify them but equally because this is how they experience them. From here, the meaning of life as a whole is reckoned. Is death the doorway to eternal life or to oblivion? If the latter, what did our life that preceded it amount to? What is lasting if ultimately nothing lasts?

In regard to what lies beyond the grave, the right interpretation of biblical statements is critical. Karl Rahner's essay "The Hermeneutics of Eschatological Assertions" sheds valuable light on this subject. Rahner makes this distinction: "To extrapolate from the present into the future is eschatology, to interpolate from the future into the present is apocalyptic. The eschatological assertion is part of man's nature and when it is concerned with the present as revealed by God's word, is Christian eschatology."[11] It is a serious mistake, he argues, to read apocalyptic visions as so many previews of coming attractions that can be cobbled together into a glimpse of the life to come. In the same vein, Jon Levenson argues, taking apocalyptic visions literally renders them prosaic. Making them prosaic betrays their truth as well.[12] Yet while such visions grow from within, they are not mere flights of fancy. Instead, they build on moments of grace within the human condition, imagining ways in which such moments might be brought to fulfillment. And one deals in images, not ideas, because imagination has the longer reach. Likewise, when such visions are reduced to the "ideas" that they contain, they are not enriched but rather are impoverished. In such visions, the human spirit soars. Grasping their truth means soaring along with them.

The Resurrection of the Dead

The right place to begin to understand the biblical meaning of the last things is with the resurrection of the dead. This stands at the heart of Christian faith and is the base point from which subsequent reflection originates and flows.

It is sometimes argued that the notion of resurrection appears late in the biblical tradition in Daniel 12:1–2 (ca. 167–164 B.C.) and is peripheral to the heart of Old Testament thought, perhaps in large measure an import from Iranian Zoroastrianism that had long nourished such hopes. Against such assumptions, Levenson argues that the resurrection of the dead is deeply rooted in Israel's traditions.[13] Intimations of resurrection stretch back to its earliest history. The prophet Elisha raises the son of a Shunamite woman from the dead (2 Kings 4:8–37). This story in 2 Kings resonates with the binding of Isaac in Genesis 22:1–15. In the case of Isaac, death is *averted;* for the Shunamite boy, death is *reversed.* Recall as well that Elijah never dies; he is expected to return as God's messenger before "the great and terrible day of the Lord" (Mal. 3:1; 4:5).

Michael Barré comments, "For the ancient Semites, life and death were not contradictory categories, but simply the opposite ends of a continuum; hence to bring a dead person back to life would represent only a further step to healing a gravely ill person."[14] In other words, there is a series of deathlike equivalents on a sliding scale: sickness, infertility, abandonment by a husband, slavery, exile, the loss of a child, and finally resurrection from the dead. They witness in different ways to God's power to reverse all such situations, revealing Yahweh as the God of life who triumphs over death. Therefore, long before the arrival of an apocalyptic framework, the resurrection of the dead was grasped as a possibility along with other miraculous interventions of God.

The resurrection also pertains to more than individuals. Israel's exile in Babylon and its subsequent restoration are nothing less than national death and resurrection. The great vision of Ezekiel 37 of the dry bones depicts the situation in just these terms. After God's judgment, the dry bones of the nation come together into a new body, a new Israel, into which God's spirit is once again poured. The servant of Isaiah 52–53, both an individual and a corporate symbol of the nation, envisions a restoration beyond the grave. The vision of Isaiah 26–27 of Israel's restoration surely anticipates the resurrection of Daniel 12. Levenson summarizes the Old Testament development this way: "What had been a rare exception in the early period became the basis for a general expectation in the late one. This is the apocalyptic expectation of a universal resurrection in a coming dispensation in which all of God's potentials would be activated in a grand finale of stupendous miracles very much at odds with the course of history."[15] He concludes, "When the belief in resurrection finally makes an unambiguous appearance in Judaism, it is thus both an innovation and a restatement of a tension that had pervaded the religion of Israel from the beginning, the tension between the Lord's promise of life, on the one hand, and the reality of death on the other."[16]

What is novel to Daniel 12:1–3 is the notion of "eternal life," the irrevocable triumph of life and the final vindication of the promise made to Israel in Deuteronomy 30:15: "I have set before you life and death, blessings and curses. Choose life so that you and your descendants may live." What follows naturally is the resurrection of the body. If moral regeneration is part of the life to come, then it must be accompanied by bodily restoration as well, a new kind of life for the whole person in the new age that God inaugurates. And the issue is here not first God's justice but rather the fulfillment of the promise made to Israel by the God of life.

In regard to the preaching of Jesus and the early church, the categories of apocalyptic are so central that I felt it necessary to treat them in the first discussion of Jesus and the preaching of the kingdom in chapters 2 and 3. To recap our conclusions: we saw that Jesus' preaching of the kingdom, clearly an apocalyptic hope, was the lynchpin that held together his words and his deeds, his life as a whole, and his death and resurrection. Apocalyptic hope was not simply the context but also the connecting thread that joined the parts together. Thus a straight line links Israel's apocalyptic expectations, Jesus' preaching of the kingdom, his resurrection from the dead, and the early church's faith that the risen Christ as the Messiah and the Son of Man would shortly return to complete his work on earth. In turn, the resurrection of Jesus lays the basis for the range of eschatological hopes that the early church will seek to articulate in subsequent centuries: the joys of the kingdom, the punishment of hell, the judgment facing humankind.[17]

The Structures of Hope

The *structures of hope* arise from Jesus' resurrection and the church's meditation on its meaning. In other words, a series of structural tensions define the future object of Christian hope and aspiration. The first axis of hope is always firmly anchored in history and human experience. The second arcs beyond this world but is based on our experience in it.

The axial structures of hope are threefold. The first and widest concerns creation and its final apocalyptic culmination in nothing less than a new creation. For Israel, the story begins at Sinai when the revelation of the divine name brings a people into existence. Second Isaiah expands God's creative act. Yahweh is the creator of the universe, and into this wider setting the exodus from Egypt is placed as a central moment. According to Genesis 1, God creates the world effortlessly by his word, pronouncing it good. Sin enters creation through the disobedience of Adam and Eve. However, they are not completely free in their action. They are seduced by the serpent, who seems to know something of good and evil before their deed. No explanation of the serpent is given. Similarly, Genesis does not offer a full and complete discussion of the origin of sin and evil; rather, it registers the fact as the beginning of the drama that now unfolds. Despite human infidelity, God will vindicate the promise of life and bring creation safely to its destiny, confirming its original goodness.

In this hope, the human person and the cosmos relate as microcosm and macrocosm. God has created Israel with a future and a destiny. Likewise, God endows each human person with the same qualities. For the individual, the future blessings of this life consist, in part, in the gift of children and a good name. But the ultimate vindication of God's creation occurs at the great battle between good and evil, not at the beginning, but at the end of time. Here the fate of the nation and of each individual is decided. In other words, the great apocalyptic vision of a new creation brings the original promise of creation to completion. Sin and death are conquered. God's kingdom of life is definitively established, not in this world but beyond it. This is the first and widest axis of hope: creation at the beginning of time, the drama of salvation, then the hope of a new creation at the end of time in which the drama is resolved.

This first axis of hope contains a second. If hope pertains to the nation and to the cosmos, it pertains also to every individual created in the image and likeness of God. These *individual* and *collective* moments cannot be collapsed into one another, because the logic of hope operates differently in each case. For the individual, the world ends with death; for the cosmos, its destiny continues until the end of time. But these hopes are also intertwined. Each person has a uniquely individual destiny. Yet each unique individual is also a member of a community, a thread in a larger tapestry. That tapestry is not complete until the last thread is sewn and its final design revealed. Thus while each individual has a unique destiny, all share a collective one as well.

The third axis of hope relates to its *present* and *future* dimensions. The great vision of Daniel 7 and its complement in Daniel 12 envision God's imminent *future* intervention to vindicate Israel before the nations and to judge each individual beyond the grave. What is unique to Jesus' preaching is his announcement that this kingdom is *now* appearing in the events of his ministry. Yet Jesus awaits its grand finale as well. Both *realized* and *future* eschatology, a present and a future dimension, run like twin threads throughout Jesus' preaching and the preaching of the early church. The resurrection represents a special point of intersection, a *present* taste of *future* glory and the offer of the same to Jesus' followers. The emphasis between future and realized eschatology shifts, but neither moment can be eliminated or absorbed into the other, although it may seem so at times. In John's Gospel, realized eschatology predominates. The preaching of the kingdom is replaced by the centrality of Jesus in our midst — in Origen's memorable phrase, Jesus as "the Kingdom in person" (*autobasilea*).[18]

These two moments of *present* experience and *future* hope continue in the church. The kingdom is present in the gift of the Spirit and the life of the sacraments. Yet the church awaits Christ's return in glory. The latter hope waxes and wanes according to its own mysterious logic. In some ages, the end of time seems palpably near; in others, it drifts to the distant future. But present and future dimensions and the tension between them are fixed axes in the structure of hope.

I do not pretend to give here an exhaustive account of the structure of hope. The tension between time and eternity runs squarely through the discussion, likewise the tension between what is imaginable and conceivable from a human point of view and how God's plans for the future may outstrip our capacities. But enough has been said to indicate how our hope of the life to come is based on experience in this life. Its unimaginable fulfillment is beyond us, but it will rivet the human imagination. But the axes of this structure and their resulting tensions remain permanent barriers against too much speculation. Instead, the last things should become the subject of meditative reflection in light of what we may surmise from the human face of hope in this life.

The Enduring Meaning of the Last Things

Since our focus in this chapter is finally on faith, I close the first half of it by stating as simply as possible the *enduring meaning* of the last things, beginning with heaven.

Heaven means, quite simply, our presence before the Triune God. That presence has been traditionally described as the *Beatific Vision,* the goal of the human intellect. Here our knowledge of the Triune God becomes transparent. Knowledge becomes vision. It has also been de-scribed as *Love,* the goal of the human will. Here the deepest longings of the human heart are satisfied. One way or another, this also means that heaven comes gift-like to all creatures and to creation. We may make some claim to reward or punishment based on our lives on this earth, but the gift of heaven exceeds all such rewards, and no one can claim it by right. And although the seeds of perfection may be sown in us in this world, they are not meant to fully blossom on earth, but only in the life to come. In other words, perfection is not a cate-gory, certainly not a helpful category, of finite human existence. Such completion is reserved to heaven as the fulfillment of a supernatural destiny given to each individual and bestowed on the cosmos as well. In larger terms, the world does not contain the natural capacity for its own completion. God, who freely created the world in the first place, freely guides the created order and each individual within it to their final destiny.

The completion that heaven brings to earth and to each individual might be likened to a series of concentric circles.[19] Our union with

God is oneness with *Christ,* who by his resurrection has opened for us the portals of heaven. Christ is the first of many brothers and sisters, and our oneness with God is the fruit of the salvation won for us by Christ, who brings us home.

Heaven means the completion of the destiny of the *church* as well. Our oneness with God means oneness with one another. Heaven therefore contains an essential ecclesial dimension. Here the communion of saints, the body of Christ, is brought to completion. Here no one is alone, and no one is a stranger.

Heaven also contains an *anthropological* dimension. Heaven means the completion of all persons individually in those capacities that are uniquely their own. Here every human heart is finally at rest in its own terms.

Heaven also contains *historical* and *cosmological* dimensions. These are the widest circles that enclose human existence and that also cry for redemption. Heaven therefore means that human history is brought to completion, not in its own terms but rather in God's. This also sets the hope of heaven apart from all utopian ideologies that claim to bring heaven to earth. Long experience has taught us that such do not bring heaven to earth. Instead, they bring us a foretaste of hell. Finally, in regard to the cosmos, heaven means that the perfection originally planted in creation at the beginning of time is brought to fruition. In heaven, this original goodness flowers and blooms.

Therefore, heaven is oneness with God in Christ and in the church in which human history and the cosmos find completion as well. Heaven gives us here on earth a grand vision of unimaginable blessing in which the promise of God's creation is brought to fulfillment.

If heaven is the presence of the Triune God, hell is God's radical absence. Levenson states that the Old Testament knows no such binary equivalents as heaven and hell.[20] Nor does the New Testament propose such. Karl Rahner observes that heaven and hell should not be regarded, in effect, as a four-lane highway, two lanes heading toward heaven and two toward hell with equal traffic in both directions.[21] Such belies the promise of creation, whose abiding nature, God pronounces, is "good." Still, the church teaches the existence and the eternity of hell. But while it names people as citizens of heaven — this is what it means to declare someone a saint — no one is by name consigned to hell. In other words, these are not to be considered binary equivalents without further ado. Rather, hell should be regarded as an anthropological limit-statement, a possibility of human existence that cannot be eliminated. In the first instance, it is a statement about human freedom. The human person can freely act against God's commandments and can remain intransigent in such deeds. And not even God's mercy can relax the human fist that has tightened around its own sin. Hell thereby becomes a statement about God's justice. God has no choice but to ratify such a freely chosen course of action. Since such actions become irrevocable, hell must be the permanent, not temporary, abode of lost souls. Hell must be eternal.

The modern era has considerable difficulty with the doctrine of hell on one principal score. When human action goes catastrophically wrong in a sinful direction, it is has become almost a reflex reaction to switch the category of its classification. We detach such actions from the area of free will and moral responsibility and reassign them to the domain of psychology for therapeutic reconsideration. A truly terrible human action is given the balm of mitigating circumstances. Such wrongful deeds may be the result of family upbringing. They may also be the sour fruit of a social environment that diminishes the worth of the individual. In effect, *sinful* human actions are now reclassified as *unhealthy* ones, the deeds of persons with a diminished capacity for right or wrong. No one of sound mind would do such things, we tell ourselves. We thereby restrict the notion of sin to a middle range of human actions, performed by people who are usually quite themselves and would seldom, if ever, perpetrate horrendous deeds. In a word, people are not free enough to commit the kind of actions that could consign them to hell for eternity. Such notions are the residues of a premodern age that misread the human situation and overestimated the capacities of free will.

But the arguments in favor of hell do not go quietly into the night, and the older logic is no less persuasive in the twenty-first century. Parenthetically, there is a sense in which heaven and hell *are* binary equivalents and both together should be placed over against their equivalent assumptions in the culture. The Christian tradition sees the human person as capable of enormous goodness for which the promise of heaven is emblematic. In other words, the tradition expands the human capacity for goodness beyond the generally accepted range of social expectations. However, it also expands the human continuum on the other side. It sees the human person as capable of great evil. It therefore warns about underestimating the range of human responsibility. If human beings are capable of heaven, they may also be capable of hell. And the Christian tradition thinks this way not on the basis of a prior theory but rather on the basis of experience.

It is ironic that the twentieth century, which declares the notion of hell an anachronism, has produced a cast of characters who seem to belong nowhere else. One can think of numerous examples from Nazi Germany in the 1930s and 1940s, above all, the perpetrators of the Holocaust. Aleksandr Solzhenitsyn's *Gulag Archipelago* provides other candidates. In other words, just as the modern era closes down the operation of hell, it produces numerous examples of people who not only belong there but who also might choose to go there. It is also clear that the therapeutic viewpoint, when applied to events as horrendous as the Holocaust, can only boomerang on itself. Such events call the therapeutic approach itself into question, revealing it as an explanatory method most aptly applied to a middle range of individual human actions. When applied to larger social evils, it trivializes them, like saying that the Holocaust was the result of tensions in the German family structure in the 1930s. The actual content of such generalizations is so vapid as to provide no satisfactory explanation at all. The truth is that evils as large as the Holocaust explode the categories of psychological explanation. They strain moral ones as well. They seem to represent evils beyond the normal range of human sinfulness. If anything, they point to the mystery of iniquity. Likewise, they should make us hesitate to say that hell has no application in the modern world. Yet having said all that, it still remains possible that all may repent and be saved (2 Pet. 3:9). God condemns no one. It is a fate of our choosing, and perhaps the promise of universal reconciliation that Origen and others glimpse may prove the deeper insight. This is a possibility and a hope. But it cannot be more.

Human imagination has not been shy about speculating about the nature of hell, from Dante's *Inferno* to the mystics, the apparitions of Fatima, and Jean-Paul Sartre. Jesus speaks of the fires of Gehenna. But fire can be a purifying medium as well. "Fire" is the heading under which Blaise Pascal describes his great experience of November 23, 1654.[22] Joseph Ratzinger has written penetrating words on this score, describing Christ's descent among the dead. The pains of the damned might be likened, he says, to the extremes of human loneliness. Here the tightly closed human fist is an apt symbol of a damned soul, a person trapped in his or her own intransigent deeds, cut off from family and friends, separated from Christ and the church, someone totally and utterly alone.[23] Here Dante may have chosen the better metaphor. A person in hell is someone frozen in ice, locked in his or her freely chosen course of action, drifting that way through eternity. Just as heaven is oneness with God in Christ and with others, hell is the opposite on every front — a person drifting alone, locked in his or her sinful deeds.

And what of the nature of judgment? John's Gospel described Jesus as truth. And judgment consists simply in the truth about ourselves and our world. François Fénelon (1615–1715) asserted that if any of us learned the real truth about ourselves, we would faint dead away.[24] That may finally be the case. That we speak of a particular and a general judgment reflects the human condition. Each of us possesses a unique destiny and an individual vocation given at birth and sanctified in baptism. We are allotted a limited number of years to fulfill that destiny within the vicissitudes of our situation. Then our lives end, and we are candidates for judgment on our own individual merits and in our own terms, and that seems right. But we are also threads in a larger tapestry, members of the human community. We also share a communal destiny, and here no judgment is possible until all threads have been sewn and each individual counted and all are judged, this time, together. Then the final shape of the human tapestry is revealed. Only then can our ultimate destiny be placed in perspective.

I close this section with the doctrine of purgatory. Eastern and Western Catholic Christianity share here a common heritage. Western Catholic Christianity has its own specific differences. It is no surprise that purgatory was as an important article of discussion at the so-called reunion councils, the Second Council of Lyons in 1274 and again at the Council of Ferrara-Florence in 1439. The Western Catholic doctrine was established by the bull *Benedictus Deus* of Pope Benedict XII on January 29, 1336.[25] There is also a difference in emphasis between

East and West. The Western emphasis is on repentance for sin, the Eastern on purification of the human person.

First, a word here about the common doctrine and then about the differences. The doctrine of purgatory springs from two sources in the church's meditation on human life, first on the nature of death and then on the function of prayer. These sources dovetail in the doctrine of purgatory. The tradition takes with great seriousness the fact that death, certainly sudden death, catches the human person woefully off guard and in an incomplete state. Although the ultimate trajectory of people's lives may be set, they often depart this life with too many trailing strings and too much unfinished business. It also seems clear that if heaven means our presence before the Triune God, we cannot appear before God until we have fully settled into that limited perfection which is ours in the first place. Purgatory designates a place only as a metaphor. It is rather a process, after death, by which we repent and shed ourselves of sin and grow into that potential which is ours so that we might fittingly appear in God's presence. The other large argument in favor of the doctrine is the long tradition of prayers for the dead, a practice going back to Judaism (2 Macc. 12:43–45) that the church unhesitatingly continues. This constant practice assumes that our prayers for the dead can actually help those who have gone before us. It assumes as well that they can continue to mature after death. The thought is not that they can launch new ventures, but rather that they can bring the business of this earth to completion.

Eastern Christianity holds to the older version in which this "intermediate state" continues for all souls until the final judgment; only then do the final states of heaven and hell commence. The Western doctrine of 1336 teaches that the souls who have no further need of purgation enter directly after death into the joys of heaven; likewise, those who die in serious sin are consigned to hell. The Western tradition still reckons with a final judgment and the resurrection of the body that occur at the end of time.

As we pull the object of faith together in its final form as the last things, the credibility of faith bends under the strain. Can all of this be true — judgment, heaven, hell, and purgatory? Must we believe it all? By the same token, it also gains credibility. Faith is, of its nature, a gamble. And the wager is not taken seriously until the cards are dealt, the game is in play, and the odds are clear. Sanitized versions of Christianity in which all scandal is removed are more acceptable in one sense but less challenging in another. Above all, they misread the nature of faith. Since they involve no risk or gamble, faith itself becomes largely unnecessary. It never takes much of an act of faith to believe in the *Zeitgeist,* the spirit of the age.

II. The Scandal of Faith

Accordingly, I describe the act of faith as delivering a series of shocks to the system of usual assumptions about ourselves and the world that we inhabit. I will speak here of a threefold scandal of faith that operates according to a certain graded symmetry. At the broadest level, faith in God delivers the first jolt. Then faith in God as a Christian and finally as a Catholic each delivers its own shock. In one sense, this trajectory comprises a single movement. Faith is not abstract and general but rather particular, specific, and personal. By the same token, it is not an individual venture but rather a communal one. In another sense, the trajectory delivers three separate jolts to the system, each of which we turn to separately and successively. The mind needs to be "broken in," in John Henry Newman's phrase, to grasp the logic of faith and these shocks are the means of accomplishing the task.

Faith in God

Newman writes, "Unless Thou wert incomprehensible, Thou would not be God. For can the infinite be other than incomprehensible to me?"[26] We take as our foil here Richard Dawkins's recent book *The God Delusion.*[27] The book delivers a sustained argument as to why belief in God is misguided, useless, and pernicious both to the individual and to society. It fairly "crackles with brio," as one reviewer put it, delivering a series of knockout punches to the "God delusion."[28] No doubt Dawkins is utterly convinced and fully sincere, a zealot in his own way. Yet a fair reader might also wonder if he has ever actually grasped the positive and sustained arguments why so many people in this age and in the past, in this culture and in others, have chosen to disregard his kind of reasoning and have decided to believe in a God. If there is one clear assumption underlying his argument, both the book's strength and its Achilles' heel, it is that Dawkins has entirely mastered his subject. Underneath this assumption lies an even more fundamental one. The human mind, working here through the categories of evolutionary biology, can curl around and encompass its object. Where even a hint of God's actual existence might extrude such limits, it is clipped off as neatly as so much extra piecrust. In a word, God is reduced to the measure of the human mind, as is all religious thinking as well.

I cited Newman to begin this section. I could have cited countless other thinkers on the same score. If there is a God at all, then God must be the measure of us and not the reverse. But this delivers a jolt to the system against which Dawkins has immunized himself. In a thousand variant forms, Newman's starting point is the usual one for serious religious inquiry. However, and here Dawkins is helpful, it does reverse the field and deliver a shock to the system.

To expand the point by way of example, Nicholas of Cusa (1401–1464) describes God as *de non aliud* — not like anything else.[29] In this regard, he would chide Anselm's proof — God is that being greater than which no being can be conceived — for thinking of God in *comparative* terms. In effect, Anselm is not thinking big enough.[30] For if God is greater than the greatest, the absolute maximum, Nicholas reckons, he must also be smaller than the smallest, the absolute minimum; if God is absolute potential, he must also be absolute actuality. God must be transcendent in the measure he is immanent, comprehensible in the measure he is incomprehensible, simple in the measure he is complex. According to Nicholas, God can only be described as the *coincidence of opposites,* beyond the law of contradiction, teetering at the edge of human comprehension, and clearly a much more suitable object of faith than reason, in the last analysis, the object of *learned ignorance (docta ignorantia).*[31] We can see here the wisdom of negative (*apophatic*) theology. We can be more certain of what God is *not* than of what God *is.* Simply put, God is not like anything around us, yet God exists.

But how is this an argument at all? What the argument does in the first instance is make a small *tear* in the seamless world that the five senses deliver and upon which human reason constructs a wall around us. Into this small tear, the argument inserts an equally small question:

What if? What if there are things beyond our comprehension? *What if* we might be encompassed by a reality larger than ourselves whose existence, much less whose nature, we can barely comprehend? *What if?* William James uses this analogy. Dogs and cats wander into our libraries, where they are surrounded by a world of ideas, contained in the books, of which they have no inkling.[32] *What if* we were in God's library in the same way? So faith insinuates a slight tear in the universe in which reason might enclose us. Then it watches the tear grow as the question itself expands.

What if the notion of God were sewn into the very fabric of the human mind? Those who would debunk the notion of God must nevertheless account for the fact that so many people in so many ages have puzzled about God's existence. Dawkins reduces it to a kind of computer virus — a "meme," in his terminology — planted long ago in the human brain, perhaps eventually to be flushed out in the evolutionary process.

But all such arguments must take into account that the question of God is pushed forward on multiple fronts. In other words, the question of God is inseparably linked to many other questions that press for an answer. Whence comes the notion of justice? How does a sense of right and wrong, of *should* and *must,* come to exist in a world of empirical facts that simply *are?* How does a sense of beauty, so integral to human aspirations, arise? How do we explain the altruism that brings people to lay down their lives not only for family and friends but also for strangers, even enemies? It is a strain to explain such deeply rooted human instincts on an evolutionary basis. What purpose do they serve in terms of personal or social utility, even reckoned in the long run, if that is their measure? Or is the measure wrong?

One way or another, why were we made to raise so many questions that we cannot answer? If the world is self-contained, why do we raise so many questions that point beyond it? Why do we seek relentlessly for answers, unless our very questions contained the intuition that somewhere, somehow answers are out there? Clear at least is this much. Admit the first small question, and a torrent of other ones tumble out. Our initial tear has now grown quite large.

The religious response is clear. What if there is an answer to such questions, and what if that answer is linked to God? Certainly, then, there would be more purpose to this world than we can discern by our five senses and by human reason. And our question is at once cosmic and personal. Not only, Is there more purpose to the universe? but also, What if there were more point to *my own* life? William James, in the conclusion of *The Varieties of Religious Experience,* suggests that religious experience may indicate that our world lies soaking in a wider one, in a dimension of reality that contains a response to dilemmas that this life poses but cannot answers.[33] What if there actually is such a dimension? But what if there is not? Such questions are answerable only within degrees of relative probability with a certain motivational push, carrying our answer across the goal line. But they are not answered conclusively in the way they are posed. Otherwise, such questions would have been answered long ago. And perhaps that is the point.

The truth is that in the end we are all believers in answers to questions that we pose but cannot answer. Those who believe in God make one act of faith. Those who believe that the world has no higher purpose, that there is no God, make an act of faith as well. Therefore, it is not as if reason were ranged on one side and faith on the other. Instead, it is a question of two kinds of acts of faith: one in favor of God, the other against. In effect, we ourselves and the world around us give off mixed signals that can never be reconciled and brought down to a simple, clear answer to which all can agree. The choice, then, is about which act of faith we wish to make. The other option is simply to ignore questions of larger purpose and live life day by day, which may suffice until something major goes wrong. Then we learn that, for most people, questions about meaning and purpose, about God, are not posed as speculative parlor games but rather because our lives are on the line and we have no choice but to ask them.

If we are leaning toward an act of faith in God's existence, this is the point at which proofs of the existence of God may make sense. In other words, in the modern era such proofs probably make sense not *before* but rather *after* the first stirrings of faith. They also make sense, above all, on an aesthetic level. Does the world *seem* more harmonious if we envision the existence of God? The argument from design continues to function powerfully in a modern scientific world. As we probe the intricate logic of DNA that we *discover,* and likewise as we probe the outer reaches of the universe, both the microcosm and macrocosm seem to more lawful and more mysterious than one would ever imagine. Yet a designer is not a creator. And all arguments from "intelligent design" must be careful not to reduce God to the level of a first engineer at the control panels of "design-project earth." God is transcendent and exists in all eternity, and such considerations make a considerable difference. The strongest argument, in my view, remains the argument from contingency. Why is there something rather than nothing? Must not there be some explanation for the universe in the first place that this passing world cannot provide? Perhaps the pre-condition of changing, earthly life is the existence of a God who is absolute and unchanging. Jim Holt frames the question in a modern cadence: "But if you think that there must be some ultimate expla-nation for the improbable leaping-into-existence of the harmonious, biofriendly cosmos we find ourselves in, then the God hypothesis is at least rational to adhere to, isn't it?"[34]

Faith in the God of Jesus Christ

There is a sense in which, once the existence of God is admitted, the desire for revelation naturally follows. Since our knowledge of God is limited to the clues planted in creation, we desire to know more. We wish that God would reveal himself. We look for revelation. Newman writes,

> When once the mind is broken in, as it must be, to the belief of a Power above it, when once it understands that it is not itself the measure of all things in heaven and earth, it will have little difficulty in going forward. . . . I say that, when once it believes in God, the great obstacle to faith has been taken away — a proud self-sufficient spirit. When once a man really, with the eyes of his soul and by the power of Divine grace, recognizes his Creator, he has passed a line; that has happened to him which cannot happen twice; he has bent his stiff neck, and triumphed over himself.[35]

As Newman observes, belief in God represents a necessary mile-stone in the forward movement of the act of faith. But it is one thing to believe in God in order to make our universe appear more harmo-nious; it is quite another to believe in the God of Jesus Christ. Belief in the God of Jesus Christ delivers its own jolt to the system and poses its own scandal. It claims that the all-powerful God has revealed himself in an utterly unique way in the life, death, and resurrection of a single historical individual, Jesus of Nazareth. While faith in God may humble the human spirit, no one is quite prepared for the claim that the Word was made flesh. There is an audacity to this claim that must be forthrightly acknowledged to be appreciated at all. Søren Kierkegaard (1813–1855) describes the incarnation as an absolute paradox that simply exceed the limits of human reason.[36] Nicholas of Cusa, who speaks of God as the coincidence of opposites, describes Christ as the *absolute intermediary (medium absolutum)*.[37] In Jesus Christ, God and human, a special coincidence of opposites appears among us.

Yet if the incarnation were only paradox that exceeds us, how would we have the capacity to understand it at all? Indeed, the paradoxical claim that the Word was made flesh speaks directly to the paradoxical dimensions of human existence. Therefore, if the incarnation defies logic on the one hand, it contains, on the other, its own apology that fits our cry for salvation. For if nature groans for redemption, those cries become articulate in the human person. Pascal describes the human person as "a thinking reed" suspended between eternity and nothingness, "a middle point between all and nothing." This unique position comprises humankind's grandeur and misery. It is also the wellspring from which our cries for salvation originate.[38]

> We are floating in a medium of vast extent, always drifting uncertainly, blown to and fro; whenever we think we have a fixed point to which we can cling and make fast, it shifts and leaves us behind; if we follow it, it eludes our grasp, slips away, and flees eternally before us. Nothing stands still for us. This is our natural state and yet the state most contrary to our inclinations. We burn with desire to find a firm footing, an ultimate lasting base on which to build a tower rising up to infinity, but our whole foundation cracks and the earth opens up into the depth of the abyss.[39]

The grandeur and the misery of human existence are the poles of the human situation to which the incarnation speaks. We claim to see in a single human existence, in Jesus of Nazareth, all the capacity for goodness, generosity, and noble purpose actually fulfilled. Most of us know such capacity only as so much empty warehouse space, so much unused potential, so much wasted talent, so often the source of our own misery. Such contains its own endless refrain: "You could have been more; it could have been otherwise." But the Gospels tell us that *once, just once,* our nature was fulfilled in all its capacity for generosity, goodness, and noble purpose. If the human person on one side is defined by an absolute openness to the infinite God, then once that absolute openness was completely filled when the Word became flesh. The incarnation therefore not only reveals God's nature; it reveals to us our own as well. Yet human nature in the incarnation does not become the measure of God. God's nature, as it fulfills our own, exceeds human capacity on every side. God becomes the measure of us. Indeed, as God comes ever closer to us, revealing himself in our own nature, he also reveals himself as radically transcendent, radically other than us. As he reveals himself, God remains ever hidden. Close up, this hiddenness becomes more apparent.

If God embraces and fulfills all human potential for goodness — the grandeur of human existence — it is only because he embraces as well the human capacity for misery. Jesus dies a human death. It certainly is no accident that the Gospels reach their climax in the story of Jesus' passion and death. Mark's Gospel underscores the utter desolation of this death. Jesus dies alone with the question of Psalm 22 on his lips: "My God, my God, why have you forsaken me?" For Mark, only in Jesus' death does his divinity shine through. Hence, the words of the centurion: "Truly, this man was God's Son!" (Mark 15:39). Mark fully grasps the meaning of Jesus' death as the climax of his life. For death represents not simply the final agonizing moment, the event of passing from this life; rather, it is tied to all the deathlike equivalents that stretch back to the beginning of Jesus' story: sickness, opposition, the random nature of human life, and, above all, sin. All of these carry a death-dealing potential. Thus at Jesus' death, the question is posed in its starkest terms. What defines human nature? Is it our potential for God? Were we truly made in the image and likeness of God as our defining mark? Or do sin and death have the final word? Were we made to endlessly pose unanswerable questions, an odd anomaly, a middle point between eternity and nothingness that belongs nowhere? In taking on a human death, Jesus embraces this dark potential of human existence. He drains the cup of human misery without himself being tainted in the process. The oldest confession says of Jesus what can be said of no one else: he is without sin. The resurrection is described as Jesus' victory over sin and death and all they represent. This victory is passed on to Jesus' followers through the gift of his Spirit so that they too might taste the new life that he has gained for us.

We should appreciate what good news this represents. If the Word has become flesh, if Jesus has conquered sin and death, then we thereby learn that we are not created with this peculiar capacity for grandeur and misery as nature's cruel joke on itself. Instead, we were created for a unique destiny, once realized in Jesus of Nazareth, who has opened for us a new kind of life that he shares with his followers.

If this is true, it tells much about our own nature, but it also tells us about our communal destiny too. The Christian community in Corinth called itself the body of Christ. By doing so, it tells us that the bonds between Christ and the individual believer also create a special link between believers. Indeed, if the risen Christ becomes a zone of personal presence, this communal dimension enjoys a certain priority. The Christian community becomes the mediator of Christ's Spirit to each individual and the repository in which the memory of Jesus is kept alive. In effect, we confess that the risen Jesus creates a church. Cardinal Newman writes that if we believe that God's Word became flesh, it is not difficult to imagine that God would have also devised the means of passing down the gospel and keeping Jesus' spirit alive. In other words, it is not much of a stretch to believe in a church, not just as a community of our making but rather as the result of God's intention in sending Jesus into the world in the first place.[40]

Faith as a Roman Catholic

We come to the final link in the act of faith. The church now enters the story, not as a generic but rather as a very specific form of Christianity in which a particular kind of Christian is cultivated, a Roman Catholic Christian. Friedrich Schleiermacher intentionally draws out the contrasts between Protestant and Catholic Christianity when he writes that Protestantism "makes the individual's relation to the Church dependent on his relation to Christ, while [Catholicism] contrariwise makes the individual's relation to Christ dependent on his relation to the Church."[41] The Second Vatican Council describes the relation less antithetically: although elements are found in other churches and ecclesial communities, the church of Christ subsists in the visible Catholic Church.

One way or another, the church bulks as an especially large item in the act of faith of a Roman Catholic. And there is no way in which this kind of faith can be mistaken for a generic brand of Christianity. On the contrary, its visible defining characteristics were and are everywhere evident. It became a commonplace that when the Catholic faith was preached by nineteenth-century missionaries in competition with their Protestant counterparts, three elements stood out: the real presence of Christ in the Eucharist, devotion to the Blessed Virgin Mary, and the centrality of the pope.

I am not sure that I would pick out these elements in quite the same order, but they are essential parts of the mix. There is a strong sense of what I will call *symbolic realism* in the Catholic faith that delivers the third jolt to the system. The foregoing examples can be ranged under this heading, which should be more closely defined. What do we mean by *symbolic realism?* At the broadest measure, it means that the Christ intended to found a church, and the present, visible Roman Catholic Church stands in historical continuity with his founding intention. Thus for Catholics, the church remains always holy as one of its defining marks, although its members may not be.

Catholics have an elevated sense of the church that manifests itself in innumerable ways. The church claims a specially endowed teaching authority, distinct from and superior to the theological views of individual theologians. Accordingly, Catholic theologians are asked to submit to its judgments not just in definitive matters but also in prudential ones. Statements of this teaching office may themselves be flawed; nonetheless, an authentic teaching office is a part of Catholic faith. Some reject it as a stumbling block. Others greet it as a guarantor of truth. But one way or another, it is there. Truth in advertising bids us be clear on the point. Yet it would not be fair to view the church, so characterized, as discharging such teaching duties in a highly authoritarian way. The traditional notion of "theological notes" witnesses to a long tradition of the graduated use of authority. Here each doctrine is assigned a "note," or doctrinal classification, on a sliding scale from "defined truth" to "common opinion." Elsewhere, I have compared the church as teacher to a golfer with five woods, nine irons, and a putter.[42] The church selects various clubs to engage different degrees of authority, and it usually does not use a driver when a sand wedge will do.

However, our concern here is less with the *use* than with the *fact* of an official teaching office. In this regard, the teaching authority connects to many other instances of symbolic realism on every level. On the level of first impressions, Catholic churches in a traditional and even modern style abound in images, crucifixes, statues, stations of the cross, and stained-glass windows. A visual imagination relentlessly seeks expression, quite apart from the quality of the product. There is no suspicion of such representational art. On the contrary, a trust in images to convey true impressions is everywhere evident.

On a deeper level, the belief in the presence of Christ in the Eucharist carries both real and symbolic dimensions. From a Catholic perspective, a merely symbolic presence, though perhaps more acceptable in one sense, remains bland and uninteresting in another sense. The world is full of symbols that never deliver the punch that they promise. Wonder bread does not make people wonderful. The breakfast of champions makes no one a champion. But a real symbol claims to convey the reality that it symbolizes. The Eucharist literally claims to give us the body and blood of Christ under the appearances of bread and wine. This both delivers a shock to credibility and renders the Eucharist a worthy object of faith.

We can range under the same heading of symbolic realism many other doctrines. For example, the Immaculate Conception and Assumption of Mary and the Virginal Conception of Jesus are heavily laden with symbolic meaning. But Catholic faith counts them as actual facts. They are the objects of faith that can become significant only if they affirmed both in symbolic and real senses. Similarly, the canonization of a saint is a statement not merely about a person's holiness but also about their presence in heaven and as worthy of our veneration here on earth. But can such be proven without question on an empirical basis? Hardly. These are objects of faith that, though based on earthly facts, soar beyond them. Likewise, the existence of heaven, hell, and purgatory, though grounded in human experience, extrapolate beyond it as objects of faith. Yet it remains a deeply rooted

Catholic conviction that the act of faith is a reasonable one. Faith does not disparage, but rather builds on, the capacities of human reason, which the Catholic tradition fully acknowledges.

On every side, the Catholic faith claims that our existence in this world is touched and surrounded by other worlds, by the church in heaven and the church on its pilgrim journey home. Further, it claims that the walls between these realities are not fixed but rather are quite permeable. It assumes also that Christ will actually come again for final judgment. It treats such as matters of fact, and therein stands its symbolic realism. It is not difficult to understand why Catholic faith delivers its own jolt to the system and makes its own special claim on faith. On the other hand, it presents an object that is fully worthy of belief.

III. The Last Question

Now the final question: Do we actually believe all of this? We noted earlier that faith was a risk, a wager and gamble that can be taken seriously only when the cards are dealt, the game is in play, and the odds are clear. We have reached that point. We understand what is at stake in believing in God's revelation in Jesus of Nazareth. We grasp the attractiveness of such belief, but we cannot banish the scandal. There is something gripping but also improbable in God revealing himself in the dimensions of a single human existence and setting up a church to boot.

At any rate, our act of faith now has content. The cards are face up on the table. We know what faith is about and what we are asked to believe. Two additional elements remain, each independent of the other. Faith requires a free act of the will on our part. No one is coerced to believe. Rational argument stops short of the goal, and we are required to make a leap of faith to bridge the intervening divide. And there is no way of reasoning one's way across this gap. Still, if we must leap, it is better to face the obstacle before us, realizing that the leap of faith is a reasonable one. The second element is a movement of the Spirit. If we leap, then someone or something catches us midway and carries us home. But we cannot be sure of this ahead of time, and we cannot presume to dictate the movements of the Spirit. Therefore, the final step is a matter of waiting. The Spirit comes at its own time and in its own circumstances, which may or may not be to our liking or at our convenience. Yet the way God's grace touches us is utterly unique. It came to Paul on the road to Damascus when a voice revealed to him that he had *already* met Christ in the Christians whom he had persecuted. It came to Augustine through a child's voice — was it a boy's or a girl's? — that told him to take and read Romans 13:13.[43] Pascal, the mathematician, recalls the exact length of his experience on November 23, 1654, from "half-past ten in the evening until half past midnight."[44] John Wesley (1703–1791) recalls that it was about a quarter to nine in the evening on May 24, 1738, while listening to Luther's commentary on the letter to the Romans, that his own heart "was strangely warmed."[45] One way or another, the Spirit comes on its own. Only then is faith complete. It may also, of course, be much more gradual and much less dramatic. There is no sense of a conversion experience with Thomas, but the reality of the Spirit surely was there. The Spirit simply chose another way of acting, and we cannot circumscribe the way the Spirit touches others. We can only wait on the way it touches us.

In the meantime, Pascal tells us that we should act as if were already believers; take holy water and have Masses said.[46] The doing of the faith creates its own inclination in the right direction. Heinrich Ott underscores something with which most would agree: the ongoing proof of God's existence is the conviction that our prayers each day are heard and answered by a merciful God who remains the constant listener to the deepest movements of the human heart.[47]

ABBREVIATIONS

ANF   *The Ante-Nicene Fathers: Translations of the Writings of the Fathers down to A.D. 325.* Edited by A. Roberts and J. Donaldson. Grand Rapids, 1978–1981.

ES   *Enchiridion symbolorum: definitionum et declarationum de rebus fidei et morum.* Edited by H. Denzinger and A. Schönmetzer. 36th ed. Freiburg, 1976.

FC   *The Fathers of the Church.* Washington, DC, 1947–.

MGH   Monumenta Germaniae Historica. Berlin, 1826–.

NJBC   *The New Jerome Biblical Commentary.* Edited by R. E. Brown, J. A. Fitzmyer, and R. E. Murphy. Englewood Cliffs, NJ, 1990.

NPNF–1   *A Select Library of Nicene and Post-Nicene Fathers of the Christian Church.* Series 1. Edited by P. Schaff. Grand Rapids, 1979–1983.

NPNF–2   *A Select Library of Nicene and Post-Nicene Fathers of the Christian Church.* Series 2. Edited by P. Schaff and H. Wace. Grand Rapids, 1979.

PG   *Patrologia graeca* [=*Patrologiae cursus completus: Series graeca*]. Edited by J.-P. Migne. Paris, 1857–1886.

PL   *Patrologia latina* [=*Patrologiae cursus completus: Series latina*]. Edited by J.-P. Migne. Paris, 1844–1864.

NOTES

Introduction

1. J. Dupuis, ed., *The Christian Faith in the Doctrinal Documents of the Catholic Church,* 6th ed. (New York, 1996), 42; *ES* 3016.

2. A. Hunt, *Trinity: Nexus of the Mysteries of Christian Faith* (Maryknoll, NY, 2005), 1–4. Hunt uses this approach to illumine the doctrine of the Trinity.

3. *Dei Verbum* §24 (A. Flannery, ed., *Vatican Council II: The Conciliar and Post Conciliar Documents* [Northport, NY, 1981]).

4. The Pontifical Biblical Commission, *The Interpretation of the Bible in the Church: Address of His Holiness Pope John Paul II and the Document of the Pontifical Biblical Commission* (Boston, 1993).

5. B. Lonergan, *Method in Theology* (New York, 1972), 302–18.

6. G. K. Chesterton, (New York, 1990), 22; see 83ff.

7. A. Schweitzer, *The Quest of the Historical Jesus: A Citical Study of Its Progress from Reimarus to Wrede,* trans. W. Montgomery ([1906] New York, 1968), 333.

8. J. Pelikan, *The Emergence of the Catholic Tradition (100–600)* (Chicago and London, 1971), 1–10.

9. Lonergan, *Method in Theology,* 295–333; K. Rahner, "The Development of Dogma," in *God, Christ, Mary and Grace,* trans. C. Ernst (Baltimore, 1963), 39–77.

10. See J. Royce, *The Problem of Christianity* (Chicago, 1968), 1:80.

11. J. H. Newman, *An Essay on the Development of Doctrine* (Garden City, NY, 1960), 411–17.

Chapter 1 / One God

1. J. N. D. Kelly, *Early Christian Creeds* (London, 1960), 195.

2. For a brief and excellent treatment of the Decalogue, see P. D. Miller, "The Place of the Decalogue in the Old Testament and Its Laws," *Interpretation* 43 (1989): 229–42.

3. A. Cody, "Little Historical Creed or Little Historical Anamnesis," *Catholic Biblical Quarterly* 68 (2006): 1–10.

4. W. F. Albright, *From the Stone Age to Christianity: Monotheism and the Historical Process* (Baltimore, 1940).

5. G. E. Mendenhall, *Law and Covenant in Israel and the Ancient Near East* (Pittsburgh, 1955).

6. K. Baltzer, *The Covenant Formulary in Old Testament, Jewish, and Early Christian Writings,* trans. D. E. Green ([1964] Philadelphia, 1971).

7. *NJBC* §75:56.

8. G. E. Mendenhall, *The Tenth Generation: The Origin of the Biblical Tradition* (Baltimore, 1973).

9. N. K. Gottwald, *The Tribes of Yahweh: A Sociology of the Religion of Liberated Israel, 1250–1050 B.C.E.* (Maryknoll, NY, 1979).

10. T. L. Thompson, *Early History of the Israelite People: From Written and Archeological Sources* (Leiden, 1992).

11. W. G. Dever, *What Did the Biblical Writers Know and When Did They Know It? What Archaeology Can Tell Us about the Reality of Ancient Israel* (Grand Rapids, 2002); *Who Were the Early Israelites and Where Did They Come From?* (Grand Rapids, 2003).

12. Cited in Dever, *Who Were the Early Israelites,* 137.

13. J. Blenkinsopp, *The Pentateuch: An Introduction to the First Five Books of the Bible* (New York, 1992), 176.

14. H. Bloom, *The Book of J* (New York, 1990).

15. R. Alter, *The David Story: A Translation with Commentary of 1 and 2 Samuel* (New York, 1999), xvii.

16. M. Weber, *The Sociology of Religion* (Boston, 1922), 51.

17. The Deuteronomistic History (a name applied to the books of Deuteronomy, Joshua, Judges, 1–2 Samuel, and 1–2 Kings) represented the first attempt to grapple with Israel's fate in the waning days of the monarchy. The history proposed that the nation's defeat was the result of the failure of successive kings to close outlying sanctuaries, where the worship of other gods might flourish, and centralize Israel's worship at the temple in Jerusalem, where its purity could be guaranteed. Sadly, the exemplary King Josiah, who did all these things, was slain by the Egyptians in 609 B.C. His death dashed reforming impulses as it revealed the weakness of this narrow interpretation of the nation's impending doom.

18. G. von Rad, *Old Testament Theology,* trans. D. M. G. Stalker, 2 vols. (New York, 1962–65), 2:206.

19. Ibid., 2:224.

20. Cited in *NJBC* §20:3.

21. von Rad, *Old Testament Theology,* 1:412.

22. In the long central section of the dialogue, Job and his friends refer to God as "El," the common word for God. When God speaks from whirlwind — and in the prologue and epilogue — it is as "Yahweh," God's name to Israel. On divine names in Job, see *NJBC* §30:7.

23. J. Miles, *God: A Biography* (New York, 1995), 318.

24. B. Janowski and P. Stuhlmacher, eds., *The Suffering Servant: Isaiah 53 in Jewish and Christian Sources* (Grand Rapids, 2004).

25. J. A. Sanders, *Torah and Canon* (Philadelphia, 1972), 31–53.

26. F. M. Cross, *Canaanite Myth and Hebrew Epic: Essays in the History of the Religion of Israel* (Cambridge, MA, 1973), 307.

27. *1 Enoch* 75:3.

28. von Rad, *Old Testament Theology,* 1:421.

29. For its effect on Judaism, see S. J. D. Cohen, *From the Maccabees to the Mishnah* (Philadelphia, 1989), 34–45.

30. "Much of the Jewish literature of the Hellenistic period follows Greek literary forms and/or the canons of Greek taste. . . . This fact is not particularly surprising for works written in Greek in the diaspora, but it is no less true for many of the works written in Hebrew or Aramaic in the land of Israel" (ibid., 43).

31. J. D. Levenson, *Creation and the Persistence of Evil: The Jewish Drama of Divine Omnipotence* (San Francisco, 1988), 14–25.

32. E. Käsemann, "The Beginnings of Christian Theology," in *New Testament Questions of Today* (London, 1969), 82–107.

33. Levenson, *Creation and the Persistence of Evil,* 50.

Chapter 2 / Jesus

1. R. Bultmann, *Jesus and the Word,* trans. L. P. Smith and E. H. Lantero ([1934] New York, 1958), 8.

2. E. Käsemann, "The Problem of the Historical Jesus," in *Essays on New Testament Themes,* trans. W. J. Montague ([1954] London, 1964), 15–47.

3. R. Bultmann, *Jesus Christ and Mythology* (London, 1958).

4. Cited in H. U. von Balthasar, *Theo-Drama,* vol. 3, *Dramatis Personae: Persons in Christ* (San Francisco, 1992), 70.

5. I should also mention Joachim Jeremias, whose work always stood apart from the skeptical discussion of the day.

6. M. Hengel, *Between Jesus and Paul: Studies in the Earliest History of Christianity,* trans. J. Bowden (London, 1983), 31.

7. I cite only a selection of Hengel's writings: *Was Jesus a Revolutionist?* trans. W. Klassen (Philadelphia, 1971); *Christ and Power,* trans. E. R. Kalin

(Philadelphia, 1974); *The Son of God: The Origin of Christology and the History of Jewish-Hellenistic Religion,* trans. J. Bowden (Philadelphia, 1976); *Crucifixion in the Ancient World and the Folly of the Message of the Cross,* trans. J. Bowden (Philadelphia, 1977); *The Charismatic Leader and His Followers,* trans. J. C. G. Greig (New York, 1981); *The Atonement: The Origins of the Doctrine in the New Testament,* trans. J. Bowden (Philadelphia, 1981).

8. L. T. Johnson, *The Real Jesus: The Misguided Quest for the Historical Jesus and the Truth of the Traditional Gospels* (San Francisco, 1997); see also N. T. Wright, *Jesus and the Victory of God* (Minneapolis, 1996), 3–124.

9. J. D. G. Dunn, *Jesus Remembered* (Grand Rapids, 2003); L. W. Hurtado, *Lord Jesus Christ: Devotion to Jesus in Earliest Christianity* (Grand Rapids, 2003); J. P. Meier, *A Marginal Jew: Rethinking the Historical Jesus,* 3 vols. (New York, 1991–2001); B. F. Meyer, *The Aims of Jesus* (London, 1979); *Christus Faber: The Master Builder and the House of God* (Allison Park, PA, 1992); N. T. Wright, *The New Testament and the People of God* (Minneapolis, 1992); *Jesus and the Victory of God* (Minneapolis, 1996); *The Resurrection of the Son of God* (Minneapolis, 2003).

10. P. Stuhlmacher, "Isaiah 53 in the Gospels and Acts," in *The Suffering Servant: Isaiah 53 in Jewish and Christian Sources,* B. Janowski and P. Stuhlmacher (Grand Rapids, 2004), 149.

11. J. Ratzinger (Pope Benedict XVI), *Jesus of Nazareth* (New York, 2007), xi–xxiv.

12. "The suggestion that the remembered Jesus was wholly insignificant, unfascinating and unintriguing, having no real impact prior to his death and resurrection is simply incredible" (Dunn, *Jesus Remembered,* 132).

13. J. D. G. Dunn, "The Historicity of the Synoptic Gospels," in *Crisis in Christology: Essays in Quest of Resolution,* ed. W. R. Farmer (Livonia, MI, 1995), 199–216. See p. 216 on the "burden of the proof" in regard to historicity.

14. B. Meyer, "Jesus," *Anchor Bible Dictionary,* ed. D. N. Freedman (New York, 1992), 3:773–96; *Christus Faber,* 59–80.

15. Stuhlmacher, "Isaiah 53," 149. Here Stuhlmacher summarizes his views and those of Hengel, Schürmann, Gerhardsson, and Riesner as well.

16. Dunn, *Jesus Remembered,* 377.

17. Meier, *A Marginal Jew,* 2:237–506.

18. Wright, *Jesus and the Victory,* 202–43; Dunn, *Jesus Remembered,* 470–87.

19. The precise phrase "kingdom of God" appears once in Wisdom 10:10 and not at all in the books of the Hebrew canon (Meier, *A Marginal Jew,* 2:243).

20. Wright, *Jesus and the Victory,* 242.

21. Dunn, *Jesus Remembered,* 789.

22. M. J. Borg, *Jesus, a New Vision: Spirit, Culture, and the Life of Discipleship* (San Francisco, 1987), 86–93, 110–12, 157–63.

23. Dunn, *Jesus Remembered,* 626–34.

24. *NJBC* §78:45.

25. Meier, *A Marginal Jew,* 2:308.

26. Stuhlmacher, "Isaiah 53," 153.

27. *Catechism of the Catholic Church: Revised in Accordance with the Official Latin Text Promulgated by Pope John Paul II,* 2nd ed. (Washington, DC, 1997), §645. See also G. G. O'Collins, "Is the Resurrection an 'Historical' Event?" *Heythrop Journal* 8 (1967): 381–87.

28. Dunn, *Jesus Remembered,* 210–12.

29. R. Fuller, *The Formation of the Resurrection Narratives* (New York, 1971), 16.

30. R. Girard, *I See Satan Fall Like Lightning,* trans. J. G. Williams (Maryknoll, NY, 2002), 137–60.

31. M. Hengel, *The Atonement,* 66.

32. K. Rahner, "The Development of Dogma," in *God, Christ, Mary and Grace,* trans. C. Ernst (Baltimore, 1963), 63–64.

33. Ibid., 64.

34. W. James, *The Principles of Psychology* (New York, 1950), 1:221–23.

Chapter 3 / Christ

1. J. D. G. Dunn, *Jesus Remembered* (Grand Rapids, 2003), 737, 724–62. Of the four uses outside the Gospels, three are quotations or allusions to OT passages. Stephen's vision in Acts 7:56 is the single titular use outside the Gospels.

2. M. Hengel, *Crucifixion in the Ancient World and the Folly of the Message of the Cross,* trans. J. Bowden (Philadelphia, 1977), 84–90.

3. J. D. Levenson, *The Death and Resurrection of the Beloved Son: The Transformation of Child Sacrifice in Judaism and Christianity* (New Haven, 1993), 222.

4. Ibid., 225.

5. Ibid., 174–75.

6. R. E. Brown, *An Introduction to the New Testament* (New York, 1997), 493.

7. L. W. Hurtado, *Lord Jesus Christ: Devotion to Jesus in Earliest Christianity* (Grand Rapids, 2003), 112.

8. G. von Rad, *Wisdom in Israel,* trans. J. D. Martin (London, 1972), 48–49.

9. M. Hengel, *Between Jesus and Paul: Studies in the Earliest History of Christianity,* trans. J. Bowden (London, 1983), 95.

10. Hurtado, *Lord Jesus Christ,* 214–16.

11. J. D. G. Dunn, *The Theology of Paul the Apostle* (Grand Rapids, 1998), 426–34.

12. Hengel, *Between Jesus and Paul,* 39–40.

13. Forty-eight times in the seven undisputed Pauline letters; fifteen times in the deutero-Pauline writings. See M. Hengel, *The Four Gospels and the One Gospel of Jesus Christ* (Harrisburg, Pa., 2000), 2.

14. Hengel, *The Four Gospels,* 76–89; F. Matera, *New Testament Christology* (Louisville, 1999), 83–88, esp. 87.

15. Brown, *New Testament,* 111.

16. Quoted in Hengel, *The Four Gospels,* 96.

17. M. Kähler, *The So-Called Historical Jesus and the Historic Biblical Christ,* trans. C. E. Braaten ([1892] Philadelphia, 1964).

18. R. E. Brown, *The Death of the Messiah: From Gethsemane to the Grave; A Commentary on the Passion Narratives in the Four Gospels* (New York, 1994), 1452.

19. Matera, *New Testament Christology,* 26.

20. Hengel, *The Four Gospels,* 112.

21. Brown, *New Testament,* 111.

22. B. Witherington III, *The Many Faces of the Christ* (New York, 1998), 158.

23. Brown, *New Testament,* 339.

Chapter 4 / How Doctrines Develop

1. J. Pelikan, *The Emergence of the Catholic Tradition (100–600)* (Chicago and London, 1971), 1–10.

2. *NPNF-2* 4:551–52.

3. H. Y. Gamble, "Canon: New Testament," *Anchor Bible Dictionary,* ed. D. N. Freedman (New York, 1992), 1:853.

4. *Against Heresies* 3.11.7–9 (*ANF* 1:428–29).

5. Hengel, *The Four Gospels,* 10–12, 34–38.

6. Gamble, "Canon: New Testament," 855.

7. Ibid., 856.

8. M. Wiles, *The Making of Christian Doctrine: A Study in the Principles of Early Doctrinal Development* (Cambridge, 1967), 41–61.

9. Ignatius, *Letter to the Magnesians* 6–7 (*ANF* 1:61–62).

10. Ignatius, *Letter to the Smyrnaeans* 8:1–2 (*ANF* 1:89–90).

11. Y. Congar, *I Believe in the Holy Spirit,* trans. D. Smith (New York, 1983), 1:65.

12. Ibid., 1:69.

13. *1 Clement* 44 (*ANF* 1:17).

14. Irenaeus, *Against Heresies* 3.3.4 (*ANF* 1:416).

15. Irenaeus, *Against Heresies* 3.3.2 (*ANF* 1:415).

16. Irenaeus, *Against Heresies* 3.20–3.23 (*ANF* 1:449–58).

17. Xenophanes writes, "But if cows and horses or lions had hands or could draw with their hands and make things men can make, then horses would draw the forms of gods like horses, cows like cows, and they would make their bodies similar to the shape to those which each had themselves" (J. Barnes, *Early Greek Philosophy* [London, 1987], 95).

18. H. Wolfson, *The Philosophy of the Church Fathers* (Cambridge, MA, 1976), 289–92.

19. P. Brown, *The Rise of Western Christendom: Triumph and Diversity, A.D. 200–1000,* 2nd ed. (Oxford, 2003), 58–60.

20. W. T. Jones, *The Classical Mind: A History of Western Philosophy* (New York, 1969), 1–8.

21. "Nevertheless, for many this official cult of the ancient gods and goddesses did not translate itself into genuine religious devotion, whence the demythologizing of the deities by the philosophers (e.g., the Stoic identification of Zeus with the *logos* or reason that pervades the universe), the appeal of newer religions from the East and/or mystery religions" (R. E. Brown, *An Introduction to the New Testament* [New York, 1997], 85–86).

22. W. H. C. Frend, *The Rise of Christianity* (Philadelphia, 1984), 212–18.

23. Ibid., 204–12.

24. Ibid., 203.

25. Pelikan, *Emergence of the Catholic Tradition,* 97–108.

26. Ibid., 107.

27. Irenaeus, *Against Heresies* 1.10.1–2 (*ANF* 1:331); Tertullian, *On the Veiling of Virgins* (*ANF* 4:27); *Prescription against Heretics* 13 (*ANF* 3:249); Clement of Alexandria, *Miscellanies* 7.17 (*ANF* 2:554–55); Origen, *On First Principles, Preface* 4–8 (*ANF* 4:240–41).

28. "In 200 though there were differences in detail, a single recognizable Rule of Faith, to which appeal could be made, circulated in the main centers of Christendom" (Frend, *The Rise of Christianity,* 284).

29. For variant forms of baptism, see Acts 8:36–38; 16:14–15, 30–34; 22:16. See also in this context Romans 10:9; 1 Timothy 6:12; Hebrews 4:14.

30. L. T. Johnson, *The Creed: What Christians Believe and Why It Matters* (New York, 2003), 30.

31. For the polemical mode, see Tertullian, *Prescription against Heretics* 13–14 (*ANF* 3:249–50). In regard to Irenaeus, J. N. D. Kelly writes, "The influence of anti-heretical motives is, on the whole, surprisingly slight, especially when we consider the polemical nature of St. Irenaeus's work" (*Early Christian Creeds* [London, 1960], 81).

Chapter 5 / The Trinity

1. Pliny, *Letters* 10.96–97 (P. R. Coleman-Norton, *Roman State and Christian Church: A Collection of Legal Documents to A.D. 535* [London, 1966], 1:1–5).

2. On the impact of Constantine's conversion, see R. MacMullen, *Christianizing the Roman Empire (A.D. 100–400)* (New Haven, 1984), 43–51.

3. I use the word *person* here in its usual sense in English as equivalent to a single individual. I do not use it in its technical, doctrinal sense. According to Catholic teaching, the second person of the Trinity bears both the human and divine natures of Christ. "Thus everything in Christ's human nature is to be attributed to his divine person as its proper subject, not only his miracles but also his sufferings and even his death" (*Catechism of the Catholic Church: Revised in Accordance with the Official Latin Text Promulgated by Pope John Paul II,* 2nd ed. [Washington, DC, 1997], §468).

4. K. Rahner, "Theos in the New Testament," in *God, Christ, Mary and Grace,* trans. C. Ernst (Baltimore, 1963), 79–148.

5. R. E. Brown, *Jesus: God and Man; Modern Biblical Reflections* (New York, 1967), 1–38. Brown revised this essay, including it as appendix 3 in *An Introduction to New Testament Christology* (New York, 1994), 171–95.

6. Brown, *New Testament Christology,* 193.

7. Pliny, *Letters* 96.

8. J. D. G. Dunn, *The Theology of Paul the Apostle* (Grand Rapids, 1998), 408.

9. Ibid., 419.

10. R. E. Brown, *The Gospel According to John I–XII* (Garden City, NY, 1966), 519–24.

11. M. Wiles, *The Christian Fathers,* 2nd ed. (New York, 1982), 15–23.

12. G. L. Prestige, *God in Patristic Thought,* 2nd ed. (London, 1975), 117–23; J. Pelikan, *The Emergence of the Catholic Tradition (100–600)* (Chicago and London, 1971), 187–88.

13. Justin, *Second Apology* 13 (*ANF* 1:193).

14. Justin, *Dialogue with Trypho* 60 (*ANF* 1:227).

15. Justin, *Dialogue with Trypho* 62 (*ANF* 1:228).

16. Justin, *Dialogue with Trypho* 61 (*ANF* 1:227–28).

17. Justin, *First Apology* 59–60 (*ANF* 1:182–83).

18. Justin, *First Apology* 13 (*ANF* 1:166–67).

19. Justin, *Dialogue with Trypho* 128 (*ANF* 1:264).

20. Irenaeus, *Against Heresies* 4.20 (*ANF* 1:487–88).

21. J. N. D. Kelly, *Early Christian Doctrines,* 2nd ed. (New York, 1960), 106. Irenaeus, along with Theophilus of Antioch, identifies the Holy Spirit with preexistent Wisdom, an identification that does not continue in the tradition.

22. E. Osborn, *Tertullian: First Theologian of the West* (Cambridge, 2003), 136–37.

23. Tertullian, *Against Praxeas* 8 (*ANF* 3:603).

24. J. H. Newman, *Tracts Theological and Ecclesiastical* (London, 1908), 167.

25. G. H. Tavard, *The Vision of the Trinity* (Washington, DC, 1981), 31–40.

26. P. Brown, *The Rise of Western Christendom: Triumph and Diversity, A.D. 200–1000,* 2nd ed. (Oxford, 2003), 59.

27. J. R. Lyman, *Christology and Cosmology; Models of Divine Activity in Origen, Eusebius and Athanasius* (Oxford, 1993), 10–38.

28. Ibid., 39.

29. L. Ayres, *Nicaea and Its Legacy: An Approach to Fourth-Century Trinitarian Theology* (Oxford, 2004); R. P. C. Hanson, *The Search for the Christian Doctrine of God: The Arian Controversy 318–381* (Edinburgh, 1988); J. T. Lienhard, "The 'Arian' Controversy: Some Categories Reconsidered," *Theological Studies* 48 (1987): 414–37; R. Williams, *Arius: Heresy and Tradition,* 2nd ed. (London, 2001); M. Wiles, *Archetypal Heresy: Arianism through the Centuries* (New York, 1996).

30. Williams, *Arius,* 234.

31. Athanasius, *First Oration against the Arians* (*NPNF–2* 4:306–43).

32. Jerome, *Altercatio Luciferiani et Orthodoxi* (Paris, 1956), 473; *PL* 23: 181b.

33. Hanson, *Christian Doctrine of God,* 202.

34. Ibid., 869–75.

35. Lienhard describes the difference as one between a *miahypostatic* and a *dyohypostatic* theology, a theology of "one substance" and of "two substances" ("The 'Arian' Controversy," 420–30).

36. On the teaching of Arius, see Williams, *Arius,* 95–116, 230–32. According to Lienhard, More significant and representative figures of this tradition are Eusebius of Caesarea (ca. 260–340) and Eusebius of Nicomedia (d. ca. 342), especially the former ("The 'Arian' Controversy," 432).

37. *ES* 126.

38. Athanasius, *On the Incarnation* 54 (*NPNF-2* 4:65).

39. "Even in medieval usage, *Veni Creator Spiritus* and *Veni Sancte Spiritus* were among the few prayers to the Spirit" (Pelikan, *Emergence of the Catholic Tradition,* 185).

40. Gregory of Nazianzus, *Oratio in laudem Basilii* 31.5 (ed. and trans. H. Bettenson, *The Later Christian Fathers* [Oxford, 1983], 113).

41. Prestige, *God in Patristic Thought,* 233–34.

42. J. T. Lienhard, "The Cappadocian Settlement," in *The Trinity: An Interdisciplinary Symposium on the Trinity,* ed. S. T. Davis, D. Kendall, and G. O'Collins (Oxford, 1999), 120.

43. Ibid., 103.

44. J. Pelikan, *Christianity and Classical Culture: The Metamorphosis of Natural Theology in the Christian Encounter with Hellenism* (New Haven, 1993).

45. "St. Basil was the first to insist upon the distinction, one *ousia* and three *hypostases* in God, and to maintain that *mia ousia, treis hypostaseis* is the only acceptable formula" (J. Quasten, *Patrology* [Westminster, MD, 1960], 3:228).

46. "More commonly, several terms, usually *physis* ('nature') and *theotes* ('deity'), as well as *ousia* designate what is one in God, and *idiotetes* ('properties') and *prosopa* ('persons'), along with *hypostasis,* are common designations for what is three in God" (Lienhard, "The Cappadocian Settlement," 120).

47. "If we compare Gregory's teaching with that of St. Basil, we notice a much stronger emphasis on the unity and *monarchia,* the one sovereignty of God, on the one hand, and on the other, a much clearer definition of the divine relations" (Quasten, *Patrology,* 3:249).

48. "According to Gregory [of Nyssa], the distinction of the three divine Persons consists exclusively in their immanent mutual relations. For this reason, their activity *ad extra* can be one and the divine Persons have it in common" (Quasten, *Patrology,* 3:286).

49. Sarah Coakley, "'Person' in the 'Social' Doctrine of the Trinity: A Critique of Current Analytic Discussion," in Davis, Kendall, and O'Collins, *The Trinity,* 137.

50. The creed of the Council of Constantinople first publicly appears at the third session of the Council of Chalcedon on October 10, 451, some seventy years after the council itself. For the issues surrounding this event and proposed solutions, see J. N. D. Kelly, *Early Christian Creeds* (London, 1960), 296–331.

51. Council of Constantinople, *The Synodal Letter* (NPNF2 14:188–90).

52. Prestige, *God in Patristic Thought,* 237.

53. G. O'Collins, "The Holy Trinity: The State of the Questions," in Davis, Kendall, and O'Collins, *The Trinity,* 9.

54. Augustine, *On the Trinity* 15.7.11 (*NPNF-1* 3:204–5).

55. Augustine, *On the Trinity* 15.17.28 (*NPNF-1* 3:215).

56. Tavard, *The Vision of the Trinity*, 80–81.

57. T. de Régnon, *Études de théologie positive sur la Sainte Trinité* in *Trinité*. (Paris, 1892–98).

58. M. R. Barnes, "Augustine in Contemporary Trinitarian Theology," *Theological Studies* 56 (1995): 238.

59. Y. Congar, *I Believe in the Holy Spirit*, trans. D. Smith (New York, 1983), 3:xvii.

60. Pelikan, *Christianity and Classical Culture*, 243.

61. Coakley, "'Person' in the 'Social' Doctrine of the Trinity," 123–44.

62. M. R. Barnes, "De Regnon Reconsidered," *Augustinian Studies* 26 (1995): 51–70; "Rereading Augustine's Theology of the Trinity," in Davis, Kendall, and O'Collins, *The Trinity*, 145–76.

63. Wiles, *The Christian Fathers*, 49–50.

64. Hunt, *Trinity*; see also O'Collins, "The Holy Trinity," 1–28.

65. Hunt, *Trinity*, 217.

66. The essay was originally published as part of the multivolume *Mysterium Salutis*, appearing separately in 1967. In regard to Rahner's own *Foundations of the Christian Faith: An Introduction to the Idea of Christianity*, O'Collins observes, "Curiously this 500-page long work has hardly anything to say about the Trinity" ("The Holy Trinity," 2 n. 5).

67. F. Schleiermacher, *The Christian Faith* ([1830] New York, 1963), 2:738.

68. K. Barth, *Church Dogmatics* (Edinburgh, 1975), 1.1:355–56.

69. K. Rahner, *The Trinity*, trans. J. Donceel (New York, 1970), 74–84.

70. Tavard, *The Vision of the Trinity*, 131.

Chapter 6 / Christ and the Church

1. D. Harrington, *The Church according to the New Testament: What the Wisdom and Witness of Early Christianity Teach Us Today* (Franklin, WI, 2001), 133–34.

2. J. Royce, *The Problem of Christianity* ([1913] Chicago, 1968), 1:80.

3. Ibid., 118.

4. John Knox, *The Church and the Reality of Christ* (New York, 1962).

5. R. Brown, *The Churches the Apostles Left Behind* (New York, 1984), 115.

6. *1 Clement* 5:2–5.

7. Shepherd of Hermas, *Visions* 2:4.

8. In regard to the role of women in the Pastoral Epistles, see F. A. Sullivan, *From Apostles to Bishops: The Development of the Episcopacy in the Early Church* (New York, 2001), 74.

9. Ignatius, *Letter to the Philadelphians* 4 (*ANF* 1:80). Here I follow the translation used in Sullivan, *From Apostles to Bishops,* 116.

10. Sullivan, *From Apostles to Bishops,* 116.

11. This insight was developed by Johann Adam Möhler (1796–1838). Möhler's thought shifted in his later work. He came to regard the office of archbishop, metropolitan, or patriarch as a secondary, administrative development. By contrast, the offices of pope and bishop were primary and essential, representing the church's center and its periphery. Möhler also grasped that the arrangement contained a certain logic, a system of checks and balances. It thereby gives the church a stable but flexible equilibrium. Möhler's earlier emphasis on the Spirit in *Die Einheit in der Kirche* (1825) gave way to a more christocentric framework in his later work *Symbolik* (1832). See M. J. Himes, *Ongoing Incarnation: Johann Adam Möhler and the Beginnings of Modern Ecclesiology* (New York, 1997), 304–34.

12. Tertullian, *Against Marcion* 28 (*ANF* 3:293).

13. J. N. D. Kelly, *Early Christian Doctrines,* 2nd ed. (New York, 1960), 209.

14. Ibid., 435.

15. Clement, *Miscellanies* 2.13 (*ANF* 2:360).

16. Origen, *Homilies on Leviticus* 2.4 (*FC* 83:45–51).

17. Tertullian, *On Repentance* 7–12 (*ANF* 3:662–66).

18. Hippolytus, *Refutation of All Heresies* 9.8 (*ANF* 5:128–31).

19. J. McGuckin, *Saint Cyril of Alexandria: The Christological Controversy; Its History, Theology, and Texts* (Crestwood, NY, 2004), 184.

20. It is also an example of the "exchange of properties" (*communicatio idiomatum*), favored in Alexandria and avoided in Antioch.

21. F. G. McLeod, *The Roles of Christ's Humanity in Salvation: Insights from Theodore of Mopsuestia* (Washington, DC, 2005); "Theodore of Mopsuestia Revisited," *Theological Studies* 61 (2000): 447–80.

22. McLeod, *Roles of Christ's Humanity,* 102–23.

23. Ibid., 152 (citing R. Norris Jr., *Manhood and Christ* [Oxford, 1963], 231).

24. Ibid., 176–205.

25. *ES* 250–64; *NPNF–2* 14:191–242.

26. Kelly, *Early Christian Doctrines,* 341; *ES* 300–303.

27. *NPNF–2* 14:242–95; *ES* 302.

28. W. H. C. Frend, *The Rise of the Monophysite Movement: Chapters in the History of the Church in the Fifth and Sixth Centuries* (Cambridge, 1972), 142.

29. Ibid. (citing *Giovanni Domenico Mansi,* Collection VII, cols. 58–60).

30. P. Brown, *The Rise of Western Christendom: Triumph and Diversity, A.D. 200–1000,* 2nd ed. (Oxford, 2003), 121.

31. The "Three Chapters," writings of Theodore of Mopsuestia, Theodore of Cyrus, and Ibas of Edessa (*ES* 421–38; *NPNF-2* 14:299–320).

32. J. Pelikan, *The Emergence of the Catholic Tradition (100–600)* (Chicago and London, 1971), 340–41.

33. Brown, *The Rise of Western Christendom,* 121.

34. By 638, works of Syriac theology, in Chinese translation, are placed in the imperial library (ibid., 285).

35. S. Coakley, "What Does Chalcedon Solve and What Does It Not? Some Reflections of the Status and Meaning of the Chalcedonian 'Definition,'" in *The Incarnation: An Interdisciplinary Symposium on the Incarnation of the Son of God,* ed. S. T. Davis, D. Kendall, and G. O'Collins (Oxford, 2002), 159. I am indebted to Coakley in this section.

36. *ES* 424–30.

37. K. Rahner, "Current Problems in Christology," in *God, Christ, Mary and Grace,* trans. C. Ernst (Baltimore, 1963), 150.

38. Coakley, "What Does Chalcedon Solve," 161.

Chapter 7 / The Western Church

1. R. Evans, *One and Holy: The Church in Latin Patristic Thought* (London, 1972), 1–3.

2. On the interpretation of chapter 4 of Cyprian's *On the Unity of the Church* (*ANF* 5:422–23), see F. A. Sullivan, *From Apostles to Bishops: The Development of the Episcopacy in the Early Church* (New York, 2001), 195–96.

3. Augustine, *The City of God* 22.1 (*NPNF-1* 2:480).

4. Evans, *One and Holy,* 103.

5. *NPNF-2* 14:287.

6. W. Ullmann, *The Growth of Papal Government in the Middle Ages: A Study in the Ideological Relation of Clerical to Lay Power* (London, 1970), 7–14.

7. Leo, *Sermon* 3.2 (*NPNF-2* 12:116–17).

8. W. Ullmann, *Law and Politics in the Middle Ages: An Introduction to the Sources of Medieval Political Ideas* (Ithaca, NY, 1975), 229.

9. J. Pelikan, *The Emergence of the Catholic Tradition (100–600)* (Chicago and London, 1971), 354; Gregory, *Epistle* 5.44 (*MGH* 1:338–43); *Epistle* 9.156 (*MGH* 2:158).

10. Gregory, *The Book of Pastoral Rule* (*NPNF-2* 12:1–72).

11. P. Brown, *The Rise of Western Christendom: Triumph and Diversity, A.D. 200–1000,* 2nd ed. (Oxford, 2003), 211.

12. E. Duffy, *Saints and Sinners: A History of the Popes* (New Haven, 2001), 63.

13. Evans, *One and Holy,* 149.

14. Duffy, *Saints and Sinners,* 69.

15. Pelikan, *Emergence of the Catholic Tradition,* 349–57.

16. J. W. O'Malley, *Four Cultures of the West* (Cambridge, MA, 2004), 84–86.

17. Duffy writes, "Of the thirteen popes elected between 687 and 752, only two, Benedict II (684–5) and Gregory II, were native Romans, or even Latins" (*Saints and Sinners,* 83).

18. E. Rosenstock-Huessy, *Out of Revolution: Autobiography of Western Man* (Norwich, VT, 1969), 503.

19. Duffy, *Saints and Sinners,* 104.

20. Rosenstock-Huessy, *Out of Revolution,* 521.

21. W. Ullmann, *A Short History of the Papacy in the Middle Ages* (London, 1972), 229.

22. H. E. J. Cowdrey, *Pope Gregory VII, 1073–1085* (Oxford, 1998), 546–50.

23. Rosenstock-Huessy, *Out of Revolution,* 539.

24. Ibid., 507.

25. O'Malley, *Four Cultures of the West,* 55.

26. Rosenstock-Huessy, *Out of Revolution,* 535.

27. R. W. Southern, *Western Society and the Church in the Middle Ages* (New York, 1973), 131–32.

28. Ullmann, *Short History of the Papacy,* 208.

29. Ullmann, *Growth of Papal Government,* 426–46.

30. Ullmann, *Short History of the Papacy,* 194, 278.

31. Rosenstock-Huessy, *Out of Revolution,* 594–606.

32. Ibid., 602.

33. Ullmann, *Short History of the Papacy,* 325.

34. Ullmann, *Short History of the Papacy,* 283; see also *Law and Politics in the Middle Ages,* 280.

35. Ullmann, *Short History of the Papacy,* 283. Aristotelian political thought provides natural arguments for the state's autonomous exercise of authority, apart from the church, with wide-ranging consequences for papal claims to universal authority. See Ullmann, *Law and Politics in the Middle Ages,* 269–306.

36. Thomas Aquinas, *Summa theologiae* I q.1, a.8.

37. F. Schüssler-Fiorenza, "Systematic Theology: Task and Methods," in *Systematic Theology: Roman Catholic Perspectives,* ed. F. Schüssler-Fiorenza and J. P. Galvin (Minneapolis, 1991), 1:27–35.

38. J. C. Livingston, *Modern Christian Thought,* vol. 1, *The Enlightenment and the Nineteenth Century,* 2nd ed. (Upper Saddle River, NJ, 1997), 342.

39. B. Welte, "Zum Strukturwandel der katholischen Theologie im 19. Jahrhundert," in *Auf der Spur des Ewigen: Philosophische Abhandlungen über verschiedene Gegenstände der Religion und der Theologie* (Freiburg, 1965), 395–409.

40. Robert Bellarmine, *De concillis,* chapter 2, book 3 (see A. Dulles, *Models of the Church* [Garden City, NY, 1974], 14–15).

41. *ES* 3683.

42. *Acta apostolicae sedis* 42 (1950), 142–47; J. Dupuis, ed., *The Christian Faith in the Doctrinal Documents of the Catholic Church,* 6th ed. (New York, 1996), 343–44.

43. *ES* 3808; *Acta sanctae sedis* 29 (1896–1897): 650.

44. *ES* 3866–73.

45. Welte, "Zum Strukturwandel der katholischen Theologie," 403–4.

46. J. W. O'Malley, *Tradition and Transition: Historical Perspectives on Vatican II* (Lima, OH, 2002), 22.

47. Ibid., 124.

48. On the notion of an "epideictic genre," see J. W. O'Malley, "Vatican II: Did Anything Happen?" *Theological Studies* 67 (2006): 21–33.

49. Walter Kasper, "Der ekklesiologische Charakter der nichtkatholischen Kirchen," *Theologische Quartalschrift* 145 (1965): 42–62. Kasper cites a tradition of magisterial documents in the recent past, beginning with statements of the Holy Office (1864 and 1865), then the encyclicals *Satis cognitum* (1896), *Mortalium animos* (1928), *Mystici corporis* (1943), and *Humani generis* (1950) (p. 43).

50. H. Vorgrimler, ed., *Commentary on the Documents of Vatican II* (New York, 1967), 1:149–52 (see p. 150 n. 29). For the various meanings of the phrase *subsistit in* and its translation as well as the use of the term in recent documents of the Magisterium, see F. Sullivan, "The Meaning of *Subsistit in* as Explained by the Congregation for the Doctrine of the Faith," *Theological Studies* 69 (2008): 116–24.

51. See also the Vatican II decree on ecumenism, *Unitatis Redintegratio* (*Restoration of Unity*) §3.

52. The formula reflects not only Catholic sensibilities but also those of other churches. From a Roman Catholic perspective, churches, strictly speaking, are those that have the episcopate in apostolic succession and valid sacraments. Some churches of the Reformation regard themselves not as churches even close to the Catholic sense but rather as correctives of the notion of church.

53. *Unitatis Redintegratio* §4.

54. *Lumen Gentium* §16.

55. *Nostra Aetate* §2 (A. Flannery, ed., *Vatican Council II: The Conciliar and Post Conciliar Documents* [Northport, NY, 1981]).

56. Vorgrimler, *Commentary on the Documents of Vatican II*, 1:150.

57. For quite different ways in which the relation between the local church and the universal church can be understood, see the exchange between Cardinal Walter Kasper and then Cardinal Joseph Ratzinger summarized in Killian McDonnell, "The Ratzinger/Kasper Debate: The Universal Church and Local Churches," *Theological Studies* 63 (2002): 227–50.

58. See the explanatory note appended to *Lumen Gentium* on November 16, 1964. For commentary, see J. Ratzinger, "Announcements and Prefatory Notes of Explanation" (Vorgrimler, *Commentary on the Documents of Vatican II*, 1:297–305). The explanatory note, says W. Kasper, "distinguishes between functions *(munera)* and powers *(potestates)*.... The concrete exercise of the functions conferred through sacramental episcopal ordination is therefore bound to the hierarchical *communio* with the pope and the whole episcopate" (*Theology and Church*, trans. M. Kohl [New York, 1989], 158).

59. See Flannery, *Vatican Council II*, 1–36.

60. *Dei Verbum* §7 (Flannery, *Vatican Council II*).

61. *Dei Verbum* §9.

62. *Dei Verbum* §10.

63. *Dei Verbum* §19.

64. *Dei Verbum* §24.

65. Quoted in G. Alberigo, ed., *History of Vatican II* (Maryknoll, NY, 2006), 5:353.

66. Ibid., 5:354.

67. *Dei Verbum* §5.

68. Alberigo, *History of Vatican II*, 5:122–77.

69. P. Hünermann, "The Final Weeks of the Council," in Alberigo, *History of Vatican II*, 5:423.

70. O'Malley, "Vatican II: Did Anything Happen?" 5. This is the fundamental assumption of a newer, more cautious interpretation of Vatican II, says O'Malley.

Chapter 8 / Mary

1. *Protevangelium of James* 1–2 (*New Testament Apocrypha*, ed. E. Hennecke and W. Schneemelcher [Philadelphia, 1963], 1:374–75).

2. *Protevangelium of James* 9 (Hennecke and Schneemelcher, *New Testament Apocrypha*, 1:379).

3. *Protevangelium of James* 6–7 (Hennecke and Schneemelcher, *New Testament Apocrypha,* 1:377–78).

4. *Protevangelium of James* 10 (Hennecke and Schneemelcher, *New Testament Apocrypha,* 1:379–80).

5. Irenaeus, *Against Heresies* 3.22 (*ANF* 1:455); 5.19 (*ANF* 1:547).

6. Irenaeus, *Against Heresies* 3.22 (*ANF* 1:455).

7. For Tertullian, the "brothers" of the Lord are the natural children of Joseph and Mary after the birth of Jesus (*Against Marcion* 4.19 [*ANF* 3:377–78]), a tradition continued in later centuries by Helvidius, Jovinian, and Bonosus but increasingly rejected as unworthy of Mary's purity. Jerome's view, that the brothers are cousins or nephews of Jesus, is preferred.

8. Origen, *Homily 17 on Luke* (*FC* 94:70–75).

9. John Chrysostom, *Homily on Matthew* 44 (*NPNF-1* 10:278–84); *Homily on John* 21 (*FC* 33:201–12).

10. Views of Bonosus and Jovinian.

11. Ambrose, *Letter 44* (*FC* 26:225–30).

12. Ambrose, *Exposition of the Gospel of Luke* 2.7 (Sources chrétiennes [Paris, 1956], 45:74).

13. Ambrose, *Letter 63* (*NPNF-2* 10:473); *Concerning Virgins* 22 (*NPNF-2* 10:374–76).

14. Ambrose, *On the Holy Spirit* 3.11 (*NPNF-2* 10:146).

15. H. Graef, *Mary: A History of Doctrine and Devotion* (New York, 1963), 1:95.

16. Augustine, *Sermon 72A* (*The Works of St. Augustine: A Translation for the 21st Century,* part 3, vol. 3, *Sermons 51–94,* ed. J. E. Rotelle [Brooklyn, NY, 1991], 287).

17. Augustine, *On Nature and Grace* 36 (41) (*FC* 86:53); *Answer to Julian* (*The Works of St. Augustine: A Translation for the 21st Century,* part 1, vol. 24, *Books: Answer to the Pelagians II,* ed. J. E. Rotelle [Hyde Park, NY, 1998], V.54, 467). The interpretation of Augustine's reply to Julian of Eclanum on this issue is controverted.

18. "For Augustine, Mary's conception of Christ stood rather for an act of undivided obedience. It recaptured the ancient harmony of body and soul, in which the will was not the maimed thing that it so soon became. A yearning for harmony and for untroubled obedience on every level, and not, as for Ambrose, the defense of a sacred inner space against a polluting world was what now held the center of Augustine's thought" (P. Brown, *The Body and Society: Men, Women, and Sexual Renunciation in Early Christianity* [New York, 1988], 407).

19. P. Brown, *The Rise of Western Christendom: Triumph and Diversity, A.D. 200–1000,* 2nd ed. (Oxford, 2003), 120.

20. R. Laurentin, *A Short Treatise on the Virgin Mary,* trans. C. Neumann (Washington, NJ, 1991), 77–88; M. O'Carroll, *Theotokos: A Theological Encyclopedia of the Blessed Virgin Mary* (Wilmington, DE, 1983), 55–57.

21. The common English translation of the accepted Latin version is "We fly to thy patronage, O Holy Mother of God, despise not our petitions in our necessities, but deliver us from all danger, O ever glorious and blessed Virgin" (O'Carroll, *Theotokos,* 336).

22. Ibid., 8.

23. L. W. Hurtado, *Lord Jesus Christ: Devotion to Jesus in Earliest Christianity* (Grand Rapids, 2003), 4.

24. Graef, *Mary,* 1:150.

25. Germanus (*PG* 98, 290–383, esp. 352A, B).

26. Graef, *Mary,* 1:50–51.

27. *PG* 120, 194A.

28. Graef, *Mary,* 1:188–89.

29. Ibid., 1:260.

30. Anselm of Canterbury, "On the Virginal Conception and Original Sin," in *Trinity, Incarnation, and Redemption: Theological Treatises,* ed. J. Hopkins and H. Richardson (New York, 1970), 63.

31. Anselm of Canterbury, "A Prayer to Mary to Obtain Love for Her and for Christ," in *S. Anselmi Cantuariensis Archiepiscopi Opera Omnia* (Stuttgart, 1968), 3:21–22.

32. Eadmer, *Tractatus de Conceptione Beatae Mariae* (*PL* 159, 306).

33. O'Carroll, *Theotokos,* 125.

34. Bernard of Clairvaux, *Epistle 174* (*PL* 333.2).

35. E. D. O'Connor, ed., *The Dogma of the Immaculate Conception: History and Significance* (Notre Dame, IN, 1958), 188–202.

36. Laurentin, *Short Treatise on the Virgin Mary,* 114.

37. Bernard of Clairvaux, *Sermon on the Twelve Stars* (*PL* 430–38, 430.1).

38. Pope Pius IX, *Ubi Primum* (1849); Pope Leo XIII, *Iucunda Semper Expectatione* (1894) (C. Carlen, ed., *The Papal Encyclicals* [New York, 1981], 1:292; 2:359).

39. Bernard of Clairvaux, *Sermon on the Aqueduct* (*PL* 183, 438–47).

40. H. A. Oberman, *The Harvest of Medieval Theology: Gabriel Biel and Late Medieval Nominalism* (Cambridge, MA, 1963), 304–7.

41. Ibid., 311.

42. Ibid., 312.

43. Ibid., 317.

44. Under the remarkable heading, "What the Blessed Virgin could do for God which God could not do for himself," Bernardine cites this example: "God could not beget anyone but God; and nevertheless the Virgin made a

Godman" (*Sermons on Feasts* I, 4 [2, 357]) (O'Carroll, *Theotokos,* 78; Graef, *Mary,* 1:316–17).

45. H. Mühlen, *Una Mystica Persona: Die Kirche als das Mysterium der Identität des Heiligen Geistes in Christus und den Christen; Eine Person in vielen Personen,* 3rd ed. (Munich, 1968), 475 (*S. Bernardini Senensis Opera Omnia,* vol. 2 [Florence, 1950], 150, 157; *Sermo LII: De salutatione angelica,* art. 1, cap. 2). "Omnis gratia, quae huic saeculo communicatur, triplicem habet processum. Nam a Deo in Christum, a Christo in Virginem, a Virgine in nos ordinatissime dispensatur" (*Acta sanctae sedis* 27 [1894–1895]: 179 [English translation from Carlen, *The Papal Encyclicals,* 2:357]).

46. Another popular preacher on the eve of the Reformation, Bernardine of Busti (1440–1513), has equally exalted notions of the Virgin. In regard to Mary's knowledge, he concludes, "She possessed all science, mechanical and liberal arts, Law, Philosophy, Medicine, Mathematics, Music and Theology" (O'Carroll, *Theotokos,* 77).

47. C. Balić, ed., *Ioannes Duns Scotus doctor Immaculatae Conceptionis,* part 1, *Textus auctoris* (Rome, 1954); O'Connor, *Dogma of the Immaculate Conception,* 202–12.

48. O'Connor, *Dogma of the Immaculate Conception,* 232. For an overview, see "The Controversy over the Immaculate Conception from after Scotus to the End of the Eighteenth Century" (pp. 213–70); also Oberman, *Harvest of Medieval Theology,* 283–86.

49. *ES* 1400.

50. *ES* 1425–26.

51. O'Carroll, *Theotokos,* 181.

52. Laurentin, *Short Treatise on the Virgin Mary,* 129.

53. O'Carroll, *Theotokos,* 181–84; R. Laurentin, "The Role of the Papal Magisterium in the Development of the Dogma of the Immaculate Conception," in O'Connor, *Dogma of the Immaculate Conception,* 271–324.

54. *ES* 2015–17.

55. O'Carroll, *Theotokos,* 182.

56. H. U. von Balthasar, *Theo-Drama,* vol. 3, *Dramatis Personae: Persons in Christ* (San Francisco, 1992), 243–44.

57. Graef, *Mary,* 2:37.

58. J. H. Newman, *Certain Difficulties Felt by Anglicans in Catholic Teaching Considered* (London, 1900), 2:26.

59. H. Graef, *The Devotion to Our Lady* (New York, 1963), 72–73. "St. Bernard had recommended this approach for those who were frightened of Christ on account of his divinity" (72).

60. A. M. de Liguori, *The Glories of Mary,* rev. ed. (Rockford, IL, 1977).

61. Balthasar, *Dramatis Personae: Persons in Christ,* 297.

62. H. Rahner, *Our Lady and the Church,* trans. S. Bullough (London, 1961).

63. K. Rahner, *Mary, Mother of the Lord: Theological Meditations,* trans. W. J. O'Hara (New York, 1963).

64. E. Schillebeeckx, *Mary, Mother of Redemption,* trans. N. D. Smith (New York, 1964).

65. O. Semmelroth, *Mary, Archetype of the Church,* trans. M. von Eroes and J. Devlin (New York, 1964).

66. R. Laurentin, *The Question of Mary,* trans. I. G. Pidoux (New York, 1964). For an analysis of the two tendencies in modern Mariology, see pp. 53–81.

67. O'Carroll, *Theotokos,* 352. H. Mühlen reports that more than five hundred council fathers ask for a solemn definition of Mary as mediatrix, and fifty of them even a definition of her role as coredemptrix as well (*Una Mystica Persona,* 461).

68. R. Laurentin, *La Vierge au Concile: Présentation, texte et traduction du chapître VIII de la Constitution dogmatique Lumen gentium consacrée à la Bienheureuse Vierge Marie, Mère de Dieu dans le mystère de l'Eglise* (Paris, 1965), 16.

69. Alberigo, *History of Vatican II,* 4:57.

70. Ibid., 4:61.

71. Ibid., 4:446–48.

72. Earlier titles: "The Blessed Virgin Mary," "Mother of God," "Mother of Men."

73. H. Vorgrimler, ed., *Commentary on the Documents of Vatican II* (New York, 1967), 1:134.

74. *Lumen Gentium* §63.

75. *Lumen Gentium* §54. The council does not intend to "give a complete doctrine of Mary" or decide outstanding theological questions.

76. Balthasar, *Dramatis Personae: Persons in Christ,* 317.

77. Ibid., 316.

78. W. Beinert and F. Schüssler-Fiorenza, eds., *Handbook of Catholic Theology* (New York, 1995), 459.

79. L.-M. G. de Montfort, *A Treatise on the True Devotion to the Blessed Virgin,* trans. F. W. Faber (New York, 1909), 191.

80. E. Johnson, *Truly Our Sister: A Theology of Mary in the Communion of Saints* (New York, 2003).

81. Balthasar, *Dramatis Personae: Persons in Christ,* 293–94.

82. S. Zimdars-Swartz, *Encountering Mary: From La Sallette to Medjugorje* (Princeton, NJ, 1991), 11. Jaroslav Pelikan lists ten: in addition to Guadalupe, December 9–12, 1531, he adds Filippsdorf (Philippsdorf), now

in the Czech Republic, January 12–13, 1866, and Pompei, Italy, July 8, 1876 (*Mary through the Centuries: Her Place in the History of Culture* [New Haven, 1996], 178–79). For this section, I am dependent on Zimdars-Swartz, *Encountering Mary.*

83. Quoted in T. Kselman, *Miracles and Prophecies in Nineteenth-Century France* (New Brunswick, NJ, 1983), 63.

84. Zimdars-Swartz, *Encountering Mary,* 52.

85. Quoted in M. Warner, *Alone of All Her Sex: The Myth and the Cult of the Virgin Mary* (New York, 1976), 251.

86. Zimdars-Swartz, *Encountering Mary,* 56–57.

87. Ibid., 82.

88. Ibid., 259–70.

89. Quoted in J. Bottum, "When the Swallows Come Back to Capistrano: Catholic Culture in America," *First Things* 66 (October 2006): 32.

90. Pope John Paul II and A. Frossard, *"Be Not Afraid!" John Paul II Speaks Out on His Life, His Beliefs, and His Inspiring Vision for Humanity,* trans. J. R. Foster (New York, 1984), 251; see also G. Weigel, *Witness to Hope: The Biography of Pope John Paul II* (New York, 1999), 413.

91. *Pilgrimage Destinations Guide* (New Providence, NJ, 2006), 21.

92. Kselman, *Miracles and Prophecies,* 200.

93. Ibid., 90–91.

94. H. R. Niebuhr, *The Kingdom of God in America* (New York, 1959), 193.

95. Warner, *Alone of All Her Sex,* 309–11.

96. Zimdars-Swartz, *Encountering Mary,* xiii.

Chapter 9 / The Last Things and Faith

1. E. Bloch, *The Principle of Hope,* trans. N. Plaice, S. Plaice, and P. Knight, 3 vols. (Cambridge, MA, 1995).

2. J. Moltmann, *Theology of Hope: On the Ground and the Implications of a Christian Eschatology* (London, 1967).

3. J. B. Metz, *Theology of the World,* trans. W. Glen-Doepel (New York, 1969).

4. P. Teilhard de Chardin, *Le milieu divin: Essai de vie intérieure* (Paris, 1958).

5. G. Greshake, *Auferstehung der Toten: Ein Beitrag zur gegenwärtigen theologischen Diskussion über die Zukunft der Geschichte* (Essen, 1969); J. Ratzinger, *Eschatology, Death and Eternal Life,* trans. M. Waldstein (Washington, DC, 1988), 104–12.

6. J. Dupuis, ed., *The Christian Faith in the Doctrinal Documents of the Catholic Church,* 6th ed. (New York, 1996), 2317, pp. 949–51.

7. Ibid., 261, 120–21.

8. H. U. von Balthasar, "Eschatology," in *Theology Today: Renewal in Dogma,* ed. J. Feiner, J. Trütsch, F. Böckle (Milwaukee, 1964), 222.

9. L. T. Johnson, *The Creed: What Christians Believe and Why It Matters* (New York, 2003), 50.

10. J. Ratzinger, *Introduction to Christianity,* trans. J. R. Foster (New York, 1973), 50–64.

11. K. Rahner, "The Hermeneutics of Eschatological Assertions," in *More Recent Writings,* trans. K. Smyth (London and Baltimore, 1966), 337.

12. J. Levenson, *Resurrection and the Restoration of Israel: The Ultimate Victory of the God of Life* (New Haven, 2006), 7.

13. Ibid., 1–22.

14. M. Barré, "New Light on the Interpretation of Hosea VI 2," *Vetus Testamentum* 28 (1978): 137–38.

15. Levenson, *Resurrection and the Restoration of Israel,* 175.

16. Ibid., 216.

17. For a fine overview of patristic eschatology, see B. Daley, *The Hope of the Early Church: A Handbook of Patristic Eschatology* (Cambridge, 1991).

18. *ANF* 10:498.

19. Ratzinger, *Eschatology, Death and Eternal Life,* 233–38.

20. Levenson, *Resurrection and the Restoration of Israel,* 83.

21. K. Rahner, *Foundations of Christian Faith: An Introduction to the Idea of Christianity,* trans. W. V. Dych (New York, 1985), 443–44.

22. B. Pascal, *Pensées* (London, 1995), no. 913.

23. Ratzinger, *Introduction to Christianity,* 227–30.

24. F. Fénelon, *Letters to Men and Women* (Westminster, MD, 1957), 140–41.

25. *ES* 1000–1002.

26. J. H. Newman, *Meditations and Devotions of the Late Cardinal Newman* (Westminster, MD, 1975), 218.

27. R. Dawkins, *The God Delusion* (Boston, 2006).

28. J. Holt, "Beyond Belief," *New York Times,* October 22, 2006, 11.

29. M. Watanabe, introduction to *Nicholas of Cusa: Selected Spiritual Writings,* trans. H. L. Bond (New York, 1997), 12.

30. W. Schulz, *Der Gott der neuzeitlichen Metaphysik* (Pfullingen, 1957), 11–30.

31. Nicholas of Cusa, *Selected Spiritual Writings,* 85–206.

32. W. James, *A Pluralistic Universe* (New York, 1947), 309.

33. W. James, *The Varieties of Religious Experience* (New York, 1958), 367–91.

34. Holt, "Beyond Belief," 11.

35. J. H. Newman, *Discourses Addressed to Mixed Congregations* (Westminster, MD, 1966), 274–75.

36. S. Kierkegaard, *Concluding Unscientific Postscript,* trans. D. F. Swenson (Princeton, 1971), 186–204.

37. Nicholas of Cusa, *Selected Spiritual Writings,* 272–76.

38. Pascal, Pensée no. 61.

39. Ibid., no. 63.

40. J. H. Newman, *An Essay on the Development of Christian Doctrine* (Garden City, NY, 1960), 95–108.

41. F. Schleiermacher, *The Christian Faith* ([1822] New York, 1999), 103 (§24).

42. H. Bleichner, *View from the Altar: Reflections on the Rapidly Changing Catholic Priesthood* (New York, 2004), 116.

43. *The Confessions of St. Augustine* (New York, 1942), 146 (book 8.12).

44. Pascal, Pensée no. 913.

45. S. E. Ahlstrom, *A Religious History of the American People* (New Haven, 1972), 325.

46. Pascal, Pensée no. 418.

47. H. Ott, *God,* trans. I. Nicol and U. Nicol (Atlanta, 1971), 79–98.

ABOUT THE AUTHOR

Howard P. Bleichner, S.S., a systematic theologian at St. Patrick's Seminary in Menlo Park, California, is a leading figure in American priestly formation. For one decade he served as President and Rector of St. Patrick's Seminary in San Francisco, and for another decade as Rector of the Theological College of the Catholic University of America. He was editor of volumes 1 and 2 of the *Norms for Priestly Formation,* and editor of the fourth edition of *The Program of Priestly Formation.* Fr. Bleichner holds a B.A. from Dartmouth College and a D.Theol. from the Catholic Faculty of the University of Tübingen (magna cum laude).

Fr. Bleichner's first book, *View from the Altar: Reflections on the Rapidly Changing Catholic Priesthood,* was hailed by reviewers everywhere for its compassionate and hopeful look at the profound changes experienced by Catholic priests from the time of Vatican II to the present.

INDEX OF NAMES

Of Related Interest

Bernard McGinn and Patricia Ferris McGinn
EARLY CHRISTIAN MYSTICS
The Divine Vision of the Spiritual Masters

The core message of the Church's early mystics, with reflections on what we can learn from them for our lives today. From the world's best-known interpreter of Christian mysticism.

0-8245-2106-4, paperback

Mark S. Massa, S.J.
ANTI-CATHOLICISM IN AMERICA
The Last Acceptable Prejudice

Now in paperback!
Since 2003, when it was first published, this astonishing study of the distinctiveness of Catholic culture and the prejudice it has generated has been hailed as a "stimulating" (*Journal of Religion*) and "eye-opening chronicle" (Catholic News Service) with "an explosion of creative insight" (Andrew Greeley).

Now with study guide!

0-8245-2362-8, paperback

crossroad

Of Related Interest

Pope Benedict XVI
THE YES OF JESUS CHRIST
Spiritual Exercises in Faith, Hope, and Love

Anyone wanting to understand Pope Benedict XVI's view of the relationship between Christianity and the world must read this eloquent book.

Secular thought has failed to answer the great questions of human existence. The "optimism" that lacks a Christian foundation ultimately cannot sustain genuine faith, hope, and love. In *The Yes of Jesus Christ,* Benedict XVI invites us to rediscover the Christian basis for hope. By exercising our spirituality through continual practice in Christian life, we hear again the distinctly Christian message that our ability to say Yes to ourselves and one another can only come from God's Yes in Christ.

"Not 'eye for eye, tooth for tooth,' but the transformation of evil through the power of love. . . . Jesus bursts our No open by means of a stronger and greater Yes. In the cross of Christ and only there this saying opens up and becomes revelation. In fellowship with him, however, it becomes a possibility for our own life too."

Other Benedict XVI books available from Crossroad include *A New Song for the Lord: Faith in Christ and Liturgy Today; Values in a Time of Upheaval.*

0-8245-2374-1, paperback

crossroad

Also by Howard Bleichner

VIEW FROM THE ALTAR

*Reflections on the Rapidly Changing
Catholic Priesthood*

"*View from the Altar* is a must-read for all who are interested in understanding the causes of the scandal of sexual abuse by members of the Catholic clergy.... I am grateful to the author for handling this sensitive topic with both raw honesty and brotherly compassion.... *View from the Altar* reminds us that spirituality must be at the core of seminary formation."   —*America*

0-8245-2141-2, paperback

Check your local bookstore for availability.
To order directly from the publisher,
please call 1-800-707-0670 for Customer Service
or visit our Web site at *www.cpcbooks.com*.
For catalog orders, please send your request to the address below.

THE CROSSROAD PUBLISHING COMPANY
16 Penn Plaza, Suite 1550
New York, NY 10001

crossroad